The Hollywood Film Industry

A Reader/Edited by Paul Kerr

Routledge & Kegan Paul
London and New York

in association with the British Film Institute
81 Dean Street, London W1V 6AA

First published in 1986 by
Routledge & Kegan Paul plc
11 New Fetter Lane, London EC4P 4EE

Published in the USA by
Routledge & Kegan Paul Inc.
in association with Methuen Inc.
29 West 35th Street, New York, NY 10001

Set in Sabon and Univers
and printed in Great Britain by
Butler & Tanner Ltd
Frome and London
Introduction and editorial matter © British Film Institute 1986
All other material © as on page ix

Library of Congress Cataloging in Publication Data

Main entry under title:
The Hollywood film industry
(British Film Institute readers in film studies)
Bibliography: p.
Includes index.
1. Moving-picture industry——United States——Addresses, essays,
lectures. I. Kerr, Paul. II. British Film Institute. III. Series.
PN1993.5.U6H5912 1986 384'.8'0979494 86-498

ISBN 0-7100-9730-1

British Library CIP Data also available

Contents

Editor's acknowledgments

I would like to thank a number of individuals and organisations for their assistance and encouragement during the preparation of this book. First of all I would like to thank Edward Buscombe and Roma Gibson of the British Film Institute Publishing Department for their editorial guidance. I am also grateful to Jane Hocking who typed part of the manuscript. More generally I am indebted to both the Education Department and the Library of the BFI and their respective staffs, and to the Society for Education in Film and Television, its members, officers, educational events and publications. Finally, I would like to express several more personal debts. To Richard Dyer, who encouraged me in the early stages of this book. And to Ruth Baumgarten, who has lived with this book as long as I have, and who, like Edward Buscombe, commented in detail on several stages of the manuscript. I would like to dedicate it to her and to the memory of one of the contributors, Lee Beaupré, who was tragically murdered while this volume was still at an early stage.

Acknowledgments

The publishers wish to thank the following for permission to reprint the copyright material listed below: the author and *The Journal of the University Film Association* for Janet Wasko, 'D. W. Griffith and the banks: a case study in film financing', *JUFA*, XXX, 1 (Winter 1978), copyright © 1978 by the University Film Association; the author and *Screen* for Edward Buscombe, 'Notes on Columbia Pictures Corporation 1926–41', *Screen*, vol. 16, no. 3 (Autumn 1975), copyright © *Screen* 1975; the author and Gloria Safier for Hugh Fordin, *'On the Town'*, from *The World of Entertainment: Hollywood's Greatest Musicals* (New York: Doubleday, 1975), copyright © Gloria Safier, Inc. 1975; the author and *The Journal of the University Film Association* for Ida Jeter, 'The collapse of the Federated Motion Picture Crafts: a case study of class collaboration in the motion picture industry', *JUFA*, XXXI, 2 (Spring 1979), copyright © by the University Film Association 1979; the author and *Wide Angle* for Janet Staiger, 'Mass-produced photoplays: economic and signifying practices in the first years of Hollywood', *Wide Angle*, vol. 4, no. 3, copyright © *Wide Angle*, The John Hopkins University Press, Baltimore; the author and *Film Reader* for Edward Branigan, 'Color and cinema: problems in the writing of history', *Film Reader*, 4 (1979), copyright © *Film Reader* 1979; the author and Redgrave Publishing Company for David Bordwell, 'Camera movement: the coming of sound and the classical Hollywood style', from *The 1977 Film Studies Annual II: Historical–Theoretical Speculations*, ed. Ben Lawton and Janet Staiger (Pleasantville: Redgrave Publishing Company, 1977), copyright © David Bordwell 1977; the author for Barry King, 'Stardom as an occupation', copyright © Barry King 1985; the author and *Film Comment* for Lee Beaupré, 'How to distribute a film', *Film Comment*, vol. 13, no. 4 (July–August 1977), copyright © 1977 by Film Comment Publishing Corporation, reprinted by the Film Society of Lincoln Center; the author and *Quarterly Review of Film Studies* for Douglas Gomery, 'The picture palace: economic sense or Hollywood nonsense?', *QRFS*, vol. 3, no. 1 (Winter 1978), copyright © 1978 by Redgrave Publishing Company; the author and SEFT for Paul Kerr, 'Out of what past? Notes on the B *film noir*', *Screen Education*, nos. 32–3 (Autumn/Winter 1979–80), copyright © *Screen Education* 1979–80; the author for Thomas Guback, 'Shaping the film business in postwar Germany: the role of the US film industry and the US state', copyright © Thomas Guback 1985.

Introduction

This book, like many others, is about 'Hollywood'. However, unlike a number of studies which often employ that term as if it was self-explanatory – a simple synonym for the films which have been made there and the film-makers who have made them – the present volume is addressed to another Hollywood. To Hollywood, that is, as the site of and byword for a history of specifically industrial structures and strategies; a Hollywood, furthermore, which is far less familiar than the frequency of references to it in film criticism (whether academic or journalistic) might suggest. To talk about the industrial Hollywood, therefore, it is necessary not only to prevent the American cinema from standing in for the industry, but also and equally importantly to prevent the industry itself from being unproblematically employed to stand in for something else, whether as a symbol of media imperialism, a synecdoche for monopoly capitalism or a symptom of cultural decline. Indeed, even to begin to discuss the industrial history of Hollywood requires considerable caution about terminology; even the most familiar formulations – 'dream factory', 'studio system' and 'culture industry' – are apt to conceal as much about Hollywood as they convey.

Of course, the tendency to confuse and conflate different definitions and conceptions of Hollywood is by no means confined to film criticism. Such confusions, however, even when they originate outside criticism in the industry itself, can have very real consequences for that criticism, for the industry, for individual film-makers and for the films themselves. To take just one early example, the formation of the Motion Picture Producers and Distributors of America in 1922 was the film industry's – or rather the major film companies' – response to a much publicised moral panic aroused by (the sensational reporting of) a series of scandals in the film-making community; of these perhaps the best known is the Fatty Arbuckle case, in which the famous comedian's career was all but ruined by allegations of the rape and murder of a young actress. The MPPDA was soon to expand its sphere of activities, however, and involve itself not only in cleaning up the public image of the film-making community but also in supervising film industry labour relations (by

way of affiliated bodies like the Studio Relations Committee)
and even in regulating film content (via the Production Code).
One of the aims of this anthology, therefore, is to try to identify
and illuminate such confusions; to begin to distinguish Hollywood as industry from those other Hollywoods, Hollywood films
and Hollywood film-makers, if only in order to secure the terrain
for future attempts to specify rather than simply assume either
their relation or the relation between American cinema and
American society – a relationship in which that industry is something of a 'missing link'.

Edward Buscombe's essay in this anthology, from which the
'missing link' formulation is borrowed, usefully begins by discussing the consequences for film criticism of the conventional
opposition which operates in our culture between the concepts
of Art and Industry. One example of that sort of opposition is
the very existence of this volume as the only one in a series of
Readers in film studies which is not addressed to the elaboration
of theoretical models for the analysis of films but is instead
concerned with the industry in and by which Hollywood films
were and are produced, distributed and exhibited. And this is
not to argue that there is a disproportionate emphasis on criticism and critical methodology in this series, but simply to acknowledge that the whole history of film studies (for and from
which these volumes are assembled) has had just such an emphasis. A look at the published surveys of film theory rapidly
reveals that attempts to elaborate a conceptual approach to the
film industry are rarely even on the agenda; all too often, indeed,
discussion of the film industry has actually been delegated to
other disciplines entirely. And this unfortunate situation has
been further exacerbated by the fact that, at least until relatively
recently, there were only a very small number of histories of
Hollywood, histories whose own slippages back and forth between films, film-makers and film industry are exemplified by
Benjamin B. Hampton's 1931 classic *A History of the Movies*,
which on its reissue in 1970 was retitled *A History of the American Film Industry* without amendment to its contents.[1]

If most journalistic accounts of Hollywood have failed to
avoid such slippages, that may be the result of their reliance on
all-too-familiar anecdotes about spoilt stars and philistine moguls, the waste of creative talent (particularly that of screen-
writers) in an art dominated by industrial assembly lines. Recent
developments in film theory, however, have also afforded a
similar conflation of films and industry in the necessary task of
reconceiving cinema as a social institution. Nevertheless, in the
absence of detail and distinctions, concepts like cinematic ap-

paratus, machine or institution or, even more simply, the term Hollywood itself can function no less than journalistic cliché to reinforce monolithic conceptions both of those films and that industry. That Hollywood has indeed been conceived of in much film criticism as an industrial monolith is evidenced by the familiarity of such ill-defined and undifferentiated formulations as the dream factory and the studio system. That it has also been classified as an aesthetic and political/ideological monolith is revealed by phrases like Godard's much quoted 'Nixon-Paramount' and 'Hollywood-Mosfilm' (however importantly polemical their original impact) and the even less specific theoretical category 'classical Hollywood cinema' with its inference of evaluation. (Perhaps a term like 'standard practice' would be preferable; it would certainly necessitate far more precision about the studio and period in question.)

That film studies has, historically, concentrated on the study of films is hardly surprising. Consequently, however, it is impossible for a volume like this to anthologise the theoretical development of analyses of industrial Hollywood; indeed, until recently the level of theoretical sophistication of such enterprises was far from impressive. That there is now an important expansion both in the quantity and quality of historical research into Hollywood as industry is encouraging. Nevertheless, this volume cannot achieve what John Caughie's Reader *Theories of Authorship* so successfully accomplishes: 'using documentation and commentary ... to follow the most significant stages in the development of theories over the past thirty years or so'.[2] A historical account of developments in the conceptualisation of the film industry over three decades – or even longer – would simply reiterate the theoretical redundancy of most of what was written in that area until the 1970s. Even those economic theories employed by film industry historians have been almost entirely derived from conventional neo-classical or Marxist models, models which have thus far usually been at the service of (respectively) either uncritically celebratory or dismissively pessimistic perspectives on the films the industry produces. But if Caughie's structure is inapplicable to an anthology on the industry, so too is the structure which Christopher Williams adopted for his volume *Realism and the Cinema*. Indeed, there would be very little to be gained by assembling such an anthology on the industry from an accumulation of 'fairly representative statements by film-makers, critics and theoreticians ... to bring out their similarities and contradictions'.[3] Until relatively recently at least, such statements as have been made by film-makers, critics and theoreticians about the film industry have tended to be both repetitively general and generally repetitive.

As an anthology about Hollywood as industry, of course, this book could also have attempted to offer 'a systematic survey of the history of the industry' as Tino Balio's *The American Film Industry* does with some success.[4] Instead, however, this collection has somewhat smaller ambitions; it makes no attempt to provide an exhaustive account of either the industry or its history, preferring instead to scrutinise several industrially and historically specific sites and moments. This then is not a systematic survey of the industry nor a historiography of critical approaches to it, but simply a selection of case studies.

Furthermore, these studies do not pretend to provide the empirical evidence, as it were, from which any easy historical or pan-industrial conclusions can be drawn. These are not 'typical' or 'exemplary' cases, though each analysis does, I think, constitute an advance both for film industrial history in particular and for film studies in general. Consequently, no attempt has been made here to assemble these individual case studies into the appearance of a collective historical or industrial chronology or comprehensiveness. There is nothing, for instance, on censorship, or marketing, media conglomerates or anti-trust legislation; there is more emphasis on the early years of the film industry than on more recent developments. No attempt has been made to compensate for these emphases and omissions editorially; nor, therefore, have schematic editorial overviews been appended to construct a context into which these case studies could comfortably be situated. Indeed, the implication of these case studies is that such a consensual history would reinforce rather than resolve the sorts of problems, both empirical and theoretical, engaged with here.

At first sight, then, a book on the American film industry seems to sit rather uneasily in a series of anthologies otherwise addressed to such serious critical debates and contentious issues of film studies as Realism, Authorship or Genre. All such concepts and critical approaches, however, have had to hypothesise the industry in some way. And so the function of this volume is by no means simply the provision of new and valuable empirical data and explanatory models for film industrial history. It is also and perhaps more importantly an opportunity to begin to unpack the orthodoxies not only of film industrial history but also of the perspectives on that history constructed by film theory. The remainder of this introduction, therefore, is devoted to a brief discussion of some of the more influential theories of (American) cinema in order to isolate and interrogate those conceptions of the industry which have historically underpinned them. Once again, no attempt has been made at an exhaustive historiography of film theory (though some of the articles anthologised here do address a number of critical approaches, notably Edward Branigan's essay on colour). Rather, a small number of specific critical approaches have been selected and their explicit or implicit conceptions of the film industry discussed. If the function of the volume as a whole is thus less to paraphrase than to problematise consensual film industrial history then the task of what follows is not yet another rehearsal of the major film theories but an attempt to address some of the ways in which those theories have historically conceived of Hollywood as industry and how those specific conceptions have occasionally impeded analysis of Hollywood both as industry and as cinema.

If it is true to say that there has been a reluctance, amongst those engaged in attempting to validate or even evaluate American cinema, to undertake any but the most perfunctory kind of analysis of the American film industry, then that reluctance cannot be unconnected to the single-minded zeal with which the detractors of that cinema have used the very existence of that industry as evidence against it. And indeed, if both cinema and industry can be comfortably accommodated under the same terminological roof, as it were, that of 'Hollywood', then the dismissal of both from the critical agenda is all the more easily achieved. It is perhaps for this reason that the proponents of the two most familiar formulations in the arsenal of the critics of the American cinema, 'the dream factory' and 'the culture industry', concentrate their analyses on a general denunciation of the industrialisation of leisure rather than on specific examples of that culture, those dreams. Whether they refer to the typical Hollywood film as a dream, drug, distraction, escape or ideology, however, the emphases of both F. R. Leavis and Denys Thompson in Britain and T. W. Adorno and Max Horkheimer in Germany are on the assembly line experiences not of Hollywood's film-makers/producers but of its filmgoers/consumers. Thus Leavis and Thompson contend that 'the repetitive monotony that results from a minute subdivision of labour ... and the substitution of machine-tending for craftsmanship'[5] have effectively impoverished the worker's imagination, leaving him or her incapable of real recreation and reduced instead to what they variously describe as 'decreation', 'distraction', 'substitute-living' and 'daydreaming'.

The theory of the Frankfurt School

The most persuasive polemic against the culture industry in general and Hollywood in particular is not to be found within what might be called the *Scrutiny* movement in Britain (indeed, Philip French in his book *The Movie Moguls* could only find a single reference to Hollywood in the whole of *Scrutiny* and that an ambivalent rather than wholeheartedly dismissive one),[6] but rather in the work of the Frankfurt School, and in particular in the writing of Adorno and Horkheimer. Since their case has, in a sense, never been either satisfactorily answered or more cogently argued, Adorno and Horkheimer's chapter on 'The culture industry' in their book *Dialectic of Enlightenment* remains probably the most sustained critical assault on that industry and its cultural products (not only American or cinematic) and for that reason alone it deserves consideration in some detail and quotation at some length:

> Amusement under late capitalism is the prolongation of work. It is sought after as an escape from the mechanized work process, and to recruit strength in order to be able to cope with it again. But at the same time mechanization has such power over man's leisure and happiness, and so profoundly determines the manufacture of amusement goods, that his experiences are inevitably after-images of the work process itself. The ostensible content is merely a faded foreground; what sinks in is the automatic succession of standardized operations. What happens at work, in the factory, or in the office can only be escaped from by an approximation to it in one's leisure time.[7]

As Marxists, Adorno and Horkheimer saw the industrialisation of culture not simply as an aesthetic but also as a political catastrophe. Of course this does not entirely distinguish their approach from that of the defenders of high culture. Nevertheless, where Leavis and particularly Thompson talked about the mass media without relinquishing the notoriously problematic concept of popular culture, Adorno and Horkheimer insist that it is precisely not a genuine popular culture but a mass culture that is produced under monopoly capitalism. Indeed, they accuse those who uncritically accept Hollywood's alibi that cinematic 'standards were based in the first place on consumers' needs' of failing to confront the uncomfortable fact that the means by which the culture industry perpetuates itself is grounded on the vertical integration of that industry. Which is to say that monopoly control of production, distribution and exhibition makes a mockery of so-called consumer choice, which it replaces with 'a circle of manipulation and retroactive need'.[8] The question of actual or apparent consumer choice, the notion that the box-office operates as some sort of aesthetic ballot, is considered in this volume in Barry King's article on the stars. But Adorno and Horkheimer don't simply contend that the industry is a monopoly – and a monolith; they go on to argue that the films which the industry produces are themselves monolithic, for 'Under monopoly all mass culture is identical.'[9]

Thus Adorno and Horkheimer's rejection of the American cinema simultaneously reinforces and is reinforced by their conception of Hollywood as industry. Both industry and cinema, in fact, are conceived as almost entirely undifferentiated monoliths; where differences are to be discovered, furthermore, they function only to conceal a more fundamental similarity:

> Marked differentiations such as those of A and B films ... depend not so much on subject matter as on classifying, organizing, and labelling consumers. Something is provided for all so that none may escape. . . .
>
> How formalized this procedure is can be seen when the mechanically differentiated products prove to be all alike in the end. That the difference between the Chrysler range and General Motors products is basically illusory strikes every child with a keen interest in varieties. What connoisseurs discuss as good or bad points serve only to perpetuate the semblance of competition and range of choice. The same applies to the Warner Brothers and Metro-Goldwyn-Mayer productions. But even the differences between the more expensive and cheaper models put out by the same firm steadily diminish: for automobiles, there are such differences as the number of cylinders, cubic capacity, details of patented gadgets; and for films there are the number of stars, the extravagant use of technology, labour and equipment, the introduction of the latest psychological formulas. The universal criterion of merit is the amount of 'conspicuous production', of blatant cash investment.[10]

Adorno and Horkheimer conclude that culture industries, including Hollywood, produce nothing more than 'cyclically recurrent and rigidly invariable' cultural commodities, both economically and ideologically at the service of a capitalism whose very production process, an automatic succession of standardised operations, is echoed in the aesthetics of its product.

If the work of Adorno and Horkheimer constitutes perhaps the most forceful critique of Hollywood – as industry and as cinema – yet mounted, it is also something of a dead end, the very definitiveness of its verdict rendering further analysis all but redundant. And yet, ultimately, any analysis which conceives of American cinema as essentially monolithic neither requires nor probably can accommodate a closer look at the complexities and specificities (including internal contradictions) that comprise that cinema and that industry; and once again, the conflation of those two concepts within the one word 'Hollywood' is perhaps at least partly responsible for allowing such a diminution to obtain. The question of differences between and within Warners and MGM is addressed both later in this Introduction and less directly in the article on the making of *On the Town*; indeed, the latter essay elaborates how certain cinematic and industrial strategies are not only specific to certain studios but also to particular production units at particular times. Similarly, the distinctions between A and B films are broached in the article on the B *film noir*, those two 'marked differentiations' actually having no more to do with the classification of consumers than they do with subject matter. Finally, Leavis and Thompson's lament about the effects of 'the substitution of machine-tending for craftsmanship' on the consumers of the dream factory's products is ironic in relation to the film industry's status as an unusually labour-intensive and perhaps anachronistically craft-based operation. Some of the implications of these apparently opposing occupational ideologies are teased out in the essays here on the collapse of the Federated Motion Picture Crafts Union and the function of stardom as an occupation. Similarly, Adorno and Horkheimer's contention that the culture industry is entirely in the hands of Wall Street and that the cultural products it circulates necessarily reinforce the ideological interests of Wall Street's monopoly capital is reprised in the famous *Cahiers du Cinéma* analysis of *Young Mr Lincoln*[11] to which Edward Buscombe refers in his essay on Columbia reprinted here.

The dream factory

In 1947, the year in which *The Dialectic of Enlightenment* was first published, an American social anthropologist named Hortense Powdermaker was spending a year in Hollywood researching a book on the social structures of the film-making community. Perhaps not surprisingly, considering her sociological background, her conclusions about the film industry's intellectual climate and cultural assumptions are strikingly similar to Adorno and Horkheimer's: 'Hollywood is engaged in the mass production of prefabricated daydreams. It tries to adapt the American dream, that all men are created equal, to the view that all men's dreams should be made equal.'[12] Powdermaker argues that Hollywood, like any other industry, attempts to rationalise its production methods and consequently discovers the desirability of rationalising its products too. At the former level, this involved a division of labour including an occupational hierarchy, the vertical integration of production, distribution and exhibition, and so on. At the latter level it involved the star system, the development of genres, cycles and stereotypes. But, she argues, there is an inherent contradiction in this process because:

> The production of movies is a creative process, and this
> characteristic does not disappear even when it is denied. It is
> illogical to carry the premises underlying the manufacture
> and merchandising of automobiles to the making and selling
> of movies, because the problems involved are essentially
> different.[13]

Here Powdermaker is taking issue with the film industry's often inappropriate conception of itself and of the films it produces, but her arguments also apply to those critics like Adorno who seem all too willing to accept the film industry's image of itself:

> Movies ... need no longer pretend to be art. The truth that
> they are just business is made into an ideology in order to
> justify the rubbish they deliberately produce. They call
> themselves industries; and when their directors' incomes are
> published, any doubt about the social utility of the finished
> products is removed.[14]

For Powdermaker, on the other hand, it is precisely this inability to conceive of a 'business' producing an 'art' which characterises the most common misconceptions about both the film industry and the films themselves:

> The product of the dream factory is not of the same nature
> as one of the material objects turned out on most assembly
> lines. For them uniformity is essential; for the motion picture,
> originality is important. The conflict between the two
> qualities is a major problem in Hollywood.[15]

Adorno and his heirs would undoubtedly describe that conflict as more apparent than real, an ideology in itself, functioning to conceal a more fundamental identity of interests. Meanwhile, for film theory as for the film industry itself, the satisfactory negotiation of that conflict remains a major problem.

Realism

Whereas the culture industry thesis still in a sense sets the agenda for any debate about the politics of popular culture and the mass media in general, probably the first theoretical dispute which could be called specific to cinema concerned the concept of realism. The first question asked of cinema in such disputes went as follows: could a medium which merely records reality be reasonably regarded as an art, or should it instead be defined as no more than a scientific device? The response of several of cinema's defenders was that it is precisely the presence of these technological devices which prevent films, even avowedly realist films, from simply recording reality and which provide cinema with its aesthetic resources. (This, for instance, is the position taken by Rudolf Arnheim in his influential study *Film as Art*.[16])

From this point the realism debate was extended to address a further question. It was argued – and still is in some quarters – that the so-called realism effect or realist aesthetic is in fact an inherent property of film and that the cinema, therefore, traces an inexorable trajectory toward some sort of Platonic pure form. In fact, several histories of the cinema have constructed a conveniently symbolic contrast between those two pioneers, Méliès and Lumière, casting the latter in the role of 'the first realist' and the former as 'the first illusionist'. This sort of approach unproblematically privileges individual inclinations and/or aesthetic destiny over other more material imperatives, not least amongst them the early industrial history of the cinema, imperatives that are neither heroic nor metaphysical.

Christopher Williams, in his anthology *Realism and the Cinema*, has described the so-called 'realist effect' of film as its apparent ability to reproduce the visible circumstances of life with almost scientific accuracy.[17] The power of realism, therefore, resides in its facility to convince the spectator that the images which are projected on to the screen have some sort of utterly unmediated and all but metaphysical relation with the world beyond and behind it. (Perhaps the most important proponent of this argument was André Bazin in his essay 'The ontology of the photographic image'.)[18] One of the central ironies of this case, of course, is that this very facility relies on the existence of the camera and the microphone and of an increasing plethora of devices, all of which have simultaneously to be exploited and repressed by realist cinema. And that technology, of course, is industrial in origin and operation. Furthermore, the very development of the aesthetic conventions we now identify as realist derive from the development of certain working practices in the film industry – as Janet Staiger's article in this volume makes clear.

Relatively recently, research like Staiger's into the imbrication of the realist aesthetic with the innovation and implementation of new film industrial techniques and technologies – notably deep focus, sound and colour – has begun to introduce the industrial dimension into what was previously perceived as an unmediated relationship between the film-maker and the object filmed. Initially such work stressed the ideological nature of realism but increasingly attention has also been paid to the economic and industrial underpinnings of the aesthetic. Thus, for example, in an afterword to an influential article about deep focus by Patrick Ogle, Christopher Williams has stressed that contrary to Ogle's account, 'technological practice and aesthetic choice' – Ogle's chosen historical protagonists – 'are neither of them independent of ideological economic choices and practices.'[19] Similarly, Douglas Gomery has criticised Jean-Louis Comolli's analysis of the ideological function of realist sound for its unproblematic reproduction of an unsubstantiated story about Warners 'risk-taking' experiment with talkies being attributable to the company's precarious economic state in which it had nothing to lose.[20] In this volume Edward Branigan discusses the relative strengths of Comolli, Gomery and Ogle in his semi-historiographical account of Hollywood's introduction of colour and considers the criteria currently employed in historical/theoretical work about aesthetic/technological change.

Meanwhile, debates about realism in the cinema continue to flourish. One common criticism of the American popular cinema, for instance, is the relative rarity of representations of the realities of ordinary life – the worlds of work and of unemployment being the two most commonly cited omissions. Such content-based criticisms have been superseded by the work of semioticians who have pointed out that one fundamental characteristic of realist films (as of realist theory) is the concealment of the materiality of their own production, their very status as products. Ironically, however, neither the radical realists nor the radical anti-realists have been quick to introduce an industrial/economic dimension into their own political/ideological critiques of dominant cinema.

Recent theoretical work deriving from semiotics has rejected both the 'ontological' premise of realist cinema and the rather less mystical 'reflection theory' which posits a more general mirroring of 'society' in realist cinema. Having done so, however, the thorny question of just how films do relate to their contexts of production and consumption has all too often been dropped from the critical agenda to be replaced by less conjuncturally specific concepts like those derived from psychoanalysis. Only relatively recently, with the resurgence of historical research into the industry, has it been possible once again to argue for such a relation without collapsing either into the reductiveness of reflection theories or the romanticism implicit in tales of transcendent talent enshrined in authorship. Edward Buscombe's suggestion that 'The history of the American film industry ... forms a kind of missing link in attempts, Marxist and otherwise, to make connections between film and society' is the cue for my own essay in this volume – an analysis of the B *film noir* which attempts to avoid the critical clichés about that genre's origins in an alleged reflection of postwar pessimism or emigré expressionism by focusing on some of the industrial imperatives that shaped it.

The auteur theory

If it is true to suggest that there is some sort of relationship between the literary and puritan side of the realist aesthetic and the rejection of Hollywood cinema in Anglo-American culture, then it is perhaps not altogether surprising that that aesthetic had to be challenged before American cinema could be seriously re-evaluated. It was not until the 1950s, therefore, roughly contemporaneous with the decline of the cinema as 'the most popular art' (and its replacement in that role by television), that some sort of reassessment of Hollywood began to get under way. *Cahiers du cinéma*'s 'politique des auteurs' provided critics for the first time with the rhetoric, if not the rigour, of a methodology for winnowing out the wheat from the cinematic chaff, and, in America, Andrew Sarris's notorious mistranslation of 'politique' as 'theory' lent this reassessment a spurious scientificity. Clearly, such a celebration of directorial artistry in the industrial terrain of Hollywood, whilst challenging the conventional dismissal of American cinema characteristic of high cultural criticism, was always in danger of duplicating the very same critical ideologies – notably via a fetishism of individual texts and a romantic championing of individual authors heroically creative in the midst of philistine market forces, both of which obliged auteur critics to exercise a very Leavis-like discrimination. Janet Wasko's case study of the role of one such 'auteur', D. W. Griffith, in film finance, and thus at both ends of this supposedly antithetical relationship, lends an invaluable distance to the assumed polarity of film as art and film as industry.

Of course, a small number of directors like Orson Welles and Fritz Lang were already admired in some highbrow circles, though usually only at the expense of exemplifying in the former case the awful predicament of the artist on the assembly line and in the latter the tragedy of the European sensibility at the mercy of the American marketplace. Thus Pauline Kael's celebration of *Citizen Kane* attributes that film's 'excellence' to the allegedly unique conditions in which it was produced. For Kael, *Kane*

was not an ordinary assignment. It is one of the few films
ever made inside a major studio in the United States in
freedom – not merely in freedom from interference but in
freedom from the routine methods of experienced directors.[21]

If for Kael the creation of *Citizen Kane* is thus something of a special case, for Adorno and Horkheimer the very existence of such exceptions simultaneously proved and perpetuated the Hollywood rule:

Whenever Orson Welles offends against the tricks of the
trade, he is forgiven because his departures from the norm
are regarded as calculated mutations which serve all the
more strongly to confirm the validity of the system.[22]

Prior to the elaboration of *Cahiers*' 'politique', therefore, for all the attention to the occasional exception, the critical consensus was that there was very little point in attempting to distinguish between what Andrew Sarris was to call the individual trees of American cinema and the general, and generally undifferentiated, forest. Sarris himself has characterised this consensus, that of the 'forest' critics, as follows:

Somewhere on the Western shores of the United States a
group of men have gathered to rob the cinema of its
birthright. If the forest critic be politically oriented, he will
describe these coastal conspirators as capitalists. If
aesthetically oriented, he will describe them as philistines.
Either way an entity called the cinema has been betrayed by
another called Hollywood.[23]

Sarris's strategy, following *Cahiers*, could accommodate a far larger number of films and film-makers than could its critical predecessor since his conception of a successful auteur did not depend on directors being free from interference – as the approach to directorial artists outside Hollywood always had. Indeed, a fundamentally monolithic conception of the industry and of the constraints on creativity which it represented is essential to Sarris's argument since 'The auteur theory values the personality of a director because of the barriers to its expression.'[24] In rescuing the American cinematic forest from a general critical lumberjacking, therefore, Sarris and his allies found it necessary to summon up a conceptual Seventh Cavalry, the auteurs – author-gods out of the Hollywood machine. For Sarris and other early auteurists, the process of film-making in Hollywood was one of creation rather than production, ideally involving an auteur transcending the banality both of his/her assignment and of the material constraints and interferences of the industry. But to celebrate such creativity it was almost obligatory for the auteur critics to ignore or forget the industry except as a constraint, a hurdle over which only Hollywood's most dexterous artists could leap. Thus, for Sarris, 'direction is a relatively mysterious not to say mystical concept of creation'[25] and it was in the interests of auteurism to keep it that way. A director 'would not be worth bothering with if he were not capable now and then of a sublimity of expression almost miraculously extracted from his money-oriented environment'[26] (just what magical agent was responsible for this miracle is necessarily mysterious: a case, perhaps, for Inspector Propp?).

This apparent contradiction between individual creativity and corporate philistinism – apparent, because while bothering the auteurists it seems not to have prevented the occurrence of a pretty enormous number of authorial 'miracles' – encouraged Robin Wood to try and recast the problematic in rather less metaphysical terms.

> There are two great contradictory truths about Hollywood and the difficulty of keeping them in reasonable balance is evidenced by the whole history of film criticism . . . (a) Hollywood is the vast commercial machine where box office considerations corrupt everyone and everything, where untrammelled artistic expression is impossible; and (b) Hollywood is a great creative workshop, comparable to Elizabethan London or the Vienna of Mozart, where hundreds of talents have come together to evolve a common language.[27]

Like Sarris's 'forest', Wood's 'workshop' is not a network of industrial structures but (following T. S. Eliot) an organic community and tradition of creative talents. Wood's formula, for all its romanticism, however, is probably no less accurate a description of Hollywood than the more familiar 'dream factory'. Nevertheless, for Sarris, Wood and the other early auteurists, Hollywood is a suitable case for critical treatment simply because people like Hawks and Hitchcock worked there and films like *To Have and Have Not* and *North by North West* were made there. (The auteurist assumption is, incidentally, that those two films are, essentially, the creation of those two directors respectively.

Occasionally, alternative authorial perspectives have been employed in attempts to transfer the occupational focus from director to screen-writer, cinematographer, art director, producer or star, but the search for a single unifying expressive signature for each film is sustained.)

Alternatively, of course, *To Have and Have Not* and *North by North West* could be considered in terms of their production companies (Adorno and Horkheimer's interchangeable Warner Bros and MGM), periods (1944 and 1959), plot-lines or generic formulae. Indeed, Robin Wood has written about *To Have and Have Not* precisely as a 'test case for the auteur theory', concluding that 'on the one hand it reveals such a multiplicity of sources and raw materials; on the other it is so consistently and intensely one of the central expressions of Hawks' personal view of life.'[28] By concentrating almost exclusively on the most visible alternative 'authors' of and 'influences' on the film, and in particular on other individual film-makers and films, however, Wood ensures that the director remains, if not the only begetter, then at least the most important one:

> *To Have and Have Not* is both a Hawks film and a
> Hollywood film, not intermittently, in some kind of
> dislocated alternation in which the director's personality can
> be seen struggling to express itself against the odds, but
> both at the same time, indissolubly, every aspect of the film
> traceable to some outside source or background information,
> yet every aspect pervaded and transmuted by the director's
> presence. Totally Hollywood and totally Hawks.[29]

If Wood's approach here is some sort of advance on Sarris it still insists on the unproblematic privileging of critical attention to Hawks rather than Hollywood. Nevertheless, there are moments where Wood's analysis begins at least to broach the question about what comprises that Hollywood, in this case discussing the impact of the thriller-in-exotic-location genre and what he calls 'Warners-style' lighting, both of which he attributes to 'the complex workings of the studio-and-star system'.[30] Such a perspective extends our attention to the industrial and cinematic specificities of Warner Bros and Metro-Goldwyn-Mayer.

Edward Buscombe has attempted to advance along this route in discussing the distinctive 'house styles' of those two companies, asking questions about the relation between those styles and the structure of the studios with which they are associated. For Buscombe, MGM's 'aesthetic style was determined by its economic hegemony':[31] 'Where Warners made a virtue out of getting a lot from a little, MGM got the most out of plenitude.'[32] Elsewhere, in examining the degree of compatibility which existed between Warner Bros and one of their contract directors, Raoul Walsh, Buscombe has begun to address the question of studio style in more detail:

> Studio style is a term which occasionally crops up in film criticism, but in a loose kind of way.... What seems to be lacking is any conception of the relations between the economic structure of a studio, its particular organization and the kinds of films it produced. For if there is such a thing as studio style it should be possible to provide some explanation of how it was formed.[33]

Buscombe argues that the elaboration of such an explanation has been blocked by film studies in two ways. Firstly, the contention that Hollywood, in the studio years, was simply and entirely in the hands of Wall Street banks and big business disallowed the possibility of specific cinematic styles being produced in specific studio situations. And secondly, the notion that an auteur's work was interesting in direct relation to the degree to which it differed from the mainstream output (of the genre being worked in or the studio being worked for) placed a critical premium on the 'exceptional'; this both endorsed and was in turn reinforced by conceptions of Hollywood industry and Hollywood cinema as almost entirely monolithic. Like Wood on Hawks, Buscombe emphasis the compatibility between the director and the context in which he worked, both in terms of the political content of the films and of their generic form. Thus Buscombe argues that Walsh, a contract director, was obliged to cast contract actors in particular and familiar kinds of roles, which meant, effectively, in particularly and familiar kinds of films, genre films:

> stars and genre were, particularly at Warners, mutually reinforcing. Because the studio had Bogart, Cagney and the rest under contract they made a lot of gangster pictures; and because they made a lot of gangster pictures they had stars like this under contract.[34]

Buscombe attempts to escape the circularity of this formulation by adding a number of other studio determinants – a 1931 administrative decision to draw subject matter from newspaper headlines; the financial success of the studio's first (early sound) examples of the genre like *Little Caesar*; 'Warner's own experience as a poverty row studio in the twenties (class on the screen being related to class off it)';[35] and finally the social background of the studio's employees – particularly those in higher executive and creative positions. There are, of course, a number of dangers here – the potential retreat back into a kind of pluralist auteurism, the reliance on biographical rather than hard industrial data, the nomination of new financial auteurs (which Buscombe him-self warns against in his essay on Columbia in this volume). Nor indeed should we wish for the 'politique des auteurs' to be replaced by a 'politique des ateliers' – the very word atelier, or studio, being almost as ideologically loaded with connotations of creativity as its predecessor. Nevertheless, the kind of detail assembled in Hugh Fordin's book on the MGM production unit under Arthur Freed (from which a chapter on the making of *On the Town* is reprinted here) importantly begins to supplement and even subtly refocus the kind of work that can and should be done on, say, Minelli and the musical.

Auteur-structuralism

The studio as auteur approach, however, was never really taken on board by film theory and in response to both the weaknesses outlined above and the romantic reductionism of classical au-teurism, a new auteur-structuralism was developed. Indeed, more elaborate conceptions of authorship were elaborated pre-cisely to avoid the sort of assumption revealed by Robin Wood's contention that *To Have and Have Not* was 'so consistently and intensely one of the central expressions of Hawks' personal view of life'.[36] Thus Peter Wollen, in *Signs and Meaning in the Cinema*, has suggested that 'The test case for the auteur theory is provided by the work of Howard Hawks ... a director who has worked for years within the Hollywood system'.[37] Wollen argues that for all the generic modes in which Hawks has worked, almost all his films

exhibit the same thematic preoccupations, the same
recurring motifs and incidents, the same visual style and
tempo. In the same way that Roland Barthes constructed a
species of homo racinianus, the critic can construct a homo
hawksianus, the protagonist of Hawksian values in the
problematic Hawksian world.[38]

Wollen is careful to distinguish between the early auteurist no-tion of Hawks the often interviewed director with a 'personal view of life', and 'Hawks' the structure of meanings to be located in the films the former is credited with directing. For Wollen, the function of auteur-structuralism, as it became known, was 'to decipher, not a coherent message or world-view, but a structure which underlies the film and shapes it, gives it a certain pattern of energy cathexis. It is this structure which auteur analysis di-sengages from the film.'[39] And thus, 'Hawks or Hitchcock, the directors, are quite separate from ... "Hawks" or "Hitchcock",

the structures named after them, and should not be methodo-
logically confused.'[40]

Wollen's 'structural approach' to auteurism was based at least
in part on the analysis of oral narratives of Vladimir Propp
and Claude Lévi-Strauss, neither of whom privilege particular
individuals as the 'tellers' of their respective 'tales'. Auteur-
structuralism, nevertheless, proceeded to apply their methods to
Hollywood films. Thus, for example, John Fell has discussed *To
Have and Have Not* together with two other Jules Furthman-
scripted films and come up with quite unorthodox (i.e. non-
Hawksian) but conventionally auteurist conclusions about that
film's structure and meaning.[41] Similarly, Wollen himself has employed a Proppian perspective in analysing the narrative of *North
by North West*.[42]

There remain two important problems here. The first is that
the absence of any ambition to displace the director (or other
individual) as punctual source of meaning can only, albeit implicitly, reinforce authorship. Peter Wollen, however, has added
a second and perhaps more serious problem:

> There is a danger . . . that by simply noting and mapping
> resemblances, all the texts which are studied (whether
> Russian fairy-tales or American movies) will be reduced to
> one, abstract and impoverished. There must be a moment of
> synthesis as well as a moment of analysis: otherwise the
> method is formalist rather than truly structuralist. Structuralist
> criticism cannot rest at the perception of resemblance or
> repetitions (redundancies in fact) but must also comprehend
> a system of differences and oppositions. In this way, texts
> can be studied not only in their universality (what they all
> have in common) but also in their singularity (what
> differentiates them from each other). This means of course
> that the test of a structural analysis lies not in the orthodox
> canon of a director's work, where resemblances are
> clustered, but in films which at first sight may seem
> eccentricities.[43]

Wollen's cautionary remarks remain a pertinent and powerful
check to the formalist excesses of structuralism. Nevertheless
they conform to and confirm the auteurist impulse and, perhaps
rather surprisingly, resist the opportunity to urge analyses of
structures beyond authorial bounds, whether generic or, indeed,
industrial. Of course, the hypothesis of multiple, often mutually
incompatible voices within a single text (notwithstanding the
notion that it is characteristically the director's voice which is
most articulate and/or interesting) does enable critical scrutiny
to supersede the apparent message and perhaps reveal contra-

dictions that are not simply author-originated, thus avoiding romantic reductionism. But it also, by means of analogy with fairy-tales and oral myths, facilitates a repression of what is already known about the very complex material conditions in which films are made. Auteur-structuralism, in fact, necessarily emphasises the consumption process rather than that of production or origin, by concentrating on the 'reading' of film texts. By revealing not just a single, coherent voice and source but instead a clash of different voices, the viewer/reader's task is transformed into that of 're-writing' the text, reconstituting a meaning for the consumer and thereby unseating the author, the writer. Such a change of emphasis, however, still fails to investigate the possibility of non-directorial auteurs and more importantly prohibits the analysis of alternative structures. Charles Eckert, for instance, once suggested that perhaps the best subject for a structural study was not the work of an individual director but 'communal blocks' assembled according to studio, production unit, period, cycle or genre as this would provide a more accurate analogy with the groups of tales studied by Propp and Lévi-Strauss.[44]

Genre

As authorship studies grew gradually more sophisticated, an alternative approach to American cinema was also being elaborated. Indeed its elaboration was almost obligatory in order that authorship could continue to operate. For if it was to be argued (as it still was by conventional auteurists) that an auteur's destiny was somehow to transcend the 'money-oriented environment', 'the vast commercial machine' that was industrial Hollywood, then the cinema that surrounded those transcendental exceptions needed to be made visible if only for the purposes of comparison. As Sarris put it, 'To resurrect Ford and Hawks, it is necessary also to resurrect the Western. To take Minnelli seriously it is necessary to take musicals seriously.'[45] In a sense, then, it was generic conventions and standard practices – in the form of specific narrative structures, iconographies, characterisations and visual styles – that began to be seen as the 'common language' that both Wood and the structuralists had hypothesised. Perhaps predictably, therefore, the first few book-length studies of Hollywood genres might more accurately be described as analyses of the cinematic careers of some of those auteurs who have worked in them. Thus Colin McArthur, in his book on the gangster film *Underworld USA*, concedes the industrial impetus of cinematic genres only to move on to their political implications and the aesthetic opportunities that they provide:

> The emergence of genres in the American cinema belongs, up to a point, to the commercial nature of Hollywood production. There is a sense in which all Hollywood movies are genre pieces, there being in Hollywood a built-in impulse to reproduce a successful formula. Thus it is possible to classify movies as sentimental comedies, social exposés, location thrillers and so on. But there are two genres which have been specially important in the development of Hollywood: the Western and the gangster film/thriller. Each genre has developed its own recurrent iconography and its own themes against which individual artists have counterpointed their personal vision.[46]

The argument here is remarkably reminiscent of Wood's, with its romantic opposition between economic necessity on the one hand and personal vision on the other. And once again, an analysis of the relationship between the industry and the critical concept at hand, in this case that of genre, is posed but then postponed in order to pursue the crucial relation between American cinema and American society, American history. Thus McArthur argues that the two major film genres have a special relationship with America, in representing, albeit in a coded mythic form, 'America talking to itself about, in the case of the Western, its agrarian past, and in the case of the gangster film/thriller its urban technological present.'[47]

Similarly Will Wright, in a structuralist study of the Western, has designated Hawks's *Rio Bravo* as a forerunner of what he calls the 'professional Western', in that its protagonists together constitute a specific economic group which Wright relates, rather schematically, to the postwar emergence of the corporate capitalist state.[48] For all the value of these kinds of approach, however, they share a conception of cinematic genre as some sort of shorthand, a ventriloquist's dummy for America and American ideology, politics or economics in general. This is not to argue, of course, that the American cinema is in any way autonomous of such determinants, but simply to suggest that the specific form of the industry which produces them is an important 'missing link' in that analysis, and furthermore that the form that industry takes is not necessarily economically in sync with the rest of American capital. Wright, meanwhile, seems simply to equate commercial success with a film's satisfaction and endorsement of its audience's ideological expectations and an underlining of its mythic pertinence. Such an approach, however, entirely fails to account for the influence of stars, publicity, competition or lack of it at the time of release, the kind of distribution the film receives, and so on. Furthermore, it takes no account of the effect of inflation on the box-office figures his analysis of best-selling Westerns is premised on, nor on the demographics of the audiences attending those films. Attention to industrial factors such as these is at least a corrective to what is otherwise a rather simplistic equation. Is it not at least possible, for instance, that research into exhibition, marketing strategies and theatre location of the kind urged and exemplified by the work of Douglas Gomery in this anthology might begin to address the question of whether the Western and the gangster film were examples of Hollywood, or rather, particular sections of Hollywood at particular times, talking to specific sections of the cinema audience – as was apparently the case with television versions of those genres in the 1950s, 1960s and 1970s? Is it not also worth considering whether Wright's 'professional' ideologies began to operate in Westerns at about the same time as, or slightly earlier or later than, similar occupational ideologies began to operate in the expanding independent sector of the American film industry? *Rio Bravo*, for instance, was distributed by Warner Bros but produced by an independent outfit, Armada. Some work has now been done on investigating the functions which specific genres and formulae may have performed for the film industry at particular times.[49] In this anthology, the essay on *film noir*, that most heavily over-determined of genres, attempts to rethink it in terms less of social malaise than of specific industrial conditions and constraints.

Rather than developing in such a direction, however, genre studies in particular and film theory in general have increasingly tended to privilege ideological and psychoanalytical factors over industrial ones. The reasons for this are clearly complex, but probably include the importance attached to the theorisation of and consequent practical production of oppositional independent film and television work. Thus Stephen Neale's book *Genre* concentrates on these two aspects of that phenomenon but concludes with an attempt to elaborate a model for incorporating industrial economies and audiential expectations into the wider process:

> On the one hand there is the economic aspect. Genres, of course, do exist within the context of a set of economic relations and practices, a fact often stressed by pointing out that they are the forms of the products of capitalist industry. On the other hand there is the fact that genres exist not simply as a body of texts, or a body of textual conventions, but also as a set of expectations.[50]

Taking the economic aspect first, Neale argues that genres are not the direct product of the industrialisation of the cinema but rather a negotiation of the necessity for profit and the need to differentiate product because of the distinction between artistic commodities and ordinary commodities. He points out that because during the studio era profitability was estimated on the basis of groups of films rather than individual films, genres provided a simple and convenient way of simultaneously maximising the use of capital assets, and minimising the risks of misjudging audiences or exhibitor expectations. Neale goes on to compare the way that this genre system distinguishes film production with car production:

> The motor car industry ... does not restrict itself to the manufacture of only one model of car. This is due not only to the fact that it comprises a number of different enterprises, each in competition with the others, and each, therefore, offering a variety of models in order to gain a bigger share of the market. It is also due to the fact that, in any event, the industry as a whole has constantly to stimulate demand. Comparing models to genres, a fundamental difference in function becomes apparent, a difference related to the nature of the commodities concerned. Whereas each individual car made according to the specifications of any one model should, ideally, be identical to all the others, each individual film belonging to a particular genre has to be different. Whereas, in other words, models in the car industry function to produce diversity, genres in the film industry function primarily to contain it.[51]

From this point, Neale's conclusion is difficult to dispute:

> Genres, therefore, are crucial to the film industry. They provide, simultaneously, maximum regularity and economy in the utilisation of plant and personnel, and the maximum degree of difference necessary for each individual product.[52]

Since the fact of genre is not simply one of economics but also one of expectations, it is easy to accept the Althusserian assumption that cinema has both an economic and an ideological face.

Textual analysis – semiotics and psychoanalysis

Growing dissatisfaction with orthodox authorial and genre-based film studies led in the early 1970s to the launch of several new theoretical initiatives, among which the name of Louis Althusser was a frequent reference. With the publication of *Cahiers du cinéma*'s lengthy analysis of John Ford's 1939 film *Young Mr Lincoln*,[53] *Cahiers* announced its abandonment not only of orthodox critical commentary, interpretation (authorial or otherwise) and simple synopsis, but also and more importantly of what it called the practice of 'mechanistic structural reading', that kind of 'demystificatory criticism' which assumes 'it is enough to re-locate the film within its historical determinations'.[54]

Before embarking on an analysis of the film itself, *Cahiers*' editors argued persuasively that:

an artistic product cannot be linked to its socio-historical
context according to a linear, expressive, direct causality
(unless one falls into a reductionist historical determinism)
but ... has a complex, mediated, decentred relationship with
this context, which has to be rigorously specified (which is
why it is simplistic to discard 'classic' Hollywood cinema on
the pretext that since it is part of the capitalist system it can
only reflect it).[55]

In the event, *Cahiers*' analysis is intentionally stronger in 'rigorously specifying' the signifying structures of the film than in identifying the socio-historical context, including the industrial structure in which it was produced, distributed and exhibited. Indeed, a single page on Hollywood in 1938–39, another on the USA in the same period, two more on Fox and Zanuck and a fifth on Ford and Lincoln, is alarmingly schematic if only because of the uncritical reception this inadequate sketch of the film's production context has all too often received. More importantly, however, *Cahiers*' cautionary words about the complexity of the text's relation with its context has been perceived not as an encouragement to increasingly rigorous research into that context but as an alibi for avoiding what was perceived as neither practicable nor desirable – and an enthusiastic if re-directed return to textual analysis. Since the project of the *Cahiers* analysis was to examine the film itself, to explore it 'symptomatically', noting its 'structuring absences' as Jacques Lacan refers to them, its 'internal shadows of exclusion' as Althusser describes them, it is perhaps unsurprising that the remarks on *Young Mr Lincoln*'s context are rather disappointing. It is not, however, merely pedantic to point out that what *Cahiers* does have to say about that context is restricted to biographical information about Ford's collaborators, thematic comparisons with other Ford films and, crucially, the unsubstantiated assumption that 20th Century-Fox supported Republicanism 'because of its links with big business'. Auteurism aside, here is a formulation in which 'causality' could hardly be more directly or reductively conceived. The value of *Cahiers'* analysis in making the film 'say not only "what this says but what it doesn't say because it doesn't want to say it"' is not at issue here. It is, however, necessary to insist that even here the anthropomorphism of the formulation implicitly enables the analysis, whether unwittingly or unwillingly, to re-authorise John Ford (or 'John Ford'). Less contentiously, perhaps, the assumption that knowledge about the economic control of a production company allows conclusions legitimately to be drawn about the politics of that company and, by extension, the politics of that company's films is addressed by Edward Buscombe in his essay in this volume.

The desire to simply and scientifically interrogate the film text has long been a characteristic of film studies. In a sense, the very strength of that desire is symptomatic of film studies' lack of academic status and self-confidence. Furthermore, the object of study is the film, not the cinema:

> film is only a small part of the cinema, for the latter
> represents a vast ensemble of phenomena some of which
> intervene before the film (the economic infrastructure of
> production studios, banks or other financing, national laws,
> sociology of the context of decision making . . .), others after
> the film (the social, political and ideological impact of the
> film on different publics, 'patterns' of behaviour or of
> sentiment induced by viewing the films, audience responses,
> audience surveys, mythology of stars, etc.).[56]

But textual analysis, for which semiotics and structuralism are undoubtedly our most supple and sophisticated tools and without which no serious attempt to elaborate the relationship between text and context could conceivably be mounted, is often either unwilling or unable to avoid resurrecting authorship. Such analyses as we already have concentrate to a perhaps surprising degree on the films of the orthodox auteur canon, and, if only by omission of other potential determinants, continue to 'credit' the director as source of meaning and decision-maker. The consequences of this for our understanding of the mechanics of signification within the film text may be minimal; the consequences for film history, on the other hand, may be far more serious. Thus, for instance, Stephen Heath's seminal semiotic analysis of *Touch of Evil* is an unparalleled and unprecedented dissection of significatory processes and structures in the Hollywood feature film; at the same time, however, it can only 'attribute' the individuating felicities of the film in question to the familiar authorial signature of Orson Welles, a signature already associated with the textual filigree of terms like 'baroque', 'expressionism' and 'chiaroscuro'.[57] It is, of course, only fair to admit that it was no part of Heath's intention to elaborate *Touch of Evil*'s relation to its context; nevertheless, Welles is credited, if only by omission. Expansion of Heath's situating remarks about Universal in 1959, on the other hand, might begin to re-locate (and re-allocate) the film in (and to) the context de-lineated in the article in this anthology on the B *film noir*. Thus Heath's estimation of the film as something of an eccentric ex-ception to 'classic narrative cinema' (rather reminiscent of Adorno/Horkheimer's verdict on Welles's tolerated infringements of standard practices) could be endorsed without echoing the implication that that difference derived from Welles alone.

Occasionally semiotics has defended itself against accusations of 'formalism' simply and indisputably by asserting the complex-ity of the semiotic task itself:

> Though the before and after of film do not interest semiotics one must not think that semiotics removes film from its socio-economic context, for this would render it a non-ideological object: thus we study neither the various pressures of production and distribution nor the ideological impact of film (these external studies being best left to sociologists, economists and psychologists) but the ideological interplay within the filmic fact itself.[58]

If the film industry is often conceived as an 'external' factor in film studies, that is not unconnected to the impact of Althusser-ian Marxism on the theory of ideology both in French and Anglo-American cultural criticism. Althusser recast Marx's famous base-superstructure metaphor and replaced it with the conception of a single social formation comprised of three dis-tinct and discrete 'levels' or 'instances', the economic, the pol-itical and the ideological. Each of these was conceived as op-erating within its own relative autonomy, with the economic apparently remaining in the classic role as the overriding deter-minant in the 'last instance'. Since Althusser's central concern, however, was with the ideological instance, film studies, freed from a denunciation of mass culture as no more than a reflection of its economic base, a denunciation common to liberal human-ist literary criticism and vulgar Marxist sociology, has followed Althusser into a relegation of the political and economic aspects of films and industry alike to a final instance, one that almost literally never materialises.

Undoubtedly, Althusser's elaboration of those three levels facilitated analyses – like that of the B *film noir* in this volume – allowing the conception of discrete and distinct categories of imperative on cinema at any specific historical moment. The advantages of this at the explanatory level are obvious; so too, with hindsight, are some of the problems. At its crudest, the model enables and even encourages film studies to conceive its object as exclusively or at least primarily ideological and, equally dubiously, to equate the film industry with economics. It is to be hoped that this volume can begin to illuminate and indeed problematise this division – for instance, in Ida Jeter's analysis of the economic and ideological origins of the political struggle between rival labour unions in the 1930s, and again in Janet Staiger's account of the multi-layered motivations for Hollywood's adoption of the photoplay in the 1920s. The impact of Althusser's work, whatever its shortcomings, included a break in the deadlock of traditional Marxist cultural criticism by refusing to reduce texts to no more than a reflection of their economic bases. Among those shortcomings, however, has been its availability as an alibi for a continued ignoring of the political economy of culture, an ignoring underwritten by the hypothesis of 'relative autonomy'. Nevertheless, without the Althusserian intervention, it is unlikely that the kind of work which is presently underway on the historical relation between those standard practices adumbrated after exhaustive textual analysis and the industrial structures within which such standards were set and monitored would ever have been begun.

A further theoretical shift which has enabled this important development to occur has been the impact on film studies of psychoanalysis. Psychoanalysis has reformulated our understanding of cinema not simply as product but as process; indeed, films themselves can now be seen to have products of their own – not just 'meanings' but pleasures produced and audiences constructed. One major influence in this field is Christian Metz, who has written in considerable detail about the symbolic (not to say symbiotic) relationship between cinema and psychoanalysis, re-applying to cinema such concepts as voyeurism, fetishism and the look. That this work, particularly in conjunction with semiotics, has crucially and critically advanced film studies is not in question. But Metz not only proposes an interrelation between cinema and the psyche; he further specifies such a relation between the psychic processes of the spectator and the infrastructures of the film industry. Thus, for Metz,

> the cinematic institution is not just the cinema industry
> (which works to fill seats, not to empty them) it is also the
> mental machinery – another industry – which spectators
> 'accustomed to the cinema' have internalised historically and
> which has adapted them to the consumption of films. (The
> institution is outside us and inside us, indistinctly collective
> and intimate, sociological and psychoanalytic. . . .) . . . The

outer machine (the cinema as industry) and the inner
machine (the spectator's psychology) are not just
metaphorically related, the latter a facsimile of the former,
'internalising' it as a reversed mould, a receptive hollow of
identical form. . . . In this way, the libidinal economy (filmic
pleasure in its historically constituted form) reveals its
'correspondence' with the political economy (the current
cinema as a commercial enterprise). . . .[59]

Metz – and psychoanalytic criticism – is here displacing the film
industry both conceptually (merging it 'indistinctly' with the rest
of the cinematic institution together with its mental machinery,
libidinal economy, another industry) and also academically (via
the promotion to a more privileged position in that institution of
the role of pleasure and hence of the analytic status of psychoanalysis). In Metz, therefore, for all the important emphasis
on the 'activity' rather than passivity' of the audience, there remain echoes of Adorno and Horkheimer in the conception of a
culture industry whose form is reflected not only in that of its
products – the films – but also in their consumers, the filmgoers.
And thus the film industry and the terminology associated with
it have been employed to stand in for another industry altogether.

None of this is to suggest that there is no relation between
the form of the Hollywood film industry and that of the cinema
that has been its product. Rather it is to argue that such a relation obtains at a level more precise, more specific, more historically and empirically concrete than the abstract generalities of
some of the more totalising theories applied to cinema have
hitherto allowed. Conversely, while semiotics, psychoanalysis
and structural anthropology have all provided methodologies for
analysing particular film texts, an equally rigorous consideration
of their production context (of Hollywood both as historically
specific industrial site and mode of aesthetic practice) has been
relegated until far too recently to narrators entirely untroubled
by theoretical or methodological questions of any kind – even
historiographical ones. Such historians have been concerned
often almost exclusively to catalogue 'great films' and to attribute them to the appropriate 'great film-makers'; their chronicles
regularly interrupted with ritual accounts of the 'constraints'
placed by industry philistines on artistic 'creativity'.

For too long, then, there has been an academic division of
labour between, on the one hand, historical (empirical) and, on
the other, theoretical (ahistorical) work. Ironically, if this division
is finally to be bridged, if these two (in fact far more than two)
approaches can be stitched together, then perhaps the cinematic

'suture' may itself be revealed not only as an ideological/psy-
choanalytic function but as the scar of a historically specific
mode of production, a particular division of Hollywood labour,
a precise allocation of technological resources.[60] The history of
Hollywood cinema – as 'superstructure' – cannot simply be read
off from its industrial conditions of existence, its economic
'base'. Indeed, it was Hollywood's commitment to a specific
mode of cinematic signification as much as to a particular mode
of production which determined the look of its films and the
ways in which they were made. If, therefore, it can be said that
the American cinema owes its style, at least in part, to the production practices of the American film industry, those practices
are themselves the consequence of a commitment to that style.
It is the ambition of this volume to provide an introduction to
and a focus on the industrial aspect of this circle; the signification of cinema and the question of film style are addressed in
other anthologies in this series. Together they may begin to
provide the perspective on Hollywood as cinema and as industry
and their interrelation that has hitherto passed all too easily for
synonymity.

Notes

1 Benjamin B. Hampton, *History of the American Film Industry* (New York: Dover Publications Inc., 1970).
2 John Caughie (ed.), *Theories of Authorship* (London: Routledge & Kegan Paul, 1981), p. 1.
3 Christopher Williams (ed.), *Realism and the Cinema* (London: Routledge & Kegan Paul, 1981), p. 3.
4 Tino Balio (ed.), *The American Film Industry* (Madison: University of Wisconsin Press, 1976), p. vii. Other book-length histories of the American film industry include Hampton (op. cit.), Robert Stanley's *The Celluloid Empire: A History of the American Motion Picture Industry* and Gorham Kindem's anthology *The American Movie Industry: The Business of Motion Pictures*.
5 F. R. Leavis and Denys Thompson, *Culture and Environment* (London: Chatto & Windus, 1933), p. 29.
6 Philip French, *The Movie Moguls* (Harmondsworth: Penguin, 1971), p. 17.
7 T. W. Adorno and Max Horkheimer, 'The culture industry: enlighten-ment as mass deception', in *Dialectic of Enlightenment* (London: Verso, 1979), p. 137.
8 Ibid., p. 121.
9 Ibid.
10 Ibid., pp. 123–4.

11 *Cahiers du cinéma* editors, 'John Ford's *Young Mr Lincoln*', in *Screen Reader 1; Cinema/Ideology/Politics* (London: SEFT, 1977).
12 Hortense Powdermaker, *Hollywood: The Dream Factory* (Boston: Little, 1950).
13 Powdermaker, op. cit., p. 44.
14 Adorno and Horkheimer, op. cit., p. 121.
15 Powdermaker, op. cit., p. 53.
16 Rudolf Arnheim, *Film as Art* (London: Faber and Faber, 1958).
17 Christopher Williams, op. cit.
18 André Bazin, 'The ontology of the photographic image', in *What Is Cinema?* (Berkeley: University of California Press, 1974).
19 Christopher Williams, 'The deep focus question: some comments on Patrick Ogle's article', in *Screen Reader 1* (London: SEFT, 1977), p. 109.
20 Douglas Gomery, 'Writing the history of the American film industry – Warner Bros and sound', *Screen*, vol. 17, no. 1, Spring 1976.
21 Pauline Kael, *The Citizen Kane Book* (London: Paladin, 1974), p. 1.
22 Adorno and Horkheimer, op. cit., p. 129.
23 Andrew Sarris, *The American Cinema* (New York: Dutton, 1968), p. 21.
24 Ibid., p. 31.
25 Ibid., p. 37.
26 Ibid.
27 Robin Wood, *Howard Hawks* (London: Secker and Warburg, 1968), pp. 8-9.
28 Robin Wood, 'To have written and have not directed', *Film Comment*, May/June 1973, p. 35.
29 Ibid., p. 30.
30 Ibid., p. 35.
31 Edward Buscombe, *MGM*, BFI Dossier no. 1 (London: BFI Publishing, 1980), p. 4.
32 Buscombe, op. cit., p. 3.
33 Edward Buscombe, 'Walsh and Warner Brothers', in *Raoul Walsh* (Edinburgh: Edinburgh Film Festival, 1974), p. 52.
34 Ibid., p. 59.
35 Ibid., p. 60.
36 Robin Wood, op. cit.
37 Peter Wollen, *Signs and Meaning in the Cinema* (London: Secker & Warburg, 1972), pp. 80-1.
38 Ibid.
39 Ibid., p. 167.
40 Ibid., p. 168.
41 John Fell, 'Vladimir Propp in Hollywood', *Film Quarterly*, vol. 3, no. 3, Spring 1977.
42 Peter Wollen, '*North by North-West*: a morphological analysis', *Film Form*, vol. 1, no. 1, Spring 1976.
43 Peter Wollen, *Signs and Meaning in the Cinema*, op. cit., p. 93.
44 Charles Eckert, 'The English cine-structuralists', in John Caughie (ed.), op. cit.
45 Sarris, op. cit., p. 30.

46 Colin McArthur, *Underworld USA* (London: Secker and Warburg, 1972), p. 17.
47 McArthur, op. cit., p. 18.
48 Will Wright, *Six Guns and Society* (Berkeley: University of California Press, 1975).
49 See, for instance, Mary Beth Haralovich, 'Sherlock Holmes: genre and industrial practice', *Journal of the University Film Association*, 31, Spring 1979.
50 Stephen Neale, *Genre* (London: British Film Institute, 1980), p. 51.
51 Ibid., pp. 52-3.
52 Ibid., p. 53.
53 *Cahiers du cinéma* editors, op. cit.
54 Ibid., p. 114.
55 Ibid., p. 115.
56 Christian Metz, *Langage et Cinéma*, quoted in Thierry Kuntzel, 'The treatment of ideology in the textual analysis of film', in *Screen Reader 2: Cinema and Semiotics* (London: SEFT, 1981), p. 187.
57 Stephen Heath, 'Film and system, terms of analysis', in *Screen*, vol. 16, nos 1 and 2.
58 Christian Metz, 'The imaginary signifier', *Screen* vol. 16, no. 2, p. 18.
59 Ibid., pp. 18-20.
60 See the 'Dossier on suture' in *Screen*, vol. 18, no. 4 for an introduction to this concept.

1 · Janet Wasko: D. W. Griffith and the banks: a case study in film financing

Journal of the University Film Association, vol. 30, no. 1, Winter 1978

'The debt that all film-makers owe to D. W. Griffith defies cal-culation.'[1] Andrew Sarris's verdict on Griffith is one of the or-thodoxies of film history: Griffith was an artist of such stature, it is often argued, that he not only created several of the Amer-ican cinema's most enduring masterpieces but also, almost single-handedly, created that cinema itself as we now know it. Inventions and innovations as various as the close-up, parallel editing, the star system, the epic film genre, indeed the very feature-length narrative film itself, have all, at one time or an-other, been attributed to Griffith. Furthermore, Griffith's career has been cited by pre-auteurist critics as exemplifying their view of Hollywood, according to which artists like Griffith, von Stroh-eim and Welles were destroyed by the philistinism of the indus-try that employed them and whose constraints their films so majestically transcended. To the auteurists, on the other hand, Griffith's career has proved something of a stumbling block, his most celebrated films having been made before the vertical in-tegration of the film industry took place and thus apparently lying outside the strict parameters of the so-called studio era which was the primary focus of magazines like *Movie* and the auteurist period of *Cahiers*.

In focusing on precisely this period, Janet Wasko's perspec-tive and project are thus doubly refreshing. Not only does she demonstrate that Griffith's 'greatest' films were made in precisely those years, the late 1910s and early 1920s, when the industry was indeed integrating, but she goes on to argue, very convinc-ingly, that far from being a passive victim of commercial philis-tinism Griffith was actually 'an active participant in the evolution of a capitalist film system'. Griffith's role as a partner in the formation of United Artists – a distribution company with no studio facilities of its own – is already a familiar part of film history. Wasko's emphasis, on the other hand, is on the far less familiar relationship between Griffith and those financial insti-tutions which were increasingly involved in investing money in his films. Of course, Griffith's long-term involvement with a var-iety of American banks and bankers could simply be seen as evidence of his status as an economic as well as aesthetic pioneer. But, as Wasko argues, Griffith's success in both fields only lasted as long as his activities either coincided with or did not by too much exceed the bounds of what was currently conceived as permissible practice. That his career came to an end in the early 1930s, therefore, is a consequence both of the financial crisis which was belatedly hitting Hollywood, and of the changing grammar of American films and the changing expectations of America filmgoers following the advent of sound.

Nevertheless and perhaps surprisingly, Wasko does not depart from the conventional conception of the conflict between 'commercial' and 'artistic' considerations in Hollywood, implying that such pressures are inherently contradictory. She concludes that 'one can't help but wonder how [Griffith's] creative potential might have developed without those commercial restrictions which contributed so greatly to his downfall'. An alternative perspective on the relationship between Griffith's creativity and the industrial environment in which he worked might reach entirely different conclusions based on the very evidence which Wasko herself has provided. If the histories of the aesthetic and entrepreneurial development of the American cinema are seen to be inextricably linked, then many of the stylistic 'innovations' attributed to Griffith could be reviewed as the strategic response of film workers to the changing imperatives of the business they were all employed in. David Bordwell's article in this anthology gives an analysis of a parallel process after the coming of sound.

Note

1 Andrew Sarris, *The American Cinema* (New York: Dutton, 1968), p. 51.

The American motion picture industry is organized as a capitalist system of production and (as is true for most other capitalist industries) relies on external financing for its survival. As various studies have shown, the motion picture business has most often relied on debt financing (i.e. bank loans) more than on stock or bond issues.[1] However, both methods have been and are still being used, and both involve relationships with banking institutions.

The extensive D. W. Griffith collection at the Museum of Modern Art in New York provides the opportunity to focus on one early film-maker and his involvement with banks and financiers. Griffith is a worthy subject for study: he was an independent producer with his own company, a partner in the United Artists Corporation, and a producer/director for several other studios. His career spanned several eras in movie history, from the Motion Picture Patents Company's early stranglehold on the industry to the introduction of sound in the late 1920s. And during that time, Griffith was involved in one way or another with at least thirty-four different banks.

His early films, especially *The Birth of a Nation*, demonstrated that film could be a powerful social force, as well as a powerful source of profit. This success led to the involvement of previously sceptical bankers and financiers, allowing Griffith to over-extend himself financially to the point that commercial considerations impinged upon and finally dominated any 'artistic' considerations. One crisis followed another, while the parameters set by the financial men became narrower and narrower. Finally, when Griffith was unable to compete, he was excluded from an industry which he had helped to create.

In 1931, Dwight MacDonald labelled D. W. Griffith a typical American product. ... [D]uring the past ten years he has gone to seed with a thoroughness possible only to the American artist ...[2] A brief look at Griffith's financial dilemmas provides an essential background for any discussion of his eventual demise.

Griffith's involvement with bankers began as early as 1908 when he began directing one-reel films for the American Mutoscope and Biograph Company.[3] His contract was signed by Jeremiah J. Kennedy, a banker who had taken over as President of Biograph after having been sent by the Empire Trust Company to investigate a delinquent $200,000 loan. Rather than liquidating the company, Kennedy stayed on as its leader, eventually becoming the dominant figure in the Motion Picture Patents Company and the General Film Company, or more simply, 'the Trust'.

For Biograph, Griffith directed at least 423 films which were largely responsible for reviving the company's weak financial condition. Yet in 1912, when he asked for Biograph stock or a share in the company's profits, Kennedy denied his requests. Griffith's desire to produce longer films was also stifled by Kennedy, who was committed to the more profitable one-reel format. The company was willing to go as far as producing a few two-reel films, but approval had to come from Biograph's executive office. Thus, when Griffith made the four-reel *Judith of Bethulia* for a cost of over $36,000, he was informed that he would either direct one-reelers or supervise other directors. Griffith officially broke ties with Biograph on 1 October 1913.

Having freed himself from Kennedy's confining policies, Griffith chose from many propositions the one which seemed to offer the most freedom plus a share of the profits. However, by aligning himself with the Mutual Film Corporation, he was still tied to men with business and financial backgrounds. Mutual had been formed in 1912 by John Freuler, an ex-banker, and Harry Aitken, one of the founders of the Federal Life Insurance Company in Chicago, with the financial assistance of two Wall Street bankers, Otto Kahn, of Kuhn, Loeb & Company, and Crawford Livingston.[4] Griffith served Mutual as head of production and directed several films, while Aitken busied himself by screening these films to financiers and 'other society people', in order to elicit more financial support.[5] But when Griffith and Aitken launched their biggest project to date – a filmed version of *The Clansman*, later known as *The Birth of a Nation* – the conservative businessmen backed away. According to Griffith's wife's account, Felix Kahn (Otto's brother) was to back the project but withdrew because of World War I. And the ex-banker Freuler limited Mutual's support as well, prompting Aitken and Griffith to form their own company to finance and distribute the film.[6]

The outcome of the venture is well known. Despite its racist content – or perhaps because of it – *The Birth of a Nation* caused a sensation, attracting huge audiences around the country, even with a $2 admission charge at some theatres, an idea which Aitken had insisted upon. The profits from the film, however, are still subject to some debate. Various accounts have cited $15 to $18 million profits during the first few years of release,[7] while in a letter to a potential investor in the proposed sound version, Aitken noted that a $15 to $18 million box-office gross was a 'conservative estimate'.[8] For years *Variety* has listed *The Birth of a Nation*'s total rental at $50 million. (This reflects the total amount paid to the distributor, not box-office gross.) This 'trade legend' has finally been acknowledged by *Variety* as a 'whopper myth', and the amount has been revised to $5 million.[9] That figure seems far more feasible, as reports of earnings in the Griffith collection list gross receipts for 1915–1919 at slightly more than $5.2 million (including foreign distribution) and total earnings after deducting general office expenses, but not royalties, at about $2 million.[10]

Despite these inaccuracies, the 'whopper myth' is perhaps more important in that the huge profits allegedly attributed to this epic film attracted the attention of hitherto uninterested financial interests, enabling Griffith to raise money for his next epic project, *Intolerance*. While many of the more than fifty investors in his new Wark Productions Company were fellow film-makers, at least one-third were in some way associated with Wall Street.[11] When the film proved to be a financial nightmare, the pressure increased for Griffith, who had taken personal responsibility for the huge debts incurred. From this point on in his career, financial problems became an increasing burden to whatever artistic capacity he had.

Meanwhile, the motion picture business was growing into a more profitable and increasingly integrated industry, thus attracting more and more interest from Wall Street and other financiers. Griffith constantly sought independence from these big studios and their financial backers, but he still wanted to benefit from the increasing profits of the growing industry. In 1919, he joined three other filmmakers in the formation of the United Artists Corporation, and the same year built his own million-dollar studio complex at Mamaroneck, New York. Even the location of this studio, however, was influenced by commercial considerations, as film historian Iris Barry noted in her well-known essay on Griffith:

> The complex financial operations that had become a part of film production were absorbing more and more of his time. He apparently felt the need to be constantly in or near New York, which was then as now the financial center and shop-window of the industry.[12]

In order to finance these additional commitments, Griffith directed three First National films, which are generally agreed to be hastily produced, shallow efforts.

Finally on 30 June 1920, the D. W. Griffith Corporation was incorporated in the state of Maryland, with a capitalization of $50 million. Listed among the company's assets were the Mamaroneck studio and property, Griffith's United Artists stock worth approximately $35,000, nearly $1 million worth of insurance policies on Griffith and his principals, and interest in all past, present and future Griffith productions. The stock issue was handled by Bertron, Griscom & Company and Counselman & Company, banking firms which were also represented on the new Board of Directors by Charles Counselman and Lee Benoist. Two banks which had previously provided Griffith with production funds were also represented: Central Union Trust Company of New York was Transfer Agent for the new corporation and Guaranty Trust Company of New York was one of the Registrars.[13]

Actually, Griffith had previously been offered several financing proposals through his association with Frank R. Wilson, Director of Publicity for the Liberty Loan Campaign of the U.S. Treasury Department. Early in 1919, Wilson had indicated a good deal of interest in the motion picture business, and by July of that year, Griffith enlisted his help in formulating a 'comprehensive plan to turn [Griffith's] great earning power into permanent investments.'[14] In several long and detailed letters, Wilson discussed attempts to amalgamate United Artists and First National in order to conquer the Adolph Zukor empire, his contacts with financial men interested in building a Griffith theatre chain, and other schemes designed to take full advantage of Griffith's name. Most of this work was done, by the way, while Wilson was still employed by the Treasury Department.[15]

In September 1919, Wilson wrote of negotiations with Kissel, Kinnicutt & Company, describing them as '... one of the strongest firms of Wall Street, Mr. Kinnicutt having formerly been a member of the firm of Morgan & Company.' The plan included the financing of Griffith's productions and a theatre building program, and was described by Wilson as follows:

> These high-class business men ... believe that the road to the
> greatest profits is one which would provide for supplying you
> with several assistant directors and turning out about thirty
> program pictures per year. The supplying of assistant directors
> would permit you to have time to devote to one or two big
> features a year which the firm will gladly finance because they
> believe these big pictures would add to the lustre of your name
> and contribute to the success of the thirty program pictures ... It
> is their belief that your name has such tremendous goodwill
> value that the opportunity best afforded for turning this goodwill
> into cash is a policy of quantity production.[16]

Another proposal in 1919 specified that twenty-four pictures would be made annually at an average cost of $125,000, yielding an average profit of $50,000 per picture. Griffith would get 75% and an unnamed banker would receive the remaining 25%. Decisions on financial affairs, investments and production expenditures would be made by a Finance Committee, which would be chosen from a 'strong Board of Directors, including men of financial standing'. The proposal stated that '... in all matters involving the artistic – such as selection of stories, the assembling of casts and the direction of production in the studio or on location – the judgment of D. W. Griffith shall be final'.[17] However, no explanation was offered as to how Griffith could carry out these artistic decisions, which would require large amounts of capital, without the approval of the Finance Committee.

This proposal was most likely the one which Wilson showed to Dennis 'Captain' O'Brien , legal counsel and a member of the United Artists Board of Directors. O'Brien advised against the proposal, noting that Griffith could obtain enough credit for his business else-

where and could 'own himself. .... He seeks an immediate and temporary advantage and mortgages himself, his future, etc., to bankers
with whom he must work and share profits indefinitely'.[18]

O'Brien's advice seemed to affect Griffith – at least, for a short
while. The next proposal offered by Wilson, in March 1920, noted:

> The objections that have been urged against a general
> incorporation heretofore have had to do with the expense of
> such an operation and the restraint which might be put upon
> your business by the participation of bankers. This plan now
> proposed does away with all these objections.[19]

In this plan, another 'group of financial men' offered to organize a
public corporation and to pay for all expenses involved in offering
its stock to the public. Wilson's efforts to persuade Griffith to accept
this proposal provide an example of the logic of finance capitalism:

> I call your attention to the fact that hardly any busines in the
> world expects to capitalize itself out of profits. .... The most
> successful businesses are the heaviest borrowers because they
> have found the way to make money by the use of other people's
> money. And other people find it profitable to cooperate with
> successful business institutions by letting them use their capital to
> make additional money.[20]

Wilson concludes with a direct appeal to Griffith's ego, pointing out
that the business depended on Griffith's personality, and upon his
death his name would be gone. But,

> If you created a great corporation under the name of 'D. W.
> Griffith Inc.,' the corporation would live on, with you or without
> you .... I feel certain that I tell you truthfully that the creation
> of a corporation very greatly minnimizes [*sic*] the hazard
> arising from the uncertainty of life.[21]

This memorandum to Griffith was dated 1 March 1920 – four months
later Griffith's name was 'immortalized' as D. W. Griffith Inc.

Griffith's loan agreements specifically reveal the pressure he experienced from banking interests. While many independent film-makers found difficulty obtaining such loans, Griffith's name and his
profit-making potential enabled him to continually gain this type of
financial support. Loan agreements in the Griffith collection date
back to November, 1919, although references to the storage of *The
Birth of a Nation* and *Intolerance* negatives at a bank indicate that
Griffith had obtained loans as early as 1917. The Central Union
Trust Company and the Guaranty Trust Company of New York
provided loans for as much as $340,000 for several productions, and
by the end of 1921, nearly $2 million had been borrowed from these
two banks alone, with interest amounting to over $43,000.

The Central Union Trust relationship began as early as 1915, and provides an example of how Griffith was able to extend his credit while being continuously restricted. Early in 1920, the Central Union Trust loans involved the assignment of negative and positive prints for specific films, together with the receipts from the sale of these films. An insurance policy for $150,000 on Griffith's life was to be payable to the bank, with premiums paid by Griffith.

As Griffith's financial involvement became deeper, additional demands were made. The negatives of pledged films were to be insured, at Griffith's expense, against fire, theft or other damage and delivered to Central Union Trust's vaults. This storage policy changed, however, with a loan in October 1921, specifying that the original negatives be stored in Griffith's studio vault, which the bank leased for a nominal fee of $1 per year. The bank had probably discovered what Guaranty Trust Company had realized the previous year, when the negative for the film *The Love Flower* was returned to the studio because the bank had learned that motion picture negatives were inflammable. An accompanying letter apologized, explaining '... that you will understand how we feel about anything inflammable in the vaults.'[22]

By 1921, the Central Union Trust loan agreements also specified that any ledgers, books, or contracts referring to the assigned firms were to be marked:

The negative and films of this photoplay, together with all
contracts and agreements for the leasing, exhibition and
distribution therefrom, are the property of Central Union Trust
Company of New York. ...[23]

A good deal of correspondence took place between representatives of the bank and the Griffith company regarding these notations, as well as arrangements for placing the negatives in the vaults. By this time, the negatives had become the exclusive possession of the bank and the vaults were checked by bank representatives.

The loans made in 1922 added several restrictions. The distributor was to be approved by Central Union Trust, which also maintained the right to call for immediate payment of the loan with interest at any time. The completed picture was to be exhibited for the bank or its designated agent, and the agreement noted that,

... in the event that [Central Union Trust] ... is not satisfied
with said picture, or any contract or contracts which may have
been or are made for sale, leasing or distribution and/or
exchange ... the loan will forthwith, without any further action
... become due and payable.[24]

Provisions added in 1923 specified that neither Griffith nor his com-

pany was to develop or produce any pictures or create any obliga-
tions without the written consent of Central Union Trust. In addition
to these added restrictions, Griffith was required to pledge additional
collateral, which included his unpaid salary from and his stock in the
Griffith company.

Of course, there were loans from banks other than Central Union
Trust and Guaranty Trust. These included similar assignments and
restrictions, although a few additional provisions were sometimes
added. A loan from Columbia Bank in July 1923, authorized that
bank to examine any distributor's books and records, as well as
specifying that if the film being financed was not finished '... with
due diligence or to its [the bank's] satisfaction', the bank had the
right to enter the Griffith studio, take possession of the picture '...
together with all apparatus and appliances in connection with the
same ...' and to complete the picture, with Griffith paying any indebtedness incurred, in addition to the original loan.[25] Then, in 1924,
a loan from the Empire Trust Company for $250,000 stated that in
case of default, the bank had the power to sell or use any negatives,
prints, contracts, as well as Griffith's name, in connection with the
film, even if it were changed or recut.[26]

By 1925, most of Griffith's indebtedness had been taken over by
the Motion Picture Capital Corporation, a company which had been
formed by a group of bankers including Jeremiah Milbank and others
connected with the Chase National Bank and other Morgan banking
interests. Griffith became a member of the Board of Directors, held
stock in the corporation, and received loans totalling over $223,000.
At the same time, the President of the company – none other than
the previously mentioned Frank R. Wilson – and his assistant became
auditors for the Griffith company and were required to sign all checks
issued.[27]

By this time, Griffith had clearly lost any chance for independence.
He had borrowed over $4.5 million through banks and other finan-
cial institutions, and more and more often loan applications were
being refused. He signed a contract to make three Famous-Players
Lasky films in order to finance a film owed to United Artists, where
he finally returned to direct his last film, aptly titled *The Struggle*, in
1931. A loan from the Federal Bank and Trust Company
was secured by the mortgage on his studio property, United Artists
stock and the film itself. *The Struggle* was released in 1932 and
withdrawn the same year as a financial disaster. The Federal Bank
and Trust loan lingered on, however, while Griffith attempted to
procure another loan on the mortgage and stock in order to settle
the matter. Finally, in March 1933, he sold his United Artists stock,

providing the necessary funds to pay the bank and several other debts.[28]

In 1932 he had resigned from the Griffith corporation, which was bankrupt by 1935. After *The Struggle*, he made only a few 'guest director' appearances, even though many other projects were discussed. As one fellow film-maker commented,

> When he had to go to work for other people to obtain money, his films suffered. He needed artistic control to make successful pictures. He failed completely whenever he deliberately set out to make a commercial movie. ....[29]

Griffith's demise was during an era when large financial interests were becoming involved with motion pictures. Through AT&T and RCA's control over sound patents, as well as through various financial ties with the film companies themselves, the Rockefeller and Morgan empires exercised both direct and indirect control over the film industry.[30] Griffith's financial difficulties did little to endear him to these forces. As one of his admirers, Seymour Stern, noted:

> ... the original crowd of cloak and suit manufacturers who gained possession of the industry in its pioneer days ... are more solidly in the saddle of power than ever before.
>
> It is worse today because now they have the big bankers behind them, who lend financial and strategic support to their position; they have successfully suppressed a single creative mind that might get out of hand and attempt to use cinema according to some other conception ... other than their own. ....[31]

While Griffith criticized Hollywood and how he had been treated, it must still be said that he had been an active participant in the evolution of a capitalist film system, even to the extent of forming his own corporation and participating in many others. Yet one can't help but wonder how his creative potential might have developed without these commercial restrictions which contributed so greatly to his downfall.

An ironic twist is that many of the great Russian directors of the same era, such as Eisenstein, Pudovkin, and others, were inspired by Griffith's style and technique, although they rejected his ideology. One wonders as well how Griffith might have grown as a film-maker if he would have accepted Lenin's invitation to work in the Soviet Union.

But Griffith died in Hollywood in 1948, having been excluded from the film business many years earlier. He had helped create a new American art-form, but he had also contributed to the growth of motion pictures as a new American industry with commercial considerations and restrictions similar to any other capitalist enterprise.

NOTES

1 See Mae Huettig, *Economic Control of the Motion Picture Industry* (Philadelphia: University of Pennsylvania Press, 1944); William Greenwald. 'The motion picture industry (PhD dissertation, New York University, 1950); and, Donald L. Perry, 'An analysis of the financial plans of the motion picture industry for the period 1929 to 1962' PhD dissertation, University of Illinois, 1966).

2 Dwight MacDonald, *Dwight MacDonald on Movies* (Englewood Cliffs, New Jersey: Prentice-Hall, 1969), pp. 70-2.

3 Background on Griffith's Biograph days based on Robert M. Henderson's *D. W. Griffith: His Life and His Work* (New York; Oxford University Press, 1972) and Gordon Hendricks' *Beginnings of the Biograph* (New York: Beginnings of the American Film, 1964).

4 Robert Grau, *The Theatre of Science* (New York: Benjamin Bloom, 1914, reissued 1969), pp. 55-6; and, Gertrude Jobes, *Motion Picture Empire* (Hamden, Conn.: Archon Books, 1966), pp. 95 and 98.

5 D. W. Griffith Collection, Museum of Modern Art, New York, letter from Harry E. Aitken to D. W. Griffith, 15 April 1914.

6 Linda Arvidson, 'How Griffith came to make *The Birth of a Nation*,' in *Focus on D. W. Griffith*, Harry M. Geduld, ed. (Englewood Cliffs, New Jersey: Prentice-Hall, 1971), pp. 81-2.

7 Arvidson, *Focus . . .*, p. 81, Maurice Bardèche and Robert Brasillach, *The History of Motion Pictures* (New York: W. W. Norton, 1933), p. 100; Iris Barry and Eileen Bowser, *D. W. Griffith: American Film Master* (revised edition, 1965), p. 20.

8 D. W. Griffith Collection, Museum of Modern Art, New York, letter from Harry E. Aitken to W. H. Kemble, 17 June 1929.

9 'All-Time film rental champs', *Variety*, 5 January 1977, p. 16.

10 D. W. Griffith Collection, 1919 General Correspondence: 'Summaries of earnings of *The Birth of a Nation*, March 1919-October 1919'.

11 D. W. Griffith Collection, 'List of stockholders and monies paid - Wark Producing Corporating,' 3 December 1920.

12 Barry and Bowser, *D. W. Griffith. . . .* p. 29.

13 D. W. Griffith Collection, letter from D. W. Griffith to Counselman & Company, 18 June 1920.

14 D. W. Griffith Collection, letter from Frank R. Wilson to D. W. Griffith, 31 July 1919.

15 D. W. Griffith Collection, miscellaneous letters from Frank R. Wilson, February to September, 1919.

16 D. W. Griffith Collection, letter from Frank R. Wilson to D. W. Griffith, 12 September 1919.

17 D. W. Griffith Collection, 1919 General Correspondence, untitled memorandum.

18 D. W. Griffith Collection, letter from Dennis ('Captain') O'Brien to Albert Banzhaf, 17 January 1920.

19 D. W. Griffith Collection, letter from Frank R. Wilson to D. W. Griffith, 1 March 1920.

20 Ibid.
21 Ibid.
22 D. W. Griffith Collection, letter from Guaranty Trust Company of New York to Albert Banzhaf, 25 May 1920.
23 D. W. Griffith Collection, agreement between Central Union Trust Company of New York and D. W. Griffith Inc., 5 October 1921.
24 D. W. Griffith Collection, agreement between Central Union Trust Company of New York, and D. W. Griffith Inc., 15 June 1922.
25 D. W. Griffith Collection, agreement between Columbia Bank and D. W. Griffith Inc., 21 July 1923.
26 D. W. Griffith Collection, agreement between Empire Trust Company and D. W. Griffith Inc., 1 July 1924.
27 D. W. Griffith Collection, minutes of meeting of Board of Directors, D. W. Griffith Inc., 10 March 1925.
28 Tino Balio, *United Artists, The Company Built By The Stars* (Madison, Wisconsin: University of Wisconsin Press, 1976), pp. 85-91.
29 Lillian Gish, 'Fade Out', in Geduld, *Focus on Griffith*, p. 153.
30 See Francis D. Klingender and Stuart Legg, *Money Behind The Screen* (London: Lawrence & Wishart, 1937).
31 Seymour Stern, 'The bankruptcy of cinema as art,' from William Perlman, *The Movies on Trial* (New York: Macmillan, 1936), p. 117.

2 · Edward Buscombe: Notes on Columbia Pictures Corporation 1926–41

Screen, vol. 16, no. 3, Autumn 1975

Edward Buscombe's essay, like Wasko's, investigates the financial control of and consequent constraints upon American cinema. But while Wasko's impulse remains ambivalently auteurist in implication, Buscombe's is resolutely anti-auteurist. Auteurism, Buscombe argues, fails to abolish the absurd distinction which obtains between film as art and film as industry, merely shifting the line of demarcation somewhat. Where Wasko contends that Griffith's 'creative potential' was first frustrated and finally destroyed by 'commercial restrictions', Buscombe counters that, at least at Columbia studio between 1926 and 1941, financial control did not necessarily imply either interference or influence.

The focus on Columbia, a production-distribution company, rather than on an individual director or a particular pan-industrial period, allows an avoidance of what might otherwise have become biographically or sociologically reductive avenues of inquiry. As Buscombe points out, in auteurism the industry only seems to exist in order to be overcome, a necessary obstacle like the hurdles in steeplejack racing; similarly, in some post-auteurist criticism of American cinema the industry has either been entirely ignored, while the wider social formation was seen as determining, or alternatively it is itself seen as totally and mechanically determining. Buscombe argues that American films have historically been seen either as the works of artists, the reflections of society or the results of mass production and notes that they have only ever been valued if falling into one or other of the first two categories.

Taking Columbia as a kind of case study, therefore, Buscombe considers whether that studio's output between 1926 and 1941 can best be understood in terms of the impact of individuals like the director Frank Capra, the studio head Harry Cohn or the banker Giannini, the social context of the New Deal, or of the imprint of the very economic and organisational infrastructure of Columbia itself. Buscombe's argument, at its simplest, is that we need to ask questions not only about whether and to what extent films reflect the dominant ideologies of their period, the creative personnel who work on them or the executives who hold the purse strings, but also about whether 'the organisation of a film text might relate to the organisation of an industry or to specific working practices'. This formulation is reminiscent of – but at the same time reverses – Adorno and Horkheimer's contention that the products of the culture industry bear the after-images of the assembly line in their aesthetic structures. For where the Frankfurt school perspective, simply by proposing such a relation, is able definitively to reject those products, Buscombe, by refusing to reject popular cinema without first examining it, is able to add the film industry to the legitimate agenda of film studies.

Buscombe concludes, convincingly, that the industry is a missing link in our attempts to relate film to society – a link which, by virtue of its very size and structural complexity, deserves close scrutiny and demands an acknowledgment of its relative autonomy both from American society and from the rest of the economy including other industries. Of course, once such autonomy is granted then analysis of the asychronicities and apparent contradictions of the film industry can begin. Edward Buscombe's discussion of Columbia provides just such a beginning.

I

'The film industry': 'the cinema'. How are these terms related in film criticism? 'The film industry' describes an economic system, a way (or ways) of organising the structure of production, distribution and consumption. Historically such organisation has, in Britain and America, conformed to the usual pattern of capitalist activity; film can be seen as an industry like any other. It has passed from the primitive stage of small-scale entrepreneurial activity to the formation of large-scale monopolies, securing their position by vertical integration, spreading from production into distribution and exhibition. Since the war the industry has, like other forms of business, developed towards diversification and the formation of multinational corporations. In other respects too film has developed like other industries. Production in particular has been based on a division of labour, of a fairly extreme kind. From early days the industry has employed the techniques of mass advertising, and it has required the injection of huge sums of capital, resulting in turn in the passing of control of the industry from its original owners and from the primary producers.

In film criticism, then, the term 'film industry' implies a way of looking at film which minimises its differences from other forms of economic activity; a way which is of course predominantly that of those who actually own the industry. Its characteristic descriptions are sufficiently indicative of a perspective: 'the trade', 'marketing', 'exploitation', a 'package', 'product'.

'The cinema' suggests something else. While the term might, notionally, encompass the industry, the pull is surely in a different direction. 'The cinema' implies film as art. As Raymond Williams has shown with convincing detail in *Culture and Society*, the opposition between art and industry has a long history in our culture. The division between the two is experienced everywhere as deep, but nowhere deeper than in film. On the one hand we are given to understand is the industry, churning out product for financial gain. On the other are artists, creating enduring works of personal expression or comment on life and society. Such an opposition has taken different forms at different times. Sometimes it has been geographical. In America there was Hollywood, the industrial system par excellence. In Europe (usually excluding Britain, apart from its documentaries) there were artists: Renoir, Dreyer, Bergman, Antonioni, etc. Later the auteur theory, as applied to American cinema, changed the emphasis. Though Hollywood was still an industry, through diligent critical work some artists could be winnowed from the chaff, artists who against the odds managed by luck, cunning or sheer genius to overcome the system, the industry. The auteur theory, whatever its 'theory' may have been, did not in practice abolish the distinction between art and industry; it merely shifted the line of demarcation.

One might suppose that a little common sense would tell us that such a distinction is nonsense, that all film is both industry *and* art, in some sense. Even the lowest, most despised products (choose your own examples) are made with some kind of art. Do they not share the same language as the acknowledged masterpieces: do they not tell a story, try to affect the spectators' emotions? They may do it more or less effectively, but isn't this a difference of degree, not of kind? Conversely, in the making of the most spiritual and sublime films grubby bank notes change hands. The film stock on which the masterpiece is recorded may come from the same batch used to shoot the potboiler on the adjoining stage.

Yet proof that the mutual exclusion of art and industry operates at a level too deep to be affected by mere common sense can be found not only in the dominant critical attitudes but in the organisation of social institutions. To give an example close to home: the British Film Institute was set up, as its Memorandum of Association states, 'to encourage the development of the art of the film'. At the same time it is stated that the BFI is not permitted 'to control nor attempt to interfere with purely trade matters'. Art not only can but must be divorced from industry. And the split is preserved even in the structure of government. Whereas the BFI is administered by the Department of Education and Science, the film industry comes under the Department of Trade and Industry. Thus the opposition art/industry has to be seen not merely as a 'mistake' in film criticism which can be easily rectified by a more careful look at the facts, but as the result of a whole practice of thinking, talking, writing and disseminating inscribed in institutions like the BFI, those parts of the education system that handle film, plus also exhibition/viewing practice – the art-house circuit and its audience(s) – the 'immaterial' thought both reflecting and being part of this apparatus; in short, as part of an ideology.

The main concern here, however, is not with the origins of such an opposition but with its consequence for film criticism. This may be baldly stated; there has been scarcely any serious attempt to think the relationship between art and industry with regard to films produced in what have historically been for us the two most important film-making countries, namely our own and the United States. Criticism has been devoted not to relating them but to separating them out, and in practice this has meant that critics have concentrated on the beauties and mysteries of art and left the industry, presumably a tougher plant, to take care of itself. Study of the industry might require knowledge of, say, economics or of how films are actually made, knowledge which critics have not been expected to acquire. The main effort of criticism, therefore, has gone into the study of film texts viewed as autonomous, self-sufficient entities; or, occasionally, as reflections of society, but certainly not as reflections of the industry which produced them, unless they are being dismissed as rubbish. Even recent work deriving from structuralism and concerned to open up the text, to 'deconstruct' it, has tended to take the film as 'given' and has ignored questions of how the organisations of a film text might relate to the organisation of an industry or to specific working practices.

It is in respect of Hollywood, the largest field of activity in both film-making and criticism, that the lack of a history of the industry is most glaring. Of course there is a certain amount of information around. Statistics have occasionally been assembled (a number of Government and trade reports on Hollywood in the 1930s are listed in the notes of Leo C. Rosten's *Hollywood: The Movie Colony, The Movie Makers*, a book which has some useful material on this period). There are one or two books, again on the 1930s, which assemble some facts about the economics of the industry (for example, F. D. Klingender and Stuart Legg, *The Money behind the Screen* and Mae D. Huettig, *Economic Control of the Motion Picture Industry*). But of course they don't attempt to make any connections between the economics and the actual films produced. There is also the ragbag of publicity releases, inaccurate box-office returns and general gossip which makes up the trade press (*Film Daily, Motion Picture Herald, Variety, Hollywood Reporter*, etc). To this may be added a host of 'biographies' (or ghosted autobiographies) of prominent industry figures, of which *Hollywood Rajah* by Bosley Crowther (on Louis B. Mayer) and *King Cohn* by Bob Thomas (on Harry Cohn) are representative examples. Little that is useful can be gleaned from such works, which mostly string together collections of anecdotes about the 'great men'. On such questions as the financial structures within which they were obliged to operate or the actual working methods of their studios they are for the most part silent. Of studio histories, properly speaking, there is none, with the possible exception of Richard Schickel's book *The Disney Version*, which is hampered by his failure to get any cooperation from the Disney studio itself; a fact, of course, that is not without its significance, since it indicates the difficulties of this kind of work.

Indeed, the neglect of industry history is not only a consequence of critical attitudes and priorities which have abandoned the field to those whose interest does not go beyond 'personalities'. It is also the result of very real practical problems. The fact is that the history of the American film industry is extremely difficult to write, because many of the basic materials that would be needed are simply not available. The statistics are incomplete and unreliable. The trade press presents only the acceptable face of the business, even when one can get access to it (the BFI Library, virtually the only collection of such periodicals in Britain, has no run of *Variety*, though there are plans to acquire one). The biographies, and studio histories, where they exist at all (for example Bosley Crowther's *The Lion's Share*, on MGM), are largely based on reminiscences. Concrete documented evidence in the form, say, of studio memoranda, accounts and other records, is almost totally lacking. If such records still exist they are mostly locked away in studio vaults. And the history of technological development in Hollywood has still to be written. Lastly, the films themselves; such prints as have been preserved are often impossible to see. The situation is little different from that which exists in relation to the history of the Elizabethan stage, with this exception, that infinitely less method and application has gone into researching it.

The result is that when Hollywood has been written about its industrial dimension has been ignored. Much of the writing has been based on an idea of history as one damned thing after another. Even such a prestigious work as Lewis Jacob's *The Rise of the American Film* scarcely rises above this, most sections being simply annotated film lists. The only principle to compete has been auteurism, which leaves film history at the stage which history proper reached in the nineteenth century when Carlyle defined it as the lives of great men. Deliberate attempts to get away from auteurism, such as Colin McArthur's *Underworld USA* (on the crime film) and Jim Kitses's *Horizons West* (on the Western) are ultimately broken-backed books. Genres may be related to aspects of American history, but in the end it is the auteurs who dominate the account.

Some recent, more promising directions have been pursued. Patrick Ogle's work on deep-focus (*Screen*, vol. 13, no. 1) or that of John Ellis and Charles Barr on Ealing Studios (*Screen*, vol. 15, nos. 1–2, vol. 16, no. 1) have from different perspectives tried to make connections between films and the nature of the industry which produced them. *The Velvet Light Trap* has brought to light valuable material on the studio system, though the use that has been made of it has often been disappointing. But the gaps in our knowledge are still enormous.

II

One consequence of the existence of such gaps has been that attempts to relate Hollywood films to the society which produced them have simply by-passed the industry altogether. The result has been a series of short circuits. Hollywood films are seen as merely 'reflecting' society. On the one hand is society, seen as a collection of facts, attitudes, psychological patterns or whatever. On the other are the films, where one sees such facts, attitudes, etc mirrored. Though it may be conceded that the mirror sometimes distorts, in so far as there is a theory behind such a view it is a naively realist one, and indeed how could it be otherwise? If there is no conception of Hollywood as an industry with its own history, specific practices, economic relationships, technological and other material constraints, if film is seen as something that somehow mysteriously appears and having appeared is simply there, fixed and given, then how is one to understand the nature of any mediation? To confine ourselves again to the period of the 1930s, a book such as Andrew Bergman's *We're in the Money* devotes a mere four pages to 'A note on the movie industry and the Depression' which ends thus: 'The preliminaries completed, we proceed to the black and white footage itself.' And in the black and white footage the social comment can simply be read off as if the films were so many sociologists' reports. Here is an admittedly rather extreme example: 'Tod Browning's 1932 MGM film, *Freaks*, had a cast made up of pinheads, human torsos, midgets, and dwarfs, like nothing ever in the movies. And what more stunted a year than 1932 for such a film?' (p. 168).

One might expect that more specifically Marxist attempts to relate Hollywood to American society would display a little more rigour and subtlety. Bourgeois cultural theories, with their assumptions about the values of artistic freedom and personal expression, are obviously ill-equipped to deal with a medium so conditioned by money, technology and organisational structures. Books such as Bergman's, which dispense with most of that theory (though never completely; some auteurs, such as Capra and Vidor, make an appearance) seem to have no theory at all to replace it. Marxism, on the other hand, proposes a sophisticated understanding of the relations between society, a system of production and the actual product. Yet such Marxist models as have been put forward for understanding Hollywood have suffered from a crudity which has had the effect of deadening further thought. The crudest model of all is that encapsulated in Godard's phrase 'Nixon-Paramount'. The model implied in such a phrase has had obvious attractions for the political avant-garde and indeed contains some truth. But the truth contained in such vulgar Marxism is so vague and general as to have scarcely any use at all. Ideological products such as films are seen as directly caused by the nature of the economic base of society. A capitalist system produces capitalist films, and that is all there is to it. Alternatively, but the slight sophistication is scarcely a modification, the products of Hollywood are bourgeois and capitalist because the particular industry which produces them is capitalist. And the more specific the model becomes the more its crudity is exposed. Thus in the first section of the *Cahiers du cinéma* text on *Young Mr Lincoln* (translated in *Screen*, vol. 13, no. 3) we are told that since Hollywood is involved with big business its ideology is not just a generally capitalist one. It supports the more reactionary wing of the political spectrum represented by the Republican Party.

The *Cahiers* text is only one example of a desire to show not only that Hollywood is a part of bourgeois ideology in general but that some Hollywood films intended to carry a specific and reactionary message which has a direct reference to a particular political situation. Another example of such over-politicisation comes in a recent issue of *Jump Cut*, no. 4, Nov.–Dec. 1974, which contains an interpretation of *King Kong* as an anti-Roosevelt tract. The article conveniently states its premises in a footnote:

This article is built round two suppositions. First, that all huge business corporations (such as RKO) are conservative Republican unless demonstrated otherwise, and that their products (like *King Kong*) will reinforce their interests instead of betraying them. Second, that the auteur theory in its standard application is not a germane approach when dealing with a political film, especially under the tight studio control of the 1930s. A political film would only be allowed release if its philosophy was in line with that of the studio which made it. Therefore, RKO studio will be regarded as the true 'auteur' of *King Kong*, despite the innumerable personal touches of its artistic crew.'

Although the phrase 'unless demonstrated otherwise' indicates that the author, Gerald Peary, is aware of the dangers of over-simple generalisations, his assumptions still seem open to two major objections. Firstly, is it not possible that even in Hollywood (not noted perhaps for its political sophistication) there were in the 1930s people who could see that the survival of capitalism (and hence of their 'huge corporations') was not necessarily synonymous with the victory of the Republican Party, especially a Republican Party so discredited as the one which had been led to electoral disaster and intellectual bankruptcy by Herbert Hoover? Secondly, what exactly *are* the interests of such corporations? In the long term, obviously, the survival of a system which allowed them to make profits. But in the short term surely it was those profits themselves. Is it to be assumed that studio executives saw the possibility of profits in attacking a leader who had so recently demonstrated his popularity at the polls (especially among the cinema-going section of the public)? Or should we assume that the political commitment of the studio executives overcame their dedication to profits?

It seems unlikely, but our ignorance about Hollywood generally and about the particular organisation of RKO is such that we cannot answer these questions. Precisely for this reason we ought to beware of assuming any answers. Even if we do assume, with the authors in *Cahiers* and *Jump Cut*, that a studio is owned by big business and that one of its products promotes the political and hence economic interests of the company (I say apparently because the actual interpretation of the films seems open to question), it does not necessarily follow that the political meaning is the direct result of who owns the studio. *Post hoc* is not *propter hoc*.

The lack of any detailed knowledge of industry history, then, suggests caution on the question of the political orientation of Hollywood in the 1930s. Firstly, is it true that the film industry was controlled by big business? And is this the same as the Republican Party (there was business influence among the Democrats too)? Secondly, if it is true can one asume a direct effect on the ideology of Hollywood films? Even the term ideology seems to pose a problem here. It is one thing to argue that, using the term in its classical Marxist sense (or as refined by Althusser) to mean a general world view or structure of thought situated primarily below the conscious level, Hollywood films are ideological expressions of bourgeois society. It is quite another to argue that they support a specific set of political attitudes. Bourgeois society is more than simply the Republican Party. And in any case Marxist theory only claims that ideological products are determined *in the last instance* by the economic relations existing at the base of society. The arguments about *Young Mr Lincoln* and *King Kong* appear to assume that facts about who controls the film industry can provide a sufficient explanation of a film's ideology, ignoring the dimension of the institutional structures which may intervene between the economic base and the final product. Without a knowledge of these structures one cannot say that these films are *not* propaganda; but if they were intended as such, as the *Cahiers* and *Jump Cut* articles imply, it is a strange sort of propaganda which requires an ingenious interpretation thirty or forty years later to make its point. Surely it would have to be demonstrated that such a reading was available to an audience at the time.

III

These problems were thrown into relief by a viewing some time ago of *American Madness*, directed for Columbia in 1932 by Frank Capra. The story of the film concerns Dickson, the manager of a small-town bank (played by Walter Huston). The directors of the bank are financiers of the old school (pre-Keynesians), dedicated to tight money policies which they pursue ruthlessly and selfishly. Dickson, however, has a different view of what the function of a bank should be. He believes that money should be put to work to create jobs and opportunities. His policy is to lend to small businessmen, trusting in his own assessment of their good intentions rather than in the security they can offer. His beliefs are put to the test when a run on the bank occurs; the run is stopped and his faith in his clients vindicated when the little people he has helped rally round to deposit money and so restore confidence in the bank.

The programme note which accompanied the screening of the film at the National Film Theatre suggested that the character of Dickson might have been based on A. H. Giannini, a California banker who was influential in Columbia's affairs in the 1930s. Such a suggestion raises one immediate difficulty, in that it seems to assume that the apparent, or manifest, meaning of the film is the only one, and ignores the possibility that the latent meaning may be quite different. The film might be about other things besides banking. It excludes, that is, the possibility of analysing the film along the lines of the *Young Mr Lincoln* text, which finds that despite the film's apparent project of supporting the Republican cause in the 1940 presidential election, the 'real' meaning of the film undermines this. (The problem of such readings, despite their obvious attractions, is that it is never explained how in practice the subversive meaning of the film becomes available to the people to whom it might be some use, i.e. the working class.) Nevertheless, the suggestion seemed worth following up because of the possibility that it might throw some light on the question of Hollywood's relation to politics in the 1930s, and on the nature of the production system generally. And this might in turn tell us something about Capra's films.

Robert Mundy, in a review of Capra's autobiography in the American *Cinema* (vol. 7, no. 1, Fall 1971, p. 65), speculates on how it was that Capra was able to make films which so closely embodied his personal ideas. He suggests two reasons; firstly, that Capra was working for a small studio where freedom was greater, and secondly, that Capra's vision 'was unusually consonant with the vision of America which Hollywood purveyed with such commercial success in the 1930s. Ideologically his films were rarely at odds with the image of life which the studios believed the public wanted to see.' Mundy avoids the facile assumption that Capra was 'in touch' with America, and that his films arise out of some special relationship to the people and the mood of the time. Instead, he suggests that his work is an expression of the point of view of his *studio*. He concludes, however, that we need to know more: 'A persuasive history of Columbia in the 1930s [is] needed before an informed critical account of Capra's work can be written.' Quite. The problem is to know where to start, given the problems of such research outlined above. Mr Giannini seemed to offer a way in.

He is referred to in a number of books about Hollywood, but as far as I know never more than in passing, as a prominent Californian banker who was involved in movie financing. In several of the references there is a curious uncertainty about his initials. Sometimes he is called A. P. Giannini, sometimes A. H. Thus Philip French in his 'informal' history of the Hollywood tycoons *The Movie Moguls* mentions him on p. 25: 'In fact the first banker to take the cinema seriously was the Californian A. P. Giannini, the son of an Italian immigrant, whose Bank of Italy (later renamed the Bank of America) has played an important part in movie finance since before the first world war.' On p. 79 we read: 'A. H. Giannini, the influential movie financier whose Bank of Italy had a special claim on Hollywood consciences of whatever religious denomination.'

The mystery of A.H. or A.P. was only cleared up when I looked up Giannini in the *National Cyclopædia of American Biography*. It appears that there were two of them. (Obviously I am not the first person since Mr Giannini *père* to be aware of this fact, but it seems as though Philip French was not when he wrote his book. Of such confusions is film history made.) It's worth giving some details of their careers, since they are relevant to Capra's film. A. H. and A. P. (or to give them their full names, Attilio Henry and Amadeo Peter) were brothers. Both their parents were natives of Italy; their father had been a hotel keeper but had come to California to try farming. Amadeo was born in 1870 and his brother four years later. The older brother had gone to work at the age of twelve in his stepfather's firm of wholesale commission agents in San Francisco, and while still in his twenties he formed the Columbus Savings and Loan Society. In 1904 he founded the Bank of Italy. Giannini's bank was at the time of a novel kind. Branches were set up in small towns across the country to attract the savings of the man in the street and Giannini even started savings schemes in schools. His bank specialised in making loans to small businesses with minimal collateral and introduced the practice of lending money for house purchase repayable in monthly instalments. He appears to have been a man of some determination and imagination; during the great San Francisco earthquake and fire of 1906, Giannini was the first to reopen his bank, setting up his desk on the waterfront while the fire still raged. By 1930 he had built up his banking interests to the point where the holding company, the Transamerica Corporation, was the largest of its kind in the world with assets of $1,000 million. Giannini's unorthodox methods did not endear him to more conservative financiers on Wall Street; particularly deplorable was his policy of encouraging wide public ownership of his corporation and of assisting his employees to become stockholders through profit-sharing schemes.

His brother Attilio (sometimes called Dr Giannini, though he abandoned medicine when made vice-president of his brother's Bank of Italy) was involved in various movie companies between the world wars. In 1920 he lent Chaplin half a million dollars to make *The Kid*. In 1936 he became president and chairman of the Board of United Artists and though he resigned from this position in 1938 he retained an influential position in the film industry by virtue of his place on the voting trust which controlled Universal Pictures. He was also involved with several so-called independent production companies such as Selznick International Pictures and Lesser-Lubitsch. It's worth pointing out that none of these organisations possessed large chains of movie theatres. It was the tangible assets of real estate which tempted the Wall Street banks into movie finance in the 1920s. Giannini does at least seem to have been more interested in making pictures.

Giannini's main importance for present purposes is his role in Columbia. The company was originally formed in 1920 as CBC, the letters standing for the names of the three men who set it up: Harry Cohn, Joe Brandt and Harry's brother Jack. All of them had previously worked for Carl Laemmle at Universal. Attilio Giannini lent them $100,000 to get started. In 1924 the company changed its name to Columbia Pictures Corporation (possibly an echo of the Columbus Savings and Loan Society?). Giannini continued to be closely involved. Although in 1929 the studio decided to establish their stock on the New York exchange, 96 per cent of the voting stock was concentrated in the hands of a voting trust. In 1932 Joe Brandt was bought out by Harry Cohn (after Jack Cohn had attempted to enlist Giannini's support in a coup against his brother) and thereafter the voting trust which controlled the company consisted of the two Cohns and Giannini. Unlike most studios at this time Columbia had no debts to the New York investment banks and instead was run as a family business.

Giannini's position was therefore a powerful one. Unfortunately one has no actual knowledge of how he used it. All that can be done is to suggest what his influence might have been given the kind of background from which he and his brother came. The Gianninis were quite separate from the New York banking establishment. Not only was theirs a different kind of business (deposit as opposed to investment banking), involving them with different kinds of clients; they were Catholics (unlike the Rockefellers and Morgans), they were second-generation immigrants, they came from the other side of the country, and their social attitudes were, as far as one can tell, less patrician. A.P.'s entry in the *National Cyclopædia* says that he 'has ever been known as a friend of the poor and struggling ' and if ever a banker could be so described it seems likely that he was.

Not surprisingly, therefore, he supported the Banking Act introduced by Roosevelt in 1935 because, he said, he preferred a measure of government control to domination of the banks by the Wall Street establishment. In 1936 he actively supported Roosevelt's campaign for a second term, at a time when Wall Street considered FDR as no better than a Communist. It seems reasonable to assume that his brother shared his liberal views.

The Gianninis might, then, be seen as a kind of contradiction in terms: populist bankers. The populists of the nineteenth century had regarded bankers as the physical embodiment of all that was evil, and believed that the agricultural problems of the Mid-West were largely caused by a conspiracy of monopolists on Wall Street keeping interest rates up and farm prices down. (Amadeo Giannini was, we are told, greatly interested in agricultural progress.) The little man, the populists contended, stood no chance against those who commanded such resources and used them for selfish purposes. But the Gianninis believed in deliberately aiding such small businessmen and farmers who got no help from Wall Street. In this respect they are in line with the policies of the New Deal, which attempted to get big business under some kind of government control while at the same time trying to raise farm prices and help small firms and individuals by encouraging banks to make loans, by refinancing mortgages and so on.

This too is Dickson's policy in *American Madness* and it seems plausible that the character is indeed based on Dr Giannini. The question then is, what do we make of it? A simple and tempting theory might be constructed: Capra's film doesn't so much capture what 'people' were thinking at the time as represent the thinking of a New Dealer on the voting trust controlling Columbia. Such a theory certainly has its attractions. Firstly, it provides a corrective to the crude assumption that Hollywood=big business=the Republican Party. Secondly, other Capra films such as *Mr Deeds Goes to Town*, *Mr Smith Goes to Washington*, *You Can't Take It With You* also embody the populism that was a powerful element in the New Deal. Thirdly, the situation of Columbia itself, quite apart from the beliefs of those in control, might well be seen as impelling it towards the New Deal coalition of anti-establishment forces. Despite the Academy Awards Capra collected for the studio in the 1930s it never entirely freed itself from its Poverty Row origins. Although the company bought its own studio in 1926 and in 1939 set up a national distribution organisation, at the beginning of the 1930s Columbia was still producing less than thirty features a year (to MGM's forty-three) and most of these were destined for the lower half of a double bill. Output increased steadily during the decade, but the studio was never in the same league as the majors. In 1935, for example, the total volume of business of Loew's, the parent company of MGM, was $85 million; Columbia's was $16 million. Thus Loew's had nearly 22 per cent of the total volume of business of the industry. Columbia only 4 per cent. And despite the characteristically violent swings in the film industry each year from profit to loss and back again, these relative percentages did not change for the rest of the decade. The reason why Columbia was unable to increase its share of business is that, unlike the major studios, it had no chain of theatres of its own which could serve as a secure outlet for its product. All the money it made came from the sale of its own pictures to theatres owned by other studios. MGM and the other majors could, and frequently did, recoup losses on their own films by profits on the exhibition of other companies' output.

But a potential advantage of this relative weakness was that Columbia preserved its financial independence. It had not had to borrow heavily from the banks to finance the acquisition of theatre chains, and as a result the studio was still in the control of the men who founded it, the two Cohns and Giannini. Its independence of Wall Street meant that it might well become the focus of anti-establishment forces, and that if it did it had the freedom to make films which reflected that, always providing of course that it could sell them to the theatres.

But caution is necessary even before trying to test out such a thesis. Capra in his autobiography devotes several pages to recording how charmed he was by Roosevelt's personality; yet, he says, this only made him 'almost a Democrat'. One might suppose that Capra, a first-generation immigrant, an Italian Catholic born in Sicily, was a natural Democrat. But the political content of his films, while embodying support for the underdog, does not attach itself to any Party. His belief in the people goes hand in hand with a classically populist distrust of *all* their leaders. And other tendencies in his films, such as a pervasive anti-intellectualism and a hostility to central government, are certainly not characteristic of the New Deal.

Nevertheless there is a kind of radicalism in his films which would certainly not have commended itself to the fiercely Republican Louis B. Mayer, for example, and it therefore seems worth pursuing the thesis that Columbia might have been a focus for Roosevelt sympathisers. Harry Cohn, who controlled the production side of the company throughout the period, appears to have had no interest in politics at all. It is true that he visited Mussolini in 1933 after Columbia had released a complimentary documentary entitled *Mus-*

solini Speaks. But Cohn seems to have been more impressed with the intimidating lay-out of the dictator's office than with his politics. When he returned to Hollywood he rearranged his own office in imitation. Capra remarked in an interview at the National Film Theatre that Cohn didn't care what the politics of his studio's films were. His concern was with their money-making potential, which he estimated with a 'foolproof device. . . . If my fanny squirms it's bad. If my fanny doesn't squirm it's good. It's as simple as that' (quoted in *King Cohn*, p. 142). If Giannini had wanted the studio to take a pro-New-Deal stance, then it seems as though Cohn would have had no particular objections.

The only way of testing whether there was such a policy, in default of any access to whatever records of the company may still exist, is to look at the films that Columbia made during the period and to find out what one can about the people who made them. It's at this point that the sheer physical difficulties of this kind of work intrude. Taking the period 1926–41, from just before the introduction of sound to a year or so after Capra left Columbia (an arbitrary choice, but less arbitrary than some, and one which corresponds very roughly to the period of the depression and the consequent New Deal, as far as World War II), Columbia, despite being one of the small studios, made on my calculations 627 feature films. (The figure may not be exact because the *Film Daily Year Book*, from which the calculation is made, lists the films of each year twice, once under each studio and once in alphabetical order for the whole industry. Titles appearing in one list don't always appear in the other.) To make those films the company employed 67 different producers, 171 directors, and 269 writers. (The figure for writers is from 1928; they are not credited in the *Year Book* before that date.) By writers is meant those credited with a screenplay. Authors of the original stories from which the films were made might amount to another two or three hundred people. There are also fifteen people whose names appear at one time or another as directors of the company, Columbia Pictures Corporation.

These are the people within the organisation whose position would have allowed them to influence the political content of the films. One might wish to argue that everyone, actors, cameramen, designers, right down to the studio policemen, had some kind of influence, however small. Melvyn Douglas, for example, who acted in many films for Columbia in the 1930s, was active in liberal causes. I have excluded these workers from consideration mainly because, given the nature of the production process, as far as one understands it, and the rigid division of labour, their control over the political content (if any) of a film would have been less. Actors didn't make up their own lines. In any case one has to stop somewhere, and it's not too easy to find out who the studio policemen were.

One is thus faced with a preliminary list of 522 people; to be precise, it is slightly less because the division of labour was not absolute and some writers directed or vice versa. But there is not much overlapping, and the total must be around 500 (this for one small studio during a mere fifteen years of its fifty-year existence). The BFI Library has a card index system which allows one to check whether the Library has entries on individuals in books, periodicals or on microfiche. I accordingly looked up everyone who worked on more than the occasional film. Very few of these names appear in the index and when they do it is often merely a reference to a tiny cutting in *Variety* recording the person's death and giving a short list of the films they worked on. (This is not a criticism of the state of the Library but of the state of film history.)

A few things do emerge. Columbia seems to have been, in the higher echelons, a tight-knit community (one precondition perhaps of a consistent policy). One of the producers was Ralph Cohn, the son of Jack. Everett Riskin, another producer, was the older brother of Robert, who wrote several of Capra's screenplays. Sam Briskin, general manager of the studio in the early 1930s and executive in charge of production from 1938 to 1942, was the brother-in-law of Abe Schneider, treasurer of the company for most of this period. Briskin's brother, Irving, was another producer at Columbia. Yet this doesn't tell us much about an industry where the pull of family relationships was always strong and where 'the son-in-law also rises' was a standard joke.

On the political affiliations of the vast majority, I found no information at all, nor even any information on their lives which would permit a guess. Some very few wrote books or had books written about them, but with the exception of Cohn and Capra their careers were peripheral to Columbia. A few more have been the subject of articles in film magazines, and from these one can glean scraps of information. Richard Maibaum, who wrote a few scripts for the studio, was the author of some anti-lynching and anti-Nazi plays before coming to Hollywood. Dore Schary, whose Democrat sympathies were well known, was also a writer at Columbia in the 1930s. So, very occasionally, were Donald Ogden Stewart, associated with left wing causes at the time, and Edward Chodorov, involved with committees for refugees from Spain and Germany and later more or less black-listed. But this scarcely amounts to much. Stewart, after all, wrote a lot of scripts for MGM.

More significant, at first sight, than the presence of 'liberals', is the fact that exactly half of the Hollywood Ten were actually employed at Columbia during the 1930s; namely Edward Dmytryk, Dalton Trumbo, Herbert Biberman, John Howard Lawson and Lester Cole. But a concerted Communist effort at the studio is hardly likely. Only Dmytryk worked there more than occasionally, and he during his time as a contract director was making routine B-feature films (musicals, horror pictures, thrillers) which, one must assume, offered little scope for the kind of social comment Dmytryk later put into *Crossfire*. There were one or two other Communists working at Columbia who testified before the House Un-American Activities Committee four years after the 1947 hearings which sent the Ten to jail. Paul Jarrico, who wrote for Columbia the screenplays of *No Time to Marry* (1938) and the *The Face Behind the Mask* (1941), was called before the Committee in 1951 but refused to testify and pleaded the 5th Amendment. Another called before the Committee in 1951 was Sidney Buchman. One of Harry Cohn's favourite writers, Buchman specialised in comedy. Among his credits for Columbia are: *Whom the Gods Destroy* (1934); *I'll Love You Always, Love Me Forever, She Married Her Boss* (1935); *The King Steps Out, Theodora Goes Wild, Adventure in Manhattan, The Music Goes Round* (1936); *Holiday* (1938); *Mr Smith Goes to Washington* (1939); *The Howards of Virginia* (1940); *Here Comes Mr Jordan* (1941). Buchman admitted that he had been in the Communist Party from 1938 to 1945, but refused to supply the Committee with the list of names of other members they required and was cited for contempt. He was found guilty and given a one-year suspended sentence and a $150 fine.

Buchman clearly occupied an influential position at Columbia. He was a producer as well as a writer and was associated with some of Columbia's greatest successes in the late 1930s and early 1940s. But if *Mr Smith* is satirical about Washington life, it retains an unswerving, even touching, faith in American political institutions, and it is difficult to see that Buchman's membership of the Communist Party had any great effect on what he wrote. Indeed many of his associates appear to have been surprised to learn that he was a Communist.

It may be that a more detailed search through such records as are available would turn up some decisive evidence. But on what has been presented so far it seems unlikely that, Dr Giannini notwithstanding, there was any deliberate policy of favouritism to the New Deal or left causes. The same conclusion seems likely to follow from the films. Here again one is attempting generalisations based on woefully inadequate knowledge, because, apart from those directed by Capra, I have seen very few of the films Columbia made during the period. Nevertheless some impressions can be gained from looking at the records. In the late 1920s and early 1930s the staples of the studio's output were adventure and action films, comedies, often mildly risqué, and the occasional exposé (one of Jack Cohn's first successes at Universal was to convince Carl Laemmle of the box office potential of *Traffic in Souls*, a sensationalist feature on the white slave trade). Westerns and thrillers made up the rest of the production schedule. Of course titles can be misleading, but a list of the films produced in 1928 probably gives a fair indication of at least the type of films being made:

That Certain Thing, The Wife's Relations, Lady Raffles, So This Is Love? Woman's Way, Sporting Age, Matinee Idol, Desert Bride, Broadway Daddies, After the Storm, Golf Widows, Modern Mothers, Name the Woman, Ransom, Way of the Strong, Beware of Blondes, Say it with Sables, Virgin Lips, Scarlet Lady, Court Martial, Runaway Girls, Streets of Illusion, Sinners' Parade, Driftwood, Stool Pigeon, The Power of the Press, Nothing to Wear, Submarine, The Apache, The Lone Wolf's Daughter, Restless Youth, The Sideshow.

Besides Capra, directors working regularly for Columbia at this time included the veteran director of serials George B. Seitz (*The Perils of Pauline*), and Erle Kenton, another veteran who had been in pictures since 1914. The policy, one guesses, was one of efficient professionalism dedicated to getting the most out of Columbia's meagre resources. Not only did Columbia make less films; they also spent less on each production than the major studios. (Few of their films at this time ran more than seventy minutes.) This would seem to leave little room for the carefully considered personal statements of the kind Capra aspired to later in the 1930s. This is not to say that there was no possibility of social or political comment, however, as the history of Warners at the same time shows.

After Capra's astonishing success with *It Happened One Night* in 1934, which won Columbia its first Oscars and enormously increased the studio's prestige, pictures of the earlier type were supplemented by the occasional more expensive production. Though Columbia had contract players of its own (for example Jack Holt, Ralph Bellamy or, in Westerns, Buck Jones and Charles Starrett), they could not compare in box-office appeal with the stars of bigger studios. Columbia could not afford the budgets which having bigger stars would have entailed. On the other hand it could never break into the big time without them. Harry Cohn's solution to this vicious circle was to invite successful directors from other studios to make occasional pictures for Columbia, pictures which would be given larger than usual budgets and which would have stars borrowed from other studios. Careful planning permitted short production schedules and kept costs down to what Columbia could afford. Capra too was given increasingly larger budgets and outside stars. Thus a number of big-name directors came to work at Columbia during the later 1930s, often tempted by the offer of being allowed to produce their own films. Among the titles produced at Columbia during the period after *It Happened One Night* were:

1934: *20th Century* (dir. Howard Hawks, with John Barrymore and Carole Lombard); *The Captain Hates the Sea* (dir. Lewis Milestone, with Victor McLaglen and John Gilbert); 1935: *The Whole Town's Talking* (dir. John Ford, with Edward G. Robinson), *She Married Her Boss* (dir. Gregory La Cava, with Claudette Colbert), *She Couldn't Take It* (dir. Tay Garnett, with George Raft and Joan Bennett), *Crime and Punishment* (dir. Josef von Sternberg, with Peter Lorre); 1936: *Theodora Goes Wild* (dir. Richard Boleslavski, with Irene Dunne); 1937: *The Awful Truth* (dir. Leo McCarey, with Cary Grant and Irene Dunne); 1938 *Holiday* (dir. George Cukor, with Cary Grant, Katharine Hepburn); 1939; *Let Us Live* (dir. John Brahm, with Maureen O'Sullivan and Henry Fonda), *Only Angels Have Wings* (dir. Howard Hawks, with Cary Grant, Thomas Mitchell and Richard Barthelmess), *Golden Boy* (dir. Rouben Mamoulian, with Barbara Stanwyck and Adolphe Menjou); 1940: *His Girl Friday* (dir. Howard Hawks, with Cary Grant and Rosalind Russell), *The Howards of Virginia* (dir. Frank Lloyd, with Cary Grant), *Angels Over Broadway* (dir. Ben Hecht and Lee Garmes, with Douglas Fairbanks Jr), *Arizona* (dir. Wesley Ruggles, with William Holden); 1941: *Penny Serenade* (dir. George Stevens, with Cary Grant and Irene Dunne), *Texas* (dir. George Marshall, with William Holden, Glenn Ford and Claire Trevor), *You Belong to Me* (dir. Wesley Ruggles, with Barbara Stanwyck and Henry Fonda), *The Men in Her Life* (dir. Gregory Ratoff, with Loretta Young).

But despite this sprinkling of prestige productions the basic recipe remained much the same as before. There were lots of low-budget Westerns (a dozen or so in 1940) directed by Lambert Hillyer, a veteran of the Columbia lot, or Joseph H. Lewis, and starring Bill Elliott or Charles Starrett. The studio made several series: a number of films based on Blondie, the cartoon character, the Lone Wolf series of thrillers, an Ellery Queen mystery series and so on. There were light comedies from Alexander Hall, more light comedies and musicals from Walter Lang, and plenty of crime films (a few titles at random from 1938: *Women in Prison, When G-Men Step In, Penitentiary, Highway Patrol, Reformatory, Convicted, I Am the Law, Juvenile Court, Smashing the Spy Ring*).

What is one to conclude from what emerges of Columbia's production policy in this period? Aware that a viewing of all the films might prove one wrong, it could be said that there is no evidence of Columbia's deliberately following a line favourable to the New Deal. Of course it could be objected that a similar scanning of the titles of Warner Brothers films of the same time would fail to reveal what an actual viewing of the films shows, a detectable if not pronounced leaning towards Rooseveltian attitudes. But this much seems likely: the policy of bringing in outside stars and directors (and writers too) for big-budget productions would have worked against the continuity required for a deliberate political policy. Whereas at Warners a nucleus of stars, writers, producers and directors was built up capable of producing pictures that fused the thrills of crime with social comment, at Columbia the occasional film (such as *A Man's Castle*, directed by Frank Borzage in 1933) which took the Depression as its subject was a one-off, with the exception of Capra. And it does seem as though Capra *was* an exception. As far as one can tell the directors who did not have his freedom at the studio did not follow him in the direction of social comment, and neither did directors brought in from outside with a similar amount of freedom. And Capra's films, after all, despite his standing within the studio, are only a tiny proportion of all the films Columbia made in the 1930s.

If one can say that the presence of Giannini on the trust controlling Columbia did not lead to films predominantly favourable to the New Deal, then can one not also throw doubt on the assumption that control of a studio by interests favourable to the Republican Party led to films (such as *Young Mr Lincoln* and *King Kong*) designed to make propaganda for that party? No one would argue that there was a total lack of correlation between ownership and the content of films. No studio in the 1930s would have tolerated outright Communist movies, or anything very close to that. (Nor for that matter would a Fascist film have stood any chance of being made.) But within these parameters considerable diversity was possibly, a diversity, moreover, which it is dangerous to reduce by the simple expedient of labelling all the films as bourgeois. The difference in political attitudes between, say *The Good Earth* (MGM, 1937) and *The Grapes of Wrath* (20th Century-Fox, 1940) – two films with not totally dissimilar subjects – are not negligible and relate to real political and social events of the time. But they cannot be explained simply in terms of who owned the studios or in terms only of social attitudes at the times. Any explanation would require that a number of factors be taken into account, and not least of these would be the exact nature of the institutions which produced them.

The history of the American film industry, then, forms a kind of missing link in attempts, Marxist and otherwise, to make connections between films and society. As we have seen, many of the materials needed to forge that link are missing, which is why the title of this essay, 'Notes on Columbia Pictures Corporation 1926–41', is intended to imply more than the customary academic modesty. The problems of producing such a history are both practical and the result of a massive ideological prejudice, and I am aware that the information I have produced on Columbia in the 1930s amounts to very little in the way of real knowledge. But this information has been the result of a few hours in the library, not of a large-scale research programme. If one considers how much has been learned, for example, about British labour history in the nineteenth century the possibilities for further research do not seem hopeless. As a subject it would appear equally as unpromising as the history of the film industry. Apart from newspapers there are few written sources and the people involved are all dead. The history therefore has to a great extent to be reconstructed from the material objects which survive: buildings, institutional structures, the customs and practices of a people. But full-time academics and research students have been working in the field for years. The study of the history of the Amer ican film industry has scarcely begun.

3 · Hugh Fordin: On the Town

From *The World of Entertainment: Hollywood's Greatest Musicals* (New York: Doubleday, 1975)

Hugh Fordin's essay on the production of MGM's musical *On the Town*, which is extracted from his book on the Freed Unit, is reprinted here for a number of reasons. First of all, the Freed Unit is one of only two Hollywood production units to which book-length studies have been devoted. (The other is Joel Siegel's volume *Val Lewton: The Reality of Terror*, on Lewton's horror unit at RKO.) Secondly, MGM is perhaps the best documented and most discussed of all the Hollywood studios and yet Fordin's book, which offers a detailed, if anecdotal, account of MGM's première musical unit and which traces the production of its entire output, is still relatively unknown and undervalued as a resource. And thirdly, the popular approach of Fordin's book offers a challenge to some texts on the industry which for all their theoretical rigour are often no more, indeed sometimes less, thoroughly researched.

A book entirely devoted to the Freed Production Unit is a particularly appropriate way of posing questions about the relationship between a single studio and a single genre by specifying a particular historical and industrial segment of that studio, MGM, and a particular film genre, the musical. The example of *On the Town* is also felicitous; the fact that the film had two directors, Gene Kelly and Stanley Donen, is already ammunition enough for the anti-auteurist critic; this, together with the overall emphasis on both the 'creative' and the 'administrative' workings of the Unit, allows a number of questions about the attribution of individual authorship to be raised. Nor is the Freed Unit itself allowed to stand in as a single, simple and harmonious author. Rather, the unit is revealed as the site of intersection of and conflict between any number of imperatives of and determinants on the film in question. Nor again is Freed himself foregrounded or his unit privileged above the forty-odd other departments at MGM at that time. Indeed, Fordin's essay isolates a number of both obvious and obscure constraints upon the unit, from the censorious recommendations of the Breen office, through the complicated chain of command which led from Louis B. Mayer and Nick Schenck down through the executive level of men like James K. McGinness, Al Lichtman, Sam Katz and Eddie Mannix and including Dore Schary, who became head of production in 1948.

The Freed Unit, then, can be seen as the site of all kinds of conflicts and contradictions: political (e.g. Schary's reputation as a 'pinko' liberal, Freed's resolute Republicanism); professional (e.g. the struggle for control over MGM between Mayer in Culver City, Nick Schenck in New York, Schary as head of production and Freed as head of a production unit favoured by Mayer which could thus afford to ignore Schary's strictures); even aesthetic (e.g. Schary's flagrant antipathy towards musicals, Freed's commitment to them as the pinnacle of motion picture art, Mayer's dispute with Freed over the kind of musicals to make). Furthermore, Fordin's essay assembles examples of both the film's standardisation to prior models (e.g. *On the Town*'s resemblance to other navy musicals like *Anchors Aweigh* and *Follow the Fleet*; the casting cannily reuniting Kelly, Sinatra and Munshin – the stars of *Take Me Back to the Ball Game*) and its differentiation from them (e.g. its distance from the stage original on which it was based, its departure from the backstage/production number kind of musical which still dominated the genre; its distinction from and alleged 'superiority' to the work of the Freed unit's main rivals in the field of 1940s prestige musicals, e.g. the reference to Powell and Pressburger's *The Red Shoes*; finally its deliberate break with the conventional studio settings of previous musicals by using extensive New York location sequences.) Similarly, the film involves an accommodation to the conventions of the star system and to the expectations associated with specific star personae. Thus the stage original had to be replotted to suit Kelly, who 'couldn't be a helpless, naive type' as the original's protagonist had been. On the other hand, Sinatra's role was such that he had to learn to expand his repertoire and even change his image, taking his hands off the mike more or less for the first time and adding dancing skills to what had previously been his almost exclusively vocal strengths in the genre.

In July 1948, when Dore Schary took over as head of production, he undoubtedly knew that he would have to deal with a small but powerful group of men who were overtly hostile toward him. Led by James K. McGinness, they were the ultraconservative, super-patriotic group around Mayer, mostly members of the Motion Picture

Alliance, an organisation founded for the purposes of 'upholding the American ideal' and eradicating communism within the film industry. They had publicly termed Schary a 'pinko'. Although not a part of this group, Katz and Lichtman resigned. Schary knew that he would not be welcomed with open arms by all of MGM.

In spite of this pressure, Mayer at first stood firmly behind Schary giving him a free hand to put his plans for reactivation of the studio's sagging production output into action. This so-called 'free hand' in his long-term contract did, however, specify that all major decisions must have Mayer and Schenck's approval.

Schary proceeded to line up a production schedule for the coming year, with a notable absence of any musicals. He had no interest in, flair for or appreciation of musical films and felt they were a luxury the studio could do without. To assert his authority, the producers were told to inform him about all their activities, including preparation of scripts, casting, production expenditures, etc., and their daily office operation. This ruling was to include Freed.

Freed had no intention of complying. He had been offered Schary's job some years before and had turned it down, preferring to work as an autonomous producer, responsible exclusively to Mayer. Schary was informed that Freed and his unit were to be left alone.

For the year 1949–50, the following projects were on Freed's schedule: *On the Town, Annie Get Your Gun, Crisis, Pagan Love Song, How to Win Friends and Influence People, Royal Wedding, The Romberg Story, Show Boat* and *An American in Paris*. And he made a deal of far-reaching consequences.

On Lillie Messinger's suggestion the studio had bought *The Day Before Spring*, the 1945 Broadway musical, with book and lyrics by Alan Jay Lerner and music by Frederick Loewe. She and Lerner became great friends and she was unrelenting in the promotion of his career.

In 1947 she went to New York for the opening of their next musical *Brigadoon* and again in 1948 for *Love Life*, which Lerner had written with Kurt Weill. By this time she had left MGM to work as a story editor at Universal Pictures but stayed in close contact with Mayer. When she learned he was going to New York, she seized the opportunity and followed him at her own expense for the sole purpose of introducing Lerner. Mayer was impressed. He called Freed in Los Angeles and the next day Lerner was on a plane to California, a territory where, until then, he had found only closed doors. After a series of meetings Lerner was signed by Metro to work exclusively in the Freed Unit. He returned to New York to develop original stories.

When Comden and Green were writing their screenplay for *The Barkleys of Broadway*, George Abbott, noted Broadway producer and director, joined them for lunch in the commissary. He told them he had been brought out to direct any picture he wished to do, and his first choice was their show *On the Town*, which he had directed on Broadway. After lunch the two writers were called to Freed's office. 'We're going to do *On the Town*,' Freed said. They were elated.

In the summer of 1944, when *On the Town* was in its formative stage, Lillie Messinger discussed the forthcoming Broadway show with Leonard Bernstein. He had not as yet written the score, but had ideas for song titles and played snatches of tunes for her. She was excited about the project and called Katz who did not respond positively. She called Mannix who was even less responsive. Mayer had been thrown by a horse and was in a hospital with a broken pelvis, but she decided to call him nonetheless. 'Something happens to your voice, Lillie, when you feel that strongly,' said Mayer. She related the story to him and mentioned the authors and the composer, 'people you've never heard of, but you will in the future. The studio bought the motion-picture rights in a preproduction agreement for $250,000, one of the first to be made.

Shortly after the show opened on 28 December 1944, Mayer, Mannix and Katz went east to attend a performance. They left the Adelphi Theatre regretting that they had had anything to do with the show.

At the time Comden and Green set out for Hollywood with their newly signed MGM contract, they had been admonished by their agents and their lawyers never to bring up the subject of *On the Town*. They had lived up to this promise; now they were dumbfounded by Freed's pronouncement. What had taken place between the Abott lunch and Freed's revelation? Most likely Gene Kelly had had breakfast with George Abbott and lunch with Arthur Freed.

The time was ripe for Kelly and Donen to codirect their first musical film. The problem of casting the three sailors was licked in thirty seconds: Kelly, Sinatra and Munshin, the trio from *Ball Game*. Sinatra had told Kelly after *Anchors Aweigh*, 'They're not going to get me into another sailor's suit!' But Kelly assured Freed that he could persuade Sinatra.

Freed never liked the score of *On the Town* and liked it even less as screen material. At the time, Bernstein's style was considered avant-garde and it did not appeal to him. He also had reservations about the book. On the stage it had been done in a campy manner, which he felt would be offensive to movie audiences. Contractually he was not obligated to use all of Bernstein's score, but Bernstein had the right of first refusal if new songs were going to be interpolated. Freed was not keen on using Bernstein to compose the new songs and Bernstein was not keen on working on the film. To satisfy the legal department, a separate agreement was drawn up in which Bernstein also waived the right of interpolation of new material in exchange for Metro returning to him all their rights, title and interest to the song titles mentioned in the original 1945 purchase agreement.[1]

In November, Freed called Comden and Green in New York and spelled out the situation: The book had to be rewritten, only a minimal part of Bernstein's score would be retained, and they would have to write new songs with Edens. For two reasons they turned him down. For one, they were in the midst of writing a new Broadway show; and for another, they were close friends of Bernstein. Freed proposed that after a couple of weeks of studio conferences they could return to New York for the major part of their work and that Edens, Kelly and Donen would be available in the East. They agreed and signed a contract which would pay them $85,000 for the rewrite and $25,000 for the new lyrics, in addition to their share of the 60 per cent of the $250,000 the studio had paid for the motion-picture rights. (Any subsidiary, motion-picture stock and amateur rights and royalties were split: 60 per cent to the collaborators on a show and 40 per cent to the investors.) Freed depended on their co-operation; without them he couldn't make the picture.

The three leading characters in the show had been a trio of innocent and simple-minded sailors, enjoying their twenty-four-hour furlough in New York City. 'With Gene as the leading character and the star of the picture,' says Comden, 'the angle of the story had to be changed. He couldn't be a helpless, naive type. The whole structure of the story had to be changed to suit the people who were going to play the characters.' The two writers completed the first half of their work and returned to the studio to write the new score and finish the screenplay.

Comden and Green came up with an ingenious device to show the passing of time in the twenty-four hours during which the picture takes place: a timestrip, running on the bottom of the screen, in the style of the *New York Times* news billboard.

The few numbers retained from the show were 'I feel like I'm not out of bed yet', the opening and closing, sung by a crane operator; 'New York, New York', the opening section of the film, sung by Kelly, Sinatra and Munshin; 'Miss Turnstiles ballet', danced by Vera-Ellen; and the taxi song, 'Come up to my place', sung by Betty Garrett and Sinatra. The new songs were 'On the Town' (all six principals); 'Prehistoric Man', featuring Ann Miller with Kelly, Munshin, Garrett and Sinatra; 'Main Street', sung and danced by Vera-Ellen and Kelly; 'You're awful', sung by Garrett and Sinatra; 'You can count on me', a novelty number with Miller, Garrett, Pearce, Kelly, Sinatra and Munshin; 'Pearl of the Persian Sea', a cooch dance performed by Kelly, Sinatra and Munshin dressed as ladies of a harem, and 'That's all there is, folks', treated as a gag.

'*On the Town* was a very happy wedding of creative spirits,' said Edens, 'and Freed turned us loose on it. I began to realize my idea of making musicals without overelaborate production numbers. Intimate musical numbers are the only way to get true entertainment. People are not entertained by chorus lines any more. The whole layout of the picture, all the numbers were unforgettably exciting for all of us to put together.'

Saul Chaplin came to work on the picture as the vocal arranger. He had worked with Kelly on *Cover Girl* (Columbia, 1944), after which he returned to New York where his close friends Bernstein, Comden and Green were working feverishly on their first Broadway show *On the Town*. He joined in by assisting them in an unofficial capacity. He later collaborated with Comden and Green on their aborted Broadway musical *Bonanza Bound* (1948). (This was the show that Comden and Green were working on when Freed first offered them the job of adapting *On the Town* for his production.)

Chaplin then went back to Columbia Pictures where he worked with Al Jolson and Larry Parks on Jolson's two-part biomusicals. Edens was deeply involved with the writing of the score and the entire production of the film. Chaplin was at liberty and so Kelly, Comden and Green asked Freed to bring Chaplin to Metro to help organise and arrange the musical material under Eden's's guidance.

When the shooting script and the songs were submitted to the Breen Office for approval the following directives were given:

Regarding the songs:

1 'New York, New York': 'It's a helluva town' is unacceptable.
2 'Prehistoric man': 'Lots of guys are *hot* for me' is
   unacceptable. 'Libido – I love that libido' is unacceptable.
   'They sat all the day just beating their tom-toms' is
   unacceptable.

Regarding the script:

1 '... we direct your particular attention to the need for the
   greatest possible care in the selection and photographing of
   the dresses and costumes of your women. The Production
   Code makes it mandatory that the intimate parts of the
   body – specifically, the breasts of women – be fully covered

at all times. Any compromise with this regulation will
compel us to withhold approval of your picture.
2 Page 20: The kissing here and elsewhere throughout this
production should not be unduly passionate, prolonged or
open-mouth.
3 Page 75: The costumes of the girls in the cooch show should
be adequate to cover them and there should be no offensive
motions in the dance routines; specifically, there should be
no grinds or bumps.

The production went into rehearsal on 21 February 1949, with the
following cast: Gene Kelly as Gabey, Frank Sinatra as Chip, Jules
Munshin as Ozzie, Betty Garrett as Hildy, Ann Miller as Claire,
Vera-Ellen as Ivy Smith, Alice Pearce as Lucy Schmeeler and Florence
Bates as Mme. Dilyovska; musical direction and orchestration by
Lennie Hayton and Conrad Salinger; vocal arrangements by Saul
Chaplin; director of photography, Harold Rosson; art direction by
Jack Martin Smith.

Kelly and Donen wanted to shoot the entire film in New York.
This was a practical and financial impossibility. However, a compromise was reached; the first unit would go to New York for most of
the exterior scenes involving the six principals.

Kelly succeeded in making Sinatra and Munshin really dance. ' I
took Frank's hands off the mike, so to speak,' as Kelly says. He
taught them the simple steps and they learned them with great good
will and gusto. But it seems that while Sinatra and Munshin at first
were not too happy with the casting of their partners, they grew to
love Garrett and Miller. 'Those girls could move – and they gave us
a lot of oomph,' Sinatra says.

Kelly and Donen rehearsed in two adjacent rehearsal halls. They
would bounce forth and back from one to the other, showing each
other what they were doing. Comden and Green would drop in and
watch; sometimes Edens came down and for a while would sub for
the rehearsal pianist; Chaplin would bring in his vocal arrangements;
Freed would visit. One day the whole group had to move to a stage
to rehearse on a set. The piano was loaded on a truck, they all
jumped on and with Chaplin crouching behind the keyboard, they
drove through the studio streets singing at the top of their lungs,
'We're going on the town. . . .'

The picture started shooting on 28 March 1949.

As soon as the production schedule was set up, permissions for
filming had to be obtained from the City of New York for the
shooting at diverse sites in New York and the Navy Department for
filming at the Brooklyn Navy Yard. The studio also had to solicit

the co-operation of the Department of Commerce and the Police Department for the clearing of traffic, etc., and the protection of the company.

Jack Smith had a conference with Kelly and Donen about the set for the Museum of Anthropological History, and he didn't lose any time seeing Gaylord and Greutart, head of special effect props and head of the sculpture department, respectively. 'I know you are busy, but this won't take too much of your time,' he began. 'We need a dinosaur resembling the *Tyrannosaurus rex*, 15 feet high, 40 feet long and 25 feet wide. You never heard of it? ... Well, of course, it must be collapsible, and make it so that it can be put together again,' Smith said and he told Greutart to make a life-size sculpture of a *Pithecanthropus erectis* in the image of Jules Munshin. 'No problem,' Greutart replied cynically. 'Just send Munshin down here for a few minutes and you'll have your apeman.'

When the scene was shot in the exhibition room of the museum, there stood the two specimens from 6000 BC. In constructing the skeleton and inventing the mechanism for its collapse, Gaylord used corrugated paper in big cubes, and with a buzz saw carved each vertebra. He then inserted wire, connecting all 283 pieces, which acted as a ripcord for the collapse and the restoration of the structure. However, the precaution of being able to restore the skeleton proved unnecessary. The scene was shot, Munshin kicked the dinosaur, it collapsed, and the first take was a print.

Scenically, the replica of the roof of the Empire State Building at night was the most challenging for the art department. Smith placed the mock-up of the observation roof in the centre of Esther Williams's swimming pool on Stage 30. By putting it into the 10-foot-deep pool, he made it an island which rose 45 feet into the air. Surrounding the edifice on three sides was a 250-feet-wide by 60-foot-high backing, with the skyline of New York (facing north) painted on it, showing both sides of Manhattan with the East River, Central Park, the Hudson River and the George Washington Bridge. He cut out tiny windows with lights behind them and miniature neon signs flashing in the streets. Putting the observation roof into the pool enabled the camera to shoot upward when Jules Munshin is hanging over the ledge of the roof, 102 storeys in the air.

This was another instance where Jack Smith manufactured reality by artificial means:

Dear Gene & Stanley:

I just ran the cut numbers of *On the Town* and they were the greatest and most inspiring works I have seen since I have been making moving pictures.

Pressburger and Powell can't shine your shoes – red, white or blue.

Much love from your proud producer.

Arthur

In April, while the shooting of the picture went along smoothly at the studio, a second unit, under director Andrew Marton and cameraman Charles Schoenbaum, went to New York to photograph process plates needed for the picture.[2]

On 5 May, when the principal photography, with the exception of the ballet, was completed, the first unit with all six principals and crew left for the New York location.

From the time Kelly, Sinatra and Munshin come off their destroyer in the Brooklyn Navy Yard for their twenty-four-hour shore leave, they covered New York from the Battery to the George Washington Bridge; from the top of the RCA Building down to the Prometheus statue in Rockefeller Center, from the Brooklyn Bridge to the Italian section of Lower Manhattan; from a tour through Central Park to Grant's Tomb; from Wall Street to the roof of the Loew's Building; from the Statue of Liberty to the top of the Empire State Building; from Washington Square in Greenwich Village to Times Square; in and out of subway entrances to the top of a Fifth Avenue double-decker bus; from the Third Avenue 'el' and back to their boat at the Navy Yard.

This was the first time any major studio sent a company to shoot musical sequences on public sites in New York. It is one thing to shoot dialogue scenes outside, even in the brouhaha of New York City streets. (If one does not get a clear dialogue track one postrecords it, – 'loop it', as the process is called.) But synchronizing action, lip-sync and dancing, or all of these, is another story. There must be a playback machine always in earshot of the director and the performers. This is not much of a problem in stationary shots; but in moving shots, in confined spaces or in long shots, it becomes quite a problem. To hear the record for synchronization, the performer has to be relatively close by, but if the loudspeaker is in earshot it often gets within camera range. In each individual shot the trio not only had to synchronize to their prerecorded voices, but had to walk in strict tempo to the music, even in the instrumental portions of the number.

An experienced, well-respected unit manager had been in New York for a couple of weeks to lay the groundwork for the location. By the time the company arrived he was unfortunately 'out of commission', and it was difficult to depend on an inexperienced assistant director. For the first days Kelly and Donen scouted locations and laid out their camera shots with their cameraman Harold Rosson.

Kelly and Donen had planned the continuity of the scenes for the opening like mosaic pieces which would have to fit together perfectly. This was imperative because each shot had to fit a certain portion of the prerecorded music track, some sections as short as fifteen to twenty feet or ten to fourteen seconds. This needed mathematical planning and for many reasons it was not possible to shoot the opening sequence in continuity. This meant jumping from one part of New York to the other, depending on traffic conditions, but more importantly on the position of the sun. A shot in a narrow street in Chinatown, for instance, could only be made during an hour or so in the forenoon; the rest of the day the street would be dim and shadowy.

The first scenes to be shot were the opening and the closing of the picture at the Brooklyn Navy Yard. In both of these a crane worker is slowly walking up the empty pier at sunrise singing, 'I feel like I'm not out of bed yet.' A Navy destroyer is moored at the pier.

The Navy had been most co-operative. They had brought the destroyer in and agreed to have it pull away and out to sea for the last shot of the film, hopefully on its own steam, and only *once*.

Donen was set up to shoot this in an extremely high shot with the camera up on a crane. Everything was ready at six o'clock in the morning. But the skyline of Manhattan was barely visible; it was foggy and drizzling and shooting that day at the Navy Yard had to be abandoned.

There were more days at the Yard and at the Brooklyn Bridge when the weather was unfavorable, and this meant hours of waiting for a change. After a couple of futile early calls, Sinatra asked to be called only if and when the camera was ready to roll. But clouds move in unpredictable and often rapid ways. Sometimes the cameraman can foretell a break in a cloud formation minutes ahead and by the time the sun breaks through he is ready to shoot; in the few minutes between clouds, so to speak, a scene can be photographed. But this possibility offered small chance of success with Sinatra resting in his hotel suite on Central Park South.

The setting of the last shot was an exact duplicate of the opening. But now the three sailors are returning to their ship, their twenty-four-hour leave is over; their girl friends arrive to bid them good-bye, and another three are coming off the ship, singing, 'New York, New York – it's a wonderful town.'

An important and rather lengthy section, taking place on the roof of the RCA Building, needed special preparation. In order to make the spectacular 180-degree shot, which Kelly and Donen had planned, it was necessary to build a monorail around the entire circumference on which the camera was attached. 'I hung upside down, strapped to the camera, to get a shot of the six principals looking down at the city,' recalls Rosson.

Other problems arose. The Police Department cleared a street in the Italian section, and as a precaution Sinatra was kept hidden when the company arrived. The very short scene was rehearsed without him. But word had got out somehow and the very minute he stepped out of a building to do the scene thousands of people poured out of doorways, stores, and hung out of windows, screaming and yelling. The police managed to keep them away for as long as it took to shoot the scene and then whizzed him off in a patrol car.

The roof of the Loew's Building presented another set of hazards. The square footage of the surface was so minimal that it could hardly accommodate the three principals, Donen, the cameraman and his assistant. The equipment had to be hooked up half a floor below; the roof itself was only bordered by a two-foot-high scalloped ledge. Munshin, afflicted by a fear of heights, at first could not be induced to even set foot on it. He began to stammer incoherently until he crawled on his knees on to the roof. While Kelly was rehearsing, practically bending over the roof's edge, Donen had a rope tied around Munshin's waist under his sailor suit. Out of camera range, a member of the crew held fast to the rope and after much coercing, in agony, Munshin managed to go through the action of the shot.

Going from one locale to another meant moving all the necessary equipment completely across town and back again, following the favourable light and other conditions. In spite of a hectic schedule, anxiety about the weather, mobs impairing activities, etc., everyone, principals as well as crew, worked without complaints of any kind.

They sang on the Brooklyn Bridge; they walked through the Jewish district; they sang at the Statue of Liberty; they rode on horseback through Central Park; they sang on Wall Street; they walked under the Third Avenue el, and they rode a double-decker bus on Fifth Avenue.

The shot on the upper deck of the bus was made in the early afternoon in the height of the day's traffic. A square block, between 60th and 61st Streets from Fifth Avenue to Madison Avenue, was cleared of traffic and, the playback machine was blaring on the bus circling the block to get on to Fifth Avenue at the right speed. The three male voices, backed by an orchestral accompaniment, pierced the air, cut through the street noises and awakened the old gentlemen at the Metropolitan Club from their behind-their-newspaper snoozes.

By the time the bus passed their building the second time they had tottered to the windows and stared in utter amazement and disbelief at the passing parade. After half a dozen tries the scene was in the can.

The company returned to the studio on 23 May to resume shooting and to resolve the pending problems concerning Kelly's ballet. According to his contract, a scenario for the ballet was to be sent to Bernstein in New York, along with requirements for music. He then was to send his sketches back to the studio to be orchestrated; after that he was to come out to the studio for five working days. When Bernstein had not received a scenario at the given time he wired Freed, expressing anxiety about the situation, 'as time was growing short.' Kelly called Bernstein and it was agreed that they would work together on the ballet during the week he was to be at the studio.

Bernstein arrived on 3 June and had meetings with Kelly and Saul Chaplin. 'It wasn't so much writing a new piece, it was reorganizing old material that he had,' recalls Chaplin. An important part of the ballet was based on a Bernstein song which was lifted from the stage show when it was out of town, titled 'Ain't got no tears left'. It eventually became one of the main themes of 'age of anxiety'.

'Leonard Bernstein talked about the ballet and I thought it should be like what Agnes de Mille did in *Oklahoma!*. So I substituted Frank and Julie with dancers and did the same with the girls, except for Vera-Ellen. One of the girls was Carol Haney,' Kelly says. The ballet, now titled 'A day in New York,' is a reflection of Kelly's experience of that day. It shows his love for Vera-Ellen, and in essence is a repeat of the overall story of the film.

The picture was completed on 2 July 1949. The entire venture, including the New York location, took all of forty-seven days. The final cost was $2,111,250.

On the Town was previewed at the Bay Theatre in Pacific Palisades on 9 September. It was a roaring success. Kelly, Donen, Edens and Simone were standing at the back of the theatre when Freed came running up the aisle, shouting. 'If it were a show it would run a year!' It had already run 463 performances on Broadway!

There was another preview at the Loew's 72nd Street Theatre in New York on 22 November 1949. This time the response was overwhelming.

The picture went into release on 30 December 1949, and grossed in excess of $4,440,000. Mayer, Mannix, Katz *et al*. had hated the show when they went to see it on Broadway. Now they could not help but say, 'Freed did it again!'

Much has been written about *On the Town*, more than about most musicals made during the past twenty years. Therefore it seems appropriate to report in this space some comments from the creators of the film:

Stanley Donen: 'Arthur just had some sort of instinct to change the musical movie from the backstage world into something else. His impulse was to do something different; he really had a basic understanding of the musical film that no other film producer had – with the exception of Roger Edens.

'In this film we tried a great many new things, aided as we were by the theme which was very cinematic. There was no stage, no theatre, simply the street. We never told ourselves, "Now we're going to do something no one has ever done before." We simply thought that this was the way one should deal with, one should conceive, a musical comedy. This is the way we felt – we didn't realize we were making any innovations. . . .'

Gene Kelly: 'It was only in *On the Town* that we tried something entirely new in the musical film. Live people get off a real ship in the Brooklyn Navy Yard and sing and dance down New York City. We did a lot of quick cutting – we'd be on the top of Radio City and then on the bottom – we'd cut from Mulberry Street to Third Avenue – and so the the dissolve went out of style. This was one of the things that changed the history of musicals more than anything.'

Arthur Freed: ' "Why adaptation?" somebody invariably asks. "I thought the play was perfect. Why did you change it all around in the movie?" Undoubtedly the producer saw the stage show himself, and the chances are he also thought it was practically perfect – as a play. But if he has learned anything at all about his own business, he knows that a play and a motion picture are two separate and widely different things. A movie is a story told by a camera, an entertainment medium much more realistic than those from which it often borrows its basic material. It's harder work and takes a little more courage to reject an obvious, literal translation – and not to have too much reverence for the story's original form – although the producer must also be careful that he doesn't "improve" it into a failure.'

New York *Herald Tribune*   Friday, 30 December 1949

10,000 WAIT TO SEE
MUSIC HALL SHOW

7-Block 2-File Line Is Called
All-Time Record

A crowd estimated at close to 10,000 persons stretched the seasonally long lines of persons waiting to see the three-hour holiday show at Radio City Music Hall to a record length of seven blocks at 11:30 AM yesterday.

The day this issue was distributed on the desks of the upper echelon, Freed, Edens and Simone entered the commissary for lunch. A prominent rival producer was overheard saying, '*Here comes the royal family.*'

Notes

1   'The nicest time of the year,' 'Ain't got no tears left', 'Lonely me', 'Sleep in your lady's arms', 'Carnegie Hall pavanne', 'Say when', 'I'm afraid it's love', 'The intermission's great', 'Got to be bad to be good' and 'Dream with me',
2   Marton also shot footage for *Annie Get Your Gun*, which was in production at the same time.

4 · Ida Jeter: The collapse of the Federated Motion Picture Crafts: a case study of class collaboration in the motion picture industry

Journal of the University Film Association, vol. 31, no. 2 (Spring 1979)

Radical and conservative critics of Hollywood cinema have regularly remarked on the relative scarcity of screen fictions whose protagonists are authentically proletarian. Much has been made, for instance, of the absence of trade union issues and indeed of work itself from the agenda of most American films. It is somewhat surprising, therefore, to discover that much of the historical analysis of the American film industry, even when conducted by Marxists, has also tended to marginalise, if not entirely exclude, any consideration of the role played in that history by organised labour. Ida Jeter's article is not only an important step in rectifying that omission but also, by dealing with a specific inter-union struggle at a particular historical moment, is able to avoid that familiarly narrow perspective which conflates and confuses economic activities with the productive process.

Jeter's subject, the Federated Motion Picture Crafts abortive strike against the Hollywood majors and the consequent collapse of the FMPC's challenge to and jurisdictional dispute with the IATSE, the International Alliance of Theatrical and Stage Employees, is an extraordinary one. By demonstrating that the FMPC were both more radical in their demands and yet at the same time perhaps more anachronistic in their attitudes – emphasising 'craft' over 'industry' and organising on a local rather than national level – Jeter implicitly problematises the assumptions shared by Leavis and Adorno that Hollywood was an industrial culture rather than a site of struggle between craft-based and industry-based practices. This craft/industry antithesis offers an historical and material explanation for the otherwise rather rhetorical opposition posed between 'creativity' and 'commerce'.

Edward Branigan's analysis of the predominant explanatory models deployed by film historians, reprinted elsewhere in this anthology, demonstrates just how often and how obstinately specific biographical subjects have been credited as the authors of historical developments – as pioneers, entrepreneurs, inventors, auteurs. Jeter's account of the 1937 dispute carefully rejects a reading of that history which would attribute IATSE-industry collaboration to individual corruption (without denying the oft-cited and undoubted criminality of IATSE officials George Browne and William Bioff), and concentrates instead on the elaboration of the concept of class collaboration. Furthermore, by discussing the structures of employment rather than the subjectivity of specific employees Jeter is able to observe that the hierarchy of Hollywood labour is a crucial underpinning of the operations of Hollywood cinema.

Friday, 30 April 1937, Hollywood painters, draftsmen, make-up artists, hairdressers, and scenic artists, all members of the newly formed Federated Motion Picture Crafts (FMPC), went on strike against the major Hollywood producers.[1] The organization demanded immediate recognition of the Federation, union shop, and separate contracts for all the affiliated crafts, which would include increased wages. Within a few days, the original picketers were joined by stationery engineers, plumbers, cooks, machinists, boiler makers, welders, and the Studio Utility Employees. But at the close of the six-week strike, with its frequent reports of violence on the picket lines,[2] only the original protesting crafts remained on the lines, all others having returned to work. When, on 10 July, the painters, make-up and scenic artists, hairdressers, and draftsmen voted to accept the agreement offered by the producers, they also dissolved the Federated Motion Picture Crafts. Thus, most of the crafts obtained contracts, but an initial goal, recognition of the Federation, was not achieved.[3]

Why did the Federated Motion Picture Crafts collapse, particularly in a period of unprecedented labor organizing and union expansion throughout the United States and the motion picture industry? The FMPC, committed to the autonomy and self-direction of local crafts, threatened the pattern of producer/international union leadership co-operation which had prevailed in the industry for eleven years. The organization of several crafts into a new competitive labor federation challenged the International Alliance of Theatrical and Stage Employees' (IATSE) plans to organize the entire amusement industry, including several crafts in the FMPC. And, to an extent, the Federated, by its structure and existence, undermined the control of local affiliates by their large international unions, most notably the International Brotherhood of Painters, Decorators, and Paper Hangers and the United Brotherhood of Carpenters and Joiners of America. In short, these internationals and the producers cooperated to eliminate the new federation and restore, to the extent possible, the status quo previous to the strike. I shall argue that this strike and the dissolution of the FMPC reveals an emerging pattern of class collaboration between the producers and international union management which commenced with the first Studio Basic Agreement in 1926 and became the dominant industrial relations strategy for both the producers and unions by the late 1940s and early 1950s.

By class collaboration I do not mean that the leaders of the large unions colluded or conspired to break the FMPC. That is possible, although the evidence does not support such a contention at this time. Rather, the producers and international union leaders shared compatible goals, the stability of both the labor and commodity markets within the prevailing system of property and production relations.[4] To understand this distinction, we must examine class collaboration in a broader context – the class conflict perspective of labor struggle.

Class collaboration

Lacking access to the means of production and possessing only its labor power, the working class sells that power to the capitalist class in order to maintain its subsistence. The source of value of commodities generating from labor, labor power also becomes the means by which capitalists increase surplus value and, hence, make a profit. The exploitation of labor and its subordination to the authority of capital constitute the principal source of class conflict, structurally inherent though at times latent in the capitalist system and most apparent in strikes and other job actions. Strikes are not an aberration in an otherwise balanced system; they are part of the capitalist structure.

However, the capitalist system also generates forces which contain incipient class struggle and redirect the consciousness of workers to an acceptance of their subordinate relationship to industry. Stanley Aronowitz in *False Promises* examines these factors, many of them peculiar to the United States, and accounts for the absence of a pervasive working class consciousness in this country. He does not blame trade unionism for the working class's failure to develop and maintain the subjective conditions in revolutionary political practice. Nonetheless, he places trade unionism in the nexus of cultural, social, political, and economic structures and practices which militate against the advances of working class consciousness. The behavior of industry and trade unions will comprise the focus of the following discussion.

Describing 'a fundamental tendency in labor relations,' Aronowitz argues that 'unions have remained useful to workers as instruments for negotiating more favorable terms in the sale of labor power, but ... have often bargained away their members' rights to retain a voice in the determination of the conditions of labor.' Trade unions in this country have become a means for integrating labor into the capitalist system. While insuring benefits for workers, they offer owners and managers a stable, disciplined work force. Management, once reluctant to turn over any control of production or the labor process, is increasingly willing to concede wages, certain health and safety benefits, and some decision-making regarding the intensity of labor. They gain a definite advantage in such concessions because they maintain 'control over labor costs as a stable factor of production in order to permit rational investment decisions.'[5]

The history of American trade unions is marked by three tendencies. Power has shifted from rank-and-file members and their shop stewards to international union officials. The rank-and-file, by virtue of their daily involvement in the labor process, tend to advance more political demands which directly affect work conditions while union management attempts to channel workers' demands into economic contract issues concerning wages and benefits. Trade unions have become committed to the stability of the labor market and are reluctant to adopt measures which might threaten their continued growth and financial security. One means of assuring a stable labor market is to remove wages and benefits from competition. Hence, the tendency on the part of unions toward expansion through organizing an entire craft or industry. Such expansion contributes to centralization; and, with increased centralization, the attention of union management has been diverted from political and social issues to contract administration, bureaucratic procedures, and union finances. Although not as highly professionalized as corporate management, 'the union leader is a business executive. His accountability is not limited to the membership – it is extended to government agencies, arbitrators, courts of law, and other institutions which play a large role in regulating the union's operations' and to the corporation with whom they share the responsibility for administration of the contract.[6]

Collective bargaining and the labor agreement illuminate the principal strategies of class collaboration. In restricting the subjects of negotiation, collective bargaining protects the prerogatives of management in the organization and direction of the labor process. The contract perpetuates hierarchies of skills, which serve owners' interests by dividing the employees into fragmented special interest groups. Grievance procedures are hierarchical and bureaucratic, involving many steps which remove control over work conditions from the site of work to higher levels of corporate and union management. Long term contracts and no strike clauses guarantee uninterrupted labor supply for the duration of the agreement. No longer seeking to profit maximize, management's goals in the era of monopoly capitalism are steady profits, growth, a strong competitive position, and high managerial incomes. They avoid risks and 'adopt an attitude of live and let live toward other members of the corporate world,' primarily other large corporations.[7]

The New Deal period provided the groundwork for an emerging alliance between corporations, government, and unions in the containment of labor struggles and the maintenance of the capitalist system. Hence, a third participant in the labor market is the state. As the federal government and industry cooperated to establish measures for recovery and continued economic growth, trade unions were recognized as an essential part of the system. Long-range planning depended on the ability to predict labor costs; hence, a stable, regulated labor market became necessary. Federal legislation, first Section 7A of the National Recovery Act and then the National Labor Relations Act[8] guaranteed labor's right to organize and bargain collectively at the same time that it established mechanisms for protecting existing property relations, containing and directing strikes or other incipient manifestations of class struggle, and formalizing procedures for the stabilization of the labor market.[9] And, as indicated, employers were becoming increasingly agreeable, though some more reluctantly than others, to collective bargaining and contractual arrangements with trade unions.

Relations in the film industry

Before moving on to the presentation on the strike, I must point out that the 1930s were a period of transition for labor, corporations, and government. None of these three organizations manifested all the characteristics outlined above. What we will see is the emergence of patterns which eventually became consolidated into institutional behavior. Several aspects of class collaboration will be demonstrated. All parties, including the Federated Motion Picture Crafts, insisted on the perpetuation of hierarchies of skill. The large international unions and producers sought the centralization of union control and contract administration at the level of the international office; rank-and-file or local initiative was discouraged. Jurisdictional disputes were generally resolved in favor of the ambitious and ever-expanding IATSE, and the fragmentation of the craft coalition into separate unions offered fertile territory for future IATSE organizing drives.

In detailing the above reasons for the dissolution of the Federated Motion Picture Crafts, I will examine relations between producers and key unions prior to the strike; conditions in the industry which rendered it vulnerable to widespread and protracted strikes; producer strategies to end the strike and what happened to the unions involved; and, the federal government's minimal participation in the conflicts.

The motion picture industry has at times been resistant to labor initiatives; however, producers have primarily adopted a posture of conciliation with large craft unions when necessary to insure the uninterrupted production, distribution, and exhibition of films. Indeed, several of the mechanisms for class collaboration between the industry and union leadership were established in the 1920s.

Since the beginning of labor troubles in Hollywood in 1916, the producers have been united in their labor relations policies, their most recent organization at the time of the 1937 strike being the Association of Motion Picture Producers. Formed in 1924, the Association was the Hollywood affiliate of the Motion Picture Producers and Distributors of America. Under the leadership of Pat Casey, the producers' labor relations representative, it pursued an open shop policy and obtained the 1926 Studio Basic Agreement, which included the nine major producers and five key unions.[10] Under the Agreement, which was renewable every five years and subject to annual adjustments, the producers would negotiate only with the presidents of international unions, not local representatives or business agents. Grievances were handled by two committees composed of producers and the international presidents. New unions could be admitted to the Agreement only with the consent of other unions. The effect of this requirement, given the many jurisdictional disputes between unions, was to limit the number of such organizations which could bargain with the producers. And until 1936, the Agreement protected the open shop. Producers maintained control over hiring and firing and the determination of crew requirements; and membership in the unions was not compulsory for employment. The Studio Basic Agreement and the Academy of Motion Picture Arts and Sciences, an employee-representation program which covered actors and other artists, comprised the foundation of producer/labor policies until 1936 and 1937, at which point the producers were forced to re-examine their situation and make adjustments in these policies.[11]

The Supreme Court decision regarding the constitutionality of the Wagner Act, rendered 12 April 1937, undermined the producers' labor policies. The producers had insisted that production was local in nature because 95 per cent of production inputs came from within the state of California. But that decision, defining the scope of federal authority to include 'any practice which has a direct objectionable effect on interstate commerce,' meant film production would be subject to federal regulation.[12] Hence, the Studio Basic Agreement, which limited the number of unions with which the producers would negotiate, was vulnerable. They would have to deal with labor organizations asserting their rights to collective bargaining.

Conditions in the film industry rendered it vulnerable to widespread union activity and contributed to the need on the part of the producers to maintain a stable labor market. Michael Conant has argued that the development of monopoly in the motion picture industry derived from the uncertainty of the commodity market. The product was not homogeneous, and audience response to films was unpredictable. This factor also necessitated industrial relations policies which would insure uninterrupted labor and controlled labor costs. Furthermore, this monopoly power in controlling supply was most effectively achieved at the level of exhibition supplemented by the distribution combination. At the level of production the control of output and maintenance of a partial certainty in the market was effected primarily through the star system and self-censorship.[13]

Because production, distribution and exhibition were closely synchronized at that time, production deadlines were critical to the steady supply of films to the exchanges. When the FMPC strike began, thirty-three pictures were in production.[14] *Variety* reported that any interruption in production would adversely affect the theaters.[15]

Confronted with these market conditions, producers had one safety valve of sorts. The increased costs of production could be passed on through higher film rentals to the public in increased admission charges. The 10 per cent wage increase stipulated in 1937 Studio Basic Agreement adjustments had already increased rentals, and *Variety* indicated that higher admissions were expected.[16]

The Federated Motion Picture Crafts

The Federated Motion Picture Crafts was formed after the yearly meeting of representatives to the Studio Basic Agreement in March 1937, at which time producer and labor committees agreed on a 10 per cent wage increase to members of IATSE, the Electrical Workers, the Carpenters, and the Teamsters. The Screen Actors Guild was denied admission to the Agreement. The Painters, who had withdrawn from the arrangement in 1932, were granted approval to rejoin with the 10 per cent wage increase provided they desist in their attempt to bring unaffiliated make-up artists, hair stylists, draftsmen, and scenic artists into the Agreement with them. They refused the offer. It subsequently became known that IATSE coveted these crafts as it did the Studio Utility Employees, which was informed it could become party to the Agreement after it worked out its jurisdictional problem with IATSE.[17]

The actors, painters, make-up artists, hair stylists, art directors, draftsmen, and laborers participated with other organizations in a meeting, on 10 April, to discuss the formation of a federated group of crafts and occupations outside the Studio Basic Agreement. This group was later named the Federated Motion Picture Crafts. The producers refused their demand for immediate recognition of the federation and the crafts under a union shop before commencing contract negotiations. Their stated position was that they would discuss recognition, wages, and other contract issues at the same time. The Federated Crafts went on strike 30 April.[18] By the end of the six-week strike, many of the crafts had obtained recognition and/ or contracts but not as affiliates of the FMPC, because the producers refused to talk with any group affiliated with that federation. Failing to receive the support it expected from other workers and unions in the industry, the Federated Crafts were unable to apply sufficient pressure on the producers to force them to recognize the organization. Hence, on 10 June, the few remaining members dissolved the Federated Motion Picture Crafts.

I am not arguing that the Federated posed a revolutionary alternative to its members or to labor organizing in the motion picture industry. After all, it manifested some of the traits attributed to trade union collaboration. The FMPC was seeking recognition as a trade federation and the right to bargain collectively. Their craft orientation secured hierarchies of skill, and their demand for union shop protected management prerogatives in hiring and firing. Nevertheless, FMPC was a threat to the producers and its structure was inimical to IATSE's policy of strict international control of locals. According to the Federated's constitution, each craft would remain autonomous, and negotiate its own contract with the support and advice of the FMPC, which would operate only in a supervisory capacity. The crafts, however, could not bargain a contract which would be detrimental to the other unions in the federation; but they would gain the advantage of support from their colleagues in emergencies.[19] The FMPC's demand for recognition of local crafts as bargaining agents challenged the Studio Basic Agreement, which established negotiation, grievance, and arbitration mechanisms based on local subordination to international union control and management/international cooperation. And, if we can take the producers' strategy of fragmenting the federation into its separate crafts as an indication of their intentions, they apparently did not want to deal with a coalition of mutually supportive yet autonomous and locally dominated craft unions. Furthermore, cooperating with the FMPC would undermine their relationship with IATSE, which wanted to bring many of the crafts in the federation under its aegis. IATSE's own membership was chafing under the tight reins of their international. The existence of a loose federation so unlike their centralized organization could potentially subvert the IATSE leadership's standing with these locals.

The producers were in a precarious position. On one hand, they had to make concessions to the striking crafts to get them back to work; and, on the other, they had to maintain existing relations with the more powerful unions party to the Studio Basic Agreement. The days of an open shop policy in the industry were over, and the Wagner Act required them to negotiate. The strike weakened the stability of both the labor and commodity markets. Important release deadlines were threatened as were substantial investments in unfinished films. Hence, they adopted a strategy which was designed to end the strike and restore, to the extent possible, the status quo before the Wagner Act. That meant breaking up the FMPC and, especially, undermining the strong alliance between the painters, make-up artists, hair stylists, draftsmen, and scenic artists.

In examining the events of the strike, principally the producers' strategy and the assistance they received from the international unions, I will outline three intersecting patterns which illustrate the producers' vulnerability to protracted labor agitation and which demonstrate certain aspects of class collaboration between producers and unions. The most prevalent pattern is, of course, the intervention by international representatives of unions to weaken or end the strike. The producers preferred to negotiate with these representatives; and, after they became involved, settlements were frequently reached and/or locals generally acceded to international union directives. Of these unions IATSE was the most active. It refused to support the strike, assisted the Screen Actors Guild in winning a contract, and exploited the strike as the justification for raiding the Studio Utility Employees. The Carpenters intervened to persuade its members to abide by the Studio Basic Agreement; and both IATSE and the Painters International were instrumental in ending the strike. Committed to the stability of the labor markets and their own standing in that market, these unions wanted their members to stay on the job or return to work, and they were willing to cooperate with each other and the producers to achieve this end.

Previous to the strike, the producers asserted that IATSE crafts 'would step in and assist them in the event of emergency.'[20] And IATSE did assist. Indeed, the strike was a means for the union to expand its jurisdiction. Earlier in 1937, IATSE publicized its intentions to organize all branches of the industry, and on 21 April it reiterated its goals, including in that announcement the complete organization of the studios. In his public statement, International President George Browne thanked the film companies for their cooperation, declaring, 'I wish to state our intention of doing everything in our power for the betterment of general business conditions in all branches of the amusement industry.' IATSE ordered its members to continue working, offered work cards and free initiation to strikers who returned to work, and replaced strikers with new employees recruited into their union.[21]

The alliance also intervened on the behalf of the Screen Actors Guild, which had been involved initially in the discussions concerning formation of the Federation. SAG delayed strike action for a week, and the night before they were set to walk out, 8 May, obtained a ten-year agreement with the producers. Prior to the settlement, the producers and IATSE repeatedly refused to recognize the Guild as the bargaining agent for the actors. However, if the Screen Actors Guild joined the FMPC picketers, one crucial means of commodity differentiation would be lost. Replacements could not be found as in the case of behind-the-scenes workers, and production would have been halted. Hence, the producers and IATSE worked toward a hasty settlement once it became clear that the actors would strike. Robert Montgomery, president of SAG, thanked William Bioff and IATSE for their assistance and said the Alliance 'had supported the movement from the start and deserved much credit for the success of the negotiations.'[22]

The second instance of IATSE's intervention illustrates how that union manipulated jurisdictional disputes to its advantage. The Studio Utility Employees Local 724 of the Hod Carriers, Builders and

Common Laborers of America had been denied entrance into the Basic Agreement until the jurisdictional dispute with IATSE was resolved. Failing in their last effort to reach an agreement with IATSE, SUE went on strike on 3 May. Even before they went out, IATSE began replacing them with their own people, some even recruited from the Studio Utility Employees. Granted a Class B grip rating, about 1,000 laborers were given a wage increase from 60c to 82½c an hour for joining the Alliance. On 21 May, the local returned to work after Joseph Marshall, international vice-president of the Hod Carriers, and George Browne agreed on a settlement and issued the following jointly signed statement: 'The International Alliance of Theatrical Stage Employees again intervened in the strained studio union situation ... Similar to their demands upon the major producers two weeks ago that the Screen Actors Guild be given recognition, the IATSE secured a union shop agreement and 15c per hour increase for the Studio Utility Employees Union.'[23] Of course, by this time there were few members remaining in SUE to benefit from the wage hike, which was even below that granted laborers who joined IATSE. Besides, most of the jobs had been taken by IATSE members.

Before the strike, the Carpenters local threatened to withdraw from the Studio Basic Agreement and affiliate with the FMPC unless given an additional 10c wage increase, denied them in the 1936 Studio Basic Agreement adjustments. However, Abe Muir, international vice-president of the United Brotherhood of Carpenters and Joiners of America, visited California and informed the local membership that such action required the sanction of the international, which was committed to the Basic Agreement. The local carpenters finally decided to petition through the international for the increase.[24]

By the fifth week of the strike, only the painters, make-up artists, hair stylists, draftsmen, and scenic designers remained in the FMPC. They were denied support from other unions, were unable to keep the Carpenters and SUE workers among their ranks, and witnessed many defections as fellow picketers returned to work. All that remained to destroy the Federated Crafts was the dissolution of the strong alliance between the few remaining crafts. Two international unions, IATSE and the Painters, became involved in this effort.

During the fourth week of the strike, George Browne claimed jurisdiction over the make-up artists, draftsmen and hair stylists and threatened 'a complete studio and theatre strike in the U.S. and Canada if the FMPC agreement [was] signed minus IATSE sanction.' Refusing to talk with any local painters' representatives, Browne stipulated that no agreement could be reached until Joe Clarke, international vice-president of the Brotherhood of Painters, Decorators, and Paperhangers, arrived in California.[25] Clarke, upon his arrival, stated that his principal goal was to get the painters and scenic artists back to work under a union shop. He then negotiated with Pat Casey and Browne, but the local painters rejected the closed shop arrangement and 10 per cent wage increase agreed upon by the three bargainers.[26]

The strike lasted one week after the contract was rejected. On 10 June, the painters, hair stylists, make-up artists, draftsmen and scenic artists returned to work. The settlement stipulated that negotiations with the separate crafts would begin within six days of the termination of the strike and arranged for union shop commencing 1 July for the crafts. The FMPC was dissolved, but *Variety* reported it had become 'ineffective some time previous to the end of the strike when George Browne ... refused to recognize its authority to negotiate with the producers as representatives of studio labor groups.'[27]

I do not think any of the producers or union representatives counted on the militance and solidarity demonstrated by the remaining members of the Federated. Hence, the timing of IATSE's announcement is crucial to the resolution of the conflict. That union's refusal to recognize the FMPC and the threat of a vertical international strike marked the point at which representatives from the Painters International intervened. Although IATSE's position posed a major threat to the kingpin of the producers' monopoly power, exhibition, and that union could shut down the studios, the Alliance's announcement served the producers' interest more than it challenged their control of the industry. The producers certainly did not want to risk the catastrophe of a major strike. Yet from the beginning they had sought the collapse of the FMPC, and IATSE's refusal to recognize the FMPC was instrumental in bringing that collapse about. Both groups wanted to restore relative labor peace, fragment the FMPC coalition, and stabilize the Basic Agreement.

The Painters International had originally been willing to re-enter the Studio Basic Agreement under the terms stipulated by the Agreement's labor and producer committees, but had supported its two Hollywood affiliates, the Studio Painters Local 644 and United Scenic Artists Local 621, when they refused to enter without the recognition of the other artists. The international had remained quiet through much of the strike, but now it had to act. If the Federated Crafts somehow managed to stay together or if a lost strike so severely weakened the Painters affiliates that they were vulnerable to being incorporated into another union, the Painters International would lose all its Hollywood members. So, Clarke announced he was willing to concede jurisdiction over the make-up artists and hair stylists, a jurisdiction the Painters International had maintained since 1932. That he initially failed to persuade the locals to agree with the compromise can be attributed to their militance. Of course, a week later the compromise became effective. The strike now broken, the crafts accepted individual settlements and the international kept the painters and, for a short while, the scenic artists.

Another reason the FMPC was unable to gain recognition as a labor organization was that other smaller crafts supporting or affiliated with the federation returned to work and reached agreements with the producers. Hence, the second principal pattern, the reverse of the producers' preference for international representatives, was that when no national or international parent union existed the producers chose to negotiate with the local crafts unaffiliated with or recently severed from the FMPC.

The Associated Motion Picture Costumers, which had delayed a vote on affiliation with the FMPC, negotiated a contract under which they won recognition, a wage increase, and specifications regarding work conditions during the early weeks of the strike. The seamstresses were also given a contract. The studio plasterers, who were present at the first meeting of the Federation but did not strike, received a 10 per cent wage increase. Machinists, plumbers, molders, and other smaller crafts which returned to work won contracts and wage increases. None of the organizations, however, was admitted into the Studio Basic Agreement.[28]

The producers apparently preferred granting wage increases and minor benefits (all of which could be passed on to viewers through higher admissions) to local unaffiliated crafts rather than negotiate with or include in the Studio Basic Agreement a strong coalition of locally controlled crafts. Fragmented and weakened, these crafts would pose no threat to standard labor relations policies. And they were vulnerable to being absorbed by established international unions, particularly IATSE, in order to protect their interests and have some input into the functioning of the industry's labor policies. Such would have the long-range effect of limiting the number of union representatives with which the producers would have to negotiate, and these representatives would, by and large, be executives of large international unions who shared the producers' commitment to the stability of the labor and commodity markets.[29]

This fragmentation of once, albeit temporarily, united crafts demonstrates the importance of jurisdictional disputes and competition between unions, prevalent in the 1930s and 1940s. As we examine what happened to the principal unions in the FMPC after the strike and the role played by the National Labor Relations Board, we will see that the jurisdictional disputes benefited the producers. Their refusal to negotiate with any union unless all disputes regarding which group would represent a job category were settled was essentially a stalling tactic. Moreover, these disputes were generally resolved in favor of IATSE, or left small, weak crafts lacking sufficient power in the labor market to gain sizeable concessions from the producers or maintain their independence, vulnerable to organization by the larger unions.

After the strike, Casey, Browne, Bioff, and the leaders of the local crafts began to negotiate, a process that lasted several months. In July, the Motion Picture Painters Local 644 received a 15 per cent wage increase and a closed shop contract, the only closed shop granted a local, after Willie Bioff approved the pay hike. The make-up artists and hair stylists, who had resisted incorporation into the IATSE, subsequently voted to affiliate with that organization and obtained contracts and sizeable wage increases.[30]

Jurisdictional disputes prevailed among the draftsmen. Three groups claimed representation rights over that occupation – the Scenic Artists, the Society of Motion Picture Set Designers, and IATSE. And the United Scenic Artists Local 621 encountered jurisdictional difficulties of its own. Its charter revoked by the International Brotherhood of Painters, some members chose to stay in an independent 621, others joined the Painters Local 644, and both IATSE and the Society of Motion Picture Set Designers claimed jurisdiction over the artists.[31]

Federal government role

The FMPC strike occurred directly after the Supreme Court confirmation of the Wagner Act, the point at which government participation in industrial relations became a regular, continuous institutionalized practice; hence, the strike was not marked by a great deal of federal intervention. Nevertheless, the state's minimal role is noteworthy.

The fledgling Regional Labor Relations Board, created by the Wagner Act and under the Directorship of Dr Towne Nylander, received several requests to mediate jurisdictional disputes. Before SUE joined the strikers, Joseph Marshall charged IATSE with raiding and conspiring with the producers to place IA members in laborer positions previously held by SUE members. Dr Nylander forwarded the charges and Casey's denial that the producers had violated the

Wagner Act to the National Board in Washington. *Variety* reported, 'Since [the] NLRB has always shied away from labor jurisdiction fights it is possible that no further cognizance will be taken of the protest.'[32] And, indeed, nothing resulted from the petition. Consideration of the several jurisdictional disputes occurred after the strike was postponed until the NLRB ruled on the Screen Writers Guild petition for an election, that ruling to address the status of writers as employees.[33]

The NLRB's delays in jurisdiction decisions can be attributed to several factors: the government's involvement under such specific legislation was a very recent development in labor relations and, consequently, the regional and national board were not yet equipped to deal with all the legal problems which resulted from the Wagner Act. Nevertheless, the delays, in effect, deferred negotiations between small crafts and producers. And these weak locals were rendered susceptible to IATSE's expansion initiative.

The Federated Motion Picture Crafts were doomed from the beginning. The alternative they offered production employees was not acceptable to the producers or the principal international unions, particularly the International Alliance of Theatrical Stage Employees with its goal of a semi-industrial union in the motion picture industry. The FMPC simply could not match the international union/ management coalition, whose aim it was to protect the policies of the Studio Basic Agreement.

Notes

1 Warner Bros., Universal, Paramount, Metro-Goldwyn-Mayer, RKO, 20th Century-Fox, Columbia, United Artists, and Hal Roach Studios.
2 Violence erupted particularly between longshoremen from California port cities who supported the FMPC and gunmen imported from Chicago by William Bioff, the representative of the International Alliance of Theatrical and Stage Employees in Hollywood.
3 *Variety*, 5, 12, 19, 26 May; 2, 9, 19 June 1937.
4 A reader familiar with motion picture history might argue the reason for cooperation between IATSE and the producers is that George Browne and William Bioff were racketeers who threatened the studios with strikes and extorted vast sums from the victimized producers. Bribery and extortion might have entered into the relationship, but not to the extent generally described by the producers and film historians. Certainly money was exchanged between the producers and IATSE, but questions regarding which party was being bribed and IATSE's usefulness to the producers in realms other than labor remain. The subject merits inquiry, but

at this time I reject the argument that extortion is the key to producer/ IATSE collaboration.

5 Stanley Aronowitz, *False Promises: The Shaping of American Working Class Consciousness* (New York: McGraw-Hill, 1973), pp. 423 and 218; Michael Shalev, 'Problems of theory in industrial relations: lessons from a comparative study of industrial conflict,' presentation at Colloquium on International Labor and Industrial Relations, University of Wisconsin-Madison, 27 February 1978; other sources for an examination of class collaboration and trade union behavior are: Irving Bernstein, *The Lean Years: A History of the American Worker, 1920–1933* (Boston: Houghton Mifflin, 1960); Irving Bernstein, *The Turbulent Years: A History of the American Worker, 1933–1941* (Boston: Houghton Mifflin, 1971); Harry Braverman, *Labor and Monopoly Capital* (New York: Monthly Review Press, 1974); Jeremy Brecher, *Strike* (San Francisco; Straight Arrow Books, 1972); Marten Estey, *The Unions: Structure, Development, and Management* (New York: St Martin's Press, 1963).

6 Aronowitz, p. 220. Union members, to be sure, still exercise a certain amount of control through elections and the national or international conventions which are generally both legislative and judicial in nature. The extent of bottoms-up government varies considerably from union to union. However, two general conditions limit this form of control. Officers, the executive board, and staff wield a great deal of authority in the actual daily operations of the union and in collective bargaining. And, by virtue of their political power within the union, tenure, skill, or expertise they can influence substantially membership decision-making. The local affiliate lacks autonomy. It is chartered by the national, and that charter can be suspended. Or the union can be put under administrative supervision (trusteeship). Under many union constitutions, locals are required to get their national's permission before calling a strike or other forms of action. Other factors contributing to the trend toward centralization in unions are: the growth of national product markets beyond the jurisdiction of local unions; the parallel centralization of a firm's decision-making such that the local managers do not have the authority to establish major employment practices and policies; and, the increasing complexity of collective bargaining.

7 Paul A. Baran and Paul M. Sweezy, *Monopoly Capital* (New York: Modern Reader Paperbacks, 1966), pp. 15–16.

8 The Wagner Act, passed in 1935, guaranteed employees 'the right to self-organization, to form, join or assist labor organizations, to bargain collectively through representatives of their own choosing, and to engage in concerted activities for the purpose of collective bargaining or other mutual aid or protection. The act created the National Labor Relations Board which functioned to prevent or remedy employers' unfair labor practices against union organizing or collective bargaining and to resolve jurisdictional controversies and hold representation elections to determine the official bargaining agent for employees.

9 The federal and state governments had intervened in labor disputes before 1930. The US Department of Labor was established as a separate federal cabinet department in 1913, and previous federal legislation dealt tangen-

tially with labor unions. Nevertheless, the Wagner Act is the principal legislation stipulating the rights of labor unions, and its passage marks a significant change in labor history in the United States. The original act does not explicitly provide mechanisms for maintaining the prevailing production relations; however, its effect and application was to protect the capitalist system and establish the procedures for stabilizing the labor market. See Aronowitz, op. cit., pp. 238–40.

10 The International Alliance of Theatrical Stage Employees and Motion Picture Machine Operators; the International Brotherhood of Painters, Decorators and Paperhangers; the United Brotherhood of Carpenters and Joiners of America; the American Federation of Musicians; and the International Brotherhood of Electrical Workers.

11 Murray Ross, *Stars and Strikes: Unionization of Hollywood* (New York: Columbia University Press, 1941). The open shop policy was first undermined in 1936 when IATSE was readmitted to the Studio Basic Agreement under the first closed shop arrangement in the industry. That union had withdrawn from the Agreement in July 1933, during an unsuccessful strike at Columbia studios and an attempted industry-wide strike over the issue of union jurisdiction over soundmen. Its membership had fallen to less than 100 as a result of their defeat. IATSE, under the new leadership of president George Browne, asserted its power in December 1935, with a brief but effective theater strike in Chicago, St Louis, Minneapolis, and Detroit. Producers not only readmitted IATSE to the agreement but informed 12,000 studio employees, all members of the Carpenters or Electrical Workers, to join IATSE.

12 'Anticipate revival of NRA in validity of the Wagner Act,' *Variety*, 14 April 1937, p. 2. The Wagner Act, and also the CIO, undermined the exclusive jurisdiction policies of the American Federation of Labor, with which IATSE and most motion picture unions were affiliated. Hence, these unions' security under the Basic Agreement was threatened. Furthermore, this period of dual unionism allows us to observe unions in a highly competitive stage of development.

13 Michael Conant, *Antitrust in the Motion Picture Industry* (Berkeley: University of California Press, 1960).

14 '33 in works as walkout came,' 5 May 1937, p. 3.

15 The studios had completed only one-third of the films contracted for release when the strike began, and the release season was already three-fourths over. The producers did not have reserves of feature films because it was not their policy at the time to hold completed films; 'Strike forcing singles?' *Variety*, 5 May 1937, p. 3.

16 See 'Pix passing labor wage increases to public,' *Variety*, 14 April 1937, pp. 2 and 66.

17 The Painters withdrew from the Agreement in 1932 because the producers refused to allow them to introduce more job classifications as participants in the Agreement. 'Wagner disturbs Hollywood,' *Variety*, 14 April 1937, pp. 1 and 2; 'Actors Guild, painters lead fight on film producers to force recognition under Wagner Act,' *Variety*, 21 April 1937, p. 2; 'Film peace this week: SAG, IATSE not backing FMPC,' *Variety*, 5 May 1937, pp. 1–2.

18 'List demands,' *Variety*, 28 April 1937, p. 5.
19 See 'Film peace this week: SAG, IATSE not backing FMPC,' *Variety*, 5 May 1937, p. 2.
20 '100% amus. unionization: AFL approves IATSE move,' 21 April 1937, pp. 1–2.
21 The FMPC had expected support from local members of the IATSE and thought dissension within the Alliance crafts would ultimately swing the workers toward them. The White Rats, a group of insurgents within IATSE, opposed the union's strike-breaking tactics and sent a resolution to the AFL calling upon that organization to support the strike. The group also petitioned the international to permit membership meetings and local elections, denied them by Browne in 1936. Such efforts were unsuccessful primarily because of strict international control of local affiliates. 'Film peace this week: SAG, IATSE not backing FMPC,' *Variety*, 5 May 1937, pp. 1–2; 'Mere 135 out, Casey insists; cites producer labor dealings as fair,' *Variety*, 5 May 1937, p. 3.
22 The producers argued that SAG did not represent a majority of actors and that negotiations with the Guild would violate the Academy agreement for actors. Once a settlement was reached, the Academy requested termination of their contract covering actors. 'Actors Guild, painters lead fight on film producers to force recognition under Wagner Act,' *Variety*, 21 April 1937, p. 2; 'Pix strife now national; picketing in 8 keys, but actors tiff patched up,' *Variety*, 12 May 1937, p. 2.
23 Before beginning negotiations with IATSE, Marshall protested against IA raiding and charged the producers and that union with conspiring to destroy SUE. After the strike, the jurisdictional struggle continued. SUE and IATSE did not agree on a satisfactory distinction between grip and laborer. In December, IATSE – temporarily weakened by state investigations and negative press coverage – relinquished control over many of the laborers. 'Coast strike settlement imminent again,' *Variety*, 26 May 1937, p. 2; 'Costumers on own,' *Variety*, 5 May 1937, p. 2.
24 In September, William Hutchinson, president of the Carpenters international, directed Cliff Mace, the business representative to the Studio Carpenters Local 946, to disband all local committees and informed him that the international officers would handle all bargaining and other local affairs. 'Wagner disturbs Hollywood,' *Variety*, 14 April 1937, p. 2.
25 'Labor arbitrator for creative end of film biz is newest idea,' *Variety*, 9 June 1937, pp. 2 and 55.
26 'Six weeks studio strike ends,' *Variety*, 16 June 1937, pp. 2 and 23.
27 'Studio labor situation easing off, makeups, stylists reach agreement,' *Variety*, 21 July 1937, p. 7.
28 Ross, *Stars and Strikes*; 'Peace looks nearer in FMPC strike on coast, but picketing continues,' *Variety*, 19 May 1937, p. 2; 'Coast strike settlement imminent again,' *Variety*, 26 May 1937, p. 2; 'Six week studio strike ends,' *Variety*, 16 June 1927, pp. 2 and 23.
29 Testifying at the California Assembly investigation of IATSE in November 1937, Pat Casey declared that if IATSE restored autonomy to its locals, the producers would consider that a violation of the Studio Basic Agreement and withdraw from that agreement. Subsequent to the strike,

IATSE repeatedly asserted its plan for one big union in the industry, though the definition of that union shifted back and forth from a loose federation of crafts to a more centralized organization much like IATSE in 1936 and 1937 (such shifts responded to IATSE's changing status in the industry). Browne explained that their goal was to protect their members from the loss of income resulting from strikes launched by other unions, particularly those guilds central to production such as actors or writers. It cannot be ignored that a large dues-paying membership contributes to the financial security of a union. Plus, IATSE members were required in 1936 and 1937 to pay an additional 2 per cent wage assessment. The timing of the Alliance's announcements of organizing drives and jurisdictional rights is suspicious. Under Browne and Bioff, the union frequently intensified organizing and/or claimed jurisdiction over a job when employees were attempting to gain recognition or negotiate with the producers independently or affiliated with another labor organization.

30 Ralph Roddy, 'Labor picture in Hollywood,' *Variety*, 5 January 1938, p. 54. A delay in negotiations occurred when Metro and Warners demanded that membership cards be issued to painters hired during the strike. Refusing to work with strikebreakers, the painters staged a 10-minute strike at Warners. The two studios withdrew their demand.

31 'Act on SAG's demand to confine talent award vote to player rank; other Hollywood crafts have plans,' *Variety*, 29 December 1937, p. 10.

32 'Screen Guild makes demands,' *Variety*, 28 April 1937, pp. 5 and 55. The Board ruled that the writers were employees, and the Screen Writers Guild won the representation election in 1938.

33 NLRB stalls off coast unions pending outcome of sub hearing,' *Variety*, 10 November 1937, p. 11; Ralph Roddy, 'Labor picture in Hollywood,' *Variety*, 5 January 1938, p. 54.

5 · Janet Staiger: Mass-produced photoplays: economic and signifying practices in the first years of Hollywood

Wide Angle, vol. 4, no. 3

Janet Staiger's essay addresses the industrial imperatives upon what have previously been perceived as exclusively aesthetic decisions about the writing of early Hollywood photoplays. More specifically, her project involves a consideration of 'how economic practices in the first years of Hollywood might be related to the development of its representational systems'. Staiger begins by suggesting that the representational strategies of early American cinema were often borrowed at a general level from the repertoire of older aesthetic forms such as prose fiction, drama, painting, and still photography. But she goes on to argue that the economic practices employed in Hollywood by the 1910s also delimited and determined the selection of such systems as well as the specific manner of their adaptation. And she proposes that within these economic practices there remained the kind of tension between the desire for differentiation and the drive toward standardisation identified in the Introduction to this anthology.

Staiger not only refuses to separate out the histories of economic and aesthetic practices in the American film industry/ cinema but also avoids relapsing into the kind of reductive model of their relation envisaged by either reflection theory or the Frankfurt School. In place of reflection, in fact, Staiger posits an inexorable opposition between two implacable forces, two irreconcilable goals: to simultaneously 'simplify, standardize and consolidate for efficiency and mass production but differentiate, direct the consumer's attention to the originality and production values of the feature product'. Hollywood is seen as a site of struggle, not simply between economic and ideological imperatives but also between different economic interests (for instance short- and long-term profit) and different ideological interests. Thus, for example, Staiger demonstrates how the 'continuity script', introduced by the companies in the early 1910s, provided a mediating concept between mode of production and mode of representation. For production, the continuity script was economic and efficient – it could be sent out at an early stage to all departments (as would have been done in much the same way forty years later for *On the Town* at MGM's Freed Unit), so that sets, props, costumes, casts, cameras and so on, not to mention the allocation of budgets, could be pre-arranged. It thus ensured and indeed reinforced the division of labour and the concomitant hierarchy of Hollywood's administration. But at the same time it also performed a kind of aesthetic quality control function, providing a 'a precheck on the quality of spatial, temporal and causal continuity and *vraisemblance*'. The continuity script thus functioned for both the cinema and the industry. And Staiger is not only careful to illustrate how these two factors influenced each other but also to ask why and when they were introduced.

Discussing the period immediately prior to the industry's and audience's acceptance of the feature film, Staiger observes that there were still restrictions within most of the companies about the amount of footage reasonably required on any project. It thus became desirable to be able to estimate accurately the length of film a particular script might be expected to occupy, as well as to ensure that such films could be produced efficiently. The early 1910s, then, with sophistication increasing throughout the decade, was the period in which both the division of labour and the studio system which we associate with it, as well the characteristics commonly attributed to 'the classic realist text', all came into being.

Staiger's emphasis on standardisation (both in mode of production and mode of representation) is balanced by an equal attention to differentiation. By 1910 a production company would be advertising its own films to distributors and exhibitors through the trade press and would be obliged to distinguish each new film both from the company's other products and from those of its competitors. It was not, apparently, unusual to find the trade press advising its readers that 'long films admit of special advertising, that is to say, special emphasis on one subject, which is more effective than equal emphasis on a number of shorter films'. Higher admission prices could be charged at the box office and generally longer films could be exhibited over a longer period – and could afford more players, production values, narrative complexity and so on. Staiger also examines the relationship between the relative expense and technical difficulty of extravagant aesthetic effects as measured against their assumed value in differentiating features and underlying their unique, special status, their novelty. Elsewhere in this collection David Bordwell's brief consideration of the re-introduction of camera movement after a period of enforced inertia with the

cumbersome technology involved in the coming of sound raises
similar sets of questions.

In a 1917 handbook for freelance writers of movies, Marguerite
Bertsch writes, 'By the subjective we mean all that takes place within
the mind or soul of a character, either in thought or feeling, influencing his future behavior.' She then describes two techniques: the
double exposure in which both the character and the subjective
thoughts are represented simultaneously in the image, and editing
with dissolves in which the subjective material is presented
sequentially in shots bracketed by the cues of dissolves. She continues: 'All subjective matter, such as a retrospection into the past, a
looking forward into the future, or the hallucinations of a troubled
mind, is possible to either, and so these two devices may be used one
in place of the other.' Of course, Bertsch is disseminating and formalizing conventions we recognize, as did she, as part of the standard
techniques of the Hollywood film of 1917.[1]

As an analyst of films, one area of research is how we explain
historically particular representational systems. An apparent explanation of films at least is that the narrative moving pictures the United
States film industry produced took theirs initially from representational systems already available in fiction, theater, pantomime,
vaudeville, opera, from systems in painting, engraving, still photography, lantern and stereoptican shows, illustrated comic strips and
so on. In other words, the industry took representational systems
available from other extant products in the culture and innovated
them where necessary to suit the moving pictures. The production of
these objects constitutes a culture's signifying practices which include
its ideologies of representation, its conventions, its aesthetics. We are
familiar with the characterization of the representational system
which Hollywood produced: a linear, 'closed' sequence of events
with emphasis on individual character psychology as motivation for
narrative action; the dominance of causal action over spatial and
temporal continuity justifying the breaking down, the analyzing of
space and time – but a continuity reconstituted through certain rules
of linkage such as matches-on-action, frame cuts, establishing and
re-establishing shots, systems of screen direction (the 180 degree rule,
shot-reverse shot, eyeline and point-of-view constructions). We are
familiar with its photographic aesthetics: valuing a 'three-dimen-
sional,' 'stereoscopic' depth; clear, steady images in which the nar-

rative event 'stands out' within the site of its occurrence; human bodies made up and lit for cultural representations of beauty, realism and typage as well as for narrative legibility. At any point of choice for this representational system other possibilities exist, and within the mode there are historical changes as well.[2]

Economic practices, the other part of this process, are also products of and producers of cultures and social institutions. These practices are the economic modes of production – the forces and relations of production. Clearly, signifying and economic practices are not separate. On the one hand, the creation of a product that signifies involves some mode of economic production, even if it is a single individual positioned in relation to a single object. On the other hand, any product of an industry (including the tools and technology produced to create the product) potentially has some signification which may be as basic as an expression of the function of the object. This object is for drinking. That one is for measuring the amount of reflected light. The difference between the two practices, really, is what part of the process one is emphasizing at the moment.

In order to make this more concrete, I want to consider how economic practices in the first years of Hollywood might be related to the development of its representational systems such as, for instance, Bertsch's statement of the equivalence of two methods to signify subjectivity. I shall concentrate on what became the dominant practices, not the options which might have been. To study this, I am going to construct, first of all, a general description of the economic practices in the society contemporaneous with the initiation of the US film industry. In this description I am going to identify a tension in the economic practices between standardization and differentiation. Second, I am going to describe some of the economic practices of the film industry between 1907 and 1917 which repeat this general tension. Third, I will suggest how and where these economic practices had an effect on the representational systems.

The contemporary economic practices

Economic practices in the United States shifted significantly during the nineteenth century. The introduction of a machine tool industry in the 1810s and 1820s permitted an industrial revolution which emphasized mass production through standardization and interchangeable parts.[3] These machines centralized the location and formalized the labor process into a factory mode of production. Companies formed to capitalize on inventions such as the telegraph and telephone, and massive capital investment in transportation systems, rapidly promoted national and international markets. Aided by state institutions in the form of laws and court decisions, a corporate business structure developed. An unanticipated effect of the four-teenth amendment was the court's decision to define business cor-porations as 'persons,' giving them due process of law.[4]

When the Standard Oil Trust was broken up in 1892, it re-incor-porated as a holding company in New Jersey, a state which had in 1889 foreseen the advantages of creating a liberal incorporation law. The New Jersey law permitted corporations, like persons, to buy and hold stock in other companies, allowing combinations to develop and to capitalize 'without regard to the actual cost of existing plant[s].'[5] From 1896 to 1904, consolidation of firms occurred at an incredible rate, the high point of which was the incorporation of US Steel for over $1,000,000,000, while Moody's listed 318 other indus-trial combinations with more than 5300 plants and a combined cap-ital of over $7,000,000,000. A thousand railroad lines were consoli-dated into six systems controlling over $10,000,000,000 in capital.[6] Supreme Court decisions made the Sherman Anti-Trust Act of 1890 almost irrelevant, except when applied to striking unions.[7] Big busi-ness produced increasing capital and goods with the United States rivalling Europe as an industrial giant.

With this came the business concept of efficiency as the means to economic success. Efficiency justified the division of labor into smaller and smaller units and the motions of the worker into more and more predetermined sequences of actions. General interest in labor conditions developed after 1900 in the United States due to attacks by labor organizations and muckrakers and by comparisons to the Europeans who adopted Taylorism before US businesses did. 'Scientific management' caught on in the early 1910s.[8]

Efficiency through economies of scale justified the creation of trusts and then holding companies and other legal business structures.[9] John D. Rockefeller sought an end to ' "idiotic, senseless destruction," "the wasteful conditions" of competition.'[10] Discussing in 1902 the reorganization and recapitalization of the railroads, M. G. Cunniff said that Huntington's and Morgan's idea of a 'community of inter-est' had brought the lines to 'the best condition they have ever known, with the cheapest freight rates, the best equipment, the fastest service, and the largest dividends in the world.'[11]

Efficiency justified the standardization of products. Trade associa-tions which dated from the Civil War provided a means of sharing information, developing standard cost accounting systems and pool-ing patents.[12] 'Efficiency' spilled over into political and legal decisions. In 1901 Theodore Roosevelt considered 'handling the tariff problem through "scientific management," '[13] and court decisions on wage rates and working conditions for women were made on the basis of business efficiency.

If efficiency justified standardization, another process was simultaneously at work – differentiation of products by advertising. Although advertising is ancient as an economic practice, in the early 1800s in the United States most goods were sold generically. By the mid-1800s companies began advertising goods by name brands, and by the 1870s retailers spent money on local and national printed materials to the consumer and began outdoor display advertising. In 1870, 121 trademarks were registered with the US Patent Office, in 1906 more than 10,000 and by 1926 over 70,000. An early advertising agent set up business in 1841 in Philadelphia, soon expanding to Boston and New York. In 1899 Ayer's became a full-service ad agency, did national campaigns, conducted market surveys and created trade names. Advertising expenditures in 1904 were over $800 million and at 3.4 per cent of the gross national product, the same percentage level current today. In the 1890s as the corporations consolidated, they moved into vertically integrated structures, directly controlling their own retailing and associated advertising to consumers. By the late 1920s only one-third of US goods went through independent wholesalers; the other two-thirds were marketed directly or through corporation-owned outlets.

Thus, the film industry begins in a general industrial structure of a well-developed corporate capitalism which is positioned between the economic practice of standardization for efficient mass production and the economic practice of product differentiation.

The economic practices of the film industry

The people who entered the film industry had these contemporary examples as their standards for successful economic competition. The formation of a moving pictures patent pool at the end of 1908 followed the general pattern of consolidation of communities-of-interest to end 'vexatious and expensive litigations.'[14] In a brief prepared by the Patents Company for the 1912 investigation by the Department of Justice into their trust, the lawyers argued that without a combination of patents no business could be conducted. A series of lawsuits had determined three patents essential to the industry which were split between three different concerns and their licensees.

The only solution for the industry to continue was cross-licensing. Lawyers cited patent pool precedents in the farm machinery industry as justification for the formation of the company.[15] At the point of organization, all significant manufacturing and importing firms were included in the company.[16] The organizing of the Patents Company seemed to indicate a stable business climate, and the individual firms, assured of regular unrestricted national and international sale of their products through the Patents Company, began to run off up to one hundred copies of each negative rather than the ten to twelve previously struck. The increased income provided capital for expanding their operations.

Unfortunately for the company, however, while patents seek a monopoly of control over an invention, publication of patent information upon application also provides knowledge for other inventors.[17] Even if the Patents Company had legal rights, the cameras and projectors were easily manufactured by others. Furthermore, the growth of the exhibition sector of the industry seemed to suggest high profits – warranting a calculated risk of being caught for patent infringement. With low barriers to entry and high profits to tempt new competitors, it is not surprising that in the next twelve months Powers Picture Plays, the Independent Motion Picture Company, the New York Motion Picture Company, Thanhouser, Rex and other films incorporated.[18]

Meanwhile, the manufacturing firms of the Patents Company followed general economic practices of vertically integrating into distributing and retailing by establishing the General Film Company in April 1910. The independents followed suit and consolidated at the distribution level.[19] In 1912 Livingston and Co., members of the New York Stock Exchange, organized the public financing of the distributing firm of Mutual Film, and $1,700,000 common stock and $800,000 cumulative preferred at 7 per cent were authorized for sale. Price, Waterhouse in 1916 issued a fifty-four-page manual on how standard accounting for the film industry should be done.[20]

The mode of production was similarly sophisticated by 1916. Once the industry seemed potentially capable of regular supply of films with a widespread demand in the exhibition sector, mass production began. Multiple shooting units for each company were created to increase the number of releases per company, thus increasing profit potentials. The 'logic' of this economic practice was described in 1911:

When an industry has reached such a magnitude that many
people are employed in its work ... some employees will develop
greater ability in some lines than in others, and the lines of

activity become so divergent that they are best cared for separately. As in any manufacturing industry, the manufacture of motion-picture films for exhibition in a modern factory has its division of labor, and a film picture is the joint product of the various departments and specialists who in turn take it and perfect it with their skills.[21]

This divided labor split into a 'line-and-staff' structure with administrators in New York or Chicago handling general operations and distributing and advertising the films, producers and studio managers administering the nationally distributed studio and on-location production units, departments handling set construction, costuming, properties, special effects, casting, developing negatives and editing, and units headed by directors doing the shooting. In late 1916, an 'efficiency system' in one studio had a four-page manual given to new employees which listed rules, regulations and the duties of every job position. Given a number within the system, the employee entered into a production schedule already organized.[22]

The pattern for the product was the scenario produced by the director and writers.[23] By 1913, detailed continuity scripts were regularly produced by scenario departments. These departments were split into two major functional operations: the writing of original screenplays for the firm and the transference of original plots from freelancers and increasingly from plays, novels and short stories. Trade papers announced as early as 1909 that manufacturers were accepting freelance contributions of stories. In a 1909 article entitled 'Motion picture play writing as an art' (three months after the new copyright law went into effect and following the court ruling that Kalem's film *Ben Hur* infringed on copyright protection), the Edison company announced the filming of Mark Twain's 'The prince and the pauper' and the hiring of famous writers to produce scenarios. By 1911 trade papers were regularly publishing articles such as 'Outline of how to write a photoplay,' and books contained sample scenarios.[24]

Producing standard scripts had at least two functions: (1) saving costs and (2) controlling quality. It is easy to see how preplanning the scenes saves costs. Since labor was paid by time not unit of production, all employees needed to be used efficiently. Furthermore, detailed scripts permitted initial estimates of the cost of the film and allowed prior trimming if the film was likely to go over budget.

The second function, quality control, relates to two events simultaneous with the development of this mode of production. Between 1910 and 1915, multiple-reel films increased in number. At the same time, Frank Woods of the *New York Dramatic Mirror* and other

writers began reviewing films and responding to patrons' questions
and reactions in the general and trade papers. This formalized network of interaction began a dissemination of rules and categories of
conspicuous skill and quality in the photoplay.

A study of some of these conceptions of quality and skill should
suggest how certain representational systems held in esteem influenced economic practices. (Again, this is a two-sided process.) As
examples, two reviews of Woods in March 1911 should indicate an
ideological reason for the development of the continuity script:

> *His Daughter* (Biograph, February 23) – ... the old father's fall
> was not convincing, and the girl's intention to leave the town
> was told only by the subtitle, as she ran out bareheaded and
> with no traveling equipment. There was also a technical error in
> the management of the scenes, exits from the interiors are to the
> right, but the immediate entrances to the exteriors are also from
> the right.[25]

> Attention has been called frequently in *Mirror* film reviews to
> apparent errors of direction or management as to exits and
> entrances in motion picture productions ... A player will be seen
> leaving a room or locality in a certain direction, and in the very
> next connecting scene, a sixteenth of a second later, he will enter
> in exactly the opposite direction. Now it may be argued quite
> logically that this need not necessarily be inartistic because the
> spectator himself may be assumed to [have] changed his point of
> view, but ... the spectator will not look at it that way. Any one
> who has watched pictures knows how often his sense of reality
> has been shocked by this very thing.[26]

What the continuity script provides is a precheck of the quality of
spatial, temporal and causal continuity and *vraisemblance*. This became more problematic as the length of the films developed and as
the aesthetics refined to include frame cuts, matches-on-action, in-
serts, cut-backs, flashes, mixing of interior and exterior sets and
narrative 'punch.'

That the industry paid attention to reviews and critics was evident
in Woods's column of 22 March 1911 in which he rather gleefully
recounts an incident of a film company arguing for half an hour,
citing Woods as an authority, whether or not the son in a photoplay
should turn toward the camera as he said farewell to his mother.[27]
The solution was that the turn was deemed realistic because of spatial positions, but that the son should avoid playing to the camera,
an acting practice Woods and others considered unnatural.

The dispersal of these standards of quality and of format was
supplemented by the appearance of trade associations in the film

industry. In July 1908 a craft union of projectionists formed, in 1911 New York motion picture exhibitors incorporated, in 1913 cinematographers in New York formed the Cinema Camera Club, in 1914 the Photoplay Authors' League was established and in 1916 the Society of Motion Picture Engineers formed with the 'avowed purpose "the advancement in the theory and practice of motion picture engineering and the allied arts and sciences, the standardization of the mechanism and practices employed therein and the dissemination of scientific knowledge by publication." '[28]

Furthermore, and this is something I want to stress, the quality control function was placed legally by the courts in the hands of the company. Two law suits in 1917 are typical of this. Charlie Chaplin sued Essanay for stretching a two-reeler of his into a four-reeler after he left. His suit was denied because, among other considerations, the photoplay was declared Essanay's property. In a second case, the director Herbert Brenon unsuccessfully contested Fox's re-editing of *A Daughter of the Gods*.[29]

If these practices provided efficient, standardized mass production of photoplays, simultaneous with them came the need to differentiate the product – to appeal to the exhibitors to order one firm's films rather than another's. It should be pointed out that direct, nationwide, organized advertising to the consumer by the producing and distributing companies did not begin until 1915.[30] At first, exhibitors chose their own films from the distributors who advertised to them, and the exhibitors created their own advertising to attract customers; newspapers, billboards and lobby displays. With the formation of the Patents Company, some aids were offered to the exhibitors. In November 1909 the ABC Company of Cleveland was delegated as official supplier of posters: 'These posters are not "fakes," made up from dead stock previously printed for some melodramatic production, but *real pictorial posters made from actual photographs of scenes in the pictures they advertise*.'[31] At the same time in Edison's catalog, 'stars' (its term) and stock players were being introduced to the exhibitors.[32] (These stars were established theatrical stars; the film companies began to develop their own about a year later.[33]) From this period on, the companies supplied cuts for newspapers and information about the actors and actresses to exhibitors so that they, in turn, could 'boom' the films.

The rise of multiple-reel films coincides with this shift in attack to more controlled advertising of individual films. What was special about each film was specified to the consumer. The concept of a *feature* film goes back at least to this 1904 advice to exhibitors by Kleine Optical Company:

The exhibitor who purchases a small quantity of films, say from 300 to 500 feet, is necessarily compelled to confine himself to short subjects. But if the purchase is 1000 feet, we advise one feature film of 400 to 500 feet, the balance from 50 to 100 feet each; if 2000 feet, there should be at least one long feature film, such as *The Great Train Robbery*, 740 feet, or *Christopher Columbus*, 850 feet. These long films admit of special advertising, that is to say, special emphasis on one subject, which is more effective than equal emphasis on a number of shorter films. The public has been educated to appreciate these long films which tell an interesting story, and need few words of explanation.[34]

In October 1909 Pathé released *The Drink* in two parts over two days. Quickly exhibitors shifted from sequential days to running the multiple reels on one day and advertising something 'extra and of more importance than the ordinary single reels.'[35] Since business was thriving, more money could be expended on these 'de luxe' films, which went together with better advertising and timing release dates to take advantage of the advertising, which permitted higher admission prices and which could pay the costs of theatrical stars and production values. As a result, the film had a longer exhibition life, providing more income to cover the geometrical increases in cost.[36] In April 1914, a year before the release of *The Birth of a Nation*, one-fifth of New York City's theaters were running multiple-reel features, and people were paying $1.00 on Broadway to see a film that cost $50,0000 to produce.[37] In 1915 Paramount, seeking higher rental rates for a feature film, decided to assist directly the exhibitors in their promotion, reasoning that to get the higher rentals they would need to increase receipts. Advised by an advertising agency to direct ads to the patrons, Paramount's New Department of Exploitation began their initial national advertising with primary demand ads - ones that emphasized the institution of movie-theater-going.[38]

In *Painting and Experience in Fifteenth Century Italy*, Michael Baxandall talks about the difficulties of determing what a patron of the arts might see in an individual work. To locate the 'period eye,' as he calls it, he examines written contracts between painters and patrons and notes that during the first part of the 1400s the quality of the materials to be used was carefully specified. By the second half of the century, what parts of the work the master artist was to paint became important. This leads Baxandall to the conclusion that cultivated people expected to be able to perceive the *conspicuous skill* of the artist.[39] These perceptible skills, of course, were formally taught by rules and categories of discussion within the culture.

What Baxandall is suggesting, I think, is generalizable to the US film industry. An historian can construct where *value* in the product lies as a means, in part, of determining the relationships between economic and signifying practices. In this mode of production, advertising is an economic practice directing consumers to the apparent areas of exchange-value in the product. In the culture in this time, novelty, originality and uniqueness are areas of heavy advertising stress.[40] Additional ones are conspicuous display of certain 'unique' personalities, specific popular genres, 'realism' and expensive means of production (for instance, spectacles in which massive sets and hundreds of people are involved).

These are parts of the catalog and review descriptions of three early films:

Life of an American Fireman (Edison, 1903, Edwin S. Porter): It will be difficult for the exhibitor to conceive the amount of work involved and the number of rehearsals necessary to turn out a film of this kind. We were compelled to enlist the services of the fire departments of four different cities ... and about 300 firemen appear in the various scenes of this film.[41]

The Great Train Robbery (Edison, 1903, Edwin S. Porter): It has been posed and acted in faithful duplication of the genuine 'Hold Ups' made famous by various outlaw bands in the far West, and only recently the East has been shocked by several crimes of the frontier order, which fact will increase the popular interest in this great *Headline Attraction*.[42]

Il Trovatore (Pathé, 1911): Pathé has an 'innovation': The novelty lies in the special music that goes with the picture. The score of the opera has been carefully arranged by a competent musician so that it times exactly with the dramatic action of the film.[43]

We have, then, in the first years of Hollywood, economic practices with a tension: simplify, standardize and consolidate for efficiency and mass production but differentiate, direct the consumers' attention to the originality and production values of the feature product.

Economic practices and filmic representational systems

In the US film industry, co-extensive with its history of economic practices is a complex history of signifying practices – ideologies, aesthetics, conventions. What might be economically cheap might simultaneously 'violate' an aesthetic of beauty or composition or a convention of *vraisemblance* or continuity or counter ideologies of value and representation. I have suggested a tension between the economic practices of standardization and differentiation. Likewise, I theorize, in general, two other tensions within the processes. First, that of economic practices versus signifying practices: the tension of low-cost – an economic goal for profit maximization – versus high-cost-ideologies of value in originality, spectacles, displays of labor and conspicuous skills such as technological tours de force. The other major tension is within the signifying practices themselves: a tension between codes of *vraisemblance*, what seems 'ordinary life,' and codes of novelty, variation, 'art,' beauty, the non-ordinary. One can begin to postulate the possibilities had the economic or signifying practices been different, had, for instance, on the broader scale, *repetition* rather than originality been valued.

This prevents a simplistic assertion that such and such economic practice determined such and such signifying practice and makes the historical representation more complex, mediated and non-linear. Locating single causes also becomes impossible. This means that in an individual instance, specific historical inquiry will be necessary to understand the impact of the particular practices operating at that time and place on the formation of specific films or groups of films. But this model likewise permits that precision without lapsing into a reflectionism.

In this concluding section, I am merely going to suggest areas in which economic practices of the period pressured the construction of certain signifying practices. I have already indicated how the mode of production, the trade media and trade associations worked toward standardizing the representational systems and how advertising and reviews promoted perception of specifiable values in the product. Now I will suggest some further sites of influence.

Cost factors promoted the reuse of sets and costumes, thus stimulating serials, genres and series. Serials like the multiple-reel films were usually shot at one time so that locations and sets were used only once even though the episodes might extend for weeks in release.[44] Price, Waterhouse, in their 1916 memorandum, advise accountants to charge all scenery and costume costs to the original film since reuse was unpredictable but would thereafter be free any time such reuse could be managed.[45] Companies often called for scenarios that would use established sets. Sometimes an extensive initial investment channeled subsequent films. William Selig's zoo, purchased in 1908 for an African safari film, was used for a series of animal films. Bison's hiring of the Miller Brothers 101 Ranch Wild West Show resulted in several years of westerns and the Civil War films using large casts.[46] Connected to this, a 1913 manual advises freelance writers:

> Unity of place is also of economic importance for the production and will permit the use of the same settings for many scenes. In this way the producer feels justified in spending more money upon the settings themselves. He is more or less limited by the owner of the motion picture company as to the outlay for each picture – and the result is more elaborate and artistic stage effects.[47]

The writer also advises creating few characters for the plot:

> At the same time more attention could be given by the director to the production; more time taken, because less wasted on supernumeraries, and more money to spend on settings and costumes and additional film, because of the reduced cost of salaries.[48]

Cost factors promoted a limited number of retakes. Price, Waterhouse suggest that there were several ways to distribute overhead costs, but the preferred method was to divide them by the number of exposed feet of negative film on the assumption that 'managers who take many feet of discarded negative are careless, wasteful, and expensive . . .'[49] Rehearsals of actors were considered cheap compared to the costs of all laborers, electricity and film stock involved in actual shooting time. Such an economic practice might also weigh against long takes which are more susceptible to error as the length of the take or its complexity increases.[50]

A more tenuous connection, but one that occasionally surfaces, is that cost factors related to techniques of style. A handbook author writes that dissolves are usually used instead of double exposures to indicate a character's thoughts because the former are cheaper, less complicated and less time consuming. The practice of having the characters 'discovered' in the scene rather than using entrances is cited as saving thirty to forty feet of film. The technique of cutbacks (the period term for cross cutting) can be used to abbreviate the length of the action and save film footage by cutting away to parallel action and then cutting back with the former action completed.[51] Obviously, there are other reasons for the cut-back: it is a means to avoid censorable material, an explicit aesthetics of variation of shots is functioning in the period and it provides a simpler, cheaper technique than a split screen or an unusual set for representing parallel action – not to mention the narrative effects of suspense and complexity which constitute a process for the subject.

Expenditures of funds on spectacles and trick work are often balanced against the effect they produce. Writers of advice to freelancers continually caution against writing photoplays that require wrecking trains, burning mansions and building extravagant sets. John Emerson and Anita Loos go so far as to advise that although night scenes can be done with 'sunlight arcs, mercury lights and spotlights,' the cost of each is $2500, and they are hard to transport. 'It is well,' they write, 'to keep your characters indoors by night.'[52]

On the other hand, the expenditures might be justified. In describing the production technology, one writer in 1913 points out that the camera is heavy and mounted on a 'massive tripod.' Despite this, it is shifted to difficult set ups:

> The body of the camera, without the tripod, may be placed upon
> the overhead beams in a studio in order to get some novel scenic
> effect below; or a special platform may be built for the camera
> and operator, when the producer is determined to get a scene on
> the side of a cliff.[53]

The reason? '... [A]n unusually strong story that justifies the special effort ...' Innovation of such effects seems motivated by this ideology of value in originality supported by the economic and signifying practices. It explains the occurrence *within the system itself of optional signifying practices* without resorting to a model of these options deconstructing the system.[54] For example, Fred Balshofer describes the decision to use a complicated camera movement rather than analytical editing in a 1915 film:

> Besides being an outstanding picture, *The Second in Command*
> contained a technical innovation ... While going over the script
> for our first picture, it seemed to us that we would have to come
> up with something new in production to match the class of our
> new star, [Francis X.] Bushman. We decided to plan the action
> of some scenes to make it possible to follow the actors, especially
> Bushman, and to move to a close-up without making a cut. We
> certainly weren't thinking of anything as elaborate as we wound
> up with. We drew a rough sketch of a platform large enough to
> set the tripod on with the camera and cameraman that could be
> moved on four wheels. When it was constructed, we found we
> would have to enlarge it to accommodate a second person. As
> the platform was pushed forward, it became difficult for Adler to
> crank the camera, watch the actors to judge distance as the
> platform moved, and to follow the focus all at the same time.
> And so it went. We were continually taking the rolling platform
> in to our small carpenter shop and having it altered to meet our
> needs as they became more and more complex.
>
> ... Making a film this way took more time but after looking at

the rushes, we thought it worthwhile. Besides, it added that
something extra to the production of the picture.[55]

Of course this sort of 'first-itis' was useful to the individual companies in promoting a studio style and identity for brand-name advertising. The reviewers and trade papers contributed to a perpetuation
of searching for novelties and innovations. One reviewer in 1912
writes:

Biograph's influence on picture production has been important. It
was the first company – at least in America – to introduce heroic
figures in its pictures. It was the first in America to present acting
of the restrained artistic type, and the first to produce quiet
drama and pure comedy. It was the first to attempt fading light
effects. It was the first to employ alternating flashes of
simultaneous action in working up suspense.[56]

Triangle initiated the use of art titles as an 'experiment' in 1916
which 'served to distinguish still further the highly individual character of the Ince plays,'[57] and in an article entitled 'Very latest thing in
photoplay subtitles,' Triangle explain that their Photographic and
Art Department head had 'set to work to develop the subtitle to a
maximum of efficiency.'[58]

Something successful was widely and rapidly imitated by the industry. Classical Hollywood films are not only typified by genres and
series but by cycles. This was made possible by short-term production plans, often made less than a year in advance even in the 1930s
and 1940s for program features. This was partially due to the standardization which made rapid production possible. In 1913, critics
were complaining that the 'time is ripe for another shift,' that everything is a 'repetition' of what had come before.[59] The search for
originality leads to some amusing results. Emerson and Loos say that
'the very latest thing' in 1920 is the 'pictorial pun. For example, in
"A virtuous vamp," a leading character says to the flirtatious heroine:
"Woman, you make me see red." The scene is instantly tinted red.'[60]
Emerson and Loos think this 'novelty' will last a couple months. Or
the case cited in 1913:

Death is seldom dramatic. It is even capable of being turned to
farce if overdone. One of the funniest stories that was ever
screened ended with the suicide of the sole remaining member of
the cast. All the others had been murdered. It was meant by
producer and author alike to be tremendously sensational, but
there is but a short step from the ultrasensational to the travesty
of sensation.[61]

Economic practices affected the signifying practices in another
way. To some writers they even became part of the aesthetic ration-

ales for the signifying practices. Victor Freeburg in the 1923 book *Pictorial Beauty on the Screen* incorporates efficiency into his theory of aesthetics: 'The pictorial beauty discussed in this book is really a kind of pictorial efficiency, and therefore must have practical economic value.' 'A practical proof is dramatic utility. The motions of a photoplay are in the service of the story. They should perform that work well without waste of time and energy.' 'One might say that the artistic efficiency of a motion picture may be partly tested in the same way as the practical value of a machine. In either case motions are no good unless they help to perform some work.'[62]

In my initial example, Bertsch's equation of the two procedures for representing subjectivity may have been a bit naive. Technically and economically, a double exposure provided more production complexity than editing with dissolves. By 1917 the perceptible value of the *novelty* of either device may have made them equivalent in signifying subjectivity with the double exposure used for production value and editing with dissolves used when the subjective sequence was extensive or not worth the additional cost. (There are also different implications about the representation of space and subject.) In either case, however, they are incorporated into a general representational mode, the classical Hollywood film. To determine the value and function of any individual practice requires an extensive construction of the history of *both* economic and signifying practices within the culture in order to provide satisfactory production of knowledge about signification by subjects.[63]

Notes

1 Marguerite Bertsch, *How to Write for Moving Pictures: A Manual of Instruction and Information* (New York: George H. Doran Company, 1917), pp. 97 and 99.
2 In using the term signifying practices, I want to emphasize that the representational systems produced have meaning in the act of the subject's constitution of the signifying object. Assumed, then, are issues of subjectivity. See Rosalind Coward and John Ellis, *Language and Materialism: Developments in Semiology and the Theory of the Subject* (London: Routledge & Kegan Paul, 1977), pp. 80–1 and 122–52 *passim*, and Stephen Heath, 'The turn of the subject,' *Ciné-Tracts* 7/8, vol. 2, nos. 3 and 4 (Summer, Fall 1979), pp. 42–5. Several instances of the characterization of the classical Hollywood mode of representation are: Jean-Louis Comolli, 'Technique et ideologie (4): caméra, perspective, profondeur de champ,' *Cahiers du cinéma*, no. 233 (November 1971), pp. 39–45; Kristin Thompson and David Bordwell, 'Space and narrative in the films of Ozu,' *Screen*, vol. 17, no. 2 (Summer 1976), pp. 42–3; and Nöel

Burch, 'Porter, or ambivalence,' *Screen*, vol. 19, no. 4 (Winter 1978/9), pp. 91–105.

3 This section relies heavily on three general economic histories: Harry N. Scheiber, Harold G. Vatter and Harold Underwood Faulkner, *American Economic History*, 9th edn (New York: Harper & Row, 1976); Alex Groner, *The American Heritage History of American Business and Industry* (New York: American Heritage, 1972); John Chamberlain, *The Enterprising Americans: A Business History of the United States*, rev. edn (New York: Harper & Row, 1974).

4 On the shift from the formation of corporations for public interests to those for private profit, see Groner, *The American Heritage History*, pp. 60 and 91. Chamberlain, *The Enterprising Americans*, pp. 132 and 154, details the court decisions and laws in the second half of the century, as does Scheiber *et al.*, *American Economic History*, pp. 299–300, and Groner, *The American Heritage History*, p. 197.

5 Chamberlain, *The Enterprising Americans*, p. 174, and see US Industrial Commission, *Preliminary Report on Trusts and Industrial Combinations* ..., 56th Cong., 1st Sess., House Document no. 476, Part 1 (Washington, DC: Government Printing Office, 1900), pp. 9–13, 16–20, 32–34 rpt. in *American Economic Development since 1860*, ed. William Greenleaf (New York: Harper & Row, 1968), pp. 216–33.

6 The government's investigation in 1900 produced a detailed description and explanation of these mergers; see US Industrial Commission, *Preliminary Report*, pp. 216–33. For a contemporary unsympathetic version which was widely read see William J. Ghent, *Our Benevolent Feudalism* (New York: Macmillan, 1902). On the findings of the Pujo Committee of Congress which investigated community-of-interest holdings in 1913, see *Great Issues in American History*, ed. Richard Hofstadter (New York: Alfred A. Knopf and Random House, 1958), pp. 298–301.

7 Groner, *American Heritage History*, pp. 198–9; Hofstadter, *Great Issues in American History*, pp. 121–2, 125.

8 On the history of scientific management in the US see Don D. Lescohier, 'Working conditions,' in *History of Labor in the United States*, ed. John R. Commons, vol. III (1935; rpt. edn New York: Augustus M. Kelley, 1966), pp. 304–15; Thomas C. Cochran and William Miller, *The Age of Enterprise*, rev. edn (New York: Harper & Brothers, 1961), pp. 184 and 243–8; Groner, *American Heritage History*, p. 217; Hofstadter, *Great Issues in American History*, pp. 242–3.

9 Magnus W. Alexander, *The Economic Evolution of the United States: Its Background and Significance* (New York: National Industrial Conference Board, 1929), p. 35.

10 John D. Rockefeller cited in Chamberlain, *The Enterprising Americans*, p. 150.

11 'Increasing railroad consolidation,' *World's Work*, 3 (February 1902), 1775–1780, rpt. in *American Economic Development since 1860*, pp. 106–15. Not everyone agreed with this assessment of holding companies; see Richard Hofstadter, *The Age of Reform* (New York: Vintage Books, 1955), p. 232, and Ghent, *Our Benevolent Feudalism*.

12 Alexander, *The Economic Evolution of the United States*, pp. 34–8;

Monte Calvert, *The Mechanical Engineer in America, 1830-1910* (Baltimore: The Johns Hopkins University Press, 1967), p. 172; Cochran and Miller, *The Age of Enterprise*, p. 243; Ray M. Hudson, 'Organized effort in simplification,' *The Annals* (of the American Academy of Political and Social Science), 87 (May 1928), pp. 1-8; and Frank L. Eidmann, *Economic Control of Engineering and Manufacturing* (New York: McGraw-Hill, 1931), pp. 261-8.

13 William Appleton Williams, *The Contours of American History* (1961; rpt. edn, New York: Franklin Watts, 1973), pp. 405-6.

14 M. B. Phillipp and Francis T. Homer for the Motion Picture Patents Co., 'Memorandum for the Motion Picture Patents Company and the General Film Company concerning the investigation of their business by the Department of Justice,' TS, 18 May 1912 (Museum of Modern Art), p. 17.

15 Phillipp and Homer, 'Memorandum,' pp. 1-17. The precedents were *Bement v. National Harrow Company*, 186 US 70 and *Indiana Manufacturing Company v. J. I. Case Threshing Machine Company*, 154 FR 365.

16 Ralph Cassady Jr., 'Monopoly in motion picture production and distribution: 1908-1915,' *Southern California Law Review*, vol. 32, no. 4 (Summer 1959), pp. 328-9, 335, 346. Page 363, Cassady lists five manufacturers not included in the company in early 1909 and another list is available in 'The independent movement,' *The Nickelodeon*, no. 1 (February 1909), pp. 39-40. The latter article gives a contemporary account of the exhibitors' reaction to the company's formation and the organisation of a counter alliance, the Independent Film Protective Association.

17 Jeanne Thomas Allen [untitled paper], The cinematic apparatus: technology as historical and ideological form, Conference at the Centre for Twentieth Century Studies, University of Wisconsin-Milwaukee, 22–24 February 1978. In the main argument of the essay Allen points out how the general business practice of standardization of technology relates to the history of the invention of the motion picture machines.

18 Robert C. Allen, 'Motion picture exhibitions in Manhattan 1906-1912: beyond the nickelodeon,' *Cinema Journal*, vol. 18, no. 2 (Spring 1979), p. 11. On contemporary accounts of the expanding exhibition industry, see 'Motion picture films,' *Complete Illustrated Catalog of Moving Picture Machines, Stereopticans, Slides, Films* (Chicago: Kleine Optical Company, November 1905), pp. 206-7, reprinted in George C. Pratt, *Spellbound in Darkness: A History of the Silent Film*, rev. edn (Greenwich, Conn.: New York Graphic Society, 1973), pp. 39-42; 'Growth of the film business,' *Billboard* vol. 18, no. 37 (15 September 1906), p. 16, reprinted in Pratt, *Spellbound in Darkness*, pp. 42-3; Joseph Medill Patterson, 'The nickelodeons: the poor man's elementary course in the drama,' *The Saturday Evening Post*, vol. 180, no. 21 (23 November 1907), pp. 10-11, 38, reprinted in Pratt *Spellbound in Darkness*, pp. 46, 48-52. The details of the formation of the independents are: Powers Picture Plays - 1909 (Anthony Slide, *Early American Cinema* [New York: A. S. Barnes & Co., 1970], p. 98); IMP - 1909 (Slide, *Early American Cinema*, p. 96); the New York Motion Picture Company - early in 1909 incorporated in New York with $10,000 capital (Fred F. Balshofer and Arthur C. Miller, *One Reel a Week* [Berkeley, California: University of California

Press, 1967], p. 22); Thanhouser – fall 1909 (Anthony Slide, *Aspects of American Film History Before 1920* [Metuchen, New Jersey: The Scarecrow Press, 1978], pp. 68–73; and Rex – 1909 by Edwin Porter, Joe Engel and William Swanson (Balshofer and Miller, *One Reel a Week*, p. 48, and Slide, *Early American Cinema*, p. 14).

19 Phillipp and Homer, 'Memorandum,' pp. 42–6; H. E. Aitken, *Reel Life*, vol. 3, no. 26 (14 April 1914), pp. 17–18; 'C. J. Hite's career,' *Reel Life*, vol. 3, no. 16 (3 January 1914), 3; 'Spectator,' ' "Spectator's" Comments,' *New York Dramatic Mirror* [hereafter *NYDM*], vol. 65, no. 1691 (17 May 1911), p. 28; for a list of 1911 manufacturers, brand names and distribution groups, see David Sherrill Hulfish, *Cyclopedia of Motion-Picture Work*, vol. I (Chicago: American School of Correspondence, 1911), pp. 277–82.

20 'Financing the motion picture Wall Street's latest move,' *Reel Life*, vol. 3, no. 22 (14 February 1914), p. 34. Other firms were organised as stock companies but without public sale; for details of early stock issues see Paul H. Davis, 'Investing in the movies [part 7],' *Photoplay*, vol. 9, no. 3 (February 1916), pp. 71–3. His series of eleven articles runs from August 1915 through August 1916. Price, Waterhouse & Company, *Memorandum on Moving Picture Accounts* (New York: Price, Waterhouse & Company, 1916).

21 Hulfish, *Cyclopedia*, vol. II, p. 76.

22 'The higher efficiency,' *Cinema News*, vol. 1, no. 1 (15 December 1916), pp. 6.

22 'The higher efficiency,' *Cinema News*, vol. 1, no. 1 (15 December 1916), p. 6.

23 For a description of the development in one company of the mode of production using the producer as quality controller and the continuity script as the pattern, see Janet Staiger, 'Dividing labor for production control: Thomas Ince and the rise of the studio system,' *Cinema Journal*, vol. 18, no. 2 (Spring 1979), pp. 16–25. The standard script format is detailed there.

24 'Motion picture play writing as an art,' *The Edison Kinetogram*, vol. 1, no. 3 (1 September 1909), p. 12; Archer McMackin, 'How moving picture plays are written,' *The Nickelodeon*, vol. 2, no. 6 (December 1909), pp. 171–3; Everett McNeil, 'Outline of how to write a photoplay,' *Moving Picture World*, vol. 9, no. 1 (15 July 1911), p. 27; Hulfish, *Cyclopedia*, vol. II, pp. 78–90.

25 'Reviews of licensed films,' *NYDM*, vol. 65, no. 1680 (1 March 1911), p. 31.

26 'Spectator,' "Spectator's" comments,' *NYDM* vol. 65, no. 1681 (8 March 1911), p. 29.

27 'Spectator,' "Spectator's" comments,' *NYDM*, vol. 65, no. 1683 (22 March 1911), p. 28. Also see 'Significant praise for "Mirror," ' *NYDM*, vol. 65, no. 1674 (18 January 1911), p. 34. Woods is undoubtedly 'biased,' but Epes Winthrop Sargent of *Moving Picture World*, William Lord Wright of *Motion Picture News* and other contemporaries continually acknowledge his (as well as their own) influence on the 'art' of the photoplay.

28 Phil Whitman, 'Western correspondent,' *Motion Picture News*, vol. 5,

no. 3 (20 January 1912), p. 35; 'Exhibitors incorporate, *NYDM*, vol. 66, no. 1718 (22 November 1911) p. 25; Lewis W. Physioc, 'The history of the Cinema Camera Club,' *Cinema News*, vol. 1, no. 5 (15 February 1917), pp. 5–6; 'Woods Heads Authors' League,' *NYDM*, vol. 70, no. 1840 (25 March 1914), p. 31; Society of Motion Picture Engineers, *The Society of Motion Picture Engineers* (New York: Society of Motion Picture Engineers, 1930), p. iii. The Cinema Camera Club was a forerunner of the American Society of Cinematographers which formally incorporated in 1919; George Blaisdell, 'Arnold Again Head of ASC,' *American Cinematographer*, vol. 20, no. 5 (May 1939), p. 198.

29 Louis D. Frohlich and Charles Schwartz, *The Law of Motion Pictures including the Law of the Theatre* (New York: Baker, Voorhis, & Co., 1918), pp. 169–71; Slide, *Early American Cinema*, pp. 92–95.

30 For a general history see John Francis Barry and Epes W. Sargent, *Building Theatre Patronage: Management and Merchandising* (New York: Chalmers, 1927), pp. 15–27; Howard Thompson Lewis, *Cases on the Motion Picture Industry* (New York: McGraw-Hill, 1930), pp. 435–43. A taste of 1915 exhibitor advertising practices may be had from Epes Winthrop Sargent, *Picture Theatre Advertising* (New York: Chambers, 1915).

31 'Advertising the pictures,' *The Edison Kinetogram*, vol. 1, no. 7 (1 November 1909), p. 14. (Their italics.)

32 'The Edison Stock Company,' *The Edison Kinetogram*, vol. 1, no. 4 (15 September 1909), p. 13; 'Our stock company,' *The Edison Kinetogram*, vol. 1, no. 5 (1 October 1909), p. 13; 'Our lobby display frames,' *The Edison Kinetogram*, vol. 1, no. 9 (1 June 1910), p. 2.

33 Anthony Slide, 'The evolution of the film star,' *Films in Review*, no. 25 (December 1974), pp. 591–4.

34 'About moving picture films,' *Complete Illustrated Catalog* (October 1904) pp. 30–1, rpt. in Pratt, *Spellbound in Darkness*, pp. 36–7.

35 'Spectator,' "Spectator's" comments,' *NYDM*, vol. 65, no. 1676 (1 February 1911), p. 29.

36 'This list does not mean to suggest any causality or priority of factors. It notes only a conjunction that worked together to promote multiple-reel films. L. F. Cook, 'Advertising the picture theater,' *The Nickelodeon*, vol. 3, no. 9 (1 May 1910), pp. 331–2; 'Laemmle plans new series of Imp Films de luxe,' *Motion Picture News*, vol. 4, no. 15 (15 April 1911); 'Spectator, "Spectator's" comments,' *NYDM*, vol. 66, no. 1709 (20 September 1911), p. 26; 'Spectator, "Spectator's" comments,' *NYDM*, vol. 66, no. 1721 (13 December 1911), p. 28; 'Spectator,' "Spectator's" comments,' *NYDM*, vol. 67, no. 1728 (31 January 1912), p. 51.

37 Most of these films were two- and three-reelers, but a shift in exhibition practices was occurring, 'The listener chatters,' *Reel Life*, vol. 4, no. 3 (4 April 1924), p. 6.

38 Barry and Sargent, *Building Theatre Patronage*, pp. 19–21; Lewis, *Cases on the Motion Picture Industry*, pp. 435–34.

39 Michael Baxandall, *Painting and Experience in Fifteenth Century Italy: A Primer in the Social History of Pictorial Style* (Oxford: Clarendon Press, 1972), pp. 14–39.

118   *Janet Staiger*

40 Leonard B. Meyer in *Music, The Arts, and Ideas: Patterns and Predictions in Twentieth-Century Culture* (Chicago: University of Chicago Press, 1967) also suggests that novelty as a value is a cultural ideological system for the West from about 1500 to now (pp. 89–133). He does not, however, tie this into the economic supports which perpetuate an appearance of novelty, assuming instead that a shift in our conception of authorship will dilute the force of 'novelty' as a value.

41 *Edison Films*, supplement No. 168 (Orange, New Jersey: Edison Manufacturing Company, February 1903), pp. 2–3, reprinted in Pratt, *Spellbound in Darkness*, pp. 29–30.

42 *Edison Films*, supplement no. 200 (January 1904), pp. 5–7, reprinted in Pratt, *Spellbound in Darkness*, pp. 34–6.

43 'Spectator, "Spectator's" comments,' *NYDM*, vol. 65, no. 1672 (4 January 1911), p. 8.

44 Epes Winthrop Sargent, *The Technique of the Photoplay*, 2nd edn (New York: Moving Picture World, 1913), p. 123.

45 Price, Waterhouse, *Memorandum*, pp. 11–12.

46 Slide, *Early American Cinema*, p. 23; 'Bison gets 101 ranch,' *NYDM*, vol. 66, no. 1720 (6 December 1911), p. 29; 'Bison Company gets 101 ranch,' *Moving Picture World*, vol. 10, no. 10 (9 December 1911), p. 810; William Lord Wright, *Photoplay Writing* (New York: Falk, 1922), pp. 105–8.

47 Eustace Hale Ball, *The Art of the Photoplay* (New York: Veritas, 1913), p. 50.

48 Ball, *The Art of the Photoplay*, p. 43; also see for example James Irving, *The Irving System* (Auburn, New York: Authors' Press, 1919), p. 159.

49 Price, Waterhouse, *Memorandum*, p. 12–15.

50 See for instance Balshofer's description below of the choice of a long take rather than analytical editing in *The Second in Command*. Another reason may be the inability of the studio to have as many final cut options available with a long take style.

51 The problem of footage length was more serious when exhibition practices limited the narrative to one, two, or three reels. Catherine Carr, *The Art of Photoplay Writing* (New York: Hannis Jordan, 1914), pp. 41–3; Ball, *The Art of the Photoplay*, pp. 52–3; Epes Winthrop Sargent, 'The photoplaywright,' *Moving Picture World*, vol. 23, no. 12 (20 March 1915), p. 1757; Irving, *The Irving System*, p. 179.

52 Sargent, *The Technique of the Photoplay*, p. 117; J. Berg Esenwein and Arthur Leeds, *Writing the Photoplay* (Springfield, Mass.: Home Correspondence School, 1913), pp. 222–4; Louella O. Parsons, *How to Write for the Movies*, rev. edn (Chicago: A. C. McClurg, 1917), p. 46; John Emerson and Anita Loos, *How to Write Photoplays* (1920 rpt., Philadelphia: George W. Jacobs, 1923), p. 55.

53 Esenwein and Leeds, *Writing the Photoplay*, p. 206.

54 After all, for example, a long take rather than editing does not in itself challenge the general Hollywood classical mode. See its classical function in Balshofer's description. Nor does analytical editing always subordinate itself to a causal chain. Without continuity links, it may function in other ways; see the obvious examples of Eisenstein and Godard.

55 Balshofer and Miller, *One Reel a Week*, pp. 117–18. Unfortunately, this description was written many years after the event, but it is still useful I think. Kevin Brownlow writes that the film had 'several beautifully executed and surprisingly intricate traveling shots. The movement was absolutely smooth, even when the camera, mounted on two dollies, slid backward and then sideways.' *The Parade's Gone By* ... (Berkeley, California: University of California Press, 1968), pp. 23–6.

56 'A blot in the "Scutcheon-Biograph,"' *NYDM*, vol. 67, no. 1728 (31 January 1912), p. 56.

57 'The wonderful year in three corners of Triangle film,' *The Triangle*, vol. 3, no. 3 (4 November 1916), p. 5.

58 'Very latest thing in photoplay subtitles,' *The Triangle*, vol. 3, no. 7 (9 December 1916), p. 1.

59 'William Lord Wright's page,' *Motion Picture News*, vol. 7, no. 16 (19 April 1913), pp. 13–14.

60 Emerson and Loos, *How to Write a Photoplay*, p. 104.

61 Sargent, *The Technique of the Photoplay*, p. 104.

62 Victor Oscar Freeburg, *Pictorial Beauty on the Screen* (1923, rpt., New York: Arno Press and *The New York Times*, 1970), pp. 10, 96 and 97.

63 I would like to thank the participants of the 1980 Ohio University Film Conference, Edward Branigan and David Bordwell, for their very useful comments on a draft of this paper.

6 · Edward Branigan: Color and cinema: problems in the writing of history

Film Reader, no. 4, 1979

Edward Branigan's article links a historical problem – how colour cinematography was first introduced in Hollywood – to a historiographical one: how that 'history' has been and might be told within the available methodological models presently dominant in film studies. Branigan's emphasis, however, is on the latter question, and he considers the respective criteria of 'cause', 'change' and 'subject' which are currently as well as traditionally to be found in accounts of technological innovation and implementation. There has been a comparatively large amount of recent writing about the advent of colour (including essays of some significance by scholars like Andrew, Buscombe, Coe and Kindem), but Branigan's intention is not to take specific critics to task or even to assemble a state of the art synthesis of such accounts. Rather, his project is to examine the assumptions and implications of particular historical methodologies – though some of them perhaps do not merit such a term. His overview, therefore, embraces four relatively diverse strands of historical writing about the cinema; these he describes as adventure history, technological history, industrial (or economic) history and ideological history.

In problematising the adventure history, for instance, in which every historical period has its own heroic protagonist, Branigan takes issue with the kind of 'great men' approach to film history which characterises Janet Wasko's nevertheless excellent account of Griffith's relationship with the banks; perhaps even Douglas Gomery's essay on the rise of the Picture Palace is obliged to make reluctant use of this model via the notion of 'creative management'. Branigan uses Gomery's work on the coming of sound to inform his analysis of what he calls a 'Gomerian' approach to the coming of colour, an approach he finds less satisfactory than Comolli's emphasis on ideological imperatives. Branigan shares Comolli's contempt for the adventure approach to film history with its individual heroics and simple narrative thrust and he quotes Comolli approvingly: 'it is to the mutual reinforcement of an ideological demand ("to see life as it is") and the economic demand to make it a source of profit that cinema owes it being.' Nevertheless, Comolli's conception of the economic and ideological instances – by virtue of its very abstraction – remains far less flexible and at the same time far less focused than Janet Staiger's.

I wish to examine the subject of color, and more specifically, the early history of color in cinema. Underlying this subject, however, is a more important issue and my major concern: the different ways in which that early history of color *has* been told or *might* be told. It should be emphasized at the outset that my purpose is not to work toward an eclecticism or pluralism where the history of color becomes the sum of all the histories of color, or all the methods of writing that history. Such a history is really only *one* more history, and a peculiarly indigestible one at that. Of much greater interest to me are the different *ways of seeing* the history of color. What forces and events are singled out by a given historian as 'significant' and how are they arranged into a narrative of time? In this manner I hope to expose the assumptions (framework, theory) which a historian uses to generate a history – all of which is normally obscured beneath apparently neutral and unassuming titles, such as 'The development of colour cinematography'[1] or 'Refinement in technique.'[2] I take this 'history of histories' approach because I'm convinced that one cannot write about the history of color without a particular conception of that history.

In a practical sense, a conception of history depends upon a set of categories which are used to analyze (break up, articulate) the world. Michel Foucault, in a preface to his history of sixteenth and seventeenth century European science, discusses the following passage from a Borges story which, in turn, quotes a 'certain Chinese encyclopaedia.' In this encyclopaedia it is written that

animals are divided into: (a) belonging to the Emperor,
(b) embalmed, (c) tame, (d) sucking pigs, (e) sirens, (f) fabulous,
(g) stray dogs, (h) included in the present classification,
(i) frenzied, (j) innumerable, (k) drawn with a very fine camelhair
brush, (l) *et cetera*, (m) having just broken the water pitcher,
(n) that from a long way off look like flies.'

What is important for us in this passage is the recognition that categories arranged in a scheme are not just a way of looking at the world but in some sense determine[4] *what we see*. The world is not out there holding a secret which at best has already been recorded in an encyclopaedia and at worst remains to be discovered by the persistent and perceptive analyst. Instead the world is constructed by the analyst in the act of analyzing. Analysis proceeds via a set of categories which are selected – consciously or unconsciously – to suit a particular purpose.

I will now examine four types of histories of color which might be constructed from the perspectives of (what I will term) adventure, technology, industrial management, and ideology. In each case I will focus on the analytical method characteristic of the approach and ask how such an approach might conceive the history of color in the cinema. In particular, what data from the early history of color might these approaches select, what arguments would be made, and how would the data be organized into a historical narrative? In this way I hope to illustrate how one might proceed in the writing of at least four different histories of color technology. These four histories, of course, do not exhaust the ways one might write the history of color.[5]

I will employ the three criteria of cause, change, and subject in order to distinguish the analytical methods of the four histories.[6] By *cause* I mean a historian's reasoning about the determinants or conditions of a state. By *change* I mean a reasoning about the difference between temporal states. That logic may appear in innumerable guises; for instance, change may be characterized in terms of a transition, evolution, progression (progress), regression, transformation, mutation, permutation, repetition, substitution (exchange), mediation, and in many other ways. By *subject* I mean that role or function ascribed to the individual with respect to a historical process. That role may run a spectrum from the individual as a psychological agent to the individual as one constructed (placed, positioned) by large-scale forces.

The adventure of color

Terry Ramsaye devotes one chapter in his history of the motion picture to color. Entitled 'Adventures of Kinemacolor,' the chapter traces the fortunes of two film companies exploiting the Kinemacolor process: Natural Color Kinematograph Co. Ltd. (England) and the Kinemacolor Company of America. The title of Ramsaye's book, with its reference to *The Arabian Nights* or *The Thousand and One Nights*, is suggestive of his method. The second sentence of the chapter states that 'the course of color history in the films has been as romantically adventurous as the story of the screen.'[7] The history of color for Ramsaye is a romantic adventure story, a tapestry of tales. This assertion is more than a metaphor or a rhetorical flourish. It reveals a way of conceiving history which is characteristic of nineteenth century historians. Such histories are structured as dramas of disclosure, with a stress on conflict and climax. They are written in a dramatic, staccato rhythm and in a vivid, even inspirational way.[8] For example, Ramsaye describes the work of the inventor Edward R. Turner, an early contributor to Kinemacolor, as follows:

Turner set to work to seek a new approach to the problem.

One day in 1902, as Urban sat at his desk nearby, there came a crash from the workshop where Turner was striving with his perplexities.

Urban ran into the room and found Turner dead on the floor.

Turner's notes, models and formulae were scattered about in confusion. No one else knew the meaning of half of them. The most of what Turner had attained died with him.[9]

Note that the first three paragraphs in the description contain only a single sentence each, and the last paragraph only three. This helps create a dramatic rhythm in which the telling of the death is more important than the date of the death. The anecdote is arranged to create suspense and surprise ('a crash from the workshop'), and its ending to perpetuate a mystery about the man and his work. It is not that the anecdote leaves something unexpressed but that it suggests the inexpressible, a mystery lingering beyond death in the ambiguity of the real.[10] (What did Turner discover? What was he thinking? If only his notes and models could speak....)

Another history of Kinemacolor – in many ways more comprehensive than Ramsaye's account – devotes one sentence to the death of Turner: 'Unfortunately Turner died of a heart attack while working in his laboratory soon afterwards.'[11] A third history says only, 'A short time later, Turner died.'[12] Ramsaye's selection of this event and his expansion of it reveals a preoccupation of nineteenth century history writing: the concentration on an event-centered time span of short duration. History is reduced to a point – often to the decision-making individual. The reduction is rendered, whenever possible, in an anecdote about an individual which serves to concentrate history further to a particular time, place, and circumstance. For example, Technicolor's abrupt (?) change from a two-color additive to a two-color subtractive process is explained in terms of a 'decisive' event, 'one terrible night in Buffalo.'[13] The event was a particular showing of the film *The Gulf Between* (1917) attended by Dr Herbert Thomas Kalmus, one of the directors of Technicolor, Inc. It is not important in this type of history writing whether the anecdote is true or false or unverifiable because even if false[14] it may yet (metaphorically) serve its purpose, which is to explicate the past as a *linear* chain of events; that is, historical cause is linear. It is not accidental that such histories choose a literary style which obeys the neo-Aristotelian unities (time, place, action); nor is the style chosen merely to capture the interest of a lay reader; rather, the drama is itself evidence of a way of seeing and articulating the world.

What then is linear narrative? Such a narrative depends on a logic of reducing the set of future possibilities by events already realized in the past and thus a 'climax' – that archetypal figure of the linear narrative – quite rightly assumes the shape of a pyramid where every element in the signifying space redoubles and builds consistently in one direction until there remains but one (inevitable) possibility. Thus, what is inevitable in a linear narrative is only the certainty of a climax or decisive event.[15] We see that the linear narrative depends on reducing signification to points – an individual, a decision, an event, the new invention, a pithy anecdote – and then linking the points one by one, through conflict and struggle, to a climax or decisive point which reveals/resolves what has gone *before*, that is, history. In this way the linear narrative is always looking back, repeating itself, summing up grandly, reducing; and most importantly, preparing the climax. Hence the charge that the linear history is 'presentist;' that is, depends on a backward projection of current events in order to seek the elements of a climax in their pure state. These elements are then arranged into a narrative which climaxes in the present. The present is also taken as an absolute reference point in order to measure *change*. Linearity, with its devices of foreshadowing, suspense, and surprise, often produces teleological overtones to the causal chain. Jacobs asserts that 'After almost half a century of progress, the American film has achieved a degree of maturity. It now moves forward toward a more profound destiny.'[16] Note the implicit view of historical change in the words 'forward,' 'progress,' 'maturity,' and 'destiny.'

If the relation of events to one another is stipulated in linear causal terms, what about long-term change? In the adventure story type of history, change is specified as an evolution, a gradualism, usually based on an organic growth metaphor.[17] Hence the common breakdown of time into the periods of birth, youth, maturity (peak), decline (sterility), death, and then perhaps rebirth. This schema may be overlaid on anything – technology, film style, genre, studio, the film industry – in order to account for change. (Witness the table of contents of many film history books.) Jacobs, for example, asserts that D. W. Griffith's career falls into three periods – apprenticeship, maturity, and decline.[18]

In summary, the adventure history is written on the assumption that historical cause is one to one; in it, a chain of pithy anecdotes and events mark a linear progression of time. Change in such histories often takes the form of an organic evolution. The source of this evolution is, again, located in a point: a decisive event, the genius of an individual, a revolutionary invention.

I now wish to consider a history which seizes on new inventions and uses their developments to model historical cause and change.

The technology of color

A second way one might approach the early history of color in cinema is to trace the technology which made it possible. In a technological reading of history, the artistic text is seen as a product of (1) the resources available, and (2) the resources preferred by the artist. From an ever-expanding pool of materials, the artist makes certain selections. This schema translates into the categories of (1) technology, and (2) aesthetics. If the project is a writing of *history*, the result combines a history of technology and a history of aesthetics. Thus is founded the autonomy of aesthetics and the search for the criteria which isolate the various arts, for example, the Russian Formalist and early structuralist search for cinematic 'specificity,' or 'pure' cinema. The aim is to discover a unique, and permanent (i.e. timeless) place for film beyond history. Hence the technological approach perpetuates a split between history and aesthetics.

Often included in the category of technology is what might be called technique. The difference between the two is that between a process, or apparatus – such as a camera dolly – and a procedure involving that apparatus in a text – such as a dolly-in or a close-up shot. The justification for blurring the distinction between technology and technique is the implicit belief that many new techniques depend on new technologies; for example, the zoom shot depends on a new type of lens. It matters little that such a connection cannot always be made so readily (what technology gave rise to the 'jump cut'?); in each case an aesthetic *form* is discovered which may receive any content. For example, Lewis Jacobs measures the developing potential of the film medium in part by what techniques have been 'invented' or 'discovered' and laid up for future film-makers like nuts in a squirrel burrow. Jacobs, in a chapter entitled 'D.W. Griffith: new discoveries,' says that with the film *After Many Years* (1908), Griffith 'saw the chance to use his new device, the close-up.' The film is important not only for adding the 'dramatic' close-up to the long shot and full shot but for 'another surprise, even more radical': breaking up a scene by cutting to a distant space, a second scene.[19] For Jacobs this means, in the broadest sense, the discovery of editing as a tool and resource. In a now famous analysis Jean-Louis Comolli demonstrates that the isolation of technique (especially from narrative) leads to a search for 'first times,' and rapidly piles up meaningless distinctions, such as the first 'enlargement' close-up, the first 'dramatic' close-up, etc.[20]

In many ways the common etymology of the words 'technology' and 'technique' provides a fortunate confusion for the writers of a technological history, because the terms reinforce each other's autonomy and obscure questions about the social and economic forces which propel technology in certain directions and the ideological investment which creates and maintains techniques. Advances in technology make possible new techniques while at the same time the desire for new forms of expression in the film medium engender advances in technology. Each justifies the other in a hermetic circularity.

An example of a technological approach is Patrick Ogle's 1972 study of the technique of deep focus. The title of his history, appropriately, points to the split between technology and aesthetics mentioned above: 'Technological and aesthetic influences upon the development of deep focus cinematography in the United States.'[21] Ogle traces how improvements and changes in design of film stocks, lenses, and lighting affected deep focus in cinema. The question now arises, if one were to write a history of color processes in technological terms, what sort of 'facts' would be selected?

First, one might attempt to list various technological and technical devices and their impact on color. Thus when Ogle notes that a new lens coating for cameras and projectors greatly increased light transmission, the color historian could immediately interject that this development would have a much greater impact on color films than on black and white films, since improved screen brightness and image contrast affects not only lightness but also the saturation of color (the colors black, white, and grey are without saturation).[22] The first commercial application of coated projection lenses was for the opening of *Gone With The Wind* (1939) in twenty-five Loew's theaters, and the color effects were stronger than any previously seen.

Along with new technology, one would also be interested in the 'discovery' by film-makers of techniques which affect color; for instance, compositions utilizing large blocks of homogeneous color, or juxtaposed primary colors, or a certain edited sequence of colors – all of which increase the perceived saturation of color and open the way for various aesthetic effects based on saturation (e.g. increased tension, unnaturalness, heightened emotion).[23] Perhaps the single most cited example of editing for color effect is the succession of colors in the ballroom scene in *Becky Sharp* (1935). As the sound of cannon fire is heard and panic begins, the colors in the scene change, principally through the costume and lighting, from cool – greys, blues, greens – to a 'climax' in the reds – yellow, orange, scarlet.[24]

Secondly, a technological history of color would examine not only new discoveries but the interaction between color and other technologies and techniques. For example, with the arrival of Technicolor came a new sort of film stock which was very slow and balanced for the blue-green of daylight. This meant that the light sources used in filming needed to be enormously increased in power, their color balance (color temperature) significantly shifted, the rate of burning made uniform, the area of illumination controlled, and, since this was also the time of the sound film, the lights had to be quiet. Technology rose to the challenge. A whole new generation of arc lamps were developed to replace Mazda incandescent lamps, and these new arc lamps were, in turn, necessary to the deep focus style of the late thirties.[25] Thus color technology was tied to deep focus.

Color technology also bore a relation with sound technology. In the early 1920s, 80–90 per cent of American films were tinted in some manner.[26] The chemical baths used in tinting, however, interfered with the sound track and so color disappeared as film-makers elected sound. The resulting flurry of activity led in 1929 to the introduction of Sonochrome by the Eastman Kodak Co., in which color was reintroduced by tints in the film stock itself. Sonochrome was a black and white positive film on one of sixteen tinted bases or a neutral base.[27]

When change is measured by 'perfection' it follows a rhythm similar to that of an evolution: inspiration, invention, modification, advance, improvement, new advance. The series can be extended in both directions: inventions are foretold by persons 'ahead of their times' (mad visionaries) and fall into disuse when replaced by bold, new inventions. The problem with the technological approach is that science does not march triumphantly along – independent and autonomous – toward perfection. This approach commonly 'explains' failure with the statement that a device 'wasn't practical' – but again, not practical with respect to what purpose? The demand for good quality, synchronous sound, for instance, is rooted in social forces larger than technology; and to say that Sonochrome is a response to the problem of tinting avoids such questions as what social and economic interests were served by color which forced its return in the form of Sonochrome (realism? profit?).

If failure is what is 'impractical,' success is often explained by the mere fact of newness, or novelty. Arthur Knight says that

At the very moment that sound arrived, a practicable color process was also ready.

And with the overwhelming success of their sound experiments, the producers were now willing to try almost any novelty.

However, only two paragraphs before, Knight explains the *failure* of early color by saying it was 'merely a novelty.'[28] What is missing is an analysis of the social forces which make a device a 'novelty' or 'merely a novelty.' It is not perfection which makes an invention successful but social and economic purpose. It is not enough to speak of the 'spirit of the age,' the movies' 'loss of innocence,' or a 'conservatism.' The last explanation is a particular favorite where a gap exists between available technology and actual practice (e.g. the very slow acceptance of panchromatic film despite its many 'technical' advantages over orthochromatic film). Ogle speaks of the film industry as 'conservative by nature,' and of the 'innate conservatism of many cinematographers.'[29]

It is true that many innovations in film – color, sound, widescreen – were imposed on the industry from outside. But to speak of the conservatism of an industry apart from an institutional and economic context explains nothing; and to speak of the conservatism of an individual leads to the construction of psychic or hereditary profiles and the view that history is generated by great men, great innovators with ideas whose time had come. In either case, the technological history is told at the expense of greater forces. Technology is not neutral or spontaneous but is a product of social and economic circumstances and only secondarily of great men.[30]

The industrial exploitation of color

I now consider a third model for writing a history of color – one suggested by Douglas Gomery with respect to sound in 'The coming of the talkies: invention, innovation, and diffusion'.[31] Like the technological model, Gomery separates out questions of aesthetics,[32] but in place of technology he employs a principle capable of a more supple analysis:

[The] advent [of sound] can be appreciated by viewing it in terms of the economic theory of technological innovation, which posits that a product or process is introduced to increase profits in three systematic phases: invention, innovation, and

diffusion. . . . In each of the three phases, the producers and
suppliers of sound equipment carried out their business decisions
with a single view toward maximizing long-run profits.[33]
Gomery, therefore, concentrates on (1) those management decisions
which (2) maximize the long-run profits of a business. The approach
is that of industrial organization economics – a branch of neo-classical economic theory.

According to Gomery's analysis the first stage of technical development is invention, which spans everything concerning the technical
device from an 'archaeology' to a time just short of commercial
exploitation. Gomery discusses the beginnings of sound and the failure of some eighty-one small companies attempting to market their
own versions of a sound system.[34] He begins with commercial
attempts to link sound and image for a viewer through the playing
of a phonograph during the projection of the images (either synchronized to the images in some way or nonsynchronized) or through
a sound-on-film method. He does not consider the development of
the phonograph itself as a commercial device, nor does he examine
the dominant method of linking sound and image in the early cinema
(i.e. live musical and/or vocal accompaniment).

When we turn from sound to the relation of color and image,
things become more complex. Do we begin with the black-and-white
photograph? An accurate color record depends on a film emulsion
which is uniformly sensitive to all the colors of the spectrum. If, for
instance, the film were not sensitive to red and yellow then those
colors would be rendered as black (absent) and there would be no
hope of distinguishing red from yellow. The silver halides in a film
emulsion are chiefly sensitive to blue, violet, and ultraviolet radiation.
(Since the human eye does not see ultraviolet, its reproduction on
film will somewhat 'distort' the other colors). The addition of certain
chemical dyes by 1884 increased the sensitivity of 'ordinary' film to
include green and brought about 'orthochromatic' film. Further advances in dyes expanded sensitivity to the reds and led to 'panchromatic' film stocks in 1903 and 1905. Color photographs from nature
were made in the late 1870s and the first commercially successful
color photographic process was the Lumière Autochrome in 1907.
Continual progress in sensitizing dyes made possible the great advances in color photography after 1930.

There are still earlier important dates in natural color photography: 1798 (the development of lithography by Senefelder), 1813
(the principle of the dye and bleach color film), and 1861 (Maxwell's
demonstration of a three-color process). In fact by the time of Technicolor film there already existed a bewildering array of color pro-

cesses and companies vying for success. There have been over 100 major color processes, about half of which originated or were used in the United States.[35] Many were rarely or never used to make a film. It is enough to note, without exploring the details,[36] that natural color processes are usually divided into two types – additive color systems (e.g. Kinemacolor, early Technicolor, and modern television) and subtractive color systems (e.g. Technicolor, Eastman Color, Kodachrome) – and that each type may be further classified according to whether it is based on a set of two or three primary colors.

So far we have considered the invention of color with respect to the photograph (natural color), but a second line of development lies closer to painting. Hand-painted daguerreotypes appeared around 1839[37] and hand-painted films appeared with the very first films in 1894.[38] Hand coloring became a large and important industry. Factories of women applied as many as six colors to each frame of the film. A variation on the technique – stenciling – existed into the 1930s. Other techniques, related to painting, involved the use of chemical baths either to dye the gelatin ('tinting,' which colors the light areas) or to replace the silver image of positive film ('toning,' which colors the dark areas) or a combination of tinting and toning. One might even add a third line of color development, closer to the theater than to either photography or painting: the use of separate, colored spotlights during the projection of a film. Griffith used the technique, which one reviewer called 'revolutionary,' in the projection of *Broken Blossoms* (1919).[39]

We see, then, that color experimentation appeared with the earliest photographs and the earliest films. The major techniques – additive color, subtractive color, painting, stenciling, and chemical baths – were all well underway in the early 1900s. In fact there is such a remarkable diversity that it is not immediately clear with which industries to begin a study of color, or how far back to go. One company, however, which was clearly involved in the invention phase of color was the Natural Color Kinematograph Co. (Kinemacolor).

Kinemacolor enjoyed considerable success in the years 1909–15. Thereafter it declined and failed. If we were to follow Gomery's model, we would not search for the failure of Kinemacolor in a failure of technology, such as the requirement of outdoor sunlight for film exposure (thus no studio shooting); excessive wear on the film due to projection at twice the speed of black-and-white films; the need for special, complicated projectors; and other problems like fringing and reduced screen illumination related to the additive process.[40] Rather, Gomery suggests that in the failure of the eighty-one or so early sound companies 'technological inferiority played only a small role'[41] or no role at all.[42] More important were such factors as a solid financial underpinning for the business, a strong research and development laboratory, and superior marketing and managerial skill.[43] It has, in fact, been claimed that poor management was a factor in the decline of Kinemacolor.[44]

Let us consider a set of data – an event in the history of Kinemacolor – and see how it might be used by different historians. In February 1912, Kinemacolor premiered its film of the Delhi Durbar of 1911 which recorded the pageantry and celebration in Bombay, Delhi, and Calcutta in honor of the coronation of King George V and his visit to India. *The Durbar at Delhi* ran two and a half hours (16,000 feet) whereas the longest films produced before 1912 were 45–60 minutes. Black and white films of the same event, which preceded the Kinemacolor film, closed after three weeks. The immensely profitable Kinemacolor film, however, ran for fifteen months and grossed three-quarters of a million dollars.[45] What can one say beyond the fact that *The Durbar at Delhi* was Kinemacolor's 'greatest success'?[46]

For Terry Ramsaye the film provides material for several stirring anecdotes, including the image of Charles Urban burying the negatives of each day's shooting and sleeping on top of them to guard against sabotage by rivals. The reels are referred to by Ramsaye as 'precious' which further prepares for the climax three sentences later: 'He slept with his treasure.'[47] Ramsaye almost certainly based his account on the typewritten notes of Urban.[48] An alternative explanation for burying the Durbar films – which would not suit Ramsaye's purpose at all – is that the films were buried to protect them from the intense heat of the Indian sun.[49]

Ramsaye also asserts that Urban lost a knighthood at the hand of the King because he fell ill and could not attend a royal showing of the Durbar film. Urban was 'on the verge of death,' says Ramsaye, and he continues: 'It was a tragedy reminiscent of the unfortunate death of Turner, the first of the color inventors, in Urban's office years before.'[50] Earlier we noted how Ramsaye portrayed Turner's death as a dramatic event, but why is it now mentioned again (and with certain details repeated) seven pages later? What is the connection between Urban's illness – from which he recovered – and Turner's death? Precisely this: to reinforce a *narrative* of history, to remind the reader of the story Ramsaye is telling – that the story connects up its events and is an organic whole. For Ramsaye, Urban is (here) a particular kind of *character* – a player in a 'tragedy'[51] and the victim of an 'unkind fate.'[52] Thus, in an important way Ramsaye's history depends on a conception of character derived from classic literary narrative. He wishes to remind us that Turner, as a character, is important to the story.

Ramsaye says that at the time of the Durbar film Kinemacolor 'was on the high tide of success.'[53] Note the use of the word 'tide.' The metaphor points to a theory of historical *change* (discussed earlier) based on an evolutionary model, more precisely, change according to an organic and natural growth process. Ramsaye does not deal with the decline of Kinemacolor (though he speaks obliquely of an 'interruption' due to World War I[54]), but instead chooses in the final page and a half of an eleven-page chapter to mention Prizma color, Kelleycolor, and Technicolor which are represented as carrying on the work of Kinemacolor ('The Kinemacolor method became in consequence the basis of practically all subsequent color processes'[55]). For Ramsaye, Kinemacolor *is* color and color is continuing to grow and evolve. The financial demise of a particular business is incidental.

How would Patrick Ogle deal with the Durbar film? He would undoubtedly cite it as proof that a certain level of technical perfection had been achieved in the camera, film stock, the projection of Kinemacolor movies. More difficult would be the question of why the company failed. Ogle might cite continuing technical problems which were never resolved, such as the frequent allegation that projection of the films near the threshold frequency needed for persistence of vision resulted in eyestrain and headaches for viewers.[56] Ogle would more likely avoid the question and concentrate on the relations of Kinemacolor technology to subsequent color processes and the eventual 'perfection' of color. Perfection in these terms would be measured against the state of color technology today or 'foreseeable' by today's standards.

Gomery would probably view the Durbar film as evidence of the long-term profit potential of the Kinemacolor enterprise, but would not attach special importance to the event because it does not provide answers to the sorts of questions he asks about financial stability, research facilities, and bold management decisions, though it does bear somewhat on the marketing of color. (Compare the Durbar film with Gomery's treatment of early sound programs and films, like *The Jazz Singer*.[57]) For Gomery the success of the Durbar film is for the most part irrelevant to the success or failure of Kinemacolor.

Although I have limited my inquiry to the early history of color, it may be useful to sketch the two phases of technological development which follow 'invention' – innovation and diffusion. In the innovative phase of sound, Gomery discusses how sound was adapted for profitable use by Warner Brothers, Fox Film Corporation, the Big Five (after the expiration of the Big Five Agreement), and RKO. It is in this phase that Gomery's criterion of 'creative management' is especially prominent. The principal hero for Warner Brothers is Waddill Catchings. The management of both Warners and Fox is characterized as 'bold,'[58] the actions of the Big Five as 'decisive,'[59] and the management of RKO as 'superior.'[60] For Gomery it is in the context of 'management' that the individual – if he is also 'creative' – has the chance to enter history.

A history of color in the innovation phase would certainly include the Technicolor Company. Its president, Herbert Kalmus, would be portrayed as 'unquestionably the man who put Technicolor over.'[61] Taken to an extreme, this reliance on the individual corporate leader leads to the following description of Kalmus in a *Fortune* magazine article:

> The Doctor shaves with a Gillette razor, likes his fried eggs done on one side only, reads a great deal of biography and physics but very little fiction.[62]

In the diffusion phase economists study how other firms in an industry react to what has become profitable for a competitor. In the diffusion of sound, Gomery includes the general adoption and conversion to sound by the large motion picture companies chiefly through mutual cooperation (the Hays Office and the Academy of Motion Picture Arts and Sciences played major roles). Smaller companies with little capital were forced out of business or merged with the majors.[63] A history of color in the diffusion phase would include the antitrust and patent problems of the Technicolor Company in the late 1940s.[64] The diffusion phase completes an economic cycle of change which is driven by a desire for long-run profit. The individual's place in such a history is one of business management.

The ideology of color

I will now consider a final approach to the writing of a history of early color. Jean-Louis Comolli, writing from an avowedly Marxist perspective, asserts in 'Technique et idéologie' that a history of technology and technical forms is not enough. He does not reject technical explanations[65] but calls for the analysis of a larger context which locates and determines technology. This larger context is composed of two social demands – the ideological and the economic. Comolli states that 'It is to the mutual reinforcement of an ideological demand ("to see life as it is") and the economic demand to make it a source of profit that cinema owes its being.'[66] Before I consider in more detail the problem of ideology, it may be useful to indicate briefly in what ways Comolli's theory of historical *cause* is nonlinear and his theory of historical *change* is nonevolutionary; that is, how Comolli differs from the sort of history written by Ramsaye.

What is the alternative to linear cause? For Comolli it is 'a history characterised by discontinuous temporality, which is recursive, dialectical, and not reducible to a single meaning but rather, is made up of types of signifying practices whose plural series has neither origin nor end.'[67] The reference to 'neither origin nor end' is crucial to Comolli because, for the traditional historian, the beginning and the end points pose special problems in the linear narrative (a special embarrassment). In Aristotle's words: 'A whole is that which has a beginning, a middle, and an end. A beginning is that which does not itself follow anything by causal necessity....'[68] To seek after beginnings and origins, then, in order to unify a historical narrative is in some sense an ahistorical inquiry: that which has no cause (a beginning) lies outside of time and history. The problem for the materialist historian is that in utilizing language to *name*, one has already cut out a point, a potential origin. The alternatives are either to no longer use language or to name a *plurality* of beginnings – a series of points which may even be contradictory – and thereby defeat the notion of an event – a coalescence of points into the master point or origin. This is what Comolli attempts by deconstructing the origin of cinema into a scattered series of events – visible and invisible, continuous and discontinuous, from yesterday to twenty-five centuries ago.[69] By naming a great many events, Comolli hopes to block the very notion of a single event, a first cause, which leads (through the neo-Aristotelian unities) to a climax.

What is the alternative to evolutionary change? For Comolli change is measured in the Marxist terms of an unremitting class struggle. He thus attacks metaphors based on evolution and natural growth, such as the 'birth' of cinema.[70] Although modern theories of biological evolution have lost much of their 'perfection' element – an organism's inherent tendency toward perfection – there remains a weak 'directional' component shaped by natural processes.[71] In this respect the Marxist notion of change is not unlike evolutionary change. Evolution, however, is still characterized by gradualism, continuity, and adaptation to the environment which is foreign to Marxism. Thus Comolli especially seizes on those 'gaps' or discontinuities in the growth of technologies and techniques which are potentially damaging to a theory of smooth evolution. One such gap, he says, is the disappearance of deep focus cinematography – widespread in early cinema – and its reappearance in the late 1930s. Another gap is the delay in moving from ordinary and orthochromatic film stocks to panchromatic films.

What is the role of the individual – the subject – in the process of history? In a system of linear cause, the individual is easily singled out: he or she is largely autonomous and often the decision-maker, the event-maker. In a system of evolutionary change, the individual again is easy to identify: change is based on the metaphor of the body – birth, growth, death. By a curious alchemy, even gaps in the evolution may be referred to the body. Thus Robert Sklar in *Movie Made America* says that D. W. Griffith's *After Many Years* is a '*rediscovery* of cinema's fundamental resources' which 'would not be *lost* again.'[72] The references to rediscovery and loss are the very figures of a linear and evolutionary history which can pose a gap or even retrogression only in such terms as a failure of 'memory,' something which was 'forgotten' but is now assured. In this way the subject is continually present and reinscribed in the traditional history.

For Comolli, on the other hand, the subject exists only in relation to *ideology*. For present purposes I shall define an ideology as a possible relation between individual consciousness and its social ground. It is a largely coherent and logical system of images, ideas, values, feelings, and actions by which, and through which, persons experience their societies at various times; for instance, a 'philosophy' or theology, although an ideology need not be formalized in this way.[73] (Strictly speaking, an ideology is not an image or an idea but a representational system through which the individual encounters the material conditions of existence.) Comolli therefore asks an epistemological question: What are the conditions that make it possible to know man? How does man represent himself to himself?

Comolli attempts to steer a middle course between those who claim that technology is neutral, independent of use (Ogle, Lebel)[74] and those who claim that technology is *inherently* ideological. In the latter group is Jean-Louis Baudry, who claims that certain features of the cinematic apparatus (lens, camera, projector) mark it with an original sin so that cinema will never truly escape bourgeois illusionism.[75] For Comolli, technology is already and always a part of an ideology and it functions along with 'institutions' to hold the members of a society in a certain set of relationships or bond. Technology is produced by and functions in an ideology; thus it is not 'neutral.' But neither is it determined forever by its past or present functions, for it may be adapted to serve in another set of social relations.

Let us consider ideology at work in the cinema through three concepts: science, art, and realism. We will then ask how color functions in each of these areas.

Comolli argues that cinema arose out of an attempt to compensate for the imperfections of the human eye by substituting the objective, scientifically accurate eye of the camera lens.[76] Cinema was vision perfected; science guaranteed the truth of cinema's reproduction of reality. According to Comolli this belief (or 'myth,' if one is outside of that ideology) was part of a complex of beliefs which shaped the development of cinema and its technology. Although Comolli does not work the argument out in detail, one can suggest evidence which would be marshalled in support of such a position. Thomas Edison or indeed, Dr Herbert Kalmus, for example, would be approached not as biographical figures but in the way in which these men *were sold to the public*.[77] Thus Edison, the man of science and invention, was almost universally referred to in his day as the Wizard of Menlo Park, or simply the Wizard – for how else to explain the miracles of science? Ramsaye's history furthers the Edison myth with such chapters as 'In the house of the wizard.' The Edison product was sold as a triumph of science. The 1902 Sears, Roebuck and Co. catalogue advertises the improved model of the Edison 1901 Kinetoscope as follows:

> This season we shall handle the Edison Kinetoscope for
> projecting moving pictures exclusively The moving picture
> apparatus is known as one of the greatest of the Edison
> inventions, and on it the Wizard of Originality has spent much
> time in the perfection of the present type of machine, embodying
> every improvement and every convenience which science,
> mechanical skill and research have been able to add to the first
> invention.[78]

The marketing of Kinemacolor, too, emphasized its scientific character and how 'the colours obtained are due to the agency of LIGHT only. No painting, hand-work, stencil-work or similar devices are used.'[79] The program for the first showing of Kinemacolor in the United States (December 1909) repeatedly stresses science, not just to differentiate its product from hand-painting and tinting but to claim a superior legitimacy derived from Science:

> It has been pointed out in an American print by a critic, who,
> by the way, had never seen the results, that 'THE MAIN
> PRINCIPLES OF THE URBAN-SMITH PROCESS WERE
> KNOWN TO THE SCIENTIFIC WORLD BEFORE EITHER
> MR. URBAN OR MR. SMITH TOOK UP THE MATTER!'
> Exactly! Messrs Urban and Smith admit the fact and take special
> pride in it. Their invention *is* based upon the solid foundation of
> established scientific truths. If it were based upon some fantastic
> notion not in accordance with the principles of pure science there

would be little hope for its future. It is just *because* Kinemacolor is based upon the solid rock of scientific fact that distinguished scientists all over Europe have been enthusiastic in its praise and have predicted a brilliant future for the young art, which has been born to the world for the entertainment and instruction of the people.

Messrs Urban and Smith's only claim is that with the expenditure of much time and money they are the *first* to take up these sound scientific principles and materialize them into practical, everyday results, and it is for that reason that the Patent offices of every civilized country in the world have granted Letters Patent for the process.[80]

The fact that cinema was taken to be a perfected form of the human eye is revealed in Ramsaye's history when he concludes his account of Kinemacolor by speaking of the 'extraordinary possibilities yet to be explored ... with light entirely below the visual range of the human eye.'[81] Ramsaye speaks of the development of a new film stock sensitive to infra-red. The ideology which links science, camera, vision, and truth is as current as today's magazines. One advertisement for a camera invites the reader to 'explore the world of 1/500 second.' The Canon camera 'can literally make you master of your visual domain.... If you want a look at a world you've never seen before, look at the AE-1.'[82]

A second center of ideology is the notion of Art (and its Aesthetics). Art is conceived to be, not a discourse, a kind of text, but a special, even sacred access to knowledge, the Human Condition, Truth (the complex, ambiguous, and ineffable), etc. Art, especially Great Art, is approached with reverence for it has universal and timeless value. Thus to the extent that cinema can become Art – and more than a 'movie' – it is able to escape history. For example, Griffith's *Broken Blossoms* (1919) was marketed in a series of elaborate ways as an Art object.[83] Its color effects were distinguished from the ordinary so as to become the very *sign* of Art. Thus cinema promised the reconciliation of science and art in a technologically precise reproduction of reality where science became the guarantor of the truths of Art.

A third area for the investigation of ideology is the insistence on realism. Since the cinema was linked to science, it became the perfect tool to record reality with precision. The 1902 Sears catalogue described the Kinetoscope as follows:

THE UNRIVALLED EDISON KINETOSCOPE, moving picture machine, giving a pictorial presentation, not lifelike merely, but apparently life itself, with every movement, every

action and every detail brought so vividly before the audience
that it becomes difficult for them to believe that what they see
before them can be other than nature's very self.[84]

Color, of course, perfectly enhances a reality effect. An ad for a 1910
hand-painted film asserted that 'the flesh tints [are] so natural that it
is hard to believe that the people are only pictures on a screen.'[85]
Natural color processes offered even greater possibilities for
realism.[86] Earlier I discussed the possible significance of Kinemacolor's *The Durbar at Delhi* for three historians. For Comolli the film
would probably be important insofar as it demonstrates the new
powers of realism provided by color. He would find significant the
comments of the Russian Dowager Empress writing to her son,
Kikolai, from London (29 April 1912) after seeing the Durbar film:

> We are lunching today with Georgie and May at Buckingham
> Palace. They both send you greetings. Last night we saw their
> journey to India. Kinemacolor is wonderfully interesting and very
> beautiful and gives one the impression of having seen it all in
> reality . . .[87]

The only danger in all this was that 'color experimenters are apt
to go arty and prevent even *natural colors from producing natural
illusions*.'[88] Many critics of early natural color processes spoke of the
dangers of 'gaudy,' unrealistic color ('garish' was another favorite
word). And Technicolor soon recognized the important investment
they had in realistic color. They insisted that anyone renting their
color equipment also hire a color consultant from the company in
order to 'properly' orchestrate color combinations.[89]

It may be useful to consider a specific set of technological changes,
related to the problem of realism, and to contrast the ways that these
changes would be seen by different historical methods. In 1936–37
new and more efficient lighting equipment, and improvements in the
laboratory processing of Technicolor film, along with new techniques
of photographing color, made possible lighting levels extremely close
to average black-and-white standards.[90] One director of photography, Ray Rennahan, testified, 'I now light almost exactly as I
would for monochrome.'[91] In 1939 Technicolor introduced a film
stock three to four times faster yet, which meant a 50 per cent
reduction in normal lighting levels (the reduction was not greater
because of the continued necessity for color filters and beam-splitting
devices in the camera). This meant that color correcting filters became practical, allowing the use of smaller, more flexible incandescent light sources (which are also softer). In addition the film offered
a wider exposure latitude and so allowed better rendition of shadows. Lighting levels approached those of black-and-white on East-

man Kodak Super X (ASA 40). Many other techniques of black-and-white photography also became feasible (e.g. the use of diffusion and of small spotlights for precise lighting of faces in close-ups) with the result that color became less garish, more natural. Director of photography Ernest Haller concluded:

Now that we have this fast film, which enables a cinematographer to use all the little tricks of precision lighting he has used in monochrome to glamorize his stars, I am sure that color is going to be more flattering than ever to the women![92]

At least the representation of women, it seems, was secure.

How might these changes be interpreted by the four historians we have discussed? For Ramsaye the data has a decidedly technical, unexciting cast about it. If he were to use it, he would want the data to coalesce about a personality or culminate in a dramatic event. One source of dramatic events in film history, of course, is the Great Film and it would be even better if some of these technical changes were *first* used in that great film. Thus Ramsaye would probably structure his presentation around the making of *Gone With The Wind*, the first production to use the faster Technicolor film and on which both Rennahan and Haller worked.

For Ogle these technological changes would be evidence of a logical, natural perfection of technique. He would assert that the changes were largely scientific and so independent of cultural demands. The resulting techniques would be neutral in that they could be used in any way: in realistic and unrealistic films. The fact that cinematographers tended to re-establish monochrome techniques – that is, to conceive color in terms of black and white – would be due to the 'conservatism' of the profession.

For Gomery the changes would be of interest to the extent that, for example, new lighting equipment might be more cost effective and techniques resulting in less 'garish' color might influence the demand for, as well as the marketing of, color. Were black-and-white techniques employed on color films because they were cost effective? How should color be introduced? Through shorts and newsreels (as in the marketing of sound) or through some combination of road-shows, cartoons, special attractions, big budget features, etc.? These marketing decisions, in turn, have aesthetic implications. Nevertheless, the general return to black-and-white techniques would have less interest for Gomery and would probably fall into the province of 'aesthetics.'

Comolli, however, would find these changes of major significance. For him it would be an illustration of technology acting to reinvest the old in new ways. Technology, here, is responding to a deeper structure – a realistic order of discourse. This argument does not contend that all black-and-white films were realist films, but only that the realist codes were by the late 1930s well worked out and well established in black-and-white. Directors and cinematographers continued to think in terms of the black-and-white codes and with the increased importance of color, the demand was there to 'improve' color film and equipment in line with the existing state of black-and-white technology. 'Improve' in this context means to make a technological change so as to be able to deploy the familiar codes.

Comolli could cite as support the detailed advice of cinematographer James Wong Howe on the best use of background, costume, rim lighting, illumination levels, light placement, colored beams, composition, and other variables in order to achieve with color the same 'illusion of naturalness'[93] as in black-and-white. Technology reveals itself, here, through color and lighting codes in the text. Hence, for Comolli, technological refinements are important in the writing of film history, but only insofar as they are related to the social and economic matrix in which they find their function. Culture, for him, is a series of codes and textual systems accessible to semiotic analysis.

In summary, Comolli points to an ideology in which man defines himself by redefining his sight in terms of the cinema. He discusses the ideology of science and how the human eye is represented as being replaced by the camera eye – by the lens of science which cannot lie. Color serves to increase the camera's claim to scientific accuracy, and when used realistically is able to repeat the dominant forms of the culture. In this sense color does not begin with Technicolor, nor even with the hand-painting of film in 1894 but much further back in Western culture: at least to the colors and linear perspective of the paintings of the Renaissance. Comolli would suggest that in order to understand color in film one must first study the uses of color in the other arts, and the forms of intelligibility they sustain.

Conclusion

The accompanying table presents in schematic form a comparison of the four types of history writing which I have explored. The problem I deal with is how one might uncover the various assumptions a historian makes about time, or rather, the social view implicated in a conception of time. Using these assumptions one can construct at least four different histories of color technology in early film. The purpose, however, is not to settle historians into categories or reveal distinctive schools of historiography. It is not uncommon for a historian to make different assumptions in different portions of the same history. (I have indicated, for example, that Lewis Jacobs has written both an adventure and a technological history in *The Rise of the American Film*.) I am not strictly analyzing what might be termed the 'style' of a particular type of writing.[94] My purpose in utilizing the criteria of cause, change, and subject is to provide a way of comparing the different types of questions that a historian may ask and thereby to reveal what kind of history arises from those questions. Thus I am primarily interested in historical logic rather than syntax.

I am not searching for the one, true, and genuine type of history writing because much can be learned from asking different sorts of questions, applying various time schemes, and using a variety of perspectives. If I tend to privilege the sort of history written by Comolli, it is because he is explicit about his method, conscious of the theoretical implications, and asks interesting questions which have produced new interpretations of certain data. Comolli attempts to use his theory at every level of his writing and in the process recasts technology, techniques, and their role in the cinematic machine.

A comparison of the assumptions of four types of historical inquiry

Aspects of historical time	Ramsaye	Ogle	Gomery	Comolli
	Adventure history	Technical history	Industrial history	Ideological history
Cause	Linear (events, anecdotes; neo-Aristotelian unities)	Relations among technologies (science)	Economic context (long-run profits; industrial organization theory)	Social and economic context (Marxist economic theory)
Change	Evolution (birth, growth, death)	Perfection of technique	Economic cycle (invention, innovation, diffusion)	Marxist class struggle (dialectical change)
Subject (role of individual)	Organic metaphor and anecdotes about individuals (psychology)	Inventors and cinematographers	Creative management	Member of economic class and subject in ideology

142   *Edward Branigan*

Notes

1 Roger Manvell (ed.), *The International Encyclopedia of Film* (New York: Crown, 1972), pp. 29–48.
2 Lewis Jacobs, *The Rise of the American Film* (New York: Teachers College Press, 1968), ch. 12.
3 Michel Foucault, *The Order of Things* (New York: Vintage Books, 1970), p. xv. Cf. Christian Metz's comments on the disorder and inconsistent methodology in film histories, 'The imaginary signifier,' *Screen*, vol. 16 no. 2 (Summer 1975), pp. 23–4.
4 It is important to qualify the word 'determine,' for if the historian is not independent of an analytical schema or language neither can we go to the other extreme and assert that the historian is fully defined by the choice of a language. It is enough to emphasize the crucial role played by the scheme in the production of a history. See generally, Dan Slobin, *Psycholinguistics* (Glenview, Ill.: Scott, Foresman & Co., 1971), pp. 120–33; Umberto Eco, *A Theory of Semiotics* (Bloomington: Indiana University Press, 1976), pp. 76–81; E. H. Gombrich, *Art and Illusion* (Princeton: Princeton University Press, 1969), pp. 181–287; Nelson Goodman, *Languages of Art* (Indianapolis: Hackett, 2nd ed, 1976), pp. 7–8.
5 Cf. Charles F. Altman, 'Towards a historiography of American film,' *Cinema Journal*, vol 16, no. 2 (Spring 1977) and the essays in *Film: Historical-Theoretical Speculations*, Ben Lawton and Janet Staiger (eds), (Pleasantville, New York: Redgrave, 1977).
6 These criteria were suggested by the remarks of Michel Foucault in his 'Foreword to the English edition' of *The Order of Things*, op. cit., pp. xii–xiv. They are useful because of their generality and because they address the logic of a historical argument.
7 Terry Ramsaye, *A Million and One Nights* (New York: Simon & Schuster, 1926), p. 562.
8 Fernand Braudel, 'Histoire et sciences sociales: la longue durée,' *Annales*, vol. 4 (Oct.–Dec. 1958), pp. 725–53 (trans. by Sian France, 'History and the social sciences: the long term,' in Fritz Stern (ed.), *The Varieties of History* [New York; Vintage Books 1973], pp. 404–29). See generally Hayden White, *Metahistory* (Baltimore: Johns Hopkins University Press, 1973); Geoffrey Nowell-Smith, 'Facts about films and facts of films,' *Quarterly Review of Film Studies*, vol. 1, no. 3 (August 1976), pp. 272–5.
9 Ramsaye, p. 563.
10 Cf. Roland Barthes, *S/Z* (New York: Hill & Wang, 1974) pp. 216–17.
11 D. B. Thomas, *The First Colour Motion Pictures* (London: HMSO, 1969), p. 10.
12 James Limbacher, *Four Aspects of the Film* (New York: Brussel & Brussel, 1969), p. 14.
13 Herbert Kalmus, 'Technicolor adventures in Cinemaland,' *Journal of the Society of Motion Picture Engineers*, vol. 31, no. 6 (Dec. 1938), pp. 565–6. This article may be found in Raymond Fielding (ed.), *A Technological History of Motion Pictures and Television* (Los Angeles: University of California Press, 1967), p. 52. Other accounts draw on Kalmus's recollections which, significantly, he views as an adventure story. See Roderick

Ryan, *A Study of the Technology of Color Motion Picture Processes Developed in the United States* (PhD dissertation: University of Southern California, 1967), pp. 133–4 (available from Focal Press, New York); Limbacher, pp. 25–6.

14 Robert Sklar repeats a 'story which may or may not be true' (in fact, almost certainly not true) because it nevertheless illustrates his theory of the importance of D. W. Griffith's years at Biograph. Robert Sklar, *Movie-Made America* (New York: Vintage Books, 1975), pp. 50–1.

15 The definition of linear narrative is derived from Edward Branigan, 'Subjectivity under siege – from Fellini's 8½ to Oshima's *The Story of a Man Who Left His Will on Film*, Screen, vol. 19, no. 1 (Spring 1978), p. 39.

16 Jacobs, p. 539.

17 Oswald Spengler develops an explicit 'organic logic' whereby cultures simply *are* organisms with the same cycles as animals, trees, and flowers; *The Decline of the West* trans. by Charles Atkinson (New York: Knopf, 1926).

18 Jacobs, p. 98 and see chs 7, 11 and 19.

19 Ibid., pp. 102–3. Griffith is still generally held to be the 'father of film technique;' Arthur Knight, *The Liveliest Art* (New York: New American Library, 1957), p. 31.

Barry Salt chronicles the 'discovery' of devices such as the 'cinematographic angle' within an explicit model of evolutionary change; 'The early development of film form,' *Film Form*, no. 1 (Spring 1976), pp. 92, 95, 96, 100 and 'Film form: 1900–06,' *Sight and Sound*, vol. 47, no. 3 (Summer 1978), p. 149.

20 Comolli, part 3, pp. 47–9 and note 12 (pp. 3.5–3.8; 3.10–3.11), see note 65 *infra*.

21 Patrick Ogle, 'Technological and Aesthetic Influences Upon the Development of Deep Focus Cinematography in the United States,' *Screen*, vol. 13, no. 1 (Spring 1972), pp. 45–72.

22 Hans Kreitler and Shulamith Kreitler, *Psychology of the Arts* (Durham, North Carolina: Duke University Press, 1972), p. 39.

23 Ibid.; Edward Branigan, 'The articulation of color in a filmic system,' *Wide Angle*, vol. 1, no. 3, pp. 20–31.

24 Rouben Mamoulian, 'Colour and emotion,' *Cinema Quarterly*, vol. 3, no. 4 (Summer 1935), p. 225 and 'Colour and light in films,' *Film Culture*, no. 21 (Summer 1960), pp. 74–5; John Gallagher and Marino Amornco, 'An interview with Rouben Mamoulian,' *The Velvet Light Trap*, no. 19 (1982), pp. 21–2; Forsyth Hardy, 'The colour question,' *Cinema Quarterly*, vol. 3, no 4 (Summer 1935), p. 232; Allen Chumley, 'The screen: movies in motley,' *New Masses*, no. 16 (2 July 1935), p. 44; Jacobs, p. 472; William Johnson, 'Coming to terms with color', in Lewis Jacobs (ed.), *The Movies as Medium* (New York: Farrar, Straus & Giroux, 1970), p. 215, n. 8.

25 Ogle, p. 52.

26 L. A. Jones, 'Tinted films for sound positives,' *Transactions of the Society of Motion Picture Engineers*, vol. 13, no. 37 (May 1929), p. 199.

27 Ryan, pp. 21–3.

28 Knight, p. 149.

144   *Edward Branigan*

29 Ogle, pp. 50, 54.
30 See in general, note 65 *infra.*; Christopher Williams, 'The deep focus question: some comments on Patrick Ogle's article,' *Screen*, vol. 13, no. 1 (Spring 1972), pp. 73–6; James Spellerberg, 'Technology and ideology in the cinema,' *Quarterly Review of Film Studies*, vol. 2, no. 3 (Aug. 1977), pp. 288–301.
31 J. Douglas Gomery, 'The coming of the talkies: invention, innovation, and diffusion,' in Tino Balio (ed.), *The American Film Industry* (Madison: Univ. of Wisconsin, 1976), pp. 192–211. Gomery draws on his more extensive study, 'The coming of sound to the American cinema: a history of the transformation of an industry,' (PhD dissertation, University of Wisconsin-Madison, 1975).

For a useful comparison between the technological and industrial management approaches to the history of sound in film, see Patrick Ogle, 'Development of sound systems: the commercial era,' pp. 198–212, and Douglas Gomery, 'Failure and success: Vocafilm and RCA,' pp. 213–21, in *Film Reader*, no. 2 (Evanston, Ill.: Northwestern University, 1977).

Other work by Gomery on the problem of sound includes the following: 'The coming of sound to the German cinema,' *Purdue Film Studies Annual*, no. 1 (Aug. 1976), pp. 136–43; 'Tri-Ergon, Tobis-Klangfilm, and the coming of sound,' *Cinema Journal*, vol. 16, no. 1 (Fall 1976), pp. 51–61; 'Problems in film history: how Fox innovated sound,' *Quarterly Review of Film Studies*, vol. 1, no. 3 (Aug. 1976), pp. 315–30; 'The Warner-Vitaphone peril: the American film industry reacts to the innovation of sound,' *Journal of the University Film Association*, vol. 28, no. 1 (Winter 1976), pp. 11–19; 'Toward an economic history of the cinema: the coming of sound to Hollywood,' paper delivered at the International Film Conference IV, University of Wisconsin-Milwaukee, 22–24 February 1978.

For criticism of Gomery's approach see Edward Buscombe, 'Sound and color,' *Jump Cut*, no. 17 (April 1978), p. 23.
32 Aesthetics is mentioned only once, Gomery, 'Talkies,' p. 210.
33 Ibid., pp. 193–4; Gomery, 'Transformation of an industry,' ch. 1.
34 Ibid., pp. 194–8; Gomery, 'Failure,' p. 213.
35 Ryan, pp. 1–2.
36 There are four major surveys of all the color processes: E. J. Wall, *History of Three Color Photography* (Boston: American Photographic Publishing Co., 1925); Joseph Friedman, *History of Color Photography* (Boston: The American Photographic Publishing Co., 1944); Ryan, op. cit.; Adrian Cornwell-Clyne, *Colour Cinematography* (London: Chapman & Hall, 1951). The first three are now available from Focal Press, New York. Three other surveys of a more summary nature are Limbacher and Manvell, op. cit., and see note 64 *infra.*
37 Thomas, p. 1.
38 Ramsaye mentions *Annabelle-the-Dancer* made in the summer of 1894 at West Orange, New Jersey, for the Edison Kinetoscope, pp. 194–5.
39 Julian Johnson, 'The shadow stage,' *Photoplay Magazine*, no. 16 (Aug. 1919), pp. 55–6 in George Pratt (ed.), *Spellbound in Darkness* (Greenwich, Conn.: New York Graphic Society, rev. edn, 1973), p. 251.

40 Thomas, pp. 31-3; Ryan, pp. 19, 132-3, 384-5.
41 Gomery, 'Failure,' pp. 213-14, 218.
42 Gomery, 'Talkies,' p. 197.
43 Gomery, 'Failure,' p. 218.
44 Thomas, p. 35.
45 Ramsaye, p. 570. Charles Urban, head of Kinemacolor and present during the filming, gives the figure of £150,000 + in typewritten notes dated 1921 quoted by Thomas, p. 27.
46 Thomas, p. 26.
47 Ramsaye, p. 570.
48 There is a striking similarity in wording between Ramsaye and the typewritten notes of Urban. Portions of the latter are presented in Thomas, pp. 26-7, 13.
49 Limbacher, p. 15.
50 Ramsaye, p. 570.
51 Ibid.
52 Ibid., pp. 570-71.
53 Ibid., p. 570.
54 Ibid., p. 571.
55 Ibid.
56 Thomas, p. 32.
57 Gomery, 'Talkies,' pp. 201-7.
58 Ibid., pp. 194, 199, 206. See also J. Douglas Gomery, 'Writing the history of the American film industry: Warner Bros. and sound,' *Screen*, vol. 17, no 1 (Spring 1976), pp. 40-53.
59 Gomery, 'Talkies,' p. 210.
60 Gomery, 'Failure,' p. 218.
61 'What? Color in the movies again?', *Fortune*, vol. 10 (Oct. 1934), p. 93.
62 Ibid., p. 166.
63 J. Douglas Gomery, 'Hollywood converts to sound: chaos or order?' in Evan William Cameron (ed.), *The Coming of Sound to the American Cinema 1925-1940* (Pleasantville, New York: Redgrave, 1979).
64 George Frost and S. Chesterfield Oppenheim, 'Technical history of professional color motion pictures' (Washington, DC: The Patent, Trademark, and Copyright Foundation, George Washington University), mimeograph.
65 Jean-Louis Comolli, 'Technique et idéologie,' six parts in *Cahiers du cinéma*, no. 229 (May-June 1971), pp. 4-21; no. 230 (July 1971), pp. 51-7; no. 231 (Aug.-Sept. 1971), pp. 42-9; no. 233 (Nov. 1971), pp. 39-45; nos. 234-5 (Dec.-Jan. 1971-2), pp. 94-100; no. 241 (Sept.-Oct. 1972), pp. 20-4.
   The first four parts are translated by Christopher Williams, 'Ideas about film technology and the history of the cinema, with reference to Comolli's texts on technology (*Cahiers du cinéma*),' British Film Institute, mimeograph, part 1 (pp. 1.1-2a.9), part 2 (pp. 2b.1-2b.10), part 3 (pp. 3.1-3.11), and part 4 (pp. 4.1-4.10). Half of the first part is translated by Diana Matias, 'Technique and ideology: camera, perspective, depth of field,' *Film Reader*, no. 2 (Evanston, Ill.: Northwestern University Press, 1977) pp. 128-40.

The reference in the text is to Comolli, part 4: pp. 40–1, 43 (pp. 4.1, 4.2, 4.5).

66 Ibid., part 1: p. 15 (p. 1.16). Edward Buscombe argues that economics can explain the necessary but not sufficient conditions for the innovation of color. He goes on to examine the needs and ideology served by color; Buscombe, pp. 24–5.

67 Ibid., part 3: p. 44 (p. 3.2); see esp. part 2: pp. 56–7 n. 13 (pp. 2b.9–2b.10).

68 *Aristotle's Poetics*, trans. by S. H. Butcher (New York: Hill & Wang, 1961), ch. VII.3.

69 Comolli, part 1: pp. 7–8, 11 (pp. 1.5, 1.6, 1.10).

70 Ibid., part 1: p. 9f. (p. 1.7f).

71 See Ernst Mayr 'Evolution,' *Scientific American*, no. 239 (Sept. 1978), pp. 47–55.

71 Sklar, p. 51 (my emphasis).

73 See Louis Althusser, 'Ideology and ideological state apparatuses', in *Lenin and Philosophy and Other Essays*, trans. by Ben Brewster (New York: Monthly Review Press, 1971), pp. 127–86; Paul Narboni and Jean-Louis Comolli, 'Cinema /ideology/criticism,' three parts in *Screen*, vol. 12, nos. 1–2 (Spring, Summer 1971), and *Screen*, vol. 13, no. 1 (Spring 1972); Terry Eagleton, *Marxism and Literary Criticism* (Los Angeles: University of California Press, 1976), pp. viii, 16–19; Philip Rosen, '*Screen* and the Marxist project in film criticism,' *Quarterly Review of Film Studies*, vol. 2, no. 3 (August 1977), pp. 273–87; Branigan, 'Subjectivity under siege,' p. 10 and 'Foreground and background: a reply to Paul Willemen,' *Screen*, vol. 19, no. 2 (Summer 1978), p. 139.

74 Jean-Patrick Lebel, *Cinéma et idéologie* (Paris: Editions sociales, 1971).

75 Jean-Louis Baudry, 'Cinéma: effets idéologiques produits par l'appareil de base,' *Cinéthique*, nos. 7–8 (1970), pp. 1–8; trans. 'Ideological effects of the basic cinematographic apparatus,' *Film Quarterly*, vol. 28, no. 2 (Winter 1974–75), pp. 39–47.

76 Comolli, part 1: p. 13 (p. 1.13).

77 Frank Taylor, 'Mr Technicolor,' *The Saturday Evening Post* (22 October 1949).

78 *The 1902 Edition of the Sears Roebuck Catalogue* (New York: Crown, 1969), p. 170.

79 Kinemacolor Programme, New York, Madison Square Garden (11 Dec. 1909), reprod. in Ryan, pp. 438–43.

80 Ibid.

81 Ramsaye, p. 572.

82 *Time* magazine (9 May 1977), p. 20. See also *Time* (13 Feb. 1978), p. 62 ('A camera can explore the world in ways your eyes can't'). The ideology of Art is also commonly invoked; see ibid., p. 5 ('For me, photography has become a magic window to two minds: my subject's and my own').

83 Vance Kepley, Jr., 'Griffith's *Broken Blossoms* and the problem of historical specificity,' *Quarterly Review of Film Studies*, vol. 3, no. 1 (Winter 1978), pp. 37–47.

84 1902 Sears catalogue, p. 156.

85 Quoted by Limbacher, p. 4.

86 See, e.g., the comments by a prominent Hollywood cinematographer on

the added realism of Technicolor, Walter Blanchard, 'Aces of the camera V: Leon Shamroy, ASC,' *American Cinematographer* (May 1941), p. 254.

87 Quoted by Jay Leyda, *Kino* (New York: Collier Books, 1960), p. 47n.

88 *Fortune*, op. cit., p. 168 (my emphasis).

89 Lansing Holden, a color designer for Selznick International, and Gilbert Betancourt, a color coordinator, offer some comments in 'Color! The new language of the screen,' *Cinema Arts*, vol 1 (July 1937), p. 64 and 'Present color trend is toward subdued hues,' *American Cinematographer* (Aug. 1937), p. 317. The color consultant was one of several tie-in services (including processing and printing) which were to cause antitrust difficulties for Technicolor. See note 64.

90 C. W. Handley, 'Advanced technique of lighting on Technicolor,' *American Cinematographer* (June 1937), pp. 230-1; William Stull, 'Technicolor bringing new charm to screen,' ibid., p. 236; Elmer Richardson, 'Recent developments in motion picture lighting,' *American Cinematographer* (Aug. 1937), p. 319; W. Howard Greene, 'Low key lighting may be as easy in color as it is in monochrome,' *American Cinematographer* (April 1938), p. 151.

91 Stull, p. 236.

92 'Faster color film cuts light a half,' *American Cinematographer* (Aug. 1939), p. 356. The faster film also allowed the use of large background projection screens which reduced the necessity for location shooting; William Stull, 'Amateur progress in 1939 exceeded professional,' *American Cinematographer* (Jan. 1940), p. 16; Barry Salt, 'Film style and technology in the thirties,' *Film Quarterly*, vol. 30, no. 1 (Fall 1976), pp. 31-2.

93 James Wong Howe, 'Reaction on making his first color production,' *American Cinematographer* (Oct. 1937), p. 411. See also, J. A. Ball, 'The Technicolor process of three-color cinematography,' *Journal of the Society of Motion Picture Engineers*, vol. 25, no. 2 (Aug. 1935). p. 136; Winton Hoch, 'Technicolor Cinematography,' ibid., vol. 39 (Aug. 1942), p. 102; and several articles in the July 1941 issue of *American Cinematographer*. The reduction of illumination levels allowed new techniques to be used to create natural effects; Arthur Miller, 'Putting naturalness into modern interior lightings,' *American Cinematographer* (Mar. 1941), p. 104.

94 There is, though, much to be learned from a stylistic analysis of historical writing; see Peter Gay, *Style in History* (New York: Basic Books, 1974) and Erich Auerbach, *Mimesis: The Representation of Reality in Western Literature*, trans. by Willard Trask (Princeton, New Jersey: Princeton University Press, 1953).

This essay emerged in part from two courses at the University of Wisconsin-Madison, Spring 1977: Tino Balio's 'History of the motion picture industry' and Russell Merritt's 'Historiography of film.' It is a revision of a paper presented at the International Film conference IV, The University of Wisconsin-Milwaukee, 22–24 February 1978. I wish to thank Douglas Gomery for his comments and Roberta Kimmel for her editorial assistance.

7 · David Bordwell: Camera movement: the coming of sound and the classical Hollywood style

The 1977 Film Studies Annual II: Historical-Theoretical Speculations, ed. Ben Lawton and Janet Staiger (Pleasantville: Redgrave Publishing Company, 1977)

Bordwell, like Branigan, looks at a technical/stylistic 'change' – in this case that of the reintroduction of camera movement after the temporary immobilisation of the camera (during synch-recording) after the coming of sound. Also like Branigan, Bordwell begins by discussing some of the several conventional kinds of explanations that arise when the simplest of questions is asked of Hollywood's history. The question Bordwell asks is as follows: Why, in spite of its relative expense as an aesthetic strategy, was camera movement re-adopted into the stylistic vocabulary? Rather than accepting conventional wisdoms about artistic innovation, technical destiny, cinematic essences or 'realism', Bordwell replaces the return of camera mobility in its historical context. Specifically, he re-situates it in the dual fields of production procedures and representational strategies and asks what sort of functions a mobile camera might have fulfilled in those two respective areas. Bordwell's answer argues a historical coincidence between the industrial need to simplify transport of the cumbersome camera, not during takes but, crucially, between them, and the aesthetic need to contribute to the conventional Hollywood illusion of reality by employing the camera as a cinematic surrogate for spectatorial mobility – a capacity which the spectator is required to relinquish on sitting down in his or her seat. (Only slightly later, the development of deep focus was intended to fulfil a comparable function.) Janet Staiger's analysis of camera movement much earlier in Hollywood's history offers an additional and perhaps contradictory pressure, by demonstrating how camera movement often functioned as a visual flourish, a sign of showmanship, of innovative individuality – one of the many characteristics deployed to distinguish a potentially 'featurable' film from competing releases.

Beginning with a simple, even naive question, may be an advantage, since the study of film history is in such a state that only a naive question has a decent chance of being answered. It is a commonplace that studio film production is ruled, at least in part, by business principles. Producers, as we say, are 'cost-conscious,' guided by budget, economy measures, and so on. But we also know that moving the camera during filming – that procedure which can produce the result we call 'camera movement' on the screen – poses certain budgetary problems. Camera movement requires a large and more alert crew; lighting is much more difficult for a moving than for a static shot; focus must be followed, viewfinding must be accurate, the movement must (or so the rule goes) be smooth. Picture Stanley Cortez filming *The Magnificent Ambersons*:

Walls moved on cue, and in went a light on a predetermined
line, all while the camera was moving ... It gave the actors a
little bit of a problem because they were trying to do their acting
in the midst of all this going on ... To add to my problems
some rooms even had mirrors. They had to be turned around on
cue and turned back on a second cue, on hinges.... (Higham,
1970, p. 108.)

Now imagine this tiresome and time-consuming procedure applied to films after the coming of sound in the late 1920s. With the arrival of sound, the cost per film increased sharply; microphones dictated camera placement; sound technology altered camera design; the blimp made cameras larger and heavier, displaced the viewfinder (creating enormous parallax problems), and made follow-focus next to impossible. Yet by 1936 all these obstacles had been overcome and all-purpose dolly and crane mechanisms were in common use.

My naive question hinges on the contradiction I've suggested: Why, given the high additional costs and the technological obstacles, was camera movement ever a dominant studio film technique *at all*?' Why, to put it more simply, did anybody bother?

One explanation readily suggests itself, though I know of no one who has advanced it in print. We can call it the Gadgeteering Theory. According to this explanation, the men at the studio shop are tinkering around, they hit on something that might be fun to try, and some adventurous director or cameraman tries it. This is not as silly as it sounds. To read the technical journals is to find recorded a certain adolescent exhilaration in trying out peculiar contraptions. Hal Mohr's description of the infamous crane he used to film Paul Fejos's *Broadway* ('That thing could do everything but bake beans'), or James Wong Howe's pride that his design for a dolly was printed in *Popular Mechanics*, exemplify the pleasures afforded by a gorgeous hunk of machinery (Maltin, 1971, p. 118). But the Gadgeteering Theory lacks plausibility. With few exceptions, a Hollywood studio does not pay grown men to dream up outlandish equipment on the chance that someone might try it out; something else is being paid for. Moreover, the Gadgeteering Theory tends toward technological determinism: because the machines are available, they will be used, and they will shape their use. Though certainly there is a basement-chemist side to the history of film technology, we shall not understand that history in its complexity if we assume it to be a haphazard tinkering.

Turn to the standard histories and you will find another answer: the Heroism Theory. The assumption is that technology is invented at the caprice of businessmen, anxious to lure the people to 'something new.' The film-maker is then forced to work within the constraints defined by the technology. But through boldness and persistence, the unusual film-maker transcends the limits of the technology. The plainest statement of this position that I have seen is to be found in the section of Arthur Knight's *The Liveliest Art* called 'Liberating the Camera:'

> It is to the eternal credit of genuinely creative and courageous
> men like Ernst Lubitsch, Rouben Mamoulian, Lewis Milestone,
> and King Vidor that they had the ingenuity and vitality to
> circumvent the experts and lift the new medium out of the rut of
> dully photographed plays and vaudeville routines into which it
> had fallen. (1957, p. 151.)

The Heroism account trades on a 'great-man' theory of history: a solitary, visionary film-maker desires something and overcomes the objections of others. ('Slowly, the sound experts of Hollywood were defeated by directors with fresh ideas about the nature of the new art – and the prestige and stamina to fight them through' [Knight, 1957, p. 154].)

The major difficulty with the Heroism Theory is that it assumes that no one but a handful of geniuses wanted the camera to move. On the contrary, the evidence suggests that the inability to move the camera was generally perceived as a serious problem. As early as 1929, William Stull asserted that practically every studio technical staff in Hollywood was aiming to do three things: '1. To do away with the [camera] booth. 2. To restore the camera's mobility. 3. To eliminate the glass window' (Stull, 1929, p. 7). Moreover, as this passage suggests, camera movement became the object of rational research. Despite romantic anecdotes about the inspired director's asking that the camera be put on a bicycle or strapped to the cinematographer's chest, in fact the studios' camera departments and the equipment manufacturing companies coolly and carefully set about innovating what were called 'camera carriages'. (These efforts were coordinated by such organizations as the American Society for Cinematographers, the Society of Motion Picture Engineers and the Academy of Motion Picture Arts and Sciences Technical Bureau.) A procession of such devices rolled through the 1930s: the Bell and Howell 'rotambulator,' the Paramount 'baby crane,' the Fox 'velocilator,' the 'perambulator,' the Fox-Fearless 'Panoram' dolly, the MGM crane of 1938. The directors were hardly fighting a recalcitrant technology; almost everyone, it seems, wanted to 'liberate' the camera.

The intense interest in camera movement and the deliberateness with which it was developed belie the Gadgeteering and Heroism hypotheses. We must pose our question again. Camera movement was enormous trouble to innovate and sustain, and a lot of money was sunk into researching it. Again, why bother?

Just because the question is naive does not mean we can answer it easily. In a sense, the question is wrongly posed; we should ask what role camera movement plays in that complex phenomenon known as cinema history. This manner of posing the question puts the emphasis on the idea that camera movement is only a part of a much larger system. Let me try to suggest the functions of camera movement within two areas of that history: that of production economics and of representation.

Both the Gadgeteering Theory and the Heroism Theory implicitly set camera movement *against* production demands. But what if the technology of camera movement in the early sound cinema partially *grew out of* concrete production demands? The constraints of sound had added as much as two or three hundred pounds to the camera bulk; the old tripods of silent cinema could not support such a heavy unit, so new camera supports were needed. Moreover, the added weight would have to be shifted around the set; no longer could the cameraman simply pick up the camera and carry it. Something had to help the cameraman change setups. Hence the development of what were then called 'mobile camera carriages' – means of simply transporting the camera easily from one point to another. At first, wheels were added to tripods; by 1929, dollies were generally available to bear the weight of the apparatus. Most important of all, these camera carriages were economical. On dollies and cranes, cameras could be quickly moved into place for shot after shot, thus saving labor and production time. According to a cameraman, the advantage of the Paramount crane was that 'it speeds up production by an hour per day' (*Journal of the Society of Motion Picture Engineers* 1935, p. 10). A Fox executive claimed that the Fox dolly was 'clearly a step toward the goal we are all striving for: better pictures at lower costs' (Seitz, 1933, p. 35). Thus there is reason to believe that the technology of camera movement was an outgrowth of rather than an antithesis to the coming of sound and that the machinery of the moving camera was welcomed as one way to trim rising production costs.

But the existence of the machinery does not mean that anyone will ever use it to film moving shots. A camera movement remains a troublesome, expensive shot. This is why we need, I think, a notion of cinematic representation – a mediation between 'the industry,' 'the machinery' and 'the film-maker'; not 'style' in the usual sense, but the entire complex of film form that exists in a wide body of films. How space is established and developed in a scene, how the human body is filmed, how the order and duration of narrative events are presented – all these matters and more are related to the difficult but necessary concept of cinematic representation. What, we should ask now, does camera movement do representationally in a film?

Elsewhere I have suggested a start toward answering this question (Bordwell, 1977). In its normal use, camera movement tends to eliminate any spatial ambiguities in the image and to specify a single profilmic layout and a unified perceptual viewing position. Perceptually, then, camera movement can be a powerful surrogate for the active locomotion which we surrender upon settling into our cinema seat. Camera movement also tends to yield an image of continuous order and duration of narrative events. All these features – coherent space, unified viewing position, narrative continuity – were canonized by the classical narrative style of film-making. We can, then, hypothesize that Hollywood seized on camera movement in the 1920s (generally, I believe, after 1925) and developed it against economic odds after the coming of sound because camera movement was needed for a specific representational system, that of an 'illusory realism' related to narrative space and time. An analogy might be made to the star system. A star may be paid out of all proportion to his/her measurable labor on a film, but what is being bought is the star as a component of representation, a figure in a textual system. Camera movement may offer a phenomenon of this kind. Only the pressure of an ideology of representation can explain the cinema's large-scale investment in camera mobility. So integral does camera movement become to the representational system 'cinema' that by 1950, when a director will not move the camera (as the early Warhol or the late Ozu won't) she/he is considered archaic, even 'uncinematic.'

A great deal, of course, remains to be done in developing this hypothesis. We must scrutinize the use of camera movement in

Lumière's films, the development of the Akeley tripod in the late teens, the technological bases and stylistic functions of camera movement in the cinemas of Italy, Germany, France, Japan, and the Soviet Union. As a test case, we might look at the relation between German experiments in camera movement (*The Last Laugh*, *Variety*) and Hollywood assimilation of those experiments (in *Seventh Heaven* and *The Crowd*), an assimilation contemporaneous with the emigration of German technicians to Hollywood; such a test case might help us concretely examine the interaction of the factors involved. Our future work on the questions posed by camera movement must take into account the larger issues of the interrelations of technology, economics, representation, and ideology.

References

Anonymous, 1935: 'Progress in the motion picture industry,' *Journal of the Society of Motion Picture Engineers*, vol. 14, no. 10.

Bordwell, David, 1977: 'Camera movement and cinematic space,' *Cine-Tracts*, no. 2.

Higham, Charles, 1970: *Hollywood Cameraman* (London: Thames & Hudson).

Knight, Arthur, 1957: *The Liveliest Art* (New York: New American Library).

Maltin, Leonard; 1971: *Behind the Camera* (New York: Signet Books) cf. Higham.

Seitz, John F., 1933: 'New camera-carriage saves time,' *American Cinematographer*, vol. 14, no. 3.

Stull, William, 1929: 'Solving the "ice-box" problem,' *American Cinematographer*, vol. 10, no. 6.

If, as Ida Jeter suggests, actors are among the labour aristocracy of Hollywood then film stars are clearly the occupational leaders of that already privileged profession. It is ironic, therefore, that for all its self-evident visibility, stardom remains the site of perhaps more contention than any other area of film studies. More has been written about the stars than about any other aspect of the American cinema or film industry and yet in many ways less is known about how they function for that cinema and that industry than about many apparently more obscure matters. Barry King's discussion begins by summarising the debate as it presently stands, polarised between those who accept the so-called consumer-sovereignty thesis and consequently conceive of stars as some sort of democratic product of the box-office 'votes' of their audience, and those who see in the phenomenon of stardom only further evidence of the manipulative powers exercised by the monopolistic film industry. King rejects both these positions, arguing that while the consumer-sovereignty thesis fails to recognise the mediating role which the industry itself plays between the stars and their fans (via distribution and exhibition strategies, casting, advertising and publicity and so on), the cultural pessimism which perceives nothing more than manipulation in the process can never adequately grasp either the audience or the industry in their complexity. Furthermore, King suggests, no manner of exploiting 'talent' can ever entirely ensure an uninterrupted run of hits or even begin to explain the differential 'electoral' success and failure of the industry's numerous nominees for stardom.

Having eliminated the conventional explanations of stardom which privilege either the audience or the industry and ignore the other, King turns his attention to that part of the process least considered by serious writing on the subject – the stars themselves. Like Bordwell, King's procedure is to re-situate the object of study into its original habitat, between the industry and the audience. Beginning with a discussion of film acting in general, which he sees as simultaneously routinised and yet artistic (both standardised and differentiated), he goes on to argue that 'stardom is a specialisation based on film acting'. Staiger's analysis of the period when such specialisations first surfaced in American cinema usefully complements King's approach here.

King concludes and confirms his argument by briefly but suggestively comparing the careers of two male stars, Clark Gable and Burt Lancaster, situating their differences in neither individual biography nor general shifts in audience taste but rather in the specific historical and industrial circumstances in which they worked – both as performers and as images.

The purpose of this article will be to lay out some of the fundamental features of stardom as part of the occupation of film acting in Hollywood. In order to situate our analysis, we shall restrict our consideration to the Hollywood of the 1930s and 1940s.

An occupation may be defined as part of the division of labour in society, that has developed a collective consciousness or a consciousness of its interests as a group.[1] Whilst the study of the occupation of film acting is an enterprise in its own right, scarcely developed since Ross's work on the process of unionization, it is nevertheless plausible to focus on stardom as a key phenomenon in the formation of an occupation of film acting.[2] This is because stars have the place of occupational leaders in the Hollywood hierarchy and their behaviour and views, for better or for worse, define the purposes and aims of film acting to the public at large as well as influencing the perspectives that entrants to the occupation have of the gains and losses involved in making film acting their career. So by focusing on stardom as a form of working within an occupation one does not exhaust all that needs to be said on the matter, but at least one does begin the specification at a pertinent point.

But there is another reason for this procedure, which is polemical. By attempting to define stardom as a part of the occupation of film acting, as a form of work, one is implicitly challenging alternative definitions that see stardom as created, not out of the exigencies of controlling the production and marketing of films, but rather by popular selection. This argument sees stardom as an arrangement forced upon producers by the enthusiasms of the public and then proceeds to elaborate what these enthusiasms are by a series of 'cultural' meditations on stars and stardom. Broadly conceived, this position, which may usefully be called the 'Zukor'[3] thesis, takes the following form:

In principle the role of stardom must be seen, if I can coin a

phrase, as that of providing a 'collective register'. This term is intended to indicate two aspects of a recurrent process. Firstly, that the
stars are taken to indicate something about the state of collective
experience, conscious or unconscious. Secondly, that what the stars
represent is otherwise suppressed by the prioritized realities of the
dominant culture. This does not mean that the stars necessarily project 'life styles' that are oppositional – consider William Holden for
example – but that the stars indicate the gap between private behaviour and public conformity and this gap in itself through being
represented furthers the 'cause of the underdog'. The stars are, therefore, agents who register collective concern and, by virtue of their
physical attractiveness and glamour, impersonate such concerns in
an exemplary form. Stars are not only an institutionally unique
means of registering the private concerns of the individual in the
'mass' – since all other means represent how common people should
behave and not how they are – but an exemplary means such that
private experience only becomes consummated in the image of the star:

> The new 'assimilable stars', stars as life-models, correspond to an
> increasingly profound desire on the part of the great mass of
> people for individual salvation . . .[4]

Again, a statement of more recent date:

> Everyone chafes at the restrictions imposed upon pleasure by
> society and one's own conscience; there is a deep satisfaction in
> identifying with someone better placed who gets away with it.
> Yet there is also resentment; retribution must come sooner or
> later . . . This explains why the most adoring fans are so eager to
> read about the private misfortunes of their idols and why, when
> a popular star dies, there seems to be something satisfyingly
> inevitable about his death, whatever grief the news inspires.[5]

Finally, in a less florid vein, Alexander Walker equates the collective
nature of film-making with representativeness:

> European films have a long tradition of expressing the viewpoints
> of their individual makers; whereas Hollywood movies, until
> recently anyhow, have generally embodied social and economic
> forces in a studio-assembled product . . . Stars *in consequence* are
> the direct or indirect reflection of the needs, drives and dreams of
> American society.'[6] (my emphasis)

What is apparent in this sort of argument is a causal emphasis on
consumer sovereignty. The star is not usefully considered as part of
a definite occupational order, defined by recurrent socio-economic
patterns of control; on the contrary, such a control can never be
finally effective since the stars 'transcend' such mundane determinations by virtue of the power of popular selection.

The point of looking at stardom as occupation is to set a limit on such essentially circular speculations. It should be apparent that such 'theories', whilst clearly identifying certain features of stardom, do not ultimately explain it. This is because in order for such relationships to operate it follows that the star system has already been constituted – in order for selection to occur as an effect there must be a range of choice in being. In other words, we are less interested in the influence of public choice, which, indeed, does have an effect, than in the processes that determine the existence of a choice set. Until we determine the latter processes – the socio-economic patterns of control that consumer sovereignty theses elide – we are unable to assess the impact of the audience on the source (Hollywood) and separate recycled corporate public relations from grounded analysis.

This much said – in short that the 'Cohn' thesis that stars can be made by good casting, careful publicity and advertising offers the most fruitful beginning – it is as well to emphasize that simplistic theories of audience manipulation will not do either.[7] The impact of audience selection on Hollywood is a complex process of interaction, marked by a large degree of inertia, channelling and predetermination, which warrants a paper in its own right. The general point that emerges from such an analysis is that it is entirely consistent with industrial survival and predominance that the public influence over film production should be restricted to the selection of stars from a predetermined list of contenders. Some of the reasons for this conclusion will become apparent below, but essentially the star system is the form of competition between the majors that is consistent with the stabilisation of monopoly control. Forms of competition which would widen the range of choice available for public selection, i.e. increase the institutional recognition of the potential range of popular taste, are incompatible with a producer- rather than audience-centred system of production.[8] Leaving a discussion of audience influence on one side for another occasion, let us see how far we can unpack the mysteries of stardom by looking at it in relation to film acting.

Film acting and stardom

Film acting and stardom have been held to be different occupations.[9] In the view taken here this position is an exaggeration but it contains an essential truth. Rather, we see film acting and stardom as different activities within one occupation, or strictly stardom is a specialization based on film acting. The first problem in characterizing stardom is therefore to produce a workable definition of film acting.

Even at the global level such a definition is problematic because of the nature of acting in general as an 'artistic' rather than scientific or routinized activity. Where the work in question is scientific then we find that creativity is defined by universalistic or objectivistic criteria and where it is routine the formal specification of creativity, though it may be an informal element, does not arise. Artistic work by contrast places a premium on creativity. This does not mean that artistic work is without controls or conventions as compared to science, which also incorporates innovation into its procedures as a norm: both are conventional activities.[10] But scientific creativity is recognized by the scientific community according to impersonal rules; whereas artistic creativity, though it may be subject to peer group evaluation, tends to be recognized by groups outside the creator group itself – critics, dealers, audiences and so on – on the basis of criteria which are partial, subjective and personalized.[11] Generally speaking, therefore, artistic work even when operating within well-established conventions and genres tends to be evaluated as, and in fact strives to be, a 'personal' statement.

Acting participates in this general tendency of artistic work but it does so under particular conditions, for it involves an unusual relationship between the creator and his product. What the actor provides is a service. The actor's product – a given performance – is inseparable from his or her physical attributes.[12] Although various fabrication processes such as make-up can supplement physical appearance, these remain a major constraint on the range of the actor.[13] Film technology, though adding the possibility of further manipulation, does not alter this basic relationship, though it may increase the dependence of the actor on the technology and those who control it. If we now ask what acting in general is we can define it as the process of subsuming the self – a personal identity, operative behind all roles and settings – into a character in a limited, e.g. written, social setting. Now it is important, if difficult, to maintain this distinction. The difficulty stems from the fact that for some social theorists the distinction between self and role is typical of all forms of social activity.[14] In this sense we are all actors. Obversely, it is also observed that the self is a plastic entity formed by the roles we are able or are permitted to play socially – the concept of socialization. For our purposes we can note that acting is that form of work in which the relation between the self and the role becomes a consciously studied process and that such a study depends on maintaining the distinction between self and character. To be clear, this does not mean that acting is restrictively defined as one form of relationship between self and character, e.g. 'Broadway' acting where an actor's identification with a part is considered to be a barrier to technical excellence, as against method acting where it is not. Rather, however the relationship between self and character is handled, the distinction itself provides the basis for technical variation. Whether the actor has an existential stake in a given character or not is adventitious to the central fact that acting is a skill in which the distinction between self and character is primary. Richard Widmark highlights the point:

Movie audiences fasten on to one aspect of the actor; they hold on to a piece of the personality for dear life, and they decide what they want you to be. They think you are playing yourself. The truth is that the only person who can ever really play himself is a baby. In each succeeding movie, you're virtually starting over. The actor is tested again each time . . .[15]

At the same time, as is well known, within all cultures there operate conventional but seemingly necessary connections between physical appearance and moral value,[16] so that the professional norm of being 'tested again' each time is an ideal rather than a reality. Actors, whether on stage or in film, are selected for the moral or personality implications of their physical type or 'body language'. This is because the personality implications of physical type allow the actor to re-inforce the apparent fusion between self and character. A minimal definition of acting therefore is the process of consciously manipu-lating a self, which is *occupationally defined* as a personality implied by appearance, to project character. A criterion for judging the extent of acting ability would therefore entail the capacity to obscure the difference between self and character and a strong test would be the extent to which an actor can assume different characters, i.e. subsume personality in a range of characters. To be clear, this is a normative stipulation; it indicates the ideal not the reality of acting.[17]

In the case of film acting the process of transcription intensifies the emphasis on the physical aspects of the actor's performance of character for at least two reasons. Firstly, for the general reason that film converts all forms of signs to indices or the physical traces of performance. This does not mean that symbols or iconic signs do not occur in films nor that they should not occur, but such acts of meaning as do occur are existentially tied to the 'materials' of per-formance.[18] Secondly, the production economy of film-making tends to centre the various effects within film on the performance of fore-grounded actors. Given, for reasons of economy, that most films are shot out of narrative sequence, the actor becomes an important factor of continuity. Barring the unusual case of an entirely fixed mise-en-scène, e.g. Ulmer's *Detour*, other factors of continuity such as camera style and genre conventions rely more on separate interfilmic under-standings. So whilst generally speaking there is a well-established tradition of representing action through the privileged medium of the individual, which predates the cinema, the cinema – as conventionally developed, at any rate – has institutionalized this tradition in physical terms.[19] Such a focus on the variously manipulated appearance or performance style of the actor, might be held to explain stardom. The cynosure effect of filming adds charisma. There are a number of problems with this position, however.

Whether we take it as a simple or extended thesis of technological determinism – whether, that is, we argue that the film medium has this effect 'naturally' or more persuasively because ideological con-ventions of viewing have been built into the cinematic apparatus – it merely identifies a necessary condition for stardom; such processing would apply to any actor who is foregrounded.[20] It does not tell us why a particular kind of actor is, in Hollywood films, persistently foregrounded. What is particular about the star is that he or she is not so much an actor in the sense defined above but a self or person-ality that behaves. To say that a star behaves does not mean that they are themselves, but rather that stars do not, as it were, surrender their public personality to the demands of characterization. As Richard Dyer has recently suggested, there is a discernible disarticu-lation between star image – by which he means the signalled person-ality of the star as a trans-filmic entity – and character as a situated component of a narrative and plot. To a large extent, unless the relationship has been purposively pre-structured as in the star vehicle, the star's image (personality image) constitutes a barrier or, at least a problem for situated characterization. In this sense, stars incarnate the principle of miscasting.[21] What this means in terms of our nor-mative definition of acting is that stars do not function as actors. This does not mean necessarily that a given star cannot act, but that acting is not essential to stardom. As an aside, however, it is worth noting that the acquisition of star status may well be a pre-condition for having enough work to develop as a skilled actor. Our observa-tions may therefore be time-dated in respect of particular stars, but this does not alter the validity of our point. Rather than acting ability being a pre-condition for stardom, the reverse may be true. To some extent Dyer's point is not new; it has been remarked upon by Edgar Morin, for example. But neither is it a groundless abstraction, since the difference between actor and star has been recognized in Holly-wood itself. Professional judgment regards character actors as repre-senting the peak of the skill hierarchy; whereas stars are at the peak, albeit short term on average, of the reward hierarchy.[22]

What we are left with is, therefore, a clear sense of the fact that stars 'transcend' the demands of situated characterization. Secondly we can say that this transcendence is not premised on acting ability, i.e. it is not meritocratic, nor on the material features of film as a medium – foregrounding alone does not explain stardom. What I now want to suggest is that it is necessary to look at the relations of ownership governing film production if we are to locate the material basis of 'stellar transcendence'. If this is so then one of the popularly felt aspect of stars, their 'Olympian divinity', is a product of quite down-to-earth economic arrangements.

Stardom: corporate regulator

As observed earlier, the nature of stardom is determined by factors of distribution. Certainly popular selection must be considered here but we have already given reasons why it cannot be primary. This understood, the nature of stardom is determined by the interaction of two phenomena: the organization of competition within Hollywood and the ownership of the star 'personality' image. Let us examine these in turn.

As is well known, since the mid-1920s the organization of competition has taken on a monopoly cartel character, with the production, distribution and exhibition of high-level profitability films being controlled by a small number of producers. In classical Hollywood, the five major studios (Warner Bros, MGM, Paramount, RKO and Fox) operated with an effectively total control over a geographically compartmentalized-balkanized-total market. (We restrict ourselves to the USA and Canada market herein.) The three minor studios – United Artists, Columbia and Universal – participated in the cartel arrangement mainly by virtue of their ability to supply routine and, periodically, successful product in a situation of overall shortage. Considering only 'A' level production, this means in effect that each major owned or had a share in the total available market for its competitors' product. Leaving on one side the need to enforce sales and pricing on independent exhibitors – accomplished by block booking and other preferential forms of negotiation – it followed that each major could only maximize its takings on a hit film by persuading its competitors to allow that film access to otherwise legally closed markets. The pertinence of time, or perishability, gives this necessity an imperative form. At the same time, whilst it is necessary to recall that there was and still is no certain relationship between the cost of a film and its ultimate earnings, this is a different matter from saying that the average earnings of any film are uncertain. On the contrary, each major, by controlling its own share of the market and/or a share of independent exhibition, was assured an average return on its product. However, in an industry where profits of a high level – sometimes double that of cost and beyond – were possible as an objective, some films – A level films – were produced precisely on the understanding that they could only become profitable if their arc of earnings was outside of the section of the market controlled by the producing company. For the minors, of course, this was a fact of life. What little we know of budgetary planning within the studios shows this to be the case. This took the form of taking gross intake for the previous year, deducting distribution and advertising as costs and retained profits as charges and then scheduling production of A, B and C films out of what is left. However these costs/charges were apportioned, their extent was determined by performance on the US total market.[23]

Looking at the global level of activity, we find that every season produces its hits, but that no particular producer can be absolutely certain of monopolizing the 'hit' product. What this means is that any season of releases resembled, at first sight, a zero-sum game with some producers having a time-dated monopoly of the total available market, theoretically speaking, since their film or films are the most popular.[24] But it is immediately apparent that if one producer (studio) has the only hit (improbable extreme) this does not mean that he alone will benefit from it. On the contrary, other producers without hits will be prepared to show such a film as exhibitors in order to write off production losses. What the lucky producer has therefore is a monopoly (copy) right to a film which will give his company access to his competitors' screen time for a price. This price – notionally the cost of distribution and/or exhibition, and usually not less than 35 per cent of the gross – is bearable precisely because of the overall gearing of costs to revenues and because, of course, such exchanges do not occur on a unilateral basis. On the contrary, what operates is a system of multilateral but unequal exchanges. For on the rough assumption, but it is always an empirical question, of a random distribution of hits, then those companies with the larger, or conversely more effectively located, number of theatres (e.g. in the 1930s and 1940s Paramount compared to MGM) would garner the higher earnings. The better the theatres or the greater the number controlled by a given company, then the larger proportions of earnings going to that company as an exhibitor of either its own or another company's product. Accordingly amortization schedules, i.e. the rate at which films recover their costs, show the majority earnings of a film accruing whilst it is within its 'own' theatres, and the companies differ, depending on holdings, on the rate of return at which this majority is reached.[25]

Post-classical Hollywood, following the consent decree in 1948, begins with the separation off of the majority of the theatres held by the majors and their formation into separate exhibition chains dealing at arm's length with all distributors. This development evidently increased the instability built into the foregoing arrangements:

> The decrees of divorcement and divestiture effectively put an end to the organised control of the industry. The bottleneck in the flow of films created by the majors' near monopoly of first-run theatres was broken. Large numbers of subsequent-run theatres received earlier access to films and were also relieved of the oppressive restrictions of block booking. Divorcement also curtailed the monopoly power of the five majors on the distribution level. Other distributors and independent producers were given freer entry to compete in the market for screen time.[26]

We now know that Conant's remarks about the decline of the majors were exaggerated, and that what in fact happened was that the majors re-established dominance over independent production either as financiers/studio lessors or as distributors.[27] In either mode there was a decisive recentring of control on distribution by virtue of four tactics which compensated for the impact of partial divorcement. Firstly, the development of a sliding scale of rental charges ensured that distributors received more on films of proven popularity. Secondly, there developed forms of *de facto* rather than *de jure* ownership by such means as the 90–100 per cent deal or the leasing of theatres. Thirdly, because distribution represented the area of least risk, distribution costs and investment being the first to be paid off, independent producers began to carry the risk of meeting overheads. Fourthly, because in a period in which theatrical revenues were declining overall, if not for specific hits, it was rational to locate control at a point where supply and demand coincided without having to bear the costs of ineffective product and unused seating. A major in distribution had the capacity to cancel out hits and misses and moreover exert a steady upward pressure on its charges to independent production companies and independent exhibition. As a result divestiture of theatres went further than envisaged in the decrees and there was a steady rise in the costs of distribution; exhibitors paid rentals at 31 per cent of box office in 1946 and by 1953 at 36 per cent.[28] In 1955 for a picture with a negative cost of $3 million, the distribution costs – including printing and advertising – would run to $2.5 million[29] and as is well known recent complaints about 'creative accounting' on overheads point, if not to the alleged fraud, to an unimpaired upward tendency in such costs.

Essentially, despite the myriad details of restabilization which cannot be pursued here, e.g. the development of telefilm production and sales, the major studios (minus RKO) in their new corporate incarnations still subtend production and exhibition under a cartel control, albeit in a more turbulent theatrical environment. Further, since the big circuits still maintain, either as the divested wings of former majors or as traditional buying circuits, strong informal ties with the new production finance-distribution complexes, the same pattern of balkanized transactions pertains or, failing that, is secured by clearance arrangements, i.e. the preferential accessing of films to exhibitors of choice.[30]

Given these broad structural specifications, we can now examine the functioning of the star system within them. The key point is to re-emphasize the extent to which the major studios need to stabilize competition within a global pattern of co-operation and to query how this might occur. The answer relates to the strategic role of production values. For accepting that each major, via block booking and related mechanisms, can dispose of average product on its own markets, such values become the means to extend the potential market from the legally controlled to the contractually negotiable limits. If a given studio can establish its supremacy over demand by virtue of the quality of its product then its competitors will be prepared to take its product into their theatres. At the same time it needs to be admitted that a periodic 'hit' was necessary to sustain block booking, even if such an arrangement reduced the need to produce so many hits to maintain a market. For normal operations, the tied aspect of the market could be assumed since establishing supremacy over a competitor's market has the same effect as stabilizing one's own. Conversely to take a competitor's 'hit' would shore up one's own tied market, since in the last analysis exhibitors are less concerned about where product comes from so long as they may have it to show. Theoretically, if a given major never produced a hit, block-booking would never have succeeded, but this is an empirical impossibility. Qualitative competition is all very well, but as the Paramount judgment established even in the vertically integrated period, no effective monopoly control over quality production had ever operated. Indeed, the absence of such a control was the *raison d'être* for the development of extensive theatre ownership, and to a degree it is difficult to assess block booking considerably abated the extent of qualitative competition.[31] So, too, in post-studio Hollywood, the existence of television outlets for routine product means that the market for film is less competitive qualitatively than a restricted focus on the theatrical film market would suggest, though there admittedly such competition has intensified. The reason for the absence of such a monopoly is integral to the nature of film itself as a collective artistic product. Not only does film-making entail the co-ordination of a large number of artistic inputs to achieve a qualitative objective, but whatever the merit of that objective it remains a scatter for subjective appraisal. This dual contingency has meant that no radical strategy of monopolizing talent can ever ensure a uniform run of compensating hits. Given such a level of uncertainty such a policy would be disastrously expensive. By the same token, a strategy of competition through technical excellence would simply increase the cost of failure without necessarily, or even probably, increasing the number of hits. The corporate resolution to this problem – the problem of the costliness of monopolizing talent and expertise – has been to develop a system of casual or picture-by-picture employment, which has affected both craft and artistic labour.[32] Casualization does and did not finally exclude the practice of permanent employment for some employees, e.g. production executives, certain directors, story department, costumers and so on, but this is an exception and a relative privilege. In the studio period the stars are notable for the fact that of all the executive level salaried employees engaged on a picture-by-picture basis (as opposed to studio-based executives), they have the status of full-time (40 weeks) salaried staff. Stars' salaries, like full-time executives', come from the fixed studio overhead charges, even though they are written into the cost structure of particular films.[33] Further, the operation of the contract system meant that stars as a category of 'creative' personnel, let alone as individuals, were more clearly tied to particular studios than other functionaries of the same rank, e.g. producers, directors, and writers, who tended to operate on a freelance basis, circulating, like John Ford, between major and minor studios. As a consequence of the circulation of freelance talent the skills of film-making tended to become generalized within the occupational community as a whole, either by the movement of personnel or by imitation.

The stars stand against this trend in two important respects: firstly, as a group they were legally prevented from working on a freelance basis unless the studio consented, determining how and by whom the stars' services are exploited (i.e. via the loan-out system). Secondly, because stars are constrained to offer services that centre on their presence rather than their performances – in terms of craft-based notions of virtuosity – their circulation does not lead to a loss of competitive edge. One might say that once a technical accomplishment is unveiled publicly, it is public property since it is usually an extension of already understood collective practices. One more appearance by June Allyson, however, is very likely to be one more appearance by June Allyson. The structuring of a star's performance on personality rather than character emphasizes what is unique to the player rather than what is generalizable to the craft and produces a performance that can only be impersonated, since it is too specific to be replicated. Since public interest has been channelled into stardom, attempts at impersonation only reinforce the 'uniqueness' of the star. In short, the ideology of stardom, with its associated individualism, protects the studio from the risk of their property becoming public domain. It is as well to recognize that the star would have a vested interest in being a personality as well. This emphasis excludes competitors and in terms of contract negotiations it would be disadvantageous to say the least to emphasize how much 'personality' relies on studio technology; rather, the star would want to highlight the uniqueness and natural quality of the elements of the image on the screen. In this light, outrageous lifestyles, temperamentalism and physical culturalism are not self-indulgent fantasies. Finally, it would not do to underestimate the extent to which stars were hoarded even within the cartel.

Thus far we can determine on deductive grounds that competition between the majors could not be routinized on grounds of technical excellence. At this point the disjunction between star and character becomes operative. To the extent that a star as a 'meaning event' is not subordinated to the technical realization process of the narrative, i.e. to the extent that the star is, unlike other actors, the bearer of a meaning that transcends the plotted meaning, then the star can function as a marker of a quality – a meta-meaning – that survives particular embodiments. In other words, stars can circulate without necessarily losing their quality of being a distinct property. In the best of all possible worlds, a star's relationship to a narrative would be one of affirmation of a personality with box-office power. But given that even within the home studio not every casting of a star is successful in those terms, the gap between star personality image and character becomes an adaptive mechanism for coping with failures and capitalizing on hits. But to capitalize on hits, it is essential that films circulate into a competitor's territory. Once again, the star avoids the problems of being overly associated with a particular studio which might if highlighted convey an invidious message of triumph. Lastly, since we are dealing with a pragmatic system of manufacture, the emphasis on the star has the virtue of providing a concrete meaning to guide the process of production, exhibition and consumption. For these reasons – and we would consider the matter of territorial circulation as most important – though the major studios had trademarks for copyright purposes emphasis in publicity has been given either to the global evocation of 'Hollywood' or to the 'stars'. Handel[34] points out that the American public do not see trademarks and story types as a reliable means for judging films for the good reason that neither of these indicate that a particular quality of filmic experience is guaranteed, whereas stars by continuity of image do. Similarly, where stars fail to honour that guarantee, there is a tendency for unsuccessful films to be transcended by the continuity of the image. Thus for example, a study of Ingrid Bergman found that her image only reflected a few of the roles she had played, inconsistent characterizations being written out.[35]

To put it as a formula, the star is that level of meaning that supports the claim to give the public what it wants without installing an unrealizable identification of such a claim with a given studio. At the same time this focus on stars and conflict over stardom provides the gratuitous benefit of providing a level of conflict consistent with reconstructing monopolistic practices and corporate power in individualistic competitive terms. It is, in short, good public relations. With the relaxation of studio control the method of contracting is transformed but the derived characteristics from that period still form the basis of stardom.

Stardom: employee/ownership relationships

We can now bring these considerations to bear on the objectives and possibilities governing the occupational role of a star. As pointed out above, the emphasis on the personality of the actor over the role has emerged as a characteristic of the popular cinema, and the star totalizes this tendency. However, this totalization is not a matter of culmination but rather an exogenous development inscribed into film acting. So far we have indicated the impress of distribution and corporate control as the cutting edge of this inscription; now we want to note its re-enforcement in the wage bargaining process. To make this clear, we saw that it is necessary to make a distinction between star personality image and character. Taking a 'natural' attitude to these variables – bracketing off the very extensive interaction between image and character that occurs throughout a career – it is apparent that the star, as a rational economic agent, would be concerned to maintain as tight a correlation between self, as appearance and personal style, and a 'viable' star personality image as is feasible. To realize this it is necessary to distinguish between the legal and physical aspects of ownership of the image. Whilst the contract for the employment of the star closely stipulates the limits on the utilization of the image and the necessity for the preservation of its physical/psychological bearer as a matter of legal ownership, nevertheless it remains factually the case that the star is ultimately the possessor of the image, because it is indexically linked to his or her person.[36] The fact that such an image may be a studio fabrication, and hence may be technically an icon not an index of its bearer, qualifies but does not refute this fundamental relationship. What this means in effect is that a legal monopoly confronts a physical or natural monopoly in a bargaining relationship. The 'good' to be exchanged is the services of the star for remuneration *and* the opportunity to further expose the stellar image. (That stardom did not represent an exchange for cash alone was recognized in the NRA period by the theory of prior repute which said that the employer materially improved the quality and value of a star by offering employment.) It could be observed, of course, that the theory of strict legality gives the employer the right to do what he will with the star, but this ignores the *de facto* situation that a star can seriously affect the costs of production by non-co-operation and other forms of temperamental 'sabotage', a risk-laden strategy, to be sure, but a manoeuvrable space.[37]

It is necessary to make a final distinction and connection. The concepts of formal and real subsumption of labour under capital were introduced by Marx to indicate two modes in the subordination of labour.[38] Formal subsumption refers to the situation in which capital as the employer does not intervene directly into the production process or labour process and expects only to receive the finished product to some agreed timetable and specification. Real subsumption refers to a situation of control in which the capitalist intervenes directly in the labour process, determining the nature and pace of production in detail. The general distinction, which admittedly needs some qualification for substantive analysis, can be applied to the star. The real subsumption process operating with stardom will lead to a systematic tendency to enforce an overlap between the star image and character, such that all potential characters are reduced to one transfilmic star personality image. This latter, for purposes of public, as opposed to private, identity, will be the star's self or personality. Such a fusion, whilst on one side oppressive, e.g. morality clauses and studio 'vetting', at the same time is in line with the star's economic interests, since the further he or she can enforce such an equation the greater his or her irreplaceability and bargaining power.

In such a circumstance the star will not be concerned with the public 'commentary' implications of a given narrative, nor to indicate the structural limits of the individual in the filmed world, but rather will be concerned to create out of such materials a *de facto* vehicle. In such a circumstance the social meaning given to stardom will tend to be transcendental and populist, i.e. of a universal human essence that says in effect that here is a person who remains the same in a variety of contexts, locations and environments.

The break-up of the studio system and the rise of sub-contractual 'putting out' of production indicates a shift from real to formal subsumption. What we would expect in the case of the star is a relaxation of the strategy of control by means of a univocal emphasis on star image and a corresponding emergent emphasis on the projection of character. There are a number of reasons for this shift operating as push factors – e.g. the economic advantages of incorporation for taxation purposes – but the key pull factor is the changing method of film financing. If films are now to be financed on an individual basis, because the hits will no longer support the failures as part of a commonly financed production budget, then it follows that each film must stand on its own merits, be competitive as an integral act of communication. This also means that a successful characterization must 'stand' in its own terms. The rise of independent production and a picture-by-picture system of contracts therefore produces a contradiction at the heart of stardom: there is a need to reproduce the distance between star image and character since the potential for failure remains. But at the same time character becomes an integral variable in its own right, no longer simply collapsible into star image. One apparent resolution is to develop an 'actorly' image, i.e. to claim technical excellence as the basis of reputation. However, this resolution is obviously limited by the fact that there is no consistent relationship between professional and commercial success. This leaves the alternative of developing a star image that indicates the 'social issues' indicated by carefully selected narratives since these issues transcend particular films.

In the development of formal subsumption, when stars start to become in effect the proprietors of their own image, we should expect that the image of the star will cease to project a simple personality and take on a reflexive, i.e. accountable, relationship to the actorly and communication aspects of his or her work. In effect, stars begin to show a distance from their own image, which becomes an object for manipulation in relation to character, and develop at the level of public interaction a self which is relatively autonomous of star image and characterizations. The social meaning given to stardom under these circumstances will be that of the professional communicator in a position of 'representative' engagement with the 'real' world of the audience through the medium of cinema. It is as well to emphasize that this nuance in the star image may not *necessarily* have any thoroughgoing material basis – stars in a situation of formal subordination are not necessarily accomplished and committed actors, nor are they closer to the concerns of their audience, since they remain a remote elite, albeit more conscious of purpose. But their image now contains the import of social representativeness; which is to say that in this situation stars no longer merely engage in a personality display whose commentary implications are a side effect construed by culture critics.

It is conventional to regard this shift as a process of politicization. However, it is important to note that what is entailed is a modulation of a particular articulation of politics. Stars, whether their image has direct or indirect political implications, have the same prominence in public culture as political functionaries, but this prominence is as a result of their personally based rather than collectively based accomplishments. As such the new 'lifestyle' stars, as Walker has called them,[39] may represent eccentric perspectives on collective politics which have not become public by virtue of being ironed out in the process of collective formulation. Formal subsumption stars certainly bring social issues on to the collective agenda, but it is apparent that that action does not automatically make their commentary politically effective for the collectivities within the audience. They may provide 'materials' to be used politically, but that is another question.

Lastly, the shift from formal to real and vice versa is a recurrent phenomenon in any situation of employment. For sharpness we use it here to highlight the shift between studio and post-studio Hollywood because it is in this transition that the different approaches to stardom become typical, rather than individual. Since at the level of film what is involved is the question of the extent to which stars are prepared either to enhance the impact of the narrative by submerging themselves in character or alternatively to enhance the impact of their image, it is clear that both approaches are to be found in the studio and post-studio periods. But it is the state of economic organization, and not the intention of specific stars, that makes these strategies dominant or subordinate options.

Clark Gable and Burt Lancaster

Having laid out some general points of analysis, we want in conclusion to show these processes working in actual cases To do this – and no claim to exhaustive demonstration is being advanced – it is useful to contrast the careers of Clark Gable and Burt Lancaster. The reasons for this selection are essentially three:

(a) Star type

Gable and Lancaster began their careers – some fifteen years apart – in the role of 'heavy' and after successive casting still retained the basic identity – based on body image – of the physically aggressive rather than romantic male lead. Of Gable's first twelve films, all made in 1931, six were gangster roles in accordance with the latest 'hit' trend and of the remaining six only two, *The Easiest Way* and *Laughing Sinners*, had Gable in non-deviant roles. Very early on the image of Gable was considered by MGM to be a replacement or substitute for another 'heavy' star, Wallace Beery, and but for these two exceptions, which show inconsistent casting, their contractee for the 1931 films was cast accordingly.[40] So decisive was Gable's image as a 'heavy' at this time, that as is well known Frank Capra demurred at using Gable in *It Happened One Night*.[41] Lancaster, considered to be another William Bendix, moved to instant stardom in 1946 in Siodmak's *The Killers* as the 'dumb Swede' and consolidated this heavy image with his role in Dassin's *Brute Force* – a title held to sum up Lancaster's image with uncanny appropriateness. These, and the later released but earlier played role of the Sheriff in *Desert Fury*, confirmed Lancaster's image as a powerful male lead, much like Gable operating on the violent fringe of the law.[42] Both actors entered the star category at a relatively late age, even for males – Gable at 30 and Lancaster at 33 – and both remained despite vicissitudes in the major league for over twenty-five years. Both actors showed early on in their careers the keynote of stardom, the capacity to draw a hit level of box office, despite casting. In the period, 1932–9 Gable was the top drawing star in Hollywood and even in his last years at MGM, from 1945 to 1954 – when he was frequently featured in inferior product that would, in the opinion of one unnamed MGM executive, have damaged the reputation of any star – was nevertheless able to average $4 million gross per picture.[43] Lancaster in roughly the same period was able to guarantee a minimum of $1 million gross. In the post-studio period both stars operated without the cast-iron benefit of block booking.

These factors of similiarity, rough and ready as they are, suggest that the comparison is not unbalanced in principle. But more important than similarities are the differences between the two stars, the specifying variables. These constitute reasons (b) and (c) for the comparison.

(b) Formal and real subsumption: low and high autonomy stars

Looked at from the point of view of the career track of a star, the patterning of formal and real subsumption becomes a question of autonomy. Gable is on any evaluation a low autonomy star compared to Lancaster. Gable's career track is determined by two factors, his signing as a contract star at MGM, in 1931 – at first on a two-year and then on a seven-year contract, with the usual six-month option – and the comparatively low salary of $350 a week on forty weeks.[44] This level of salary, whilst arguably an effect of a mood of salary cutting that affected bargaining in the 1930s, is also an indication of MGM's attitude towards Gable's potential as a star. John Gilbert, for example, a star on the wane, was receiving $520,000 a year at this time. Within the year, despite evidence of spiralling popularity, Gable was loaned out twice, to Warners for *Night Nurse* and to First National for *The Finger Points*. Both roles were considered to be damaging to anyone seeking stardom and it seems that MGM were more concerned with the short-term gain of the loan-out than with building a long-term investment. Probably it is correct to say that the Depression dictated such a policy, but it is worth noting that this did not hit the industry until 1932 and even then MGM stayed within profit. Even though a cost-cutting exercise was in operation, Gable's popularity would have justified forgoing the earnings of damaging loan-outs if the studio had been convinced of his star potential. But apparently the studio was not. This initial lack of conviction appears to have dogged his career and it seems plausible to relate this to the fact that Gable as an actor was unusually dependent on studio resources, e.g. directors, to maintain his performance and appearance as a star. Whether this was because of factors of disposition – his insecurity about his ability – or as an over-reaction to the threat of dismissal and exclusion from motion pictures by L. B. Mayer when he staged a walk-out in 1932 for more pay or, finally, because of his attachment to the prestige of MGM, we need not speculate.[45] But the fact is that despite rough treatment and under-valuing by MGM, Gable became a virtual company man there for nearly a quarter of a century. Ironically it was not until Gable gained an Oscar in 1935, for the role he did not want (and was given as a punishment) in *It Happened One Night*, that MGM began to pay Gable a salary of star dimensions and gave him his own unit to work with.[46] But for all that, his salary, initiated at such a low starting point, lagged behind that of comparable stars and in spite of his being one of the most successful box-office stars on the MGM roster.[47]

It was no doubt something of a pointed demonstration of his 'relative deprivation' that Gable's third wife, Carole Lombard, was able as a freelance actress to earn $465,000 in 1937 and the right to a percentage share in her pictures. Whilst it is true that one year's earnings may be eccentric it is nevertheless significant that in 1938 as a straight salary Gable reported earnings of $272,000. It was not until after his contract with MGM expired in 1954, when as the longest-serving contract star ever he was earning $7500 a week on forty weeks, that Gable was to command what he had long been seeking: a flat fee and a percentage. Given that in Hollywood the association between earnings and prestige was high, this long-suffering acceptance of lower earnings is striking.[48]

Lancaster, by contrast, was never to experience the process of real subsumption, since he secured a degree of autonomy over his career at the moment of its inception. His first contract was with Hal B. Wallis productions, which operated as an independent under a sub-contract with Paramount. Lancaster was to receive $1100 a week whilst preparing for a test, $10,000 for passing it and $1250 a week when working thereafter. What is crucial about this signing was the nature of the career choice it consciously entailed. Alternative offers – said to be six in all – were for the seven years' contract with a major studio with the usual six-month renewable option. Lancaster signed with Wallis on a similar seven-year basis, to make two pictures a year with the unusual feature that the star could make one picture a year with any other company.[49] From the start, then, Lancaster made the decision to distance himself from any particular company. In the first year of his contract with Wallis, he made three films, with a small showcase part in Paramount's all star *Variety Girl*. Significantly the first film of Lancaster's to be released, *The Killers*, was done at Universal for Mark Hellinger, and his second, *Brute Force*, once more for Hellinger and again at Universal. So in effect, as his contract for Wallis began he was already associated with another producer. In fact the Wallis production of *Desert Fury* was made before but released after these two star-making films, rejigged to give the Lancaster character greater prominence. Following these 'tough lead' image-establishing performances, Lancaster made *I Walk Alone* with another Wallis contractee, Kirk Douglas, which continued the work of image confirmation. But then, presumably as an exercise of his option, he took a reputedly large salary cut to make Arthur Miller's *All My Sons* with Edward G. Robinson at Universal, in an effort to counter criticisms of his inability to turn in expressive performances.[50] This modulation of contractual and option roles and the counterpart of efforts to modulate between star image and character was to emerge as an established pattern following the formation, with his agent Hecht, of Norma Productions in 1948, later metamorphosed into Hecht-Hill-Lancaster and not dissolved until 1959. In effect, then, within less than two years Lancaster realized his ambition, defined before his rise to stardom, to become an actor-producer. In order not to over-emphasize the high autonomy shape of his career, it is as well to note that even by 1953 Lancaster was contractually obligated to Wallis. According to one source, for his part in *From Here to Eternity* Lancaster received $73,000, and Wallis received from Columbia the equivalent of $330,000.[51]

(c) Image-character relations

Looking at Gable and Lancaster in terms of star image and character, we find a different pattern of relationship that marks off the two stars more certainly than differences in ability. Lancaster has been less content to be a personality and has sought the accolade of 'actor', whereas Gable certainly did not. It is not the aim here to offer an opinion on Lancaster's success in this aim or for that matter Gable's failure – if it is such – but rather to emphasize the difference in orientation between the two stars.

Gable's attitude towards his image, I would argue, stems from his position of dependency. This is best exemplified in the interview he gave at the beginning of his career in 1933 to *Photoplay*:

> My advice has never been asked about a picture. I have never
> been consulted about what I'd like to play. I just work here . . .
> the company has an investment in me. It's my business to work,
> not to think . . . I read in the paper that I was going to play
> *Susan Lennox*. I walked on the lot one day and was told I was
> to play *Red Dust* in place of John Gilbert.[52]

This statement was considered frank enough to be dangerous and the studio thereafter began to 'protect' Gable from further unguarded utterances (especially of the kind that would suggest that the star was not the demiurge of the cinematic process as publicity suggested). We can take it that the state of affairs depicted by Gable in 1933 was to set the 'tone', albeit not the detail, of subsequent producer-star relations, because Eddie Mannix of MGM has put the matter on record:

> Clark ... after he became a star was the name player who gave
> directors the least trouble. He felt that the director was the
> captain of the ship and that it was his job, as a member of the
> crew, to take the captain's orders. He could be talked into doing
> things if you could convince him what you wanted made sense.[53]

What is interesting about this observation is that it occurs after Gable had been given his own 'unit' and it is served up to explain Gable's disastrous performance in *Parnell* (1937). What that film indicates is a conflict between star image and character, with the star failing to protect his image from inappropriate casting, under reportedly great pressure from L. B. Mayer. The fact that Gable gave in here is less important than the fact that Gable shows up the strategy appropriate to real subsumption, the jealous protection of image. This sensitivity to star image as a 'value' to be protected comes out periodically through Gable's career in a tendency to demur – even under threat of potential loss of earnings through suspension, which he took seriously – at playing roles that were to have a decisive impact on his popularity: *Red Dust, It Happened One Night, Gone With the Wind* and *Mutiny On The Bounty*. The first two were objected to because he felt he was being downgraded by the role or the loan-out and the others because he felt exposed to the charge of being a poor actor. It is of course paradoxical that these roles, more than any others, were to re-enforce his star image, but this does not invalidate his basic approach so much as his judgment.

The best available evidence we have is one of Gable's rare public observations on his career, given retrospectively after he had gone freelance:

> At one time if I was given a line to speak that wasn't in
> character I'd say Clark Gable wouldn't say that, Clark Gable
> doesn't act that way. But now it's different. Now I'd play
> anything. Dope fiends, drunks, cowards, Marlon Brando's father.
> I should say I could go on playing romantic roles until I was 65.
> Maybe longer. Maybe till 80. Who knows?[54]

What the statement basically shows is that for Clark Gable playing a character is playing star image. As argued here this approach is comprehensible and rational in the context of real subsumption:

> Though he never analysed his acting, Gable kept a sharp eye on
> his public image and was quick off the mark to protect it. The
> gravest threat to it was any situation which subordinated him to
> a woman. This is why he was particularly riled by the publicity
> slogan 'Gable's back and Garson's got him'.[55]

To which we can add that Gable was also shy of roles that would require him to act in the normative sense of losing himself in a character. This emphasis puts Gable unequivocally in the position of a low autonomy star. One fond appreciation of him elevates this strategy position to an indicator of great acting:

> He would be highly suspicious of anyone who called him a Brechtian actor, yet he unknowingly was one. His detachment was miles away from the Stanislavskian school of acting by identification, brought to films by Brando, Steiger, and the Actor's Studio crowd. Gable did not live the part but often merely showed it, held it before the audience by keeping himself one or two steps removed.

The writer continues, almost in contradiction,

> He was a very good actor, blessed and cursed with such projection of personality that he was often accused of merely playing himself. This is not true at all: in thirty years and sixty-six films, he played Gable, a finely tuned instrument of infinite variety. It belonged to him, but was not really he. The real Gable is another matter, another man.[56]

Such are the shifts of self, character and star image in the case of real subsumption. The same author provides a useful description of Gable's basic personality image:

> Ears too big, manners too rough, he emerged as the populist thirties Everyman. Men could identify with him as he went about dispensing vicarious thrills such as telling the boss where to get off or bringing the haughty down a peg, or for women, he was the promise of the powerful, earthy sexuality that could hopefully be found at the Woolworth counter.[57]

If this description is bearable as describing what Gable does, what he is – the 'populist' hero constant in all social contexts – emerges as an extension of the strategy of reducing all character to the star image personality.

In contrast to Gable, Lancaster presents a process of distancing from image, with a career-track tendency to modulate personality reproduction with a projection of characters that indicate social concern for the film's 'message' and actorly range. This drive is perhaps best indicated in his early decision to take the part of Chris Keller in *All My Sons*. The role of Keller met with objection from Wallis on the grounds that it would harm Lancaster to play a son who 'betrays' his father, albeit for high moral purpose. Gable in a parallel situation needed, as we saw, no reminding, but for Lancaster the part was an opportunity for a public statement:

> I wanted to play him because he had the courage to make his

father realise that he was just as responsible for the deaths of many servicemen as if he had murdered them. I had been in the Army, I had no difficulty in duplicating Chris' feelings. I believe that each person shares a responsibility for the welfare of others.[58]

So, as pointed out above, after two years of stardom Lancaster was prepared to introduce ambiguity into his stellar image and, moreover, share the foregrounding of the action with other actors. This process of counterpointing 'man of action' with 'thinking' roles was to become a persistent feature of Lancaster's career. In 1951 *Ten Tall Men* interfaces with *Jim Thorpe – All American*; in 1952 *The Crimson Pirate* with *Come Back Little Sheba*; in 1954 *Vera Cruz* with *Apache*; in 1957 *Gunfight at the OK Corral* with *The Sweet Smell of Success*; in 1968 *The Scalphunters* with *The Swimmer*; in 1977 *The Cassandra Crossing* with *Twilight's Last Gleaming*. The box-office success of these films is variable, as are their creative merits – though a rule of thumb would give the former to the first film and the latter to the last – but what is important is that each role shows a play-off of star and character. We are not then dealing with an absolute break with the approach of Gable, but a manipulation of the relationship. The material basis of this manipulation is certainly to be found in Lancaster's activities as a producer, in which role he becomes the proprietor, under subcontract to major studios, of his own image as well as the caretaker of his professional reputation. Again it would not do to over-idealize Lancaster's commitment as running wild of commercial astuteness. In this connection, it is worth recalling that *Marty*, made by Hecht-Hill-Lancaster in 1955, which established their reputation as 'realists' once and for all, was conceived as a tax loss.[59] Further, it is important to note as an indicator of a conscious strategy that Lancaster's approach to stardom was not simply a matter of suffering stardom for contractual purposes and producing 'thinking' films in his own right. On the contrary, and sensibly, Lancaster uses his own company sometimes to bolster his star image and enhance his bargaining power for creative control in the long term:

I'll go on making swashbucklers for my own company. But in my outside pictures, I want to do things that will help me as an actor against the time when I have to give up jumping around.[60]

This statement, following Lancaster's unsuccessful casting in *Come Back Little Sheba*, needs balancing against another made at the same time:

[For *Come Back Little Sheba*] I got extraordinarily interesting reviews for the first time. The tendency of the reviewer is to

regard you in the image you had before. In other words I was
the leading man or the swashbuckler, blah-blah-blah. And
suddenly they began to think of me as a serious actor and that
was a progression in my career.[61]

For Lancaster, then, the image is not an absolutely essential public
identity but a resource to be manipulated to gain autonomy:

If you make good films, you're a good businessman. Being a
businessman, a producer, is like giving birth to a baby. I enjoy
the business side of the films I make with Mr Hecht more than
the acting. You feel it's more yours – as an actor you're at the
whim of the producer. Someone else is laying down the rules. I
prefer to be in the driver's seat.[62]

At the same time, stardom is seen as a limited accomplishment:

In terms of popular appeal what counts is appearance and
personality. Skill as an actor, that's something extra.[63]

With its own definite requirements:

People go to the movies to see the star. Whatever you are
playing they come looking for you. The real you, the star's
unique personality, must never be submerged.[64]

The limitations of stardom are therefore partially transcended (and
commercial possibilities exploited) by producing. Failing that, an
actor must be prepared to take risks and forgo a particular kind of
success:

Every actor, in order to learn his trade, has to subject himself to
experience that might perhaps be beyond what he feels he can
encompass. I've always tried to do different things, things I
wasn't even sure I could do ... People like Clark Gable and Gary
Cooper played, for the most part, themselves, and did it
successfully. That kind of success was not what I was after. It
depends on the individual actor, what his needs are and what he
feels he has to do about his own work.[65]

This perception of the limits of stardom means that Lancaster's involvement in the films he undertakes is not primarily to protect his
image but also, where this is compatible with the plot, if not the
desire of the director, to make the maximum effectiveness out of a
given dramatic situation. This approach has led to Lancaster's
apparently deserved reputation as a 'difficult actor'. Though it is
mainly a complaint voiced by directors, it is interesting to note
Jeanne Moreau's observation:

Burt Lancaster! Before he can pick up an ashtray, he discusses
motivation for an hour or two. You want to say, just pick up the
ashtray and shut up.[66]

Thus, as opposed to Gable, Lancaster is concerned less with conflict over image than with conflict over characterization. This conflict, evidently an aspect of his involvement as a producer – and rarely as a director – is basically an expression of a persistent drive to maintain a position of formal subsumption within film work. As a consequence Lancaster is omnivorously interested in the production process of film:

He has always felt that it was his job as a star to be involved with production and scripts have always been his primary concern. He is thoroughly honest and his candour can be brutal, but he is critically and constructively valuable at production conferences.[67]

This interest can at times take on a high tone:

Films in their way are history making. Like all good art they illuminate something. This doesn't mean that all films should be serious things. There's a good deal of room for the pleasant fun film. But people need to be made more aware. In the final analysis, the direction life takes will fall into their own hands. They will have to make the decisions as to how they want their society to move. So all art must take that into consideration – and film can be one of the great art forms.[68]

That Lancaster took this social commentary role seriously is probably best borne out by his explanation for the dissolution of Hecht-Hill-Lancaster:

We had built up an organization that was too big for the things we wanted to do. We had taken on some of the overhead-aches of a major studio, and could no longer afford to operate the way we wanted to. You can't spend two or three years preparing for a film that will have limited appeal when your overhead is the size of ours.[69]

Success was beginning to undermine the project of 'serious' film-making and rather than submit himself to the subsumption constraints of stardom – to become in effect an employer-employee pursuing Gable-style objectives – Lancaster chooses to shed these pressures in favour of his own interests in the social meaning of characterizations.

What marks Lancaster off from Gable as a star is not therefore an absolute break, a rejection of the vehicle, but a calculating use of star image that turns on the discontinuities of character. The meaning of Lancaster's image is thereby transformed into a form of realist reference to external events – using the term realist to imply 'consciously interpretative in relation to a particular viewpoint.'[70] Rather than evaluate this viewpoint, which co-ordinates with Democratic Liberalism, the point to emphasize is that the image of Lancaster has shifted from being self-sponsorship towards the sponsorship of themes of social concern. This does not mean that Lancaster is prepared to forgo his position of star – guarantor of sales for production – but that his stardom is given the status of an expert in providing awareness through entertainment. If the stardom of Gable is a form of 'being there', the stardom of Lancaster begins the turn towards advocacy.

Conclusion

As far as it goes the analysis of Gable and Lancaster bears out the expectations prompted by the analysis of changing production relations. The tentativeness in this statement stems mainly from the fact that a more detailed study of their careers might introduce qualifications into the final reckoning. For all that, it is too much to expect that further analysis would do more than temper the sharpness of the contrast drawn here. The *reductio ad absurdum* of this sort of structural explanation would be to claim that such changes are merely an expression of the differences in the personality of Gable and Lancaster. That such a difference must be considered can be readily admitted – it might for example become important in examining the different strategies of stars in the same era of film organization. But the choice of Gable and Lancaster has been made to present the strongest possible case; personality differences are a necessary but not sufficient condition for the changes indicated. It should always be recalled in considering stars that they are highly selected phenomena. Before any star – out of the large number present – can meet with public approval he or she must be selected by those governing the current organization of production. Indeed, it is a consistent position that the former is governed as a possibility by the reality of the latter. Lancaster is able to capitalize on changed production conditions, but no more than Gable could he create those conditions.

This does not imply that Lancaster's pronouncements are mere attitudinizing; it means that as far as we know his private personality fits with the organizational reality as he encountered it. Or rather, his action is part of the process in which such realities are encountered, defined and tested. In this respect the presentation above, for reasons of definition, is too sharply drawn since the formation of a star image and the allied strategy is an emergent process.

Lastly, the shift from personality to character has been explained in terms different from the usual one of audience sophistication. The changes indicated in fact occurred before the changing interests of the audience were registered in Hollywood. Indeed, Hecht-Hill-Lancaster are a part of this process of registration. Correspondingly, the change in the form of stardom predates the impact of the tastes of the 'youth audience' of the 1960s.

Notes

1 Elliot Krause, *The Sociology of Occupations* (New York: Little, Brown, 1971).

2 Murray Ross, *Stars and Strikes* (New York: Columbia University Press, 1941).

3 See Adolph Zukor, *The Public Is Never Wrong* (London: Cassell, 1953).

4 Edgar Morin, *The Stars* (New York and London: Evergreen Books, 1961), p. 34.

5 Marianne Sinclair, *Those Who Die Young* (London: Plexus, 1979), p. 13.

6 Alexander Walker, *Stardom* (Harmondsworth: Penguin, 1970), p. xi.

7 See Ezra Goodman, *The Fifty Year Decline and Fall of Hollywood* (New York: Simon & Schuster, 1961), p. 277. Cohn as the head of a 'Poverty Row' studio evidently had more reason than most to denigrate stars' abilities.

8 These and other points are more extensively elaborated in my thesis: 'The Hollywood star system: the impact of an occupational ideology on popular hero-worship', PhD thesis, University of London, 1984.

9 Richard Schickel, *The Stars* (New York: Dial Press, 1962), p. 10.

10 H. Becker, 'Art as collective action,' *American Sociological Review*, vol. 39, no. 6, p. 767f.

11 Krause, *The Sociology of Occupations*, especially p. 270f.

12 See Karl Marx, *Theories of Surplus Value*, Part I (Moscow: Progress Publishers, n.d.), pp. 166-7.

13 Leo Rosten, *Hollywood* (New York: Harcourt Brace, 1941), pp. 333-4.

14 See Erving Goffman, *The Presentation of Self in Everyday Life* (Harmondsworth: Penguin, 1969).

15 Cited in Schickel, *The Stars*, p. 15.

16 See D. Efron, *Gesture, Race and Culture* (The Hague: Mouton, 1972).

17 This is to admit that the specification of acting remains difficult because of the diffuse nature of the occupation. A definition like this one is analytically severe in order to be operational in an area of confusion.

18 It was the error of Siegfried Kracauer in *Theory of Film: The Redemption of Physical Reality* to suppose that it was.

19 See David Thomson, 'The look on the actor's face', *Sight and Sound*, vol. 46, no. 4, Autumn 1977. It may be thought that photogenicity is an absolute precondition for stardom, but such a condition is notoriously vague and is in any case an attribute possessed by more actors than the few who achieve stardom.

182   *Barry King*

20 I am alluding to the analysis of suture and the tutor code.
21 See Richard Dyer, *Stars* (London: BFI Publishing, 1979), p. 99f. and 'Four films of Lana Turner', *Movie*, no. 25, pp. 30–52.
22 Hortense Powdermaker, *Hollywood, the Dream Factory* (New York: Little, Brown, 1950).
23 M. C. Levee, in J. Tibbets, *Introduction to the Photoplay* (Shawnee Mission, Kansas: National Film Society Reprint, 1977), p. 247.
24 Mae D. Huetigg, *Economic Control of the Motion Picture Industry* (Philadelphia: University of Pennsylvania Press, 1944), shows (p. 89) that the question of theatre ownership was important as a determinant of performance. MGM has a consistently high performance, though interestingly United Artists shows an even higher performance on average.
25 W. Greenwald, 'The motion picture industry: an economic study of the history and practices of a business', PhD thesis, New York University, 1950, p. 111f.
26 Michael Conant, *Anti-Trust in the Motion Picture Industry* (Berkeley: University of California Press, 1960), p. 219.
27 David Gordon, 'Why the movie majors are still major', *Sight and Sound*, vol. 48, no. 3, Summer 1979.
28 J. Brogan, 'Aspects of the changing economic structure of the motion picture industry in the United States, MA Thesis, University of California at Los Angeles, 1971, pp. 45, 64–6.
29 F. Lincoln, 'The comeback of the movies', in Tino Balio (ed.), *The American Film Industry* (Madison: University of Wisconsin Press, 1976), p. 379.
30 See Conant, *Anti-Trust*, pp. 218–20 and also Lee Beaupré, 'How to distribute a film', included in this volume.
31 Conant, *Anti-Trust*, p. 39.
32 See Anthony Dawson, 'Patterns of production and employment in Hollywood', *Hollywood Quarterly*, vol. 14, no. 4, Summer 1950, p. 346. The terms 'craft' and 'artistic' are unfortunately too dichotomous, since both forms of labour have routine and creative elements. For convenience we stick to common usage.
33 H. Love and T. Carter, *Collective Bargaining in the Motion Picture Industry* (Berkeley: University of California Institute of Industrial Relations, 1955), pp. 5–6.
34 Leo Handel, *Hollywood Looks At Its Audience* (Urbana: University of Illinois Press, 1950), chapter 2.
35 James Damico, 'Ingrid from Lorraine to Stromboli', *Journal of Popular Film*, vol. 4, no. 1, 1975.
36 See the details of Clark Gable's contract in 1935, given in L. Tornabene, *Long Live The King* (London: W. H. Allen, 1977).
37 See National Recovery Administration, Sol A. Rosenblatt, *Report Regarding the Investigation to be Made by the President* (Washington: Government Printing Office, 1934), pp. 6–7.
38 Karl Marx, *Capital*, vol. I (Harmondsworth: Penguin, 1976), p. 1019f.
39 Walker, *Stardom*, Part 7, *passim*.
40 Rene Jordan, *Clark Gable* (New York: Pyramid, 1973), p. 21f.

41 Frank Capra, *The Name Above The Title* (New York: Macmillan, 1971), p. 164.
42 T. Thomas, *Burt Lancaster* (New York: Pyramid, 1975), p. 20f.
43 See P. Bachlin, *Histoire économique du cinéma* (Paris: La Nouvelle Edition, 1946) and *Evening News*, 17 November 1960.
44 See *Views and Reviews*, vol. 3, no. 3, 1971–2, p. 7.
45 These various possibilities are advanced by Charles Samuels, *The King of Hollywood* (London: W. H. Allen, 1962), pp. 113–15 and 119; Capra, *The Name Above The Title*, pp. 164–5; Gavin Lambert, *GWTW: The Making of Gone With The Wind* (New York: Bantam Books, 1976), p. 100. It is worth recalling also that MGM preferred to build stars – a strategy of home-growing for dependency.
46 Samuels, *The King of Hollywood*, p. 124.
47 Rosten, *Hollywood*, p. 342.
48 Samuels, *The King of Hollywood*, pp. 132–3 and Tornabene, *Long Live The King*, p. 25. At the same time Gable's personal stinginess must be seen in the context of the fact that stardom is an occupation in which it is rational to seek to maximize short-term earnings. The fact that he did not do well in this respect is more grist for the dependency argument.
49 Thomas, *Burt Lancaster*, p. 20.
50 James R. Parish, *The Tough Guys* (New Rochelle: Arlington House, 1976), p. 191.
51 Thomas, *Burt Lancaster*, p. 58. Parish, *The Tough Guys*, p. 206 gives Lancaster as receiving $120,000 and Wallis $70,000.
52 Samuels, *The King of Hollywood*, p. 145.
53 Ibid., p. 135.
54 *Evening Standard*, 17 November 1960. It is as well to emphasize the distance Gable felt from his image, as this statement implies. He may have been subordinated, but it is clear he was not beyond ridiculing the system in his own way. As Alexander Walker points out, Gable delighted in poking fun at his 'sweetheart of the world' image by appearing toothless in public – though not when it mattered. Further, and more interesting, Gable is reputed to have deliberately muffed lines so that technical crews would get overtime for retakes. Such instances do not disprove subordination, but they do demonstrate that it is never total.
55 Walker, *Stardom*, p. 296.
56 Jordan, *Clark Gable*, pp. 5 and 8.
57 Ibid, p. 5.
58 Thomas, *Burt Lancaster*, p. 30.
59 *TV Times*, 15 March 1973.
60 Parish, *The Tough Guys*, p. 206.
61 Ibid., p. 203.
62 *Daily Express*, 26 September 1958.
63 *Evening Standard*, n.d. 1958.
64 *Daily Express*, 26 September 1958.
65 Thomas, *Burt Lancaster*, p. 10.
66 Parish, *The Tough Guys*, p. 233.
67 Writer R. Kibbee, cited in Thomas, *Burt Lancaster*, p. 138.

68 Cited in Gordon Gow, 'Energy', *Films and Filming*, vol. 19, no. 1, January 1973.
69 Parish, *The Tough Guys*, p. 221.
70 Raymond Williams, 'A lecture on realism', *Screen*, vol. 18, no. 1, Spring 1977.

9 · Lee Beaupré: How to distribute a film

Film Comment, vol. 13, no. 4, July/August 1977

There remains a remarkable tendency in academic writing about the American cinema to assume an unproblematic equation between the (economic) profitability of any film and the degree to which it can be said to have satisfied or failed to satisfy the (ideological) expectations or needs of its audience. Much the same has been said about the relation of both genres and stars to returns at the box office. The inherent fallacy of this kind of approach, apart from its painful reductiveness, is not that box-office figures are irrelevant to an understanding of how an audience can be said to 'read' a film but rather that, like television ratings, they are neither reliable nor adequate data on which to rest such propositions. In film studies the most familiar response to an admission of these difficulties has been a relieved return to the text. Lee Beaupré, however, suggests that textual analysis can still be complemented by an awareness of box office success if such additional considerations as competitive release, advertising, time and season of release, manner of distribution and so on are borne in mind.

Beaupré's article on the distribution practices of Hollywood in the 1970s is excerpted from a 400-page report commissioned by Francis Ford Coppola in preparation for the release of *Apocalypse Now*. One of Beaupré's examples is *Jaws*, and the account he offers of that film's distribution complements but also importantly counterpoints and contradicts some of the conclusions reached in textual analyses. Thus, according to Beaupré, *Jaws*'s success as a film cannot be separated from the best-seller status of the novel on which it was based or from the television advertising of the film immediately prior to its 'saturation' release in 400 theatres. Stephen Heath, on the other hand, in an extremely suggestive and influential piece about the film, attributed its success to two distinct ideological levels of operation, as a Watergate film and as a white male misogynistic myth which coincided with the last summer of the Vietnam War. Neither an exclusive emphasis on the textual-ideological nor on the contextual-industrial is adequate; nor, again, are these two approaches necessarily irreconcilable. Thus it is not simply sufficient to point out that *Jaws* enjoyed a 'saturation' release to explain its success; saturation as a distribution device was neither new nor infallible. Rather, as Beaupré argues, saturation was simply one strategy among many which for this film proved particularly appropriate to the aesthetic strategies of the text itself.

Some of Beaupré's assumptions and assertions about industrial history are perhaps suspect (for instance, his comments about the role played by 'chasers' in the 1910s have been challenged by several American scholars); similarly, his attribution of the innovation of most distribution strategies to one man, Hodkinson, is but another example of the 'great man' school of film history which Branigan discusses in his article on the historiography of film colour. On the other hand, however, Beaupré's overview provides the context for both Gomery's article on the picture palace and Kerr's essay on the B *film noir*.

Finally, a brief note on the terms in which Beaupré's article is written and on the language that most trade press discussions of the industry employ. Film studies has often, not always unfoundedly, been accused of using academic and impenetrable jargon. That all specialist disciplines and professions deploy specialist and equally impenetrable vocabularies is revealed here by Beaupré's use of terms like 'look', 'air' and 'underbelly break'. That Beaupré actually attempts to explain, rather than simply assume our understanding of, these terms, however, is exemplary in several senses. First of all, because it reminds both film theorists and their critics that such arcane vocabularies are neither unusual nor untranslatable; and secondly and perhaps more importantly, because it emphasises that the industry should no more be taken at face value than are its products. Indeed, if concepts like 'house nut' and 'distributor guarantees' are not grasped by film students then it is all too easy to confuse gross and net takings (for instance) and consequently to facilitate the kinds of fallacious equations between box-office returns and popularity described above.

Considering the radical changes in American business practices over the past fifty years, it is remarkable (if not downright appalling) that modern film distribution still bears so many fundamental resemblances to methods developed by the 1920s and refined in the following two decades. Periodic media promotion of a 'new' Hollywood to the contrary, the only truly dramatic difference between sales practices in the 1930s and today, resulted not from innovative corporate managements but from a 1948 Supreme Court decision that forced the major film companies to dismantle and reorganize their vertically integrated operations.

To understand current distribution procedures, then, it is useful to take a brief backward look at the infancy and adolescence of the motion picture industry. This child, more than most, was certainly father to the man.

Past precedents

The first motion pictures were one-minute snippets of film exhibited in cabinets known as Kinetoscopes; by inserting a penny and peering through a slit, a spectator could ogle Fatima's famed Egyptian shimmy or chortle at *Fun in a Chinese Laundry*. Enterprising businessmen bought slews of Kinetoscopes and installed them in converted storerooms, then lured customers into their 'penny arcades' with the help of garish posters and obstreperous sidewalk barkers. Films were bought outright from a small number of American and European manufacturers and exhibited in the cabinets until their sprocket holes shredded.

The Kinetoscope soon gave way to the Vitascope, a machine capable of projecting film images on a screen and thus enlarging the number of people who could simultaneously watch these moving pictures. For the first few years, screen-projected films were a virtual monopoly of urban vaudeville theaters, but eventually the reasonably sophisticated customers at these music halls tired of the novelty. Once the prime attraction, movies were demoted to the role of 'chaser,' serving to clear the theater between shows or to fill time between live acts.

The penny-arcade owners, suspecting the market for 'living pictures' had barely been tapped, soon bought their own projectors, partitioned off the rear section of their arcades, installed chairs and a screen, upped the admission price of five cents and thus inaugurated the nickelodeon age. The hunch more than paid off. While vaudeville patrons may have tired of the moving-picture 'fad,' the less jaundiced working class flocked to the makeshift theaters. By 1908 an estimated 8,000 nickelodeons had opened across the country.

At first the demand for films far outstripped the supply, and the fledgling nickelodeon owner would buy any piece of celluloid that was available. After playing a picture for several days, he might then 'bicycle' the print to another house for further showings before destroying it. In response to the economic folly of purchasing prints outright for showings in only a few houses, a trading system between exhibitors evolved. Exchanges were opened in many cities; theater owners could rent prints for a fraction of their purchase price, then return them for other prints. As a given print became increasingly worn from repeated showings in the community, its rental cost was lowered.

Development of the exchange system established a line of communication between the audience and the growing number of film producers. Customer compliments or complaints about particular films were passed from the exhibitor to the exchange heads, who in turn passed the word to the producers from whom they had bought or leased the films. However inadvertently, the public began to affect the film-making process.

Although weekly nickelodeon attendance reportedly hit 14,000,000 by 1908, the burgeoning motion picture industry did not capture the interest or the imagination of successful businessmen, most of whom were repelled by the gaudiness and seeming ephemerality of the storefront enterprises. The new theater and exchange owners were predominantly Jewish immigrants quick to see the moneymaking potential of the new medium and sensitive to the entertainment needs of the lower-class customers who thronged to the arcades and nickelodeons. These former garment workers, furriers, clothing-store managers, and jewelers helped create one of the most profitable industries of the early twentieth century, but they neglected to involve knowledgeable businessmen in their empires until it was too late to revoke anachronistic practices.

From the very outset chaos reigned in the motion picture industry. There was no standard for film rental prices, and exhibitors frequently quarreled with exchanges that they suspected were giving competitors a better deal. Jealousy of the success of neighboring houses, constant scheming to be the first exhibitor in a new district, and the illegal 'duping' of prints were all regular occurrences. Commercial ethics were unknown in the squawling young industry.

To gain control of this mushrooming business, the Edison Company joined forces with its leading competitors and formed the Motion Picture Patents Company in 1909. Claiming that they alone owned patents governing the photographing, developing, and printing of motion pictures, the ten partners promptly declared a monopoly on film production and threatened to take legal action against any infringing producers. The Patents Company then set up its own distribution arm, the General Film Company, by buying the best-organized exchanges already in existence.

The trust had a stranglehold on the entire film industry. General Film announced that all theaters would henceforth be classified and charged a standard rental; the better houses would pay $100–125 per week for daily changes of programs, while the smallest theaters would pay $15. Release dates, the specified days on which films would be made available for exhibition, could no longer be 'jumped' by eager exhibitors. And all theaters would be charged a weekly license fee of $2 for their projectors at that time manufactured only by the Patents Company's members.

Five years of bitter fighting ensued between the prosperous Patents Company on the one hand and the many stifled producers and badgered exhibitors on the other, until the combine was felled by an antitrust decision in 1915. During this long fracas a number of independent producers and distributors nonetheless managed to remain in business, at the same time effecting some innovations in the sales practices codified by the trust. They offered their pictures at prices both above and below the prevailing General Film rates, based on a given film's popular merits. They also introduced the star system and the feature-length film to the industry, thereby facilitating their efforts to obtain larger-than-normal rental fees.

Meanwhile, one of the trust's own associates, William Wadsworth Hodkin, son of its San Francisco exchange, argued against its rigid sales policies. Standardization of film length, a fixed rental scale, and daily changes of program were all retarding the industry, in his opinion. He maintained that an above-average film could run for two or even three days, thus capitalizing on favorable word-of-mouth and earning higher rentals than if exhibited for only a single day. When he tested this classification of 'first class' and 'second class' product in his territory, he was rebuked by General Film so strongly that he resigned to open his own network of western exchanges.

The first tangible confirmation of Hodkinson's 'outrageous' theories came with the 1913 exhibition of *Quo Vadis*, a nine-reel Italian epic acquired for US distribution by George Kleine, one of the trust's founding members. When General Film refused to distribute the film outside its normal system, Kleine opened the picture himself at New York's Astor Theatre. Admission was set at $1, ten times the previous high charged for a motion picture, and the deal called for Kleine to receive 10 per cent of the gross receipts. The first roadshow proved a smash, and within a few months it was playing in nearly two dozen US cities on the same basis.

The success of *Quo Vadis* paved the way for other feature-length films. Adolph Zukor launched the four-reel *Queen Elizabeth* through a network of state's-rights distributors, unaffiliated exchanges franchised to handle the local release of an independent film or program of films made by a company lacking a national distribution apparatus. *Queen Elizabeth's* success led to Zukor's formation of the Famous Players Film Company, and undoubtedly spurred vaudeville producer Jesse Lasky's concurrent creation of the Jesse L. Lasky Feature Play Company. In short order, both Zukor and Lasky signed with Hodkinson's newly formed Paramount Pictures Corp. to handle national distribution of their features.

Whereas General Film had charged the best houses about $125 a week for seven programs of four to eight reels, Paramount rented its five-reel features for as much as $700 for a full week's playoff in the largest theaters. Despite this hefty rate boost, exhibitors joined the Paramount bandwagon as quickly as possible, and within a few years more than 5,000 theaters were contracted. Average gross rentals soon escalated to $125,000 per picture, of which Hodkinson's Paramount retained 35 per cent as a distribution fee. (D. W. Griffith's *The Birth of a Nation*, released in 1915 through state's-rights distributors, far surpassed all other films of the era with a staggering $3,500,000 in rentals upon its initial release.)

So successful was the Hodkinson-Zukor-Lasky operation that other combinations of exhibitors, state's-rights exchanges, and producers were soon formed. None of the earliest entrants survived very long, but within a few years most of the companies that were to dominate the motion picture industry for the next fifty years had been seeded: Metro-Goldwyn-Mayer, a combination of three small production companies wedded to the Loew's theater circuit; Fox Film Corporation; Warner Brothers; and several smaller distributors (Columbia Pictures, United Artists, and Universal) that lacked the theatrical holdings eventually amassed by the larger companies. RKO Radio, the last of the theater-holding majors, was not born until 1929.

Most of the distribution practices that were to become traditional in the film business originated with Hodkinson, however. He graded all houses on the basis of their size and importance, established different rental levels for them, and gave each theater clearance, or protection against exhibition by nearby houses of the same picture for a specified period. First-run theaters were primarily located in the downtown center of the amusement district, second-run (or neighborhood) situations were smaller houses located in residential districts, and subsequent-run (or sub-run) theaters were either less substantial or located in less desirable areas.

When Mary Pickford's star skyrocketed and she demanded a heftier salary, Zukor (who had since ousted Hodkinson and taken control of Paramount) separated her films from the rest of his company's product and charged a higher rental price for the series. Exhibitors squawked, but they met 'Little Mary's' price. A few years later another Pickford film, United Artists' *Pollyanna*, successfully sought a percentage of gross receipts rather than a flat rental fee from exhibitors, thereby establishing a distribution policy that became standard for most better-grade pictures by the mid-1920s (*Quo Vadis* had earlier played New York on a percentage basis, but this policy was not maintained in its later playdates around the country.)

Just as the Pickford films had commanded higher rental fees than other Paramount productions, so the contracted percentage of gross receipts increased for films with greater production costs or commercial potential. By the 1930s the exhibitor might pay anywhere from 25 per cent to an infrequent 60 per cent of his box-office gross as rent for a feature. The introduction of double bills during the Depression triggered the manufacture of so-called 'B-films' to play the bottom half of the program; flat rentals were paid for these features.

As long as the major studios also owned large circuits of theaters, it was relatively academic what percentage of gross receipts was to be remitted to the distributor: many of the first-run houses showing MGM films, for example, were owned by Loew's, its parent corporation. A gentleman's agreement that prevailed among the major distributors further insured mutually agreeable terms between one company's distribution arm and another's theatrical chain. When the US Justice Department successfully enforced the divorcement of exhibition from production-distribution in 1948, however, the rental percentage assumed greater importance.

To alleviate theater losses on disappointing grossers, the sliding scale was instituted in the post-divorcement era. The percentage of box-office receipts due the distributor as a rental could vary from, say, 25 per cent to 60 per cent depending on the week's gross: receipts of $25,000 or more might require remission of 60 per cent to the distributor, receipts of $20–24,000 might require 50 per cent, etc.

The unfavorable antitrust decision in 1948 slowly but irrevocably shifted power and profitability from the hands of the producer-distributors to the exhibitors. With this increased potency came the look, a modification of the sliding-rental scale that favored the theater owner. Under this practice, an exhibitor reviews the results of a film engagement; unilaterally decides whether the contractually determined rental percentage leaves him with a sufficient amount of income; and then, if he feels that rental is too high, begins a lengthy period of 'renegotiation' with the distributor aimed at reducing his rental payment. In most cases a rental payment (variously called a settlement or adjustment) lower than that required by the contract is established.

Although this 'look' at the rental percentage has no basis in contractual law, distributors have for many years been reluctant to pursue their legal rights in these renegotiations. It seemed a self-defeating practice to institute lawsuits against customers, for fear of losing not only the one theater or circuit in question but also other theaters that might fear similar contretemps with the distributor. Furthermore, years of antitrust litigation have persuaded the major companies that mutual action aimed at enforcing exhibition covenants would only expose them to further Justice Department intervention.

These developments, then, are the background for distribution practices in today's motion picture industry. Certainly the past few years have witnessed dramatic changes in the terms and negotiations attendant upon booking major releases, and these are detailed below. What remains remarkable, however, is the minor deviation in actual distribution (as opposed to sales) tactics employed by modern companies from those used by their forerunners back in Hollywood's 'golden age.'

Preliminary product analysis and market research

The first decision made concerning a film's distribution is also the most important: the kind of playoff the picture will be given. To some extent this initial decision can be later modified or refined, but instances of total reversal are historically rare. Since a film's commercial success depends greatly on the aptness of its chosen playoff pattern, it would seem essential that the film 'product' and its potential market be thoroughly researched and analyzed before making this determination. In actual practice, however, most films are distributed on the basis of crudely assimilated past experiences and seat-of-the-pants hunches, without knowledgeably answering some questions before a particular playoff approach is adopted for any film.

1. *How much advance interest do audiences have in the picture?*

Advance interest in most films is minimal. The Yankelovich Report, a 1967 study of industry marketing practices prepared for the Motion Picture Association of America, noted that prerelease publicity 'seems unable to create extensive public awareness' for films lacking 'a tie-in with a very familiar book or play or music.' At that time the researchers questioned a representative cross-section of the American public about their awareness of six heavily publicized but then-un-released pictures. Only *Camelot* was familiar to a majority (58 per cent) of those interviewed; the degree of awareness for the other five films ranged from 37 per cent for *Doctor Dolittle* to 6 per cent for *Tony Rome*.

Public familiarity, needless to say, is hardly the same as ticket-buying interest, and the same study suggested even less advance interest in attending these six pictures. Almost none of the interviewed sample knew the stars of any of the films in question, and in many cases there was a complete misconception of their contents. *The Comedians*, a Richard Burton–Elizabeth Taylor melodrama set in politics-infested Haiti, was almost universally described as a comedy, possibly starring Jerry Lewis. *Far from the Madding Crowd*, John Schlesinger's adaptation of the Thomas Hardy novel, was presumed to be 'about hippies.' And *Doctor Dolittle*, the big-budgeted family musical starring Rex Harrison, was frequently labeled as a story about Dr Tom Dooley.

If public familiarity and knowledge about upcoming motion pictures was so low in 1967, advance awareness is probably even lower in 1975, given the intervening demise of such mass-media communications as *Life* and *Look*. Obviously, everything possible should be done to maximize advance interest in all films, but even the heartiest ballyhoo cannot stir much public awareness of upcoming pictures lacking such presold ingredients as a popular property or major stars.

When there is evident public interest in a motion picture (or when it seems likely that a pre-opening campaign will excite that interest), a broad national launching could well be most appropriate. *Jaws*, a national hard-cover bestseller for ten consecutive months and the beneficiary of massive production publicity, certainly had a substantial audience waiting for its release, and its visual material lent itself to effective television promotion shortly before its simultaneous opening in 460 theaters. The two *Godfathers* and *The Trial of Billy Jack* also had sizable built-in audiences that warranted a widespread launching.

Most pictures, however, are virtually unknown quantities the day they open, and other marketing prongs (critical reception, word-of-mouth, follow-up campaigns) assume greater importance in their successful distribution. In these cases a slower playoff may be necessary, with a few low-key openings needed to launch the picture and offset the previously non-existent audience interest in these films.

2. What are the likely responses to the film from various audience segments?

Favorable word-of-mouth is essential to the success of most films, big and small. An occasional motion picture can be exploited with sufficient fanfare to entice a profit before audience disgruntlement drowns out the ballyhoo, and such films are best served by mass-saturation bookings that allow the film a few brief weeks of artificially induced importance before the word leaks out. The difference between this kind of saturation booking and the kind of widespread playoff accorded a *Jaws* is often fine, apart from the prestige and importance of the theaters involved; the intention is to 'buy' short-lived grosses on a film like the Charles Bronson *Breakout* by feigning stature through heavy advertising.

For the most part, however, it is vital to attract at the outset those customers who will be most vociferous in their praise of a film's merits, thus creating the climate for enthusiastic word-of-mouth. If market tests indicate the picture holds its greatest appeal for teenage girls, certainly initial bookings should include few inner-city houses and should ideally occur in the summer. If the best audience reaction comes from black men, on the other hand, it is hardly logical to book the picture in white suburban houses.

Such truisms may seem self-evident, but the principle is ignored more often than one would expect. Few producers wish their films to be characterized as appealing to a particular audience segment, and instead prefer the fantasy that their efforts are aimed at 'the general audience.' Such fuzzy thinking ignores the fact that television long ago usurped movies' position as the American mass entertainment medium. In the past two decades, only a few motion pictures have been theatrically viewed by even one-third of the combined US–Canadian population, and attendance by as little as 10 per cent of that population can yield domestic theatrical rentals in the vicinity of $25,000,000. There is much profit in defining and reaching a specialized segment of the potential audience.

The initial selection of theaters, then, should be based on their accessibility to the given film's core audience, whether defined in chronological, sexual, regional, economic, racial, or educational terms. Once that audience is tapped successfully, the word-of-mouth can fan out to other audience segments, and so can the kind of theatrical bookings.

3. *What theatrical atmosphere will most effectively enhance audience reaction?*

A secondary factor to be considered in determining the ideal first-run bookings for a film is the desired theatrical atmosphere. Motion pictures can play very differently in different houses, even assuming both theaters are filled to capacity. To give just one possible example, I saw *Nashville* in New York at the Cinema Two, a 291-seat theater of greater width than depth and with an extremely austere interior design. I found the 157-minute film almost continually engrossing and involving, and so did the audience with which I saw it. On the other hand, friends who saw the same picture in Los Angeles at the 1535-seat, narrow, long, and ornately decorated Village Theatre in Westwood have complained about the picture's longueurs and emotional coldness, adding that the audience reaction seemed equally tepid.

Admittedly the difference may just be one of taste, but it seems equally likely to me than an intimate and lengthy mosaic like *Nashville* suffers in a larger theater rife with distractingly ornamental detail. Conversely, a film as loud and obstreperously visual as *Tommy* undoubtedly plays much more effectively in New York's 1200-seat Ziegfeld or Los Angeles's 1408-seat Fox Wilshire than in a 713-seat Minneapolis house that is one-third of a modernized triplex.

4. *Which promotional technique will maximize the size of the total audience?*

The final factor to be considered while designing a playoff pattern is the method to be used in marketing the picture. Will the bulk of the advertising dollar be spent on television or on print media? How much will be spent? How much of the advertising will be national as opposed to local? What forms of publicity seem most attainable?

These questions are usually answered concurrent with a final decision on the film's playoff. Obviously it makes no sense to make expensive national television buys when the film will be playing simultaneously in only a small number of cities, and it makes no sense to spend a great deal of advertising money in a city where the film is appearing only in one theater with a small grossing potential. The likelihood of major national publicity breaks concurrent with the picture's opening, on the other hand, might make a broader immediate playoff seem more expeditious.

Playoff alternative

Once a film's core audience is defined, the most suitable kinds of theaters determined, and the marketing strategy defined, the playoff pattern can be selected with some confidence. Basically there are four kinds of first-run (initial) bookings, exclusive, day-and-date, multiple, and saturation.

An exclusive first-run involves opening the picture in only one theater in a metropolitan market. Until recently almost all important pictures were launched in this manner, but increases in advertising costs and a continuing geographic spread of suburban perimeters have made this a generally uneconomical method of opening a film in the bigger markets.

A day-and-date first run signifies the simultaneous launching of a picture in two or three theaters within a community, with these houses usually located in diverse sections of the metropolitan area. In Los Angeles it is now common to open a picture in Westwood (for the western Los Angeles area), in Hollywood (for the eastern Los Angeles area), and in Costa Mesa or La Habra (for the southern portion of the Greater Los Angeles area). In Manhattan films frequently open day-and-date at a Broadway house and an East Side theater, and a third site on the Upper East Side (around 86th Street) is also often added.

The advantage in day-and-date openings is the maximization of immediate box-office gross, much of which can offset heavy initial advertising costs. The disadvantage is that a smaller percentage of the total gross may well be remitted to the distributor as film rental (on a standard 90/10 deal) than if the film had opened in only one theater.

To illustrate this latter point, here are the day-and-date figures for Paramount's *The Longest Yard*, which opened in August 1974 at three Manhattan houses:

Week	State One	Orpheum	Tower East
1	$31,365	$16,646	$ 6,929
2	$39,729	$21,618	$14,268
3	$35,317	$18,539	$12,710
4	$30,000	$15,111	$10,407
5	$30,194	$11,015	$ 8,313
6	$24,066	$11,144	$ 8,500

Under the 90/10 deal, an exhibitor first recoups his contractually specified operating expenses (house nut) from the gross before remitting 90 per cent of the average to the distributor as film rental, while retaining the other 10 per cent as his profit. (All house nuts are conceded to have a certain amount of air that ensures a profit for the theater even before this 10 per cent is added.)

The 'nut' for the State One was a reported $16,500. Since each of the six weeks saw box-office receipts in excess of that operating overhead, Paramount earned 90 per cent of sums ranging from $23,229 (Week 2) to $7,566 (Week 6), or a total film rental of $82,504 from this one theater alone. However, box office grosses fell below the Orpheum's $16,000 'nut' in Week 4 through 6 and below the Tower East's $8,000 nut in Week 1, thus precluding Paramount from any share in these weekly takes. So we apply the 90/10 formula only to the 'profitable' weeks at these houses, and find remissions to Paramount of $7,923 from the Orpheum and $12,6778 from the Tower.

This six-week, three theater booking thus yielded film rentals of $103,204 on a box-office gross of $345,871. Had *The Longest Yard* played exclusively at the State One and not the other two theaters, it would have had to gross only $23,000 more than it actually did there (or only 15 per cent of the customers diverted to the other two theaters) to return the same rental income to the distributor. In other words, Paramount effectively subsidized the other two houses for these six weeks by giving them a film that could cover their operating expenses without producing much additional revenue for the distributor.

The remaining two forms of first-run bookings, multiple and saturation, both involve opening a picture in a sizable number of theaters at the same time. Multiple first-runs (known in New York as flagship) occur in a relatively limited number of better-grade theaters, often including some normally exclusive or day-and-date houses, and are supported with a major advertising campaign. (*Jaws* in Los Angeles is a good recent example.) Saturation first-runs (known in New York as showcase) presume a larger number of simultaneous openings in lesser theaters, usually including a smattering of drive-ins.

A number of variations exist for subsequent playoff of a film after it has completed its first-run engagement. It may move over to another house normally used for first-run bookings; this method is generally employed for a successful picture forced out of its original theater because of a previous commitment to open another film on a given date (a locked booking). It may broaden into a multiple (or flagship) run; if that playoff maintains a high commercial profile, a subsequent intermediate run may intervene before the broadest possible saturation break. Or it may move directly from first-run to showcase, often supported in the latter dates by a second feature. At the end of the line is the so-called underbelly break.

The pacing of this theatrical hopscotch is one of the more important decisions reached by sales-distribution executives. If a film moves from first-run to multiple too quickly, it may lose its cachet of exclusivity and cease to seem an important event. On the other hand, a sluggish ride from first-run to multiple or saturation may dissipate the earlier interest of filmgoers too far removed from the first-run site(s) or too budget-conscious to pay the higher first-run admission price.

As each step of this ladder is descended, certain promotional questions also arise. Even if the advertising-publicity campaign has proved enormously successful, it may be advisable to broaden the pitch beyond the first-run periphery. It may also seem a good idea to introduce more 'commercial' sales techniques and advertising tools aimed at snaring the presumably less sophisticated second- and third-run audiences. Study of earlier grosses, audience responses, and the general nature of the entire film market should provide suitable approaches to these subsequent-run bookings.

Terms and bids

A print of a motion picture is leased to a theater for a specified rental, although (as noted) these contractual terms remain vulnerable to the theater owner's 'look' and the distributor's resultant 'adjustment.' In the past few years, the major distributors have had increasing success in enforcing the terms of exhibition contracts, and it is no longer unusual for a contract to contain a no review provision. In such cases the distributor and exhibitor often strike an under-the-table agreement to exchange contractual adherence on one film for promised 'flexibility' on a forthcoming picture. (The best-known recent example of this involved the disappointing *Jonathan Livingston Seagull*, for which consenting exhibitors were rewarded with unofficial 'rebates' on Paramount's subsequent *Don't Look Now*.)

There are several standard kinds of film-rental terms. The contract may call for a specified percentage of the box-office gross (for example 50 per cent of gross receipts in the first week, 40 per cent of gross receipts in the second and third weeks, 35 per cent of gross receipts in the fourth week, 30 per cent thereafter). It may specify a sliding scale in which the applicable percentage of gross receipts due as film rental depends on the size of the gross (for example, 60 per cent of the box-office take if the week's gross is $25,000 or more, 50 per cent if the gross is $20,000–24,999, 40 per cent if the gross is $115,000–19,999, etc.).

The current blockbuster era has seen both these formulas replaced by periodic use of the 90/10 formula that was once reserved for first-run theaters in only a few cities like New York and Los Angeles. When first adopted unilaterally by Manhattan first-run houses, the 90/10 deal was considered the bane of distributors' existence. It was not uncommon, especially in the later weeks of a film's initial engagement, for the gross to dangle precipitously close to the nut, thus yielding the distributor little or no rental for his merchandise. Before the 90/10 deal went national, however, the major producers added a new wrinkle known as floor to ensure against minimal payments for disappointing releases. The floor is a specified percentage of total box-office gross below which the exhibitor cannot pay, regardless of application of the 90/10 formula.

The following two examples illustrate application of the 90/10 formula with a hypothetical floor of 70 per cent for two different theaters having the same house nut of $5,000.

		'A'	'B'
(1)	Box-office gross	$50,000	$15,000
(2)	House nut	$ 5,000	$ 5,000
(3)	Rental base (1–2)	$45,000	$10,000
(4)	90/10 (90% of 3)	$40,000	$ 9,000
(5)	70% (70% of 1)	$35,000	$10,500

Since the 90/10 deal yields more than the 70 per cent floor for Theatre A, this house pays the distributor a film rental of $40,000 (according to the 90/10 formula, line 4). However, the 90/10 deal results in less than 70 per cent of Theatre B's gross receipts, so it pays the distributor $10,500 (according to the 70 per cent floor, line 5). If one assumes that it truly costs Theatre B $5,000 a week to remain open, this contract has led to a $500 operating deficit for the week. Fortunately, active concession-stand business will usually offset that theoretical loss.

In addition to these various percentage formulas, films are also sometimes licensed on a flat-rental basis, in which the theater is charged, say, $100 for a week's playtime regardless of the gross receipts. Such deals generally occur only on second-feature or final-run pictures and are normally reserved for the theaters of minimal grossing potential.

It is now quite common for distributors to request competitive exhibition bids for the right to play an important picture. This procedure starts with a bid letter mailed to all theaters in a given market, announcing the availability of a film for a specific opening date and requesting that each interested exhibitor make an offer before a specified deadline.

This letter specifies minimum requirements for an acceptable offer: the number of guaranteed playing weeks, the percentage terms, and the size of a cash guarantee or advance required prior to the release of the print. The distributor will also determine the 'clearance' sought by the theater, i.e., the kind of exclusivity wanted in the theater's area. This clearance may be expressed in terms of distance (no simultaneous booking within specified geographical boundaries) or time (no bookings at certain theaters until, say, a month after the conclusion of the bidding theater's engagement).

The theater in a given area that bids the most will usually get the picture, although the distributor retains the right to reject all bids or accept one that may seem less advantageous on the surface. Acceptance of an 'inferior' bid may be based on legitimate factors, such as the greater grossing potential of a theater offering a smaller up-front guarantee. Legal recourse is available to losing theaters only if they can establish that sheer favoritism cost them a film on which they had placed a higher bid than the one accepted.

Two recent aspects of blind bidding – the bidding on an unseen picture – have attracted trade attention. According to Justice Department regulations, distributors are allowed to blind-bid only three releases a year. To protect the smaller circuits and independent theater owners against such large chains as General Cinema (approximately 500 screens), United Artists Theater Circuit (500), Mann Theaters (250), Commonwealth (200), ABC Theaters (1985), and Cinemette (150), the law stipulates that no picture on which blind bids are sought can have possibly been seen by any of the competing bidders.

Both Universal and Columbia were recently charged with violating this edict. *Jaws*, *Bite The Bullet*, and *The Fortune* had all been screened, or sneaked, primarily to market-test advertising approaches and assess audience reactions, and these showings had inadvertently allowed some exhibitors an advantageous view of the finished pictures. Both companies were obliged to withdraw their acceptance of all bids and reopen the entire bidding process.

The other aspect of blind bidding that has garnered considerable trade interest recently has been the steady mushrooming of large cash advances and guarantees on unseen pictures. Advances differ from guarantees in that the former can be renegotiated later if the picture fails to perform as expected, while guarantees are non-returnable. In the past few years several pictures have stocked up reportedly huge advances and guarantees: $30,000,000 for *The Godfather*,

Part II, $25,000,000 for *The Towering Inferno*, $20,000,000 for *Earthquake* and *Jaws* and $16,000,000 for *The Great Gatsby*. The effect of these impressive cash outlays is to involve exhibitors in the financing of motion pictures, but once the theater owners are singed badly by this experiment, this distribution gravy train will stop rolling.

Do-it-yourself distribution

The recent publicity accorded exhibition deals struck for a few big-budgeters should not camouflage the fact that most films are booked in most theaters on a one-to-one basis and on fairly reasonable terms that will yield huge rentals only if the box-office grosses are commensurately big. It is also worth repeating that systematic analysis of the particular film and its most productive niche in the market-place is still more important than a few lavish deals made with possibly inappropriate theaters six months in advance of its premiere.

Typically the major distributors carry a domestic overhead of about $5,000,000 each, which they can thus offset by 25 per cent distribution fees on annual gross rentals of only $20,000,000. Proponents of the competitive free-enterprise system maintain that multiplicity of distribution outlets is essential to the motion picture industry's continued health. Others retort that merchandise in many other industries is handled by jobbers who successfully distribute competing manufacturers' product; in their view several of the existing distributors could effectively combine their operations and thus reduce the overhead that must be charged against skyrocketing production costs.

Film-makers' traditional hostility to distribution companies – the presumed manglers of a film and embezzlers of its profits – has long made self-distribution seem an attractive alternative. The assumption is that a successful producer or distributor can release his own pictures at a cost below that charged by the major companies and then bank the difference. Most film-makers are content to complain while this utopian idea evaporates in the Polo Lounge smoke, but a few have taken the plunge and learned too late just how deep the distribution waters can be.

1. Setting up a national distribution company is very costly. Even a so-called 'minor' such as Allied Artists, with only twelve exchanges and a limited number of management executives, carries an annual overhead in excess of $3,000,000. Certainly no less than $5,000,000

should be earmarked for the launching of a new distributor, and the size of that initial outlay virtually demands public financing.

It is possible, of course, to set up a handful of sales offices across the country and buttress this skeletal organization with territorial sub-distributors for a much smaller investment. But since most regional 'subs' get 20 to 25 per cent of the distributor's share of box-office gross as a commission, it is hard to see how this approach would save much money.

2. A distribution company's continuing overhead demands periodic feeding of film product. In order to offset this $3–4,000,000 burden, a distribution company needs to distribute enough films to amass gross theatrical rentals in the annual vicinity of $12–20,000,000. Given the chaotic and unpredictable nature of today's theatrical film market, that is no easy chore.

Over the past five years, only a handful of independent films acquired after completion of production have earned even $4,000,000 in domestic rentals, and these few hits will continue to be offered first to the surviving six majors or the few successful minors. The search for commercially viable independent pictures is a long, frustrating tour through more cinematic garbage than most people know exists – a fact to which I can attest after one year of such fruitless wading while working for Levitt-Pickman Film Corp. The declining appeal of foreign-language pictures in the US further mitigates against a successful acquisition program.

The only alternative, then, is for the new distributor to produce its own releases, which requires even greater capital and carries even larger risks. As long as the Federal government remains disposed to the recently popular tax-shelter scheme, some of the risks in production financing can be alleviated. The rub, needless to say, is that tax shelters also reduce potential profitability to the film-maker.

3. Running a distribution company is a time-consuming business. Unless a film-maker intends to desert the creative arena for the mercantile world (as appears the case with Roger Corman since he formed New World Pictures in 1970), it is essential that most areas of responsibility be delegated to other executives. Relinquishment of active control is difficult for any owner and/or founder of a business, and it may lead to the film-maker's feeling as alienated from his own company as he previously did from the major distributors.

4. Most small distributors lack the clout needed to collect the bulk of their billings. Exhibitor-distributor contracts are seldom worth the paper on which they are written, and receivables remain the curse of the film industry. A major distributor is able to strong-arm most theater owners into settlements reasonably reflective of contractual

terms because the distributor has more major product for the future. A small distributor, on the other hand, generally lacks an upcoming lineup sufficient to compel recalcitrant exhibitors' prompt remission of monies due the company. It has been said, perhaps apocryphally, that Allied Artists took its $7,000,000 *Papillon* plunge in order to accelerate collections on its *Cabaret* billings.

In short, self-distribution is a trap for the unwary. As far back as the 1940s, David O. Selznick learned the hardships of owning one's own distribution company when he formed Selznick Releasing Organization and launched the firm with his blockbuster *Duel in the Sun*. In one of his incessant directives (reprinted in *Memo from David O. Selznick*), he claimed that Selznick Releasing Organization 'proved that it was unnecessary to make pictures that nobody wanted to see in order to absorb production overheads, which are in most cases absurdly inflated, and in order to keep feeding an excessively expensive distribution method.' Nonetheless, his company released only a half-dozen pictures in a four-year period, after which Selznick 'decided that the burden was altogether too great.'

More recently, Tom Laughlin formed his own distribution company to oversee the reissue of *Billy Jack* and the launching of the *The Trial of Billy Jack* and *The Master Gunfighter*. Laughlin soon tacitly acknowledged his operation's defects by transferring secondary playoff of *Trial* to Warner Bros., the company he earlier faulted for its alleged 'mishandling' of *Billy Jack*. And it is well known throughout the industry that Taylor-Laughlin's skirting of bankruptcy depended on the substantial success of *Gunfighter*.

Notwithstanding the above provisos, I believe there is a place for another major distribution company in the film business, one that would function more systematically and economically than most of the existing batch and one that would concentrate on the kind of specialized or problematic films that no longer interest our blockbuster-obsessed majors. A good deal of care and study should precede such a high-risk venture, however, or its fate will probably echo the prevalent industry view that 'there just ain't room for another major in today's market.'

10 · Douglas Gomery: The picture palace: economic sense or Hollywood nonsense?

Quarterly Review of Film Studies, vol. 3, no. 1, Winter 1978

Like Beaupré's examination of film distribution, Gomery's article on exhibition is an attempt to redress the balance both of film studies in general and of film history in particular by looking at that side of the industry which is most often ignored by critics and academics alike. Gomery addresses one of the oldest orthodoxies of film history, the notion that the picture palaces of the 1920s were an irrational and uneconomic indulgence, indeed, that they were an unmitigated disaster. Just as theoretical work about film texts has increasingly imported concepts from other disciplines (anthropology, linguistics, psychoanalysis), so too Gomery assembles his argument and evidence from well beyond the boundaries of conventional film studies. By borrowing from studies of retail location and the history of urban geography Gomery is able to argue a convincing case about the picture palaces, a case which is of some consequence for film studies for two reasons. Firstly, Gomery encourages us to investigate the most taken-for-granted 'facts' about Hollywood's history as an industry by considering picture palaces not in terms of their apparent inappropriateness today but in terms of the functions they might have served when they were built; and secondly, having asked questions about the precise economic function of the picture palaces it becomes possible to at least place on the agenda other equally pertinent questions, questions of the kind with which Gomery concludes: 'What effect, if any, did big-city theaters have upon the product created by Hollywood? What effect did they have upon the way audiences reacted to films?' Such questions are not simply historical or empirical, they also problematise the very premise upon which much of the theoretical work on Hollywood and ideology rests – the assumption that ideologies and meanings reside in and can be read out of texts, without recourse either to the mode of production or the mode and moment of consumption. Such questions are also addressed in Paul Kerr's analysis of the B *film noir* in which he attempts to reconstruct that genre's origins in specific production and exhibition strategies in the 1940s and early 1950s.

Branigan's discussion of the dominant available models for understanding the process of innovation and implementation in film history includes some observations about Gomery's method which he compares (unfavourably) with that of Comolli. Branigan explains this preference on the grounds that Comolli 'is explicit about his method' and because he privileges the role of ideology in his account of film history. In this article, however, Gomery is equally clear about his methodology and is specific about his understanding of the impact of ideology. In order to answer questions about the relationship between exhibition and the film product on the one hand and exhibition and the audience on the other, Gomery argues that 'one needs a much more complex and adventurous method of working than I have been using here, and one has to address more directly the problem of American ideology.... My point here has been that the models so far developed to help us understand film's ideological functioning have been too casual in treating the material basis of the industry.' It is that very casualness which Gomery's article so successfully unsettles.

Our knowledge of the history of the American film industry has grown significantly during the last ten years. Yet historians cling to the old models of analysis. One outcome of this lack of new methodology is that we know much about how films were made, and precious little about the conditions under which they were shown. It is typical, for example, to find historical texts devoting several pages to the rise of Hollywood's 'Big Five' in the 1920s, and then noting in a sentence or two that also during this period a large number of picture palaces were built. Authors simply describe the size and extravagance of such theaters, and then assert that picture palaces served principally as a means to create an atmosphere of escape and fantasy.[1] A small number of historians have begun to examine the picture palace as an example of popular architecture, yet none asks a more basic question: why would profit-conscious movie entrepreneurs build so many large, elaborate theaters? Was it just a waste of money, the overindulgence of monopoly capitalists?

Only Robert Sklar discusses this seemingly irrational behavior. In his book *Movie-Made America*, Sklar argues that 'the picture palaces were economic white elephants,' simply ornate, gaudy monuments perpetrated by ambitious movie moguls. Sklar appeals to our common sense; such theaters were too large to keep constantly filled and much too costly to run.[2]

Unfortunately, Sklar goes no further; what is needed, and what I have attempted to provide in the following paper, is a systematic account of the economic function of the movie palaces for the period in which they were built. This will help explain why motion picture exhibitors saw fit to build so many 'wonder' theaters during the 1920s. In fact, the principles of retail location theory, urban geography, and microeconomics all lead to the conclusion that the picture palace was the most sensible economic activity large-city motion picture entrepreneurs could have undertaken. Data to support this claim comes from a variety of sources: newspapers, motion picture trade papers, antitrust suits, city directories, and studies of urban history, geography, and recreation.

Two assumptions precede my analysis. First, I assume that the picture palace was principally an American urban phenomenon.[3] I define a picture palace as a large theater built to screen films and to accommodate live shows, seating over 1,500 people, constructed with a fan-shaped auditorium and much nonfunctional decoration.[4] There were about 1,000 such theaters in the United States, and all were in cities. Second, I assume that theater entrepreneurs tried to maximize their profits; the selection of locations and the size of theaters were the key decisions in this process. Exhibitors would then place the most popular movies they could get into these theaters. Analyzing this investment decision is the key to explaining why such large theaters came to be, where they were located, and what role these theaters played in the complex pattern of American city life during the 1920s.[5]

I

Most of the first great picture palaces were built in the central business districts of American cities with populations over 100,000 in 1920. Desire for monopoly power provided the motivation. By the early 1920s motion picture entrepreneurs realized that first-run films coupled with elaborate stage shows could generate extraordinary profits. Many movie-goers preferred to see a film *now* rather than later. A stage show would draw others from competing vaudeville and burlesque attractions. To take advantage of this short-run monopoly, and turn it into 'monopoly profit,' motion picture entrepreneurs built larger and larger theaters in which to present imposing stage shows and the latest Hollywood films.[6] The central business district was the most obvious location for such large theaters. It was easy to travel there because America was still in an age of mass transit; all streetcar lines led to 'Main Street' or the center square.

Moreover, since downtown was the average city's largest shopping center and home of many other commercial recreation activities, city dwellers could combine their shopping and recreation activities all in one journey. Soon the new picture palaces (initially modeled on European or American legitimate or vaudeville theaters) became the flagships, the most profitable theaters in large regional chains: Loew's (New York City), Stanley (Philadelphia and Washington, DC), Balaban and Katz (Chicago), Saxe Bros. (Milwaukee), Finkelstein and Runin (Minneapolis), North American (San Francisco and Seattle), and West Coast (Los Angeles).[7]

Unlike today, all downtown picture palaces offered a smorgasbord of movies, live acts, and music during the two-hour show. Since live entertainment accounted for only one-sixth of a complete show, such theaters were able to charge prices 50 per cent lower than nearby vaudeville houses. A typical 1920s 'movie show' began with a ten-minute overture, usually foreshadowing the theme music presented with the feature film. Orchestras sometimes numbered over seventy members. Next came a live prologue or presentation. A comedy short, newsreels, and a feature film followed in that order. However, even the biggest theaters did not present a full orchestra with 'shows' at 12:00 noon, 2:00 p.m., 4:00 p.m., 7:30 p.m., and 9:30 p.m. The noon and late afternoon 'shows' normally employed only a grand organ. These organs could imitate an orchestra, any single instrument, and also provide varied sound effects.[8]

By 1925, live entertainment had become such an important part of downtown movie palace fare that three fairly rigid formulae had evolved. Labeled 'presentations' in industry jargon, the first type was the 'pure' presentation, a revue-like spectacle with a troupe of dancers and several specialty acts of vaudeville built around one particular theme. One week it might be 'Great Moments from Grand Opera,' and next 'Just Girls.' One particular type of the 'pure' presentation became very popular: the 'prologue.' Here the presentation's central theme was linked to a theme or motif from the feature film. So a nautical motif would be used with Buster Keaton's *The Navigator*, including a singer costumed as a diver suspended from cables surrounded by girls in sailor suits. Stage designers working for Chicago's Balaban and Katz chain pioneered the 'pure' presentation. Los Angeles exhibitor Sid Grauman championed the 'prologue.' New York's Samuel Rothaefel (Roxy) offered an alternative mode, the 'variety show,' in which two or three highly paid vaudeville acts filled the twenty minutes. Marcus Loew tendered yet a third type, the 'headliner method'; one vaudeville star, for example a singer like Gilda Gray, or even a popular band like Paul Whiteman's, performed for the complete twenty-minute period. Many times such headliners proved more popular than the feature film. It is no wonder that big-time vaudeville began to decline dramatically as early as 1923. Picture palace entertainment signaled the death of vaudeville; the coming of sound to motion pictures just insured its burial.[9]

Thus it is not surprising that with the best locations, a large seating capacity, the newest films, and top live entertainment, the downtown picture palaces became the cornerstone of American film exhibition between 1925 and 1950. The basis for the Supreme Court's decision in the famous Paramount case was the profitability of first-run theaters, which by 1930 were controlled by Hollywood's majors. The record of that case established, over and over again, that such theaters provided the bulk of the industry's revenue. For example, as early as 1926 an average of 50 per cent of each week's audience attended the approximate 2,000 key theaters (first- and second-run) in the seventy-nine American cities with populations over 100,000. In other words, these downtown picture palaces, prior to the Great Depression, were *not* white elephants, but very profitable business enterprises.[10]

II

By omission, film historians have led us to believe that all the important picture palaces were downtown. Their examples are always the same: New York's Roxy, Paramount, Loew's State and – later – Radio City Music Hall. However, New York is not a typical American city; in the late 1920s it was really five cities: Manhattan, Brooklyn, Bronx, Queens and, to a lesser degree, Richmond. Moreover, Manhattan represents only one type of city, what retail location theorists label a 'rectangular' city, one which is much longer than wide. There are two other basic types: the square-shaped city, and the fan city. In the 1920s a huge expansion took place in American cities, and because of this growth, the shape of a city became the vital component determining where retail and recreational activity would take place.[11]

A square city is the simplest type. It usually had its origin as a rural trading center. Denver, Dayton, San Antonio, and Indianapolis provide examples. During the 1920s a square city could expand on all sides, and still have most of its population near the central business district. There would be only minimal pressure to create new large outlying shopping and entertainment districts. Two examples illustrate how few picture palaces there were in square cities. South

Bend, Indiana, grew from 71,000 to 104,000 during the 1920s, a 47 per cent increase. Yet, because growth occurred equally on all sides, South Bend's three picture palaces were all located downtown within a block of each other. There were two other theaters downtown, and six houses of about 500 seats, scattered in equal proportions in South Bend's residential neighborhoods.[12] South Bend was typical of medium-sized, square cities in which all picture palaces were downtown.[13]

To the south of South Bend lay one of America's largest square cities: Indianapolis. A major city of 314,000 in 1920, Indianapolis grew to 364,000 during the 1920s. Yet, Indianapolis had only four theaters seating more than 1,500, only one more than South Bend, and all were located downtown. Where Indianapolis differed was in its vast number of theaters seating between 1,000 and 1,500. Three of these mini-palaces were downtown; nine were located in outlying business centers. These centers ringed Indianapolis at a distance of from one-half to one and one-half miles, and defined the edge of the most densely populated part of the city. The key variable for location (and city growth) was the trolley line. All the outlying mini-palaces were located on major trolley lines, most at the intersection of two or more lines. Yet because Indianapolis was a square city, people could take these same trolleys downtown. Thus, there developed no large outlying picture palaces, the Hollywood majors did not take over the outlying theaters (Publix and Loew's dominated downtown), the mini-palaces regularly featured only second-run films, and no outlying theaters offered elaborate presentations as part of their regular shows. The development of large outlying picture palaces could only occur in different shaped cities.[14]

A rectangular city is a square type compressed in two directions by rugged topography, or a body of water. Here, as the city expanded during the 1920s, each new addition had to be further and further from the central business district. In general, rectangular cities, as they grew, developed one or more large outlying business and recreational centers. Again, two cities serve to illustrate a minimum and maximum case. Madison, Wisconsin, was a typical, small rectangular city during the 1920s. Built between two lakes, it contained nearly 58,000 people, about three-quarters of the population of South Bend. As a consequence, Madison had only two picture palaces, both downtown, as compared to South Bend's three. In terms of other downtown theaters and neighborhood houses, Madison had three-quarters the number of South Bend.[15]

There was one exception. Madison had one mini-palace, located about two miles from Madison's downtown. Because Madison's central business district was not at the center of the isthmus between the two lakes but nearer its western edge, as the city grew during the 1920s more and more residents of the 'East Side' found themselves at a greater distance from downtown. Thus at the 'East Side's' major streetcar junction, 'Schenk's Corners,' an outlying business district took shape. Anchored around a local department store, the Winnebago-Atwood corner soon included lawyers' offices, a large bank, insurance offices, variety stores, drugstores, a bowling alley and arcade, and from 1914 on, a small neighborhood movie theater of about 300 seats. To promote their enterprises and increase the attraction of the Atwood-Winnebago center, the East Side Business Men's Association pooled funds and built a small picture palace in 1928. They invested $200,000, and even hired Chicago's most famous theater architects, C. W. and George Rapp, to design the Eastwood (1,000 seats), Madison's first and only atmospheric theater – complete with stars and clouds. The Eastwood also had an adjacent parking lot for 200 cars. Opened in December 1928, when sound movies were already commonplace, the Eastwood did not have to offer stage shows to compete; instead it presented Paramount, MGM, and Warner Bros.' films, all, of course, second-run. Madison was about as small as a rectangular city could be and still generate the population for an outlying picture palace.[16]

On the opposite end of the scale was America's largest rectangular 'city,' the borough of Manhattan. Of course, Manhattan is even more of a special case because it is an island; growth can proceed only so far. Moreover, Manhattan, unlike the other cities considered in this article, reached a peak in terms of population in 1910 and experienced a *decline* in population during the 1920s. Population fell 18.2 per cent from 1920 to 1930; it was to Queens and the Bronx that people moved for the suburban life. Only the area north of 145th street at the upper end of Manhattan grew during the 1920s.[17] Motion picture entrepreneurs opened over 300 theaters all over the island. By 1930 Manhattan had ten theaters which held over 3,000 people. Yet because of the rectangular shape of the island, and despite available rapid transit, only four were in the central entertainment area (i.e., Times Square): The Roxy (5,889 seats), the Capital (5,486), the Paramount (3,664), and Loew's State (3,327).[18] The others were on the upper-middle-class east side: Loew's Seventy-Second (3,200), RKO's 86th Street (3,186), and RKO's 58th Street, on Union Square, Fox's Academy of Music (3,515), and in the uppermost tip of the island: Loew's 175th Street, and RKO's Coliseum (3,107) at 181st and Broadway. Likewise of Manhattan's twenty-nine movie theaters seating 2,000 or more, only six were in Times Square. By and large the movie theaters in the Times Square area were converted legitimate or vaudeville houses, and seated from 1,000 to 2,000.[19]

In general, picture palaces in Manhattan were spread equally throughout the island, with certain understandable exceptions. There were none near the southern tip around Wall Street; this was due to the largely transient population. Despite Times Square, there were no more than the population would demand from 14th Street north to Central Park. This area had about 38 per cent of the picture palaces, and about 38 per cent of the people. Up to 145th Street the proportions remained about the same, with the Upper East Side having slightly more than its share, probably due to its high density and middle- to upper-income families with much income to spend on leisure activities. But it is north of 145th Street, 5 to 8.5 miles from Times Square, in an expanding, middle-class area, with a large number of people between 15 and 30, in which there was a disproportionate number of picture palaces. That section of the island had only 2.5 per cent of the people, but had over 14 per cent of those picture palaces with over 2,000 seats. These outlying picture palaces presented elaborate stage shows, and second-run films. A film would reach the upper tip of Manhattan at the same time it played the 'downtowns' of Queens, Brooklyn, and the Bronx. Here the distance from Times Square helped generate the need for large, outlying picture palaces, the same conditions which helped foster Madison's lone outlying mini-palace.[20]

III

It is the third type of urban pattern – the fan-shaped city – which provides the most extreme decentralization of retail and recreational activity during the 1920s. These cities, built along bodies of water, have their downtown adjacent to that water. Examples are Chicago, Cleveland, St Louis, and Milwaukee. In such cities, with the central business district already located at the city's periphery, most of the population growth of the 1920s took place at a greater and greater distance from downtown, and thus provided a strong incentive for decentralization of retail, social, and recreational activity. Since the greatest development of the outlying picture palace was in these cities, I will concentrate my analysis on this most extreme case. In addition I will focus on America's largest fan-shaped city during the 1920s: Chicago (1930 population: 3,376,438). All other fan-shaped cities demonstrate the same trends, only to a lesser degree. Moreover, since 1920 Chicago has been the most studied city in the world. Social scientists, principally from the University of Chicago, have examined and re-examined all forms of social change in this 'urban laboratory.' Thus, it is much easier to locate data concerning Chicago for the 1920s than any other American city.[21]

Chicago's population increased by 25 per cent during the 1920s. The population of new communities just outside the city's borders tripled, giving Chicago a suburban population of over one million by 1930. The extension of mass transit served as the basis for such growth. Gradually Chicago's middle and upper-middle classes moved further and further from 'the Loop.' The shift in population was large enough by the 1910s to motivate newly developing chain stores to seek outlets near where these customers lived. In Chicago, forty outlying stores could be rented for the same cost as one in the 'Loop.' The Columbia drug chain was the first to expand; in 1910 it leased twenty-five lots near streetcar transfer points. As a major drug chain, it could easily find the capital for such a massive investment. In turn it drove up the rent for such prized locations, forced independent entrepreneurs to poorer sites and, consequently, only other chains could profit from the increasing advantages of retail amalgamation. Thus by the mid-1920s such familiar merchants as the Atlantic and Pacific Tea Company, United Cigar stores, Woolworth and Kresge variety stores, Walgreen Drugstores, and Sears-Roebuck department stores, were common sights to Chicago shoppers in large business centers near their homes.[22]

By 1930 there were twenty important 'outlying business centers' in the city of Chicago, whose total volume of retail sales exceeded the Loop. All centered around major streetcar transfer corners, or points where the elevated, trolley, and other mass transit lines intersected. These centers, familiar to Chicagoans of the 1920s by neighborhood name, e.g., Uptown or Englewood, or major intersections, e.g., 63rd and Cottage Grove, or Madison and Crawford, soon became more than just the location of chain stores. Local entrepreneurs set up banks and other financial institutions to facilitate expansion. Manufacturers and wholesale warehouses relocated nearby the increased supply of workers and new prospering retail establishments. Moreover, each center had its large dance halls, high-class restaurants, cabarets, 'smart' hotels, amusement arcades, and bowling alleys. Throughout the 1920s the cycle continued: more of the middle and upper-middle class moved to the city's periphery; entrepreneurs opened retail and recreational establishments to serve these new residents; the outlying business and recreational centers expanded.[23]

The basis for all this growth rested on transportation. Mass transit continued to reach out further and further in all directions; railroads set up connecting commuter lines. One major innovation was added to this transportation matrix during the 1920s; the new 'suburbanites' purchased automobiles in great numbers, usually from dealers set up in 'outlying shopping centers.' Between 1920 and 1930 the total number of motor vehicle registrations in the United States grew threefold; ownership was concentrated in the middle and upper-middle classes. Although neither the central business district nor the outlying business districts were set up to handle the congestion and parking problems caused by the massive numbers of cars in the 1920s, the outlying centers gained a short-run advantage. They required a much shorter drive, provided relatively less congestion, and more parking. Most large chain department stores located in outlying centers provided a parking lot. Land was still cheaper in the outlying centers than in the Loop.[24]

By 1929, University of Chicago sociologists had recognized this new urban phenomenon, and labeled these outlying centers, 'satellite Loops ... "bright light area(s)" attracting citywide attendance.'[25] In the mid-1930s five key centers formed a semicircle about five miles from the Loop. To the north was Uptown – at Lawrence and Broadway; to the northwest – Lincoln-Ashland Belmonth; to the west – Madison and Crawford; to the southwest – 63rd and Halsted (Englewood), and to the south – 63rd and Cottage Grove. The others filled in the gaps of this semicircle. There was a greater proportion on Chicago's wealthier north side, especially near the 'Gold Coast' on Chicago's lake shore. Immediately surrounding the five major outlying centers were large numbers of apartment buildings, nearly half of which were built during the 1920s. Beyond this ring of apartments came rows and rows of new single-family bungalows. These five centers, in particular, formed the core of small 'cities' within Chicago itself.[26]

Chicago's motion picture entrepreneurs quickly recognized the growth of these outlying business and recreation centers. In 1921 Chicago's most important exhibitors, Balaban and Katz (B & K), built the massive Tivoli Theater (3,984 seats) at 63rd and Cottage Grove. With the immediate success of this enterprise, B & K and others constructed massive 'wonder theaters' at all the major outlying centers. By 1925 it was clear that most of Chicago's picture palaces would be built in outlying business centers, not downtown. In 1930, of Chicago's twelve largest movie theaters, all seating over 3,000 people, only two were in the Loop. Of the six largest – each over 3,700 seats, among America's largest – two were in the Loop, the Chicago (3,840) and the Oriental (3,900); one on the south side, the Tivoli; one on the north side, the Uptown (4,307), then and now Chicago's largest; and two on the west side, at Madison and Crawford, the Marbro (3,939) and Paradise (3,700).[27] By 1930, B & K owned all six theaters, thus dominating Chicago's movie exhibition market. Chicago's remaining palaces were all built in smaller out-lying business centers and, in sum, roughly formed an arc which defined the border of the densely settled area of Chicago in 1930.[28]

Picture palaces built in outlying business centres were in the opti-mal location: midway between the new rich living at the edge of the city and the lower and middle classes still living in Chicago's inner city. Mass transit and automobiles made the journey to such theaters inexpensive and convenient. Nearby restaurants, cabarets, dance halls, and arcades provided entertainment before and after the movie show. Moreover, Hollywood's run-zone-clearance system of distri-bution guaranteed such theaters films only three to four weeks after their first run at the Chicago, Oriental, or other major Loop houses. These outlying theaters were also the only houses outside the Loop to provide live entertainment – vaudeville performers and huge orchestras to accompany the films. Thus, with admission prices two-thirds as high as first-run Loop theaters, B & K's outlying palaces generated immense revenues and, despite high costs, helped B & K earn huge profits during the late 1920s. Again, the numerous antitrust cases provide case after case to support such a claim.[29]

The growth of such profitable enterprises was not limited to Chicago. All fan-shaped cities with more than 50,000 people also saw the development of outlying business and recreation centers during the 1920s. In smaller fan cities, however, the outlying theaters never grew as large or profitable as they did in Chicago. In such cities as large as Milwaukee (578,000 in 1930) and as small as Racine, Wis-consin (68,000 in 1930), outlying theaters usually held between 1,000 and 2,000 people. Still it was not surprising that Hollywood's 'Big Five' would try to merge or affiliate with chains of theaters which included large outlying picture palaces. Paramount took over B & K in 1926. Then, during the next five years, Hollywood companies took over almost all outlying picture palaces; for example, in 1928 Warner Bros., through the Stanley merger, acquired outlying palaces in Philadelphia; one year earlier Fox had acquired half the outlying houses in Milwaukee through its takeover of the Saxe chain. The prospect of larger profits provided a strong incentive for Hollywood's majors.[30]

IV

The picture palace was hardly an economic blunder. Although such theaters were costly to run, they generated more than sufficient revenues to cover costs. In fact, with the monopolies of location, popular live entertainment, and first- or second-run films, they were among the most profitable enterprises in the film industry. Motion picture entrepreneurs understood the changing American city of the 1920s and constructed picture palaces both downtown and, depending on the size and shape of the city, in outlying business and recreation centers. Fan-shaped cities possessed the greater number of picture palaces relative to their population; rectangular cities had less; square cities even fewer. Later events – the Great Depression, the rise of television, further growth in American cities, and antitrust decisions – destroyed the basis of monopoly profit on which the profitability of the picture palace rested. Only today do these theaters seem to have been part of a 'nonsense world' perpetuated by Hollywood movie moguls during the 1920s.

But when the seeming contradiction between the size of theaters and the nature of the business has been cleared up, certain questions immediately pose themselves: What cultural implications are to be found in the ornate style and architecture of the palaces? What effect, if any, did big-city theaters have upon the product created by Hollywood? What effect did they have upon the way audiences reacted to films? To answer such questions one needs a much more complex and adventurous method of working than I have been using here, and one has to address more directly the problem of American ideology. At that level of inquiry, contradictions would indeed proliferate and become real. My point here has been that the models so far developed to help us understand film's ideological functioning have been too casual in treating the material basis of the industry. My aim has been to offer a modest first step toward a truer understanding of this basis.

Notes

1 See Lawrence Kardish, *Reel Plastic Magic* (Boston: Little, Brown, 1972), pp. 101–2, for a typical treatment of the picture palace.

2 Robert Sklar, *Movie-Made America* (New York: Random House, 1975), pp. 149–52.

3 I wish to write a history of *American* motion picture exhibition, thus this narrow assumption. England and Australia certainly had their share of picture palaces. See Dennis Sharp, *The Picture Palace* (New York: Praeger, 1969), and Ross Thorne, *Picture Palace Architecture in Australia* (South Melbourne: Sun Books, 1976).

4 Some argue that the lower capacity was 1,800 seats. See Charlotte Herzog, 'Movie palaces,' *Film Reader* vol. 2, 1977, p. 185.

5 William A. Johnson, 'The structure of the motion picture industry,' *Society of Motion Picture Engineers Transactions*, XI (1927), p. 667; *Variety*, 5 December 1926, p. 7; Martin Quigley, ed., *Motion Picture Almanac* (New York: Quigley Publications, 1934), pp. 890–9.

6 That is, 'monopoly profit' is that additional profit which accrues above and beyond normal profits because the monopolist is the only seller. See Richard A. Bilas, *Micro-Economic Theory* (New York: McGraw-Hill, 1967), pp. 186–8.

7 Maurice D. Kann, ed., *The Film Daily Yearbook – 1927* (New York: Film Daily, 1928), pp. 649–71, 905; *Variety*, 12 May 1926, p. 5; Raymond E. Murphy, *The American City: An Urban Geography* (New York: McGraw-Hill, 1974), pp. 345–78.

8 Eric T. Clark, 'An exhibitor's problems in 1925,' *Transactions of the Society of Motion Picture Engineers*, January 1926, p. 49; Charles Hoffman, *Sounds for Silents*, (New York: Drama Bookstore Publications/ Drama Book Specialists, 1970), pp. 26, 39; Ben M. Hall, *The Best Remaining Seats* (New York: C. N. Potter, 1961), pp. 186–98; Reginald Foort, *The Cinema Organ* (Vestal, NY: Vestal Press, 1970), p. 87; Erno Rapee, *Encyclopedia of Music for Pictures* (New York: Belwin, 1925), pp. 23–4.

9 Clark, 'An exhibitor's problems in 1925,' p. 49; *Variety*, 1 April 1926, p. 36; *Variety*, 10 March 1926, p. 35; Lewis W. Townsend and William W. Hennessy, 'Some novel projected motion picture presentations,' *Society of Motion Picture Engineers' Transactions*, XII (1928), p. 349; Kann, *Yearbook – 1927*, p. 509.

10 United States v. Paramount Pictures, 70 F. Supp. 53, 60 (SDNY, 1947), Findings 146, 148(a)–148(c); United States v. Paramount Pictures, 334 US 131, 168, passim; Johnson, 'The structure of the motion picture industry,' p. 667.

11 Richard L. Nelson, *The Selection of Retail Locations* (New York: F. W. Dodge Corporation, 1958), p. 10; William H. Wilson, *Coming of Age: Urban America 1915-1945* (New York: John Wiley & Sons, 1974), pp. 34–6.

12 For the size, location, and other information concerning the movie theaters of South Bend, and the other cities discussed in detail below – Indianapolis, Madison, Wisconsin, Manhattan, and Chicago – the principal sources of data were the following: Maurice D. Kann, ed., *The Film Daily Yearbook – 1930* (New York: Film Daily 1931); Maurice D. Kann, ed., *The Film Daily Yearbook – 1934* (New York: Film Daily 1935); *Motion Picture Directory – 1929* (New York: Siebert, 1929); *Motion Picture Trade Directory – 1928* (New York: Siebert, 1928). I took the cutoff date as December 1929. Additional sources will be cited in the sections concerning each city.

13 Donald J. Bogue, *Population Growth in Standard Metropolitan Areas, 1900-1950* (Washington, DC: Housing and Home Finance Agency, 1953), p. 70; Dean R. Esslinger, *Immigrants and the City* (Port Washington, NY: Kennikat Press, 1975), passim; Louis V. Bruggner, *South Bend, Mishawaha, St Joseph County, Indiana* (Map) (South Bend, 1944).

14 Bogue, *Population Growth*, p. 65; Gene Gladson, *Indianapolis Theatres*

from A to Z (Indianapolis: Gladson Publications, 1976), passim; Edward A. Leary, *Indianapolis: The Story of a City* (Indianapolis: Bobbs-Merrill, 1971), pp. 180–99; *Indianapolis Railroads, A Map for Going Anywhere in Indianapolis by Street Car, Trackless Trolley, Bus* (Indianapolis, 1945); sources cited in note 13.

15 Nelson, *The Selection*, pp. 10–13; Bogue, *Population Growth*, p. 66; Ben Koenig (comp.), *Guide for Sales Executives – 1933* (Milwaukee: Milwaukee Film Board of Trade, 1933), pp. 14–15; sources cited in note 13.

16 *Wright's Madison City Directory – 1929*, vol. 20 (Milwaukee: Wright's Directory Company, 1929), pp. 28, 875, 1183; *Wright's Madison City Directory – 1925*, vol. 18 (Milwaukee: Wright's Directory Company, 1925), pp. 825, 1081; *Standard Historical Atlas of Dane County, Wisconsin* (Madison: Cartwell Publishing Company, 1911); Federal Writer's Project, *Wisconsin* (New York: Random House, 1939), pp. 222–3; Ladislas Sogoe, *Comprehensive Plan of Madison, Wisconsin and Environs*, 2 vols (Madison: Trustees of Madison Planning Commission, 1938), vol. 1, pp. 46–9, 53–4, vol. 2, Book 9, pp. 8–19; Kimball Young, John L. Gillin and Calvert L. Dedrick, *The Madison Community*, University of Wisconsin Studies in the Social Sciences and History no 21 (Madison, 1934), pp. 7–70; 'Thousand at dedication of beautiful Eastwood Theatre,' *Capital Times* (Madison, Wisconsin), 28 December 1929, p. 3; 'Crowds jam new theatre at dedication,' *Wisconsin State Journal*, 28 December 1929, p. 2; 'Advertisement for Eastwood,' 28 December 1929, *Wisconsin State Journal*, p. 3, Gilmore, Frank A., *The City of Madison* (Madison: Madison Board of Commerce, 1916), pp. 100–1.

17 Walter Laidlow, *Population of the City of New York, 1890–1930* (New York: Cities Census Committee, 1922), pp. 51–3, 85; Consolidated Edison Company of New York, *Population Growth of New York City by Districts, 1910–1948* (New York: Consolidated Edison Company, 1948), p. 2; Harold M. Lewis, *Transit and Transportation*, Regional Survey, vol. 4 (New York: Regional Plan of New York and Its Environs, 1928), pp. 19–69; Thomas Adams, Harold M. Lewis and Theodore T. McCrosky, *Population, Land Values and Government*, Regional Survey, vol 2 (New York: Regional Plan of New York and Its Environs, 1929), pp. 74–6, 149–50.

18 The Radio City Music Hall (6,200) did not open until 1932. I did not count the Hippodrome (5,105) because it was, largely, a vaudeville house during the 1920s. See Norman Clarke, *The Mighty Hippodrome* (New York: A. S. Barnes, 1968), pp. 113–31.

19 Mary C. Henderson, *The City and the Theatre* (Clifton, NJ: James T. White & Co., 1973), pp. 199–284; Michael Miller, 'Proctor's Fifty-eight Street Theatre', *Marquee*, 5, no. 3, Third Quarter, 1973, pp. 7–11; Federal Writers Project, *New York City Guide* (New York: Random House, 1939), pp. 226–52; sources cited in note 13.

20 A market survey, *New York Herald, The New York Market* (New York: New York Herald, 1922), pp. 60–3, 68–79, provided important information about population and housing stock. See also Allan Nevins and John A. Krout, eds, *The Greater City: New York, 1898–1948* (New York: Columbia University Press, 1948) pp. 148–54, 170–4, Federal Writer's

Project, *New York City Guide*, passim, and *New York Times*, 15 December 1929, p. 5.
21 Bogue, *Population Growth*, p. 62; Nelson, *The Selection,* pp. 11–12; Homer Hoyt, *One Hundred Years of Land Values in Chicago, 1830–1933* (Chicago: University of Chicago Press, 1933), p. 225. For a review of the literature of studies of Chicago see Irving Cutler, *Chicago: Metropolis of the Mid-Continent,* 2nd edn (Dubuque, Iowa: Kendall/Hunt Publishing Company, 1976), pp. 197–203 and Harold M. Mayer and Richard C. Wade, *Chicago: Growth of a Metropolis* (Chicago: University of Chicago Press, 1960), pp. 475–94.
22 Harold M. Mayer, 'Patterns and trends of Chicago's outlying business centers,' *The Journal of Land and Public Utility Economics,* 18 (February 1942), pp. 4–6; Hoyt, *One Hundred Years,* pp. 225–9, 249–55; T. V. Smith and Leonard D. White, eds, *Chicago: An Experiment in Social Science Research* (Chicago: University of Chicago Press, 1929), pp. 116, 127; Bogue, *Population Growth,* p. 62; James L. Davis, 'The elevated system and the growth of northern Chicago,' *Studies in Geography,* no. 10 (Evanston, Ill.: Northwestern University Press, 1965), pp. 11–49; Boris Emmet and John E. Jeuck, *Catalogues and Counters: A History of Sears, Roebuck and Company* (Chicago: University of Chicago Press, 1950), p. 348.
23 Hoyt, *One Hundred Years,* pp. 227–31; Smith and White, *Chicago,* pp. 113–18; Miller McClintock, *Report and Recommendations of the Metropolitan Street Traffic Survey* (Chicago: Chicago Association of Commerce, 1926), passim; Malcolm J. Proudfoot, 'The major outlying business centers of Chicago,' (PhD dissertation, University of Chicago, 1936), pp. 16–50, 100–224; Mayer, 'Patterns,' pp. 4–6.
24 R. D. McKenzie, *The Metropolitan Community* (New York: McGraw-Hill, 1933), pp. 271–6; James J. Flink, *The Car Culture* (Cambridge, Mass.: MIT Press, 1975), pp. 143–4; James H. Madison, 'Changing patterns of urban retailing: the 1920s,' *Business and Economic History,* 2nd series, vol. 5, March 1976, pp. 106–7; Hoyt, *One Hundred Years,* pp. 223–41; McClintock, *Report,* p. 57.
25 Smith and White, *Chicago,* pp. 116–17.
26 Louis Wirth and Margaret Furez, eds, *Local Community Factbook, 1938* (Chicago: Chicago Recreation Commission, 1939), pp. 3, 6, 26, 42, 68; Harvey W. Zorbaugh, *The Gold Coast and the Slum* (Chicago: University of Chicago Press, 1929), passim; Nancy Banks, 'The world's most beautiful ballrooms,' *Chicago History,* 2, no. 4 (Fall-Winter 1973), pp. 206–15; Mayer and Wade, *Chicago,* pp. 344–8; Chicago Plan Commission, *Forty-Four Cities in the City of Chicago* (Chicago: Chicago Plan Commission, 1942), pp 10–13, 22–4, 39–40, 58–9.
27 Size is capacity at opening day from records of the Cook County Assessor's Office from Chicago Historical Society, Arthur G. Levy Collection, 'Largest motion picture theatres in Chicago and vicinity,' 12 July 1935 (mimeo), n.p.
28 Michael Conant, *Antitrust in the Motion Picture Industry* (Berkeley: University of California Press, 1960), pp. 154–5; Levy, 'Largest,' n.p.; Chicago Recreation Commission, *The Chicago Recreation Survey, 1937, vol. 2,*

Commercial Recreation (Chicago, 1938), pp. 37–8; McKenzie, *Metropolitan*, pp. 188–90; Hoyt, *One Hundred Years*, p. 262; Carrie Balaban, *Continuous Performance* (New York: A. J. Balaban Foundation, 1964), pp. 53–5.

29 Proudfoot, 'The major centers,' pp. 202–6; Conant, *Anti-Trust*, pp. 58–83; *Chicago Tribune*, 1 December 1929, part 7, p. 4; *Chicago Tribune*, 20 December 1929, pp. 32–3; *Chicago Tribune*, 31 December 1929, pp. 10–11; *Chicago Tribune*, 2 January 1930, p. 18; *Chicago Tribune*, 5 January 1930, part 7, p. 4; *Chicago Tribune*, 11 January 1930, p. 14.

30 Conant, pp. 21–32; Kann, *Yearbook – 1930*, pp. 802–3; Douglas Gomery, 'A history of Milwaukee's movie theatres,' unpublished Ms (Milwaukee: 1976) and Thomas M. Stroschein, 'A history of the Racine movie theatres and their effects on Racine's urban growth,' unpublished Ms (Milwaukee: 1976). Population figures from Bogue, *Population Growth*, pp. 66–8.

11 · Paul Kerr: Out of what past? Notes on the B film noir

Screen Education, nos. 32-3, Autumn/Winter 1979-80

Where Hugh Fordin's essay about *On the Town* starts with the Freed Unit at MGM and proceeds to chronicle chronologically that Unit's production of the film from conception to release, the following article addresses the subgenre known as the B *film noir* and attempts to trace back from the films to the industrial determinants from which they emerged.

Attempts to relate films to society reach their peak of productivity and absurdity with *film noir*. This article reconsiders the genre not as a reflection of a social/psychological/political *zeitgeist*, nor as the triumphant achievement of a number of émigré artists, but rather as the product of a complex and often contradictory coincidence of forces operating in and around the American film industry at a particular period in its history. In brief, the argument is that ideological, economic and political determinants at all levels of that industry (i.e. in distribution and exhibition as well as production) encouraged both differentiation within certain generic areas of the B film from the then dominant representational mode (which was characterised variously by the A film, by deep focus, by colour cinematography, by linear narration and later by the advent of television and the precariousness of the production code) and the simultaneous standardisation of aesthetic devices, which was obligatory in the industry even among what might be called upwardly mobile B films.

The article owes a great deal to the influence of Althusser which was so crucial in shifting film studies away from the economic determinism which a previous generation of radical scholars had been unable to avoid. Thus, for this author, 'An analysis of *film noir* as nothing more than an attempt to make a stylistic virtue out of economic necessity – the equation, at its crudest, of low budgets with low key lighting – is inadequate.' Furthermore the B *film noir* is the consequence not only of 'accommodation to restricted expenditure' but also of 'resistance to the realist aesthetic'. If this, perhaps rather mechanical, application of Althusserian categories, for all its disadvantages, does dispel the liberal pluralism apparent in almost all other accounts of the genre's origins, the idealist implications of hypothesising autonomous economic, ideological and political instances remain inescapable. Once cinema is placed in the category of the ideological (for example), the very possibility of thinking through its economic and political meanings and modes is severely diminished. For the tendency of the Althusser model, indeed one that is inherent in the strength of its approach – a refusal of economic reductionism in the conception of any cultural question – is to identify specific cultural institutions with specific Althusserian instances.

If the political instance is perhaps conspicuous by its absence from the following then it is worth amending the account by noting that the 1940 Consent Decree eliminated both blind selling and block booking; thus, for the first time, necessitating trade shows for every film (and not just A films as had previously been the case) and encouraging an increasing differentiation of product especially at the most threatened end of the industry, that of the smaller independent studios and the B units. Finally, in the light of David Bordwell's article in this volume, it is worth pointing out here that while certain *noir* characteristics might appear uneconomic, the expenditure they obliged would probably have been accepted as a legitimate strategy in order to distinguish the final product from its competitor releases, and from contemporary Hollywood's aesthetic norms.

Ever since the publication of Borde and Chaumeton's pioneering *Panorama du Film Noir Américain* in 1955, there has been a continuing dispute about the genre's precise cultural sources and critical status.[1] In their attempts to provide *film noir* with a respectable pedigree, subsequent studies have cited not only cinematic but also sociological, psychological, philosophical, political, technological and aesthetic factors amongst its progenitors. What they have not done, however, is to relate these general – and generally untheorised – notions of 'influence' to the specific modes of production, both economic and ideological, upon which they were, presumably, exercised; in this case, those structures and strategies adopted by certain factions within the American film industry over a period of almost two decades. Instead, these archaeologists of the genre have excavated a wide range of 'ancestors' for *film noir* – the influx of German *émigrés* and the influence of expressionism; the influx of French *émigrés* and the influence of existentialism; Ernest Hemingway and the 'hard-boiled' school of writing; Edward Hopper and the 'ash can' school of painting; pre-war photo-journalism, wartime newsreels and post-war neorealism; the creators of *Kane* – Citizens Mankiewicz, Toland and Welles; the Wall Street crash and the rise of populism; the Second World War and the rise of fascism; the Cold War and the rise of McCarthyism. Finally, several critics have pointed, in passing, to a number of even less specific sources, such as general American fears about bureaucracy, the bomb and the big city, as well as one or two more substantial ones, including the industrialisation of the female work-force during the war and the escalating corporatism of American capital throughout the 1940s.[2] However pertinent some of these suggestions, attempts to establish a 'family tree' have usually revealed less about the formation of *film noir* in particular than about the poverty of film history in general. This article, therefore, is an attempt to refocus the debate on the specifically film-industrial determinants of the genre by concentrating on one important, industrially defined, fraction of it – the B *film noir*.

As I have indicated, most explanations have tended to credit either particular people (such as ex-employees of UFA and *Black Mask*) or events (the Depression and the war, for example) with the creation of – or, more accurately, a contribution to – *film noir*. Thus, in the first category, auteurists discuss the genre as if it were simply the chosen canvas of a few talented individuals, whether they were directors (Siodmak, Tourneur, Ulmer), writers (Chandler, Mainwaring, Paxton) or cinematographers (Alton, Musuraca, Toland). Similarly, genre critics generally consider *film noir* either in terms of its function as social myth or, more simply, as no more than a symptom of social malaise.[3] Borde and Chaumeton begin their chapter on sources with an account of *film noir*'s literary and cinematic precursors, so endorsing an evolutionary model of film history, but they go on to propose a much more interesting industrial origin in Hollywood's 'synthesis of three types of films which at that time had developed such an autonomy that each studio had its own specialities from among them; the brutal and colourful gangster film, whose style carried over to other productions at Warner Bros; the horror film over which Universal acquired a near-monopoly; and the classic detective film of deduction which was shared by Fox and Metro-Goldwyn-Mayer.'[4] Having gone this far, though, Borde and Chaumeton fail to ask why such a synthesis should ever have taken place, if indeed it did. There are, I think, only two other theories which have been seriously put forward *vis-à-vis* the relationship between *film noir* and the film industry, both of which are equally untenable. The first argues that the genre was the cinema's unmediated reflection of an all-pervading postwar gloom and the second, that it was the expression of a community finally freed from its Depression duties as a dream factory by an audience that no longer needed cheering up.[5] In spite of their diametrically opposing views of postwar American 'morale', both theories employ a conception of Hollywood as monolithic, its products either entirely determined by American ideology or entirely autonomous of it.

Clearly, if we want to go on using the notion of 'determination' rather than relying on the dubious concept of 'derivation', it is necessary to approach the classic base/superstructure formulation with some caution. Indeed, Raymond Williams has remarked that

... each term of the proposition has to be revalued in a particular direction. We have to revalue 'determination' towards the setting of limits and the exertion of pressure and away from a predicted, prefigured and controlled content. We have to revalue 'superstructure' towards a related range of cultural practices and away from a reflected, reproduced or specifically dependent content. And, crucially, we have to revalue 'the base' away from the notion of a fixed economic or technological abstraction, and towards the specific activities of men in real social and economic relationships, containing fundamental contradictions and variations and therefore always in a state of dynamic process.[6]

This article, then, taking its cue from the oft-cited specificity of *film noir* as a genre, will attempt to relate it not to the general American social formation (as some species of 'reflection'), nor to a monolithically conceived film industry, but rather to particular, relatively autonomous modes of film production, distribution and exhibition in a particular conjuncture. What follows, therefore, is an exploratory rather than an exhaustive analysis of the reciprocal relation which obtained between *film noir*'s primary determinants – the economic and the ideological. (The third determinant, at least in Althusserian terms, is that of the political, the effectivity of which with respect to the *film noir* would have to include the production code, the antitrust suits and the Hollywood blacklist. The political instance, for reasons of brevity, has here been subsumed within the other two categories.) This analysis attends in particular to the relatively autonomous and uneven development of the B *film noir*, a category constituted, I will argue, by a negotiated resistance to the realist aesthetic on the one hand and an accommodation to restricted expenditure on the other. Of course, none of these terms – relative autonomy, non-synchronicity, realism (not to mention *film noir* itself) – is unproblematic; their employment here, however, is a necessary condition of any discussion which hopes to account for the

existence of a genre at different times and in different places with a
number of different inflections. The crucial theoretical formulation
here is that of 'determination' itself, since the identity of the infamous
'last instance' though classically considered to be the economic will
actually fluctuate, at least in the short term. Thus, in the long term,
Hollywood's ideological and economic aims are complementary: the
reproduction of the conditions necessary for continued cinematic
production and consumption – in other words, the perpetuation of
the industry. In the short term, however, these determinants may be
less compatible, and it is the shifting balance of relations between
the two which accords Hollywood's 'superstructure' its relative autonomy from its economic 'base'. Furthermore, the economic or ideological space opened up for the American cinema in this way is in
direct proportion to the urgency with which ideological or economic
priorities in the industry are negotiated.

   To take an example, Antony Easthope has argued that 'in the early
Thirties Hollywood production was determined ideologically or even
politically rather than economically'[7] but his argument, like so many
others, hinges on a reading of American history in general and not
that of the film industry. In fact, it seems equally plausible – if
equally schematic – to suggest that Hollywood's product was domi-
nantly determined economically only in periods of economic crisis in
the industry (like the early 1930s when several studios were actually
bankrupted by a combination of reduced receipts and excessive cap-
italisation), whilst in eras of relative economic stability but marked
ideological and/or political unrest (like the mid-1940s, when receipts
rose to a new high but both international and industrial relations
were of crucial importance) that product would have tended to be,
primarily at least, ideologically determined. In modification of this
latter formulation, however, it is necessary to add that low-budget
and blockbuster film-making, neither of which was really established
across the industry until the latter half of the 1930s – having their
origins in precisely those economic conditions outlined above – might
have been more vulnerable to economic imperatives ('masking' and
'flaunting' their respective production values) than the admittedly
slightly hypothetical 'mid-budgeted' mainstream A products of the
studios at that time. This privileging of the economic imperative on
the B film, in a period of film history which was otherwise primarily
ideologically determinate (at least until about 1947), might begin to
account for the presence of several aesthetically (and therefore ideologically) unorthodox practices within the B *film noir*.

Towards a definition

Before a discussion of such suggestions can legitimately begin, however, some kind of critical consensus about these 'practices' and the period in which they were pursued is needed. The authors of the *Panorama* focus their own analysis on those films produced between 1941 and 1953 but more recent critics have broadened these bounds somewhat to include films made from the beginning of the 1940s (and sometimes even earlier) until the end of the following decade. If we employ the more elastic of these estimates and allow an additional – and admittedly arbitrary – margin at the beginning of the period, we may be able to reconstruct at least some of the industrial determinants of the genre. Furthermore, several critics have tried to demonstrate that *film noir* comprises a number of distinct stages. Paul Schrader, for example, has outlined 'three broad phases' for the genre: the first lasting until about 1946 and characterised by couples like Bogart and Bacall and 'classy' studio directors like Curtiz; the second spanning the immediate postwar years, when shooting began to move out of the studios and into the streets; and the third and final phase in which both characters and conventions alike were subject to extraordinary permutations. Perhaps film history will ultimately explain the industrial underpinnings of such 'sub-generic' shifts as well as the primary determinants and eventual demise of the wider genre itself.[8] Until then, whether the period of *film noir* production is relatively easily agreed upon or not, the volume of that production is decidedly more difficult to ascertain. This is due, to some degree at least, to the primacy of the economic and relative autonomy of the ideological instances of the *film noir*. Equally important is its controversial status as a genre at all, since it is usually defined in terms of its style rather than – as most genres are – in relation to content, character, setting and plot. Further difficulties derive from its relative inaccessibility as an object of study: retrospectives are all too rare and there are still no book-length analyses of the genre in English – even the *Panorama* remains untranslated. *Film noir*, therefore, has still not received its due in terms of either critical or archival attention.

Despite such difficulties, it still remains possible to offer at least an outline of the genre's defining characteristics.[9] Primarily, *film noir* has been associated with a propensity for low key lighting, a convention which was in direct opposition to the cinematographic orthodoxy of the previous decade. In the 1930s the dominant lighting style, known as high key, had been characterised by a contrast ratio of approximately 4:1 between the light value of the key lamp on the one hand and the filler on the other. *Noir*, with a considerably higher range of contrasts, is thus a *chiaroscuro* style, its low key effects often undiffused by either lens gauzes or lamp glasses – as they certainly would have been in conventional high key style. Instead, *noir* sets are often only half or quarter lit, with the important exception of those brief sequences in the *'blanc'* (that is, 'normal') world which are sometimes employed as a framing device at the beginning and end of the narrative. Otherwise, shooting tends to be either day-for-night or night-for-night and the main action has a habit of occurring in shadowy rooms, dingy offices, overlush apartments and rainwashed streets. In such settings both actors and decor are often partially obscured by the foregrounding of oblique objects – shutters and banisters, for instance, casting horizontal or vertical grids of light and dark across faces and furniture. Meanwhile, the arrangement of space within the frame is often equally irregular, both in regard to its occupation by actors and props as well as to the width and depth of focus. This can lead to a 'discomposition' of the image (and consequent disorientation of the spectator) in terms of the neo-classical conventions of composition generally used and, indeed, reinforced by Hollywood. These kinds of disorientation can be accentuated by the use of 'perversely' low and high camera angles (a perversity defined entirely in relation to contemporary realist criteria) and the virtual elimination of those other staples of realism, the establishing long shot and the personalising close-up. In fact, the latter is often used ironically in the *film noir* in soft focus treatment of male villainy (signifying feminine decadence) whilst women, the conventional 'objects' of such attention, are often photographed in harsh, unflattering and undiffused light with wide angle distorting lenses. Such an emphasis on unconventional camera angles and lighting set-ups, however, is often achieved at the (literal) expense of camera movement and classical editing. A number of other realist conventions, including the shot-reverse-shot alternation of points of view and the 180 degree rule, are also occasionally infringed by the *film noir*.[10] Finally, there is a great deal of reliance on such fragmented narrative structures as the flashback, which lend an additional sense of inevitability to the plot and helplessness to the characters. Hitherto, most definitions of the genre have more or less rested at this point, tending to ignore that plot and those characters. One recent critic, however, has assembled what he calls a 'rudimentary working prototype' of characteristic content for *film noir* along the following lines:

> Either because he is fated to do so by chance, or because he has
> been hired for a job specifically associated with her, a man

whose experience of life has left him sanguine and often bitter meets a not-innocent woman of similar outlook to whom he is sexually and fatally attracted. Through this attraction, either because the woman induces him to it or because it is the natural result of their relationship, the man comes to cheat, attempt to murder or actually murder a second man to whom the woman is unhappily or unwillingly attached (generally he is her husband or lover), an act which brings about the sometimes metaphoric but usually literal destruction of the woman, the man to whom she is attached and frequently the protagonist himself.[11]

This schematic summary of *film noir* will have to suffice for our purposes here, if only as a result of the extremely tentative account of the genre's determination outlined below.

The coming of the B feature

The B film was launched as an attempt by a number of independent exhibitors to lure audiences back into their theatres at a time of acute economic crisis in the industry. Along with the double bill these independents had already – by the beginning of the 1930s – introduced lotteries, live acts, quizzes, free gifts and several other gimmicks in order to build up bigger audiences and, at the same time, keep those patrons they already had in their seats a little longer, so boosting both box-office takings and confectionery sales whilst re-legitimising admission prices. The double bill, however, had the additional – and, as it proved, crucial – advantage of enabling independent exhibitors to accommodate their programme policies to the majors' monopolistic distribution practices (such as blind selling and block booking) and allowing them to exhibit more independent product at the same time. Of the 23,000 theatres operating in the United States in 1930, the five majors (MGM, RKO, Fox, Warners and Paramount) either owned or controlled some 3,000 – most of that number being among the biggest and best situated of the first-run theatres; these 3,000 theatres, though comprising less than 14 per cent of the total number then in operation, accounted for nearly 70 per cent of the entire industry's box-office takings that year. This left the independents with some 20,000 theatres in which to screen what were either second-run or independent films. By the end of 1931 the double bill, which had originated in New England, had spread its influence on programme policy right across the country, establishing itself as at least a part of that policy in one-eighth of the theatres then in operation. In 1935, the last of the majors to adopt double bills in their theatres – MGM and RKO – announced their decision to screen two features in all but two of their theatres. By 1947, the fraction of cinemas advertising double bills had risen to nearly two-thirds. In normal circumstances, of course, any such increase in the volume of films in exhibition would have led to a similar increase in the volume of film production but this was not the case. Overproduction by the majors since the advent of sound had accumulated an enormous backlog of as yet unreleased material. It was not, therefore, until this reservoir of ready-made second features had been exhausted that it became necessary to set up an entirely new mode of film production – the B unit.

While those units within the vertically integrated majors virtually monopolised the independent exhibition outlets a number of B studios established to meet the same demand were compelled to rely on the so-called States Rights system, whereby studios sold distribution rights to film franchises on a territorial basis. Lacking theatre chains of their own, several independent production companies were forced to farm out their product to a relatively unknown market. Monogram and Republic did eventually set up small exchanges of their own in a few cities and their main rival, PRC, even acquired some theatres of its own in the 1940s but the distinction between such venues and those owned by the majors should not be forgotten. Certainly, the producers of the B films themselves would have been acutely aware of the kind of cinemas in which the bulk of their products would have been seen and this may have been as influential a factor in B film production as the picture palaces undoubtedly were for the As. Mae D. Huettig,[12] for instance, has described how Los Angeles's eleven first-run theatres exhibited 405 films in the year 1939/40 of which only five were the product of independent companies, all but one of that five being shown at the bottom of a double bill. Wherever such double bills were programmed, however, few exhibitors could afford the rentals of two top quality (i.e. top price) products at the same time. The double bill, therefore, was a combination of one relatively expensive A film and one relatively inexpensive B, the former generally deriving from the major studios and costing, throughout the 1940s, upwards of $700,000 and the latter being produced by low budget units at the same studios as well as by several B studios, at anything less than about $400,000.[13] In general, the A feature's rental was based on a percentage of box-office takings whilst the Bs played for a fixed or flat rental and were thus not so reliant on audience attendance figures at all – at least, not in the short term. In the long term, however, these B units would be compelled to carve out identifiable and distinctive styles for themselves

in order to differentiate their product – within generic constraints –
for the benefit of audiences in general and exhibitors in particular.

In most cases the B *film noir* would have been produced – like all
Bs – on a fixed budget which would itself have been calculated in
relation to fixed rentals. In illustrating the effects such economies
exercised on these Bs I have restricted reference, as far as possible,
to one large integrated company, RKO, and one small independent
company, PRC.[14] At the beginning of the decade the budgets of
RKO's most important production unit in the B sector were approximately $150,000 per picture; at PRC, several years later, most units
were working with less than two-thirds of that amount. To take two
examples: Val Lewton's films at RKO had tight, twenty-one-day
schedules whilst Edgar G. Ulmer's at PRC were often brought in
after only six days and nights. (To achieve this remarkable shooting
speed nightwork was almost inevitable and Ulmer's unit used to
mount many as eighty different camera set-ups a day.) Props, sets
and costumes were kept to a minimum, except on those occasions
when they could be borrowed from more expensive productions, as
Lewton borrowed a staircase from *The Magnificent Ambersons* for
his first feature, *The Cat People*. Nick Grinde, a veteran of B units
in the 1940s, has described how a producer would resist charges of
plagiarism on the grounds that 'the way he will shoot it no-one will
recognise it for the same set. He'll have his director pick new angles
and redress the foreground ... [and] ... will even agree to shoot at
night ...'[15]

Night shooting, of course, was an obvious and often unavoidable
strategy for getting films in on short schedules as well as fully exploiting fixed assets and economising on rentals. (It also suited those
employees who sought to avoid IATSE overtime bans.) Mark Robson, an editor and later director in Lewton's unit, has recalled that 'the
streets we had in *The Seventh Victim*, for instance, were studio streets
and the less light we put on them the better they looked.'[16] Similarly,
expensive special effects and spectacular action sequences were generally
avoided unless stock footage could be borrowed from other films.
This 'borrowing' became known as the 'montage' and involved the
use of 'a series of quick cuts of film'. As Grinde has explained,

> You can't shoot a first-rate crime wave on short dough, so you
> borrow or buy about twenty pieces of thrilling moments from
> twenty forgotten pictures. A fleeing limousine skids into a street- car,
> a pedestrian is socked over the head in an alley, a newspaper
> office is wrecked by hoodlums, a woman screams, a couple of
> mugs are slapping a little merchant into seeing things their way.
> And so on until we end up on a really big explosion.[17]

Not all such 'thrilling moments' were 'borrowed' from 'forgotten pictures', however. Fritz Lang, for example, has noted that footage from *You Only Live Once* (UA 1937), including a classic bank robbery sequence, found its way into *Dillinger* (Monogram 1945).[18]

The exploitation of borrowed footage and furniture was only really possible as long as films were still being shot inside the studios. Until the middle of the 1940s location shooting was extremely rare and even independents like Monogram and PRC had their own studio facilities. As fixed and variable costs began to escalate at the end of the war, however, production units were encouraged to go out on location and this practice was extended by the prolonged studio strikes of 1945-47. In 1946, the abolition of block booking encouraged the appearance of a number of small studio-less independent production companies and these also contributed to the 'street' rather than 'studio' look in the latter half of the decade. Constraints at both the production and distribution ends of the industry meant that the running length of Bs fluctuated between about fifty-five and seventy-five minutes; raw footage was expensive, audiences had only limited amounts of time and of course, exhibitors were keen to screen their double bills as many times a day as possible. In 1943 the government reduced basic allotments of raw film stock to the studios by 25 per cent and once again it was the B units which were hardest hit. Consequently 'montages' became even more common. Casts and crews on contract to B units were kept at a manageable minimum, so prohibiting plots with long cast lists, crowd scenes and complicated camera or lighting set-ups. Similarly, overworked script departments often produced unpolished and occasionally incoherent scripts. (Film titles were pretested with audiences before stories or scripts were even considered.) Despite such drawbacks, however, the B units, throughout the 1940s and as late as the mid-1950s, employed the same basic equipment as their big budget rivals, including Mitchell or Bell and Howell cameras, Mole Richardson lighting units, Moviola editing gear and RCA or Western Electric sound systems. Such economies as B units practised, therefore, were not related to fixed assets like rents and salaries but to variable costs like sets, scripts, footage, casual labour and, crucially, power.

RKO's production of *noir* Bs seems to have been inaugurated in 1940 with the release of Boris Ingster's extraordinary *Stranger On The Third Floor*. The studio had emerged from receivership at the end of the previous decade – a period of some prosperity for the other majors – to make only minimal profits of $18,604 in 1938 and $228,608 in 1939. In 1940 the studio lost almost half a million dollars and began to augment its low budget policy with B series like *The Saint* and *The Falcon*. It was not until 1942, however, when RKO plunged more than two million dollars into debt that the trend towards the B *film noir* became really evident. In that year, George Schaefer was fired as president and replaced by his deputy, Ned Depinet, who immediately appointed Charles M. Koerner – from RKO Theatres Inc. – as vice-president in charge of production. It was at this point that Val Lewton was brought to the studio to set up his own B unit. Within the limitations I have outlined, as well as the generic constraints of having to work in the 'horror' category, Lewton's unit, and others like it, were accorded a degree of autonomy which would never have been sanctioned for more expensive studio productions.[19] At PRC the situation was rather different. The company had been formed in March 1940 by the creditors of its predecessor, the Producers' Distributing Corporation, and with the cooperation of the Pathé Laboratories. The new Producers' Releasing Corporation had five separate production units and the Fine Arts Studio (formerly Grand National). At first the emphasis was on comedy and westerns; PRC produced forty-four films, mostly in these genres, in the 1941/42 season. By 1942, however, PRC had acquired twenty-three film exchanges and with the replacement of George Batchelor by Leon Fromkess as production head, there was an increased diversification of product. While most units concentrated on comedies and musicals, others began to turn out cut-rate westerns and crime thrillers. It was also in 1942 that Edgar G. Ulmer began work for the studio. Allowed only about 15,000 feet per picture, Ulmer's unit, like Lewton's, economised with stock footage (as in *Girls in Chains* PRC 1943) and minimal casts and sets (as in *Detour* PRC 1946).

Artistic ingenuity in the face of economic intransigence is one critical commonplace about the B *film noir* (and about people like Lewton and Ulmer in particular). Against this, I have suggested that a number of *noir* characteristics can at least be associated with – if not directly attributed to – economic and therefore technological constraints. The paucity of 'production values' (sets, stars and so forth) may even have encouraged low budget production units to compensate with complicated plots and convoluted atmosphere. Realist denotation would thus have been de-emphasised in favour of expressionist connotation (in *The Cat People* RKO 1942, for example). This 'connotative' quality might also owe something to the influence of the Hays Office, which meant that 'unspeakable' subjects could only be suggested – *Under Age* (Columbia 1941), although concerned with the criminal exploitation of young girls, could never actually illustrate that exploitation. Similarly, compressed shooting

schedules, overworked script editors and general cost cutting procedures could well have contributed to what we now call *film noir*.
Nevertheless, an analysis of *film noir* as nothing more than an
attempt to make a stylistic virtue out of economic necessity – the
equation, at its crudest, of low budgets with low key lighting – is
inadequate: budgetary constraints and the relative autonomy of many
B units in comparison with As were a necessary but by no means
sufficient condition for its formation. It was, I have suggested, constituted not only by accommodation to restricted expenditure but
also by resistance to the realist aesthetic – like the B film generally,
it was determined not only economically but also ideologically. For
instance, the double bill was not simply the result of combining any
two films, one A and one B, but often depended on a number of
quite complex contrasts. *The Saint in New York*, for example, was
billed with *Gold Diggers in Paris*, *Blind Alibi* with *Holiday*. According to Frank Ricketson Jr, the tendency of both distributors and
exhibitors was to ensure that

> Heavy drama is blended with sparkling comedy. A virile action
> picture is mated with a sophisticated society play. An all-star
> production is matched with a light situation comedy of no-star
> value. An adventure story is contrasted with a musical
> production.[20]

Initially, of course, B films had been little more than low budget
versions of profitable A releases but as the industry was rationalised
after the Depression this imitative trend was partially replaced by
another differentiation. Thus, while early Bs had tended to remain in
the least expensive of successful genres – westerns, situation comedies, melodramas, thrillers and horror films – the exhibitors themselves began to exert a moderating influence (by means of intercom-
pany promotions like Koerner's within the integrated companies; by
means of advertisements in the trade papers among the independents). By the end of the 1930s, therefore, double bills were beginning
to contrast the staple A genres of that decade – gangster films, biop-
ics, musicals, screwball comedies, mysteries and westerns – with a
number of Poverty Row hybrids, mixtures of melodrama and mystery, gangster and private eye, screwball comedy and thriller (and,
later, 'documentary' and drama). In part, of course, this hybrid quality is explicable in terms of studio insecurities about marketing their
B products; nevertheless, the curiously cross-generic quality of the
film noir is perhaps a vestige of its origins as a kind of 'oppositional'
cinematic mode. Low key lighting styles, for example, were not only
more economic than their high key alternatives, they were also
dramatically and radically distinct from them.

Stylistic generation

In considering the concept of stylistic differentiation it is useful, at this point, to introduce the work of the Birmingham Centre for Contemporary Cultural Studies on 'the process of stylistic generation'.[21] Although specifically addressed to the 'styles' adopted by such subcultural groups as Teds, punks and Rastas, this work seems to me to be applicable, with some reservations, to the style of the B *film noir*. Whether or not one can legitimately describe Poverty Row as a subculture is clearly a matter for serious debate but, until we have some kind of social history of Hollywood, a final decision on the matter is premature. Lacking such knowledge, it remains striking how appropriate some of the Birmingham conclusions are for the present study. In their analysis the authors make admittedly eclectic use of Lévi-Strauss's concept of bricolage; but whereas Lévi-Strauss is concerned with situations and cultures where a single myth is dominant, John Clarke concentrates on the 'genesis of "unofficial" styles, where the stylistic core (if there is one) can be located in the expression of a partly negotiated opposition to the values of a wider society.'[22] (I will return to the notion of 'negotiated opposition' later.) Clarke proposes a two-tiered theory of stylistic generation, the first axiom of which states that the generation of subcultural styles involves differential selection from within the matrix of the existent and the second, that one of the main functions of a distinctive subcultural style is to define the boundaries of group membership as against other groups. I hope that the pertinence of these two axioms (the first 'economic', the second 'ideological') to the group which I have designated the B *film noir* will become apparent. Clarke even goes on to discuss the process whereby such subcultural styles are assimilated into/recuperated by the dominant culture; a process which Raymond Williams refers to as 'incorporation'. The defusion and dilution of the B *film noir*'s unorthodox visual style within the aesthetic of the A film clearly fits this kind of pattern, with the most economically secure studios at that time – MGM, Fox and Paramount – tending to produce not only fewer films in the genre than their competitors but also more lavish ones like *The Postman Always Rings Twice*, *Laura* and *Double Indemnity*. Furthermore, it was Fox who were to launch and lead the break-away police procedural strand at the end of the 1940s, a strand which emanated from and to a certain extent replaced that studio's location-based *March of Time* series.[23]

Meanwhile, the monopoly structure of the industry – which had been initially, if indirectly, responsible for the B phenomenon – was

234   *Paul Kerr*

being challenged. In May 1935 the Supreme Court voted to revoke
Roosevelt's National Industrial Recovery Act (under which *A Code
Of Fair Competition For The Motion Picture Industry* had more or
less condoned the industry's monopoly practices) on the grounds that
it was unconstitutional. Opposition to motion picture monopolies
was mounting, not only among the independent companies but also
in the courts and even in Congress itself. Finally, in July 1938, the
Department of Justice filed an Anti-Trust suit against the majors,
United States versus Paramount Pictures Inc. *et al.*, so launching a
case which was to reach the Supreme Court a decade later. In the
suit the majors were accused of separate infringements of Anti-Trust
legislation but, in November 1940, the case was apparently abandoned;
in fact it was merely being adjourned for the duration of hostilities,
the government being unwilling to provoke Hollywood at a time
when the communications media were of such crucial importance.
The suit was settled out of court with the signing of a modest Consent Decree, the provisions of which included an agreement by the
majors to 'modify' their use of block booking, to eliminate blind
selling and to refrain from 'unnecessary' theatrical expansion. Most
important of all the Decree's requirements, however, was the majors'
agreement to withdraw from the package selling procedures which
had compelled independent exhibitors to screen shorts, re-issues, ser-
ial westerns and newsreels with their main features. The last provision expanded the market for low budget production almost overnight. Whereas at the end of the 1930s there had been very few
independent companies, by 1946 (the year in which block booking
was finally abolished) there were more than forty. The Anti-Trust
Commission never entirely dropped their case against Hollywood,
however, and finally, in 1948, the five fully integrated companies
were instructed to divest themselves of their theatrical holdings. Paramount was the first to obey this ruling, divorcing its exhibition arm
from the production/distribution end of its business in late 1949.
RKO followed in 1950, 20th Century-Fox in 1952, Warner Bros. in
1953 and MGM in 1959. Rather ironically, the divorce meant the
demise of many independent studios which had thrived on providing
films for the bottom half of the bill; quite simply, low budget productions could no longer be guaranteed fixed rentals in exhibition.
Consequently, one of the first casualties of divorcement was the
double bill. The majors cancelled their B productions and the independents were forced to choose between closure and absorption. In
1949 PRC was absorbed by Rank and transformed into Eagle Lion;
the following year it ceased production altogether and merged with
United Artists. In 1953 Monogram became Allied Artists Pictures

Corporation and began to operate an increasingly important television subsidiary. Republic, whose staple product had always been westerns and serials, was finally sold to CBS in 1959 and became that network's Television City studio.

It was thus between the first filing of the Anti-Trust suit in 1938 and the final act of divorcement in 1959 that the B *film noir* flourished. Obviously, however, the trend towards media conglomerates and away from simple monopolies was by no means the only 'political' determinant on cinematic modes in that period, a period which witnessed American entry into the war, the rise of McCarthyism and a series of jurisdictional disputes in the labour unions.[24] During the Second World War the international market for American films shrank drastically and the domestic market expanded to take its place. By 1941, the cinemas of continental Europe, where the majors had earned more than a quarter of their entire box office in 1936, were no longer open to American distributors. Even in Britain, where most cinemas remained open throughout the war and where attendance actually rose from a weekly average of nineteen million in 1939 to more than thirty million in 1945, the Hollywood majors were unable to maintain even prewar profits. The introduction of currency restrictions severely limited the amount that American distributors could remove from the country; thus, only half their former revenues – some $17,500,000 – were withdrawn in 1940 and only $12,900,000 in 1941. Meanwhile, however, American domestic rentals soared from $193,000,000 in 1939 to $332,000,000 in 1946. By the end of the war, average weekly attendance in the US was back at about 90,000,000, its prewar peak. As the majors' profits rose, the volume of their production actually fell: having released some 400 films in 1939 the big eight companies released only 250 in 1946, the balance being made up by a flush of new B companies. This geographically – but not economically – reduced constituency may have afforded Hollywood the opportunity to take a closer look at contemporary and specifically American phenomena without relying on the 'comfortable' distance provided by classic genres like the western or the musical. That 'closer look' (at, for instance, urban crime, the family and the rise of corporations) could, furthermore, because of the national specificity of its audience and as a result of the 'dialectic' of its consumption (within the double bill), employ a less orthodox aesthetic than would previously have been likely.

The aesthetic orthodoxy of the American cinema in the 1940s and 1950s was realism and so it is necessary to relate cinematic realism to the *film noir*. Colin MacCabe has suggested its two primary conditions:

(1) The classic realist text cannot deal with the real as contradictory.

(2) In a reciprocal movement the classic realist text ensures the position of the subject in a relation of dominant specularity.

These two conditions, the repression of contradiction and the construction of spectatorial omniscience, are negotiated through a hierarchy of narrative discourses:

> Through the knowledge we gain from the narrative we can split the discourses of the various characters from their situation and compare what is said in these discourses with what has been revealed to us through narration. The camera shows us what happens – it tells the truth against which we can measure the discourses.[25]

Elsewhere MacCabe has restated this notion quite clearly: 'classical realism ... involves the homogenisation of different discourses by their relation to one dominant discourse – assured of its domination by the security and transparency of its image.'[26]

It is this very 'transparency' which *film noir* refuses; indeed, Sylvia Harvey has noted that 'One way of looking at the plot of the typical film noir is to see it as a struggle between different voices for control over the telling of the story.' From that perspective, *film noir* represents a fissure in the aesthetic and ideological fabric of realism. Thus,

> Despite the presence of most of the conventions of the dominant methods of film making and storytelling, the impetus towards the resolution of the plot, the diffusion of tension, the circularity of a narrative that resolves all the problems it encounters, the successful completion of the individual's quest, these methods do not, in the end, create the most significant contours of the cultural map of film noir. The defining contours of this group of films are the product of that which is abnormal and dissonant.[27]

Gill Davies, on the other hand, has suggested that such 'dissonance' can quite comfortably be contained by the 'weight' of generic convention.

> The disturbing effect of mystery or suspense is balanced by confidence in the inevitability of the genre. Character types, stock settings and the repetition of familiar plot devices assure the reader that a harmonious resolution will take place. This narrative pattern pretends to challenge the reader, creates superficial disorientation, while maintaining total narrative control. Our knowledge of the genre (supported, in the cinema, with the reappearance of certain actors and actresses in familiar roles) takes us through a baffling narrative with the confidence that all problems will ultimately be solved.[28]

In terms of *film noir*, however, I would argue that the 'surplus' of realist devices catalogued by Harvey and Davies indicates an attempt to hold in balance traditional generic elements with unorthodox aesthetic practices that constantly undermine them. *Film noir* can thus be seen as the negotiation of an 'oppositional space' within and against realist cinematic practice; this trend could only be effectively disarmed by the introduction of a number of stock devices derived from other genres (such as melodrama or the detective story). It is not an object of this article, though, to gauge the degree to which that resistance was or was not successful. Rather, its task is to begin to establish those historically contemporaneous strands of realism – Technicolor, television and the A film – against which any such resistance would necessarily have defined itself.

Television and Technicolor

In 1947 there were only 14,000 television receivers in the United States; two years later that number had risen to a million. By 1950 there were four million and by 1954 thirty-two million. In the face of such swiftly escalating opposition and as a consequence of the impending demise of the double bill (in the aftermath of the Anti-Trust decision), several of the smaller studios began renting theatrical films for television exhibition and even producing tele-films of their own. Thus, in 1949, Columbia formed a subsidiary, Screen Gems, to produce new films for and release old films to the new medium. In 1955, the first of the five majors, Warner Bros., was persuaded to produce a weekly ABC TV series, to be called *Warner Brothers Presents*, based on three of that studio's successful 1940s features: *King's Row* (1941), *Casablanca* (1944) and *Cheyenne* (1947). It is perhaps worth pointing out that *Cheyenne* was the only one which lacked elements of the *'noir'* style and also the only one to enjoy a mass audience; indeed, it was ultimately 'spun off' into a seven-year series of its own while the other two 'thirds' of the slot were quietly discontinued. In December of 1955 RKO withdrew from film production altogether and sold its film library to a television programming syndicate; two years later, the old RKO studio itself was in the hands of Desilu, an independent television production company owned by ex-RKO contract player Lucille Ball and her husband Desi Arnaz. In fact, Lucille Ball's comedy series *I Love Lucy* had been the first 'filmed' (as opposed to live) series on American television; it was only dislodged from its place at the top of the ratings by another filmed series, *Dragnet*. The latter, characterised by high key lighting, sparse shadowless sets and procedural plots, was to provide a model for television crime fiction for more than two decades. It is particularly ironic, therefore, to note that *Dragnet* derived from a 1948 B *film noir* produced by Eagle Lion, *He Walked By Night*, a film which contains what is perhaps the most dramatically *chiaroscuro* scene ever shot in Hollywood. In 1954 Warner Bros. released a cinematic spin-off from the series, again called *Dragnet*, but this time without a trace of the stylistic virtuosity which had characterised its cinematic grandparent. (The fact that this film proved unsuccessful at the box office, far from invalidating my thesis about the relationship between television and the *film noir*, actually corroborates my account of the different 'spaces' occupied by the discourse of realism in television and the cinema.) Very simply, the low contrast range of television receivers meant that any high contrast cinematic features (like *films noirs*) were inherently unsuitable for tele-cine reproduction.

If *film noir* was determined to any degree by an initial desire to differentiate B cinematic product from that of television (as A product was differentiated by colour, production values, 3D, wide screens and epic or 'adult' themes), as, too, its ultimate demise relates to capitulation to the requirements of tele-cine, that 'difference' can also be seen as a response to the advent of colour. The first full-length Technicolor feature, *Becky Sharp*, was released in 1935 (by RKO), and its director, Rouben Mamoulian – one of the few professionals in favour of colour at that time – has described in some detail the aesthetic consensus into which the new process was inserted:

For more than twenty years, cinematographers have varied the
key of lighting in photographing black-and-white pictures to
make the visual impression enhance the emotional mood of the
action. We have become accustomed to a definite language of
lighting: low key effects, with sombre, heavy shadows express a
sombrely dramatic mood; high key effects, with brilliant lighting
and sparkling definition, suggest a lighter mood; harsh contrasts
with velvety shadows and strong highlights strike a melodramatic
note. Today we have color – a new medium, basically different
in many ways from any dramatic medium previously known ...
Is it not logical, therefore, to feel that it is incumbent upon all of
us, as film craftsmen, to seek to evolve a photodramatic language
of color analogous with the language of light with which we are
all so familiar?[29]

Mamoulian's implicit appeal to a 'logic of the form' might well have impressed some of the 'creative' workers associated with A film productions but it is unlikely to have been heard sympathetically among employees of the Bs. Indeed, the advent of colour actually exacerbated the situation he had outlined: the Technicolor process demanded 'high key effects, with brilliant lighting and sparkling definition' as a very condition of its existence. It is, therefore, hardly surprising that a cinema of 'low key effects, with sombre heavy shadows' flourished in counterpart to it. Furthermore, the films actually employing Technicolor were often characterised by exotic locations, lavish sets, elaborate costumes and spectacular action sequences (generally of the musical or swashbuckling variety) and so fell into an expanding group of 'colour-specific' genres – westerns, musicals, epics, historical dramas, etcetera – leaving melodramas, thrillers, and horror films to the lower budgets of black and white. Finally, in 1939 the really decisive blow for the industrial endorsement of colour was struck by the unprecedented success of *Gone With The Wind*. However, wartime economic and technological restraint frustrated much further movement to colour for several years – as it also postponed the rise of television – and perhaps the very 'dormancy' of the Technicolor phenomenon in those years encouraged people engaged in and/or committed to black and white to continue to experiment. If the war years saw no great increase in Technicolor features (from eighteen in 1939 to twenty-nine in 1945), the postwar period witnessed a rapid acceleration of colour production; in 1949 *Variety* confidently predicted that 30 per cent of all forthcoming features would be in colour and on 15 July 1952 *Film Daily* announced that well over 75 per cent of features in production were shooting in colour.

At the other end of the colour quality spectrum, but perhaps equally influential on the *film noir*, was the development of a number of low budget, two-colour processes. In 1939, the first of these, Cinecolor, became available and the following year the first full-length Cinecolor feature – Monogram's *The Gentleman From Arizona* – was released. Costing only 25 per cent more than black and white stock and considerably less than Technicolor and with the additional advantage of overnight rushes, Cinecolor (and other 'primitive chromatic' processes like it – Vitacolor, Anscocolor, Trucolor) naturally appealed to and was rapidly adopted by certain genres at the low budget end of the industry. By 1959, Allied Artists, Columbia, Eagle Lion, Film Classics, MGM, Monogram, Paramount, 20th Century-Fox, United Artists and Universal had all made some use of the process. Meanwhile, on the A front, Technicolor did have its disadvantages. For instance, because of the prism block between the back element of the lens and the film gates, neither wide angle lenses nor those with very long focal lengths could be accommodated by the new three strip cameras. Indeed, even the introduction of faster (black and white and colour) negative stock in 1938 was unable to produce any depth of focus without wide angle lenses and, for Technicolor, faster film stock necessitated stronger floodlighting throughout the late 1930s, the 1940s and into the 1950s; floodlighting which in turn made for a flatter image and a marked lack of contrast. For black and white, on the other hand, the introduction of faster film stock allowed a decrease in lighting levels and aperture openings commensurate with previously impractical *chiaroscuro* effects. Single source lighting became steadily more feasible and was attractively economic – cheap on both power and labour. Similarly, night for night shooting, which generally involved the payment of prohibitive overtime rates, was particularly applicable to B units which paid set rates for all hours worked.

Apart from colour, perhaps the most important technological development in the late 1930s was the introduction of a new range of Fresnel lenses which, for the first time, made it possible to place large diameter lenses close to a powerful light source without loss of focus. Consequently, spotlights began to replace floodlights for key light functions. While colour stock still needed diffused high key lighting, the new fast black and white stock opened the way for smaller lighting units – such as Babys or Krieg Lilliputs – which permitted lower lighting levels. In 1940, small spotlights with Fresnel lenses and 150- or 300-watt tungsten incandescent bulbs began to outmode heavier, less mobile Carbon Arc lamps. The combination of swinging keys, lightweight spots and mobile military cameras made unorthodox angles possible but involved the erection of previously unnecessary set ceilings. It was for precisely this reason that Sid Hickox, Howard Hawks's cameraman on *To Have And Have Not* (1944),

> had a problem with his set ceilings: in wanting to hang the
> incandescent lights low, he had to remove most of the ceilings,
> but the camera shooting from the floor would reveal the lights
> themselves. So he set up ready-made three quarter ceilings of
> butter muslin, just sufficiently dark to conceal the incandescents
> massed behind them, with the other incandescents only a fraction
> beyond the range of vision.[30]

There were also important developments in camera production in this period. The Mitchell BNC – produced in 1934 but not used in Hollywood until 1938 – enabled synch-sound shooting with lenses of 25 mm widths for the first time. The only new 35 mm camera introduced in the 1940s in any quantity was the Cunningham Combat Camera, a lightweight (13 lb) affair which allowed cinematographers to move more easily whilst filming and to set up in what would previously have been inaccessible positions. Even more appropriate

for hand-held and high or low angle shooting, however, was the
Arriflex, which was captured from German military cameramen.
(The subjective camera opening sequence of Delmer Davies's *Dark
Passage* in 1947, inspired by the previous year's *Lady In The Lake*,
was shot with a hand-held Arriflex.) In 1940 the first practical anti-
reflective coatings became available, coming into general cinematic
currency after their use in *Citizen Kane*. These micro-thin coatings,
known as Vard Opticoats, together with twin-arc broadside lamps
which were also developed for Technicolor, minimised light loss at
the surface of the lens (through reflection or refraction) and at the
same time accelerated shutter speeds and facilitated the use of good
wide-angle lenses – though once again only with black and white.
So-called Tolandesque deep focus was therefore only technologically
possible from 1938 when the new fast 1232 Super XX Panchromatic
Stock could be combined with Duarc light, 25 mm wide-angle lenses
and considerably reduced apertures. Wide-angle lenses were extensively used thereafter until they were somewhat anachronised by the
advent of wide screens in 1953 and the accommodation to television
standards later in that decade. In the same way, the use of deep focus
photography continued until it was necessarily abated by Hollywood's brief romance with 3D which lasted from 1952 until 1954.
The first CinemaScope murder mystery – Nunnally Johnson's *Black
Widow* (1954) – suffered from its screen size just as much as those
3D thrillers released at the same time – *I, The Jury* (1953) and *Dial
M For Murder* (1954), all of which illustrate precisely how such
processes militated against projects which might, only a few months
earlier, have been *films noir*.[31]

This line of argument should not, however, be mistaken for a
covert reintroduction of the tenets of technological determinism.[32]
Indeed, these various 'innovations' were all either side effects of the
(profoundly ideological) desire for ever-increasing degrees of verisi-
militude (Technicolor, Deep Focus) or were determined by a negotiated differentiation from and resistance to that realism (exemplified
by the A film, by television and by Technicolor itself) in accordance
with economic constraints. I would like, finally, to suggest that it
was, specifically, the absorption of a colour aesthetic within realism
which generated the space which *film noir* was to occupy. Indeed,
just as the advent of radio in 1924 had provoked a cinematic trend
away from realism until it was reversed in 1927 with the coming of
sound to the cinema, so while colour originally signified 'fantasy'
and was first appropriated by 'fantastic' genres, it too was soon
recuperated within the realist aesthetic. Compare, for instance, the
realist status of black and white sequences in *The Wizard Of Oz*

(1939) and *If* (1969). The period of this transition, the period in which the equation between black and white on the one hand and realism on the other was at its most fragile, was thus the period from the late 1930s – when television, Technicolor and the double bill were first operating – to the late 1950s, when television and colour had established themselves, both economically and ideologically, as powerful lobbies in the industry, and the double bill had virtually disappeared. That period, of something less than twenty years, saw the conjunction of a primarily economically determined mode of production, known as B film-making, with what were primarily ideologically defined modes of 'difference', known as the *film noir*. Specific conjunctures such as this – of economic constraints, institutional structures, technological developments, political, legal and labour relations – are central to any history of film; they represent the industrial conditions in which certain representational modes, certain generic codes come into existence. This is not to argue that cinema is somehow innocent of extra-industrial determinants but simply to insist that Hollywood has a (so far unspecified) relative autonomy within the wider American social formation, however theoretically unsatisfactory that 'relativity' remains. The point of this article, therefore, has been to map out an influential fraction of that Hollywood terrain and, as part of that process, to challenge the conceptual catch-all of 'mediation' with the concrete specificities of industrial history.

Notes

1 Raymond Borde and Etienne Chaumeton, *Panorama du Film Noir Américain* (Paris: Les Editions de Minuit, 1955). I use the term 'genre' in this article where others have opted for 'subgenre', 'series', 'cycle', 'style', 'period', 'movement', etc. For a recent discussion of critical notions of (and approaches to) *film noir*, see James Damico 'Film noir: a modest proposal' in *Film Reader* no. 3, 1978.
2 In an article on 'Woman's place: the absent family of film noir' (in E. Ann Kaplan, *Women In Film Noir* (London: British Film Institute, 1978) p. 26), Sylvia Harvey has described how 'the increasing size of corporations, the growth of monopolies and the accelerated elimination of small businesses' all contributed to an atmosphere in which it was 'increasingly hard for even the petit bourgeoisie to continue to believe in certain dominant myths. Foremost among these was the dream of equality of opportunity in business and of the God-given right of every man to be his own boss. Increasingly, the petit bourgeoisie were forced into selling their labour and working for the big companies, instead of running their own businesses and working for themselves.' Other genres have been

analysed in this way: for example, Will Wright's *Sixguns and Society* (Berkeley: University of California Press, 1975) treats the development of the Western as a (generically coded) reflection of the development of American capital.

3 This is not to deny the possible efficacy of such approaches, but rather to insist on their being predicated on the sort of industrial analysis attempted here.

4 Borde and Chaumeton's chapter on 'The sources of film noir', translated in *Film Reader*, no. 3, p. 63.

5 An example of the first is Paul Schrader, 'Notes on film noir' in *Film Comment*, vol. 8, no. 1, Spring 1972, p. 11; of the second, Raymond Durgnat, 'Paint it black: the family tree of film noir' in *Cinema*, nos. 6–7, August 1970.

6 Raymond Williams, 'Base and superstructure in Marxist cultural theory', in *New Left Review*, no. 82, November–December 1973.

7 Antony Easthope, 'Todorov, genre theory and TV detectives', mimeo, 1978, p. 4.

8 The poverty of film history already referred to is less material than conceptual. For a useful contribution to the historical debate see Edward Buscombe's 'A new approach to film history', published with other papers from the Purdue University Conference in the 1977 *Film Studies Annual*.

9 Much of the stylistic detail in this outline is indebted to J. A. Place and L. S. Peterson, 'Some visual motifs of film noir' in *Film Comment*, vol. 10, no. 1, January–February 1974.

10 For further examples of such infringements see Stuart Marshall, '*Lady in the Lake*: identification and the drives', in *Film Form*, vol. 1, nos. 1–2, 1977; Stephen Heath, 'Film and system: terms of analysis', in *Screen*, vol. 16, nos. 1–2, Spring/Summer 1975; Kristin Thompson, 'The duplicitous text: an analysis of *Stage Fright*', in *Film Reader*, no. 2, 1977; and idem, 'Closure within a dream: point-of-view in *Laura*', in *Film Reader*, no. 3, 1978.

11 Damico, 'Film noir: a modest proposal'.

12 Mae D. Heuttig, *Economic Control of the Motion Picture Industry* (Philadelphia: University of Pennsylvania Press, 1944)

13 These figures are, of course, approximate – several of the smallest B companies actually produced films on budgets of less than $100,000 – but they do at least indicate the degree of economic difference between the various 'modes'.

14 Producers' Releasing Corporation: for information on this see Todd McCarthy and Charles Flynn (eds), *Kings of the Bs* (New York: Dutton, 1975); Don Miller, *B Movies* (New York: Curtis Books, 1973); idem, 'Eagle-Lion: the violent years', in *Focus on Film*, no. 31, November 1978.

15 Nick Grinde, 'Pictures for peanuts', in *The Penguin Film Review*, no. 1, August 1946 (reprinted London: Scolar Press, 1977, pp. 46–7).

16 Mark Robson, interviewed in *The Velvet Light Trap*, no. 10, Fall 1973.

17 Grinde, 'Pictures for peanuts', p. 44.

18 Peter Bogdanovich, *Fritz Lang in America* (London: Studio Vista, 1967).

19 For information on the Lewton unit see Joel Siegel, *Val Lewton, The Reality of Terror* (London: Secker & Warburg/BFI, 1972). For further

detail on RKO see the special issue (no. 10) of *The Velvet Light Trap*. On production in general see Gene Fernett, *Poverty Row* (Satellite Beach, Florida: Coral Reef, 1973).

20 Frank Ricketson Jr, *The Management of Motion Picture Theatres* (New York: McGraw-Hill, 1938), pp. 82–3.

21 Stuart Hall and Tony Jefferson (eds), *Resistance Through Rituals: Cultural Studies*, nos. 7–8, Summer 1975; reprinted London: Hutchinson, 1976.

22 John Clarke, 'Style', in ibid., pp. 175–92.

23 Fox's *March of Time* series lasted from 1934 until 1953 and its photo-journalistic aesthetic carried over into that studio's 'documentary' fictions in the late 1940s. Similarly, MGM's series of shorts, *Crime Does Not Pay*, which ran from 1935 until 1948, also complemented Metro's own output in that genre.

24 For one account of the effect of these pressures on the cinema see Keith Kelly and Clay Steinman, '*Crossfire*: a dialectical attack', in *Film Reader* no. 3.

25 Colin MacCabe, 'Realism and the cinema: notes on some Brechtian theses', *Screen*, vol. 15, no. 2, Summer 1974, pp. 10–12.

26 Colin MacCabe, 'Theory and film: principles of realism and pleasure', *Screen*, vol. 17, no. 3, Autumn 1976, p. 12.

27 Sylvia Harvey, 'Woman's place', p. 22.

28 Gill Davies, 'Teaching about narrative', *Screen Education*, no. 29, Winter 1978/79, p. 62.

29 Rouben Mamoulian, 'Controlling color for dramatic effect', in *The American Cinematographers*, June 1941, collected in Richard Koszarski (ed.), *Hollywood Directors 1941–1976* (New York: Oxford University Press, 1976) p. 15.

30 Charles Higham, *Warner Brothers* (New York: Charles Scribner's Sons, 1975) p. 157.

31 The major sources of technological history drawn on here are Barry Salt, 'Film style and technology in the thirties', in *Film Quarterly*, vol. 30, no. 1, Fall 1976 and 'Film style and technology in the forties', in *Film Quarterly*, vol. 31, no. 1, Fall 1977; and James Limbacher, *Four Aspects of the Film* (New York: Brussel & Brussel, 1968).

32 See, in this respect, Patrick Ogle 'Technological and aesthetic influence upon the development of deep focus cinematography in the United States' and Christopher Williams's critique of that article's elision of notions of ideology and economy. Both are anthologised in *Screen Reader*, 1 (London: SEFT, 1977).

12 · Thomas Guback: Shaping the film business in postwar Germany: the role of the US film industry and the US state

This is a completely rewritten and expanded version of material first presented in the author's book *The International Film Industries* (Bloomington: Indiana University Press, 1969)

The following essay is a case study of American involvement (economic, political and ideological) in the German film industry between 1945 and 1962. Using 'the question of government-business relationships as a way of ordering and analysing a moment in the development of the American motion picture industry's foreign market', Guback teases out the relationship between the film industry and the state and takes up the question of American media imperialism in the historically specific circumstances of postwar Germany. In the course of his analysis, Guback traces the tension between economic (film industrial) and political (governmental) pressures, a tension which, he suggests, was resolved in terms of ideology. Thus Guback quotes Spyros Skouras's proposal that Hollywood should adopt some sort of missionary spirit in its foreign policy – a proposal which epitomises that tension: 'This will not only be of great importance to the motion picture industry economically but it will also enable us to diligently discharge the sacred duty of our medium to help enlighten humanity.' Skouras goes on to elaborate that this 'sacred duty' involves 'indoctrinating people into the free way of life' and taking part in 'the worldwide ideological struggle for the minds of men'.

Guback argues that it was the ideology of escapist entertainment which enabled this 'indoctrination' to be accompanied together with a return on investment. Indeed, it was the assumption of the film industry that any closing of the gap between itself and the government would damage both the credibility of the films and their profitability at the box office. In the words of Eric Johnston, then president of the Motion Picture Export Association, 'Hollywood is not in the business of grinding out pictures neatly labelled for use in the propaganda war ... Hollywood is in the entertainment business, and that's precisely why our films are loved and believed by people abroad.' Clearly the implication here is that people 'believe' entertainment (which may offer a smooth passage to ideology) while resisting 'propaganda' (which is always labelled as such). It is precisely because entertainment films are not 'obvious propaganda' that Hollywood could perform such an apparently crucial role in the re-education programme in postwar Germany. Basing his analysis on Congressional records, Senate hearings, Department of State bulletins, transcripts and studio records Guback satisfactorily explains the fundamental 'coalescence of interests' between the state and the American film industry.

In the course of this analysis, Guback also glosses Wim Wenders's oft-cited remark about the enthusiastic reception accorded to American cinema in occupied Germany: 'The fact that US imperialism was so successful over here was highly favoured by the Germans' own difficulties with their past. One way of forgetting it, and one way of regression, was to accept the American imperialism.'

Whether this 'regression' contributed to the collapse in 1961 of UFI, a company which throughout the 1950s had attempted to compete with American imports by producing expensive star-laden films which failed at the box office and had unsuccessfully campaigned for import quotas, is difficult to determine. More certainly, UFI's collapse, the same year as the publication of the Oberhausen Manifesto (which prefigured the launch of the New German Cinema), was clearly connected to the question of American influence. So, too, ironically, was the New German Cinema itself, since, in Wenders's own words, 'The Americans had colonised our unconscious.' It is curious to consider whether without the efforts of Skouras and others Fassbinder's fascination with Sirk or Wenders's with Ray and Fuller would ever have been aroused. Certainly all three of these American 'auteurs' are directors whose 'authorisation' relies primarily on their work in the 1950s – the period in which textual excess flourished perhaps more than at any other time in the history of Hollywood and in which the American domination of distribution in Germany was at its height.

The relationship between the state and the private sector in a capitalist society has stimulated considerable speculation and debate, stemming not only from different ideological perspectives but also from the different levels of analysis on which this problem can be approached. Often, the discussion has been on a theoretical plane of such generality that its application to specific cases, in particular historical circumstances, has been difficult to achieve satisfactorily.

The purpose of the present article is not to explore in detail the dimensions of this debate, but to use the question of government-business relationships as a way of ordering and analyzing a moment in the development of the American motion picture industry's foreign market. At the same time, the details of this case study can help to inform the debate about government-business interaction.

To provide a context for looking at how the American film industry and the United States government cooperated in the postwar German market, it is necessary at first to lay out major contrasting lines of theory, although to do so with great brevity here entails the obvious risk of simplification and glossing over of essential intricacies.

One basic approach with roots in the development of classical liberalism centuries ago views the state as inherently inimical to private interest, because the state is seen to function for maintaining its own arbitrary power at the expense of legitimate individual interests. This notion of an adversarial relationship clearly grew from the frustrations and problems of the rising class of individual entrepreneurs, as nascent capitalism struggled to extract itself from, and eventually eradicate, a constraining feudal economic order. In the place of absolute political privilege, classical liberals insisted upon opening the political process to participation by their own kind, which initially meant the property-owning class. What were considered the proper functions of the state were redefined in this process. Communication, too, began to assume new objectives and uses, one of which was to assist the multiplication and accumulation of capital. As opposed to the feudal state, the capitalist state then came to be seen as the site in which relatively co-equal groups with differing opinions could debate and form public policy. The state, if left out of control and beyond vigilance, still had the propensity for aggrandizing its own power. But as long as it was open and democratized (according to the classical liberal definition), the state was proclaimed to be a neutral, autonomous institution in which competing ideas worked themselves out. The impartial pluralist state, it was said, played no favorites and represented no interests.

In contrast to pluralist theory stand other approaches that posit a much different identity for the state. It is no longer defined predominantly as an adversary or even as a neutral institution. It is not just a state in capitalist society, but a *capitalist* state in a capitalist society, one constructed on a particular foundation of productive relations, and one that assumes the legitimacy of those relations. As a consequence, the state does have an identifiable set of interests to protect and foster.

The way in which the state goes about this is explained by two different theoretical positions that can hardly be discussed in depth here. One argues that the state is essentially a captive of ruling-class interests, and that it therefore becomes an instrument for serving the needs of that class. The state mechanism is directed in this purpose, for example, by elected or appointed government officials who are from that class or friendly to it. Think tanks and research centers operated for the interest of that class provide agendas on which the state acts, while public and private advisory boards channel state policy in desired directions. Special interest legislation and favorable tax laws also further the needs of particular segments of the ruling class.

Another perspective, on a different level of abstraction, argues that the state in a capitalist society exhibits considerable autonomy and that it cannot be described as a mere tool of ruling class interests, which themselves are often diverse and mutually contradictory. The state, according to this view, functions to maintain its own existence, as well as that of the economic system on which it is based, by sorting and adjusting competing needs of the private sector. In order to achieve the long-range viability of the system, the state may have to postpone or even act against special short-range demands of one or another part of the capitalist sector. While the state might be hostile to some particulars, it is always cordial to the generalities, however.

These two perspectives on state-business relationships in a capitalist society are customarily posed as either-or propositions. That is, they are seen as contrasting, if not conflicting, interpretations one must choose between. It would be more productive for analytical purposes, however, to see them not as competing but as complementary explanations that together establish the variety of levels on which a capitalist state serves and perpetuates a capitalist system. Seen in this way, the perspectives are not mutually exclusive, but mutually supportive.

The circumstances of postwar Germany display many unique features, but they need to be seen in a somewhat larger context. The United States emerged from the war as unquestionably the most powerful nation in the world. Economically and militarily - and hence politically - it was in a position to dominate the globe's reconstruction, and to set the terms of debate and the agenda of priorities in international bodies created in the postwar era. Among many points, American policy called for eliminating restrictions on international trade, the strengthening of private enterprise economies throughout the world, the containment of Soviet power, and the suffocation of the left in any country that showed signs of a political shift in that direction. With particular reference to Germany, the objectives also included re-educating the populace away from Nazi ideas, and establishing a private enterprise economy on a competitive basis.

Worthy of note is the American government's position toward the global flow of information, a subject that had received almost no attention in US foreign policy before the war. The position took shape during the early 1940s and, as hostilities drew to a close, was implemented in specific acts on the national level and in international fora. This information policy was prompted as much by obvious ideological and propaganda concerns as by commercial considerations, which the business sector was only too willing to call to government's attention. The main thrust of this policy was to strike down any foreign barriers to the flow of information and entertainment from the United States, to codify the principles of unrestrained flow in various international treaties and declarations, and to assist the American private media in capturing markets abroad in which to sell products. International bodies, whose agendas could be dominated by the United States and its allies, were called up for duty to assist global implementation of America's definition of what constituted adequate information flow. As Senator William Benton pointed out in 1950,

> If we work through UNESCO, we cannot be charged with cultural imperialism. Indeed, there are many areas where UNESCO can be far more effective than can the United States alone. Germany may be such a one, where UNESCO can work across the zonal boundaries.[1]

The broad plan for information was based on the principle that the main instruments for circulating American ideology would be American commercial media. Mr Benton, when Assistant Secretary of State for Public Affairs in 1946, described it succinctly:

> We in the State Department know that private interests are eager to do more than they have ever done. They are seeking world markets. The total volume of their efforts represented by news carried by the commercial wire services, by foreign editions of magazines and books, by movies, tourists, and commercial contacts will amount to vastly more than the Government's contribution. The Government's job will be merely to fill the gaps ... [such as reaching] small groups far too few in number to provide a profitable market for American private enterprise.[2]

An additional role for the government was particularly crucial, as Assistant Secretary Benton realized:

> The State Department plans to do everything within its power along political or diplomatic lines to help break down the

artificial barriers to the expansion of private American news
agencies, magazines, motion pictures, and other media of
communications throughout the world.[3]
In this respect, the interests of government and business were entirely
compatible and complementary. Access of private media representatives to the highest levels of political power insured favorable government treatment on their behalf. Ellis Arnall, president of the Society
of Independent Motion Picture Producers, told the Motion Picture
Industry Council in 1949:

> Some while ago, I visited the President of the United States
> [Harry Truman] and undertook to convey to him the idea that
> American motion pictures are the best salesmen of American
> democracy, the best ambassadors of good will, the best trade
> developers available to our government; that while the
> government is spending billions of dollars for ECA [Economic
> Cooperation Administration], millions of dollars for the Voice of
> America and programs designed to sell Democracy to the rest of
> the world, our government is leaving unused the most effective
> medium at its disposal – quality American pictures. This medium
> can be utilized by our government absolutely free of cost. The
> President readily agreed that our government has a responsibility
> to see to it that American-produced motion pictures be utilized
> to the fullest in carrying the message of Americanism and
> Democracy to the rest of the world. He expressed these views to
> the Secretary of State, Mr [Dean] Acheson, and requested Mr
> Acheson to take such steps as feasible to the end that foreign
> countries would not discriminate against American-produced
> pictures and would maintain no unreasonable quotas or unfair
> restrictions against them.[4]

The postwar anti-communism hysteria was a major cornerstone of
American international communication policy, just as it provided the
basis for the foreign aid program. Senator Benton was not alone in
understanding the connection:

> The Marshall plan has been no mere containment of
> communism. It has aimed at a positive rollback for communism,
> an ideological as well as an economic defeat for communism ...
> With this success before us, is it not time – and past time – for
> us to create a world-wide Marshall plan in the field of ideas?[5]
>
> We are not yet using the motion picture and the radio and the
> printing press in the international field. For all practical
> purposes, it may be said we are not using them at all. Their
> impact today in our interests, is that of a midget. I make an
> exception of the Hollywood motion picture, with its varying

types of impact. They do have the potential strength of a giant, and my plea today is that we give them a chance.[6]

The dimensions of the postwar international ideological, economic and political struggle, carried out on the level of the state, clearly made the state favorably disposed to using motion pictures for propaganda purposes. Additionally, their international distribution would have a positive commercial effect on the American film industry by allowing it to consolidate its position in foreign markets and extract revenue from them. These ideological and financial advantages obviously appealed to American production and distribution companies. They understood that postwar assistance from the state, amplifying the very basic kinds of commercial help it provided in the prewar period, could be invaluable for re-establishing and expanding markets overseas. Consequently, the film companies were eager to second the general policy lines of the state and to reaffirm its belief in the propaganda value of Hollywood's products. Typical in this regard was Spyros Skouras, president of 20th Century-Fox, who urged the industry to 'work harder and harder to create [a] missionary spirit.' 'This will not only be of great importance to the motion picture industry economically,' he declared, 'but it will also enable us to diligently discharge the sacred duty of our great medium to help enlighten humanity.' Mr Skouras believed that

it is a solemn responsibility of our industry to increase motion
picture outlets throughout the free world because it has been
shown that no medium can play a greater part than the motion
picture in indoctrinating people into the free way of life and
instilling in them a compelling desire for freedom and hope for a
brighter future. Therefore, we as an industry can play an
infinitely important part in the worldwide ideological struggle for
the minds of men and confound the Communist propagandists.[7]

Mr Skouras did not seem to need any empirical research evidence to substantiate his claim about film's effects, for at this point in time there was less worry about social science validity than about the future course of world capitalism.

Although the government was explicit about why American films needed to be distributed overseas, representatives of the industry usually were a bit more guarded in their public pronouncements. Those of the state reflected the generalized needs of the capitalist sector as a whole, while statements from film industry executives had to take into account not only the political climate of the time, but also audiences at home and abroad who would consume these films. Whereas the political atmosphere called for declarations of staunch patriotism and militant anti-communism, market considerations attenuated such claims as far as films' content was concerned. Motion picture companies did not continuously draw attention to the overt propaganda characteristics of their products because they preferred to avoid any insinuation that they were manipulating content to meet government specifications. In a broad way, their cooperation with the state was on the level of erasing undesirable aspects from pictures, rather than intentionally incorporating elements that propaganda concerns would have demanded. The basic assumption was that commercial motion pictures already represented Americanism and no additional steps needed to be taken to enhance their content.

Naturally, this approach reflected the fundamental business motives of the companies, which was the production of pictures for the production of profit. If, in carrying out this mandate, international political aims of the state also could be advanced, then a double purpose would be served. At risk here was also the tradition of separation of the state from operation of the communication system, particularly when media content was involved.

'Hollywood is not in the business of grinding out pictures neatly labeled for use as weapons in the propaganda war,' Eric Johnston once said, when he was president of the Motion Picture Association of America. 'Hollywood is in the entertainment business, and that's precisely why our films are loved and believed by people abroad.'[8] Accordingly, closing the gap between state and business could serve neither party because both credibility and profit might decline. Film industry representatives stressed that commercial pictures could achieve ideological objectives abroad without any change in the production context in which they were made, and that meant no direct state involvement. Further, the companies had no intention of finding themselves in the position of making two sets of pictures, one for domestic consumption, and another for foreign audiences who needed to be manipulated ideologically.

The motion picture industry was eager to cooperate, but on its own terms, as Eric Johnston explained to a Senate committee in 1953:

> Pictures give an idea of America which it is difficult to portray in any other way, and the reason, the main reason, we think, is because our pictures are not obvious propaganda. They are completely free pictures, and they reflect the freedom under which they are made and the freedom under which they are shown.[9]
>
> We have advised foreign managers to be careful and set up some criteria as to what pictures should be sent to areas and they have done that on their own. I know they have a keen awareness ... of what pictures should go into what areas, and whether a picture is harmful and whether it will do a great deal

of good. They are doing the screening themselves ... There are a
good many of our pictures that are not shown overseas.[10]

Senator J. William Fulbright, who was a member of the committee
to which Mr Johnston testified, sought to uncover the motives for
exportation:

Senator Fulbright: What determines whether a picture is sold
abroad or not? It is a commercial determination, is it not – what
you think will sell?

Mr Johnston: Yes. Drama sells abroad better, but I am not an
expert ...

Senator Fulbright: You don't have to describe it. What I mean is
that your test, the criterion you use, is whether or not it will
make money. Isn't that your objective?

Mr Johnston: Of course, we are a commercial enterprise.[11]

The sensitivities of foreign audiences apparently were considered to
some unspecified extent by producers in presentation of themes and
characterizations. But, as Y. Frank Freeman, vice president of Paramount Pictures, implied, the effort in this case was really to create a
saleable product.

We try to find out whether the subject matter that we are
handling would be an offensive matter in the area where our
Government is having problems, and, if so, not to do it. We try,
where we can, to inject things that will be an expression of
friendliness in relation to that country and those people. We do
that as Americans. We do not do it under the demand or under
the control of anybody in the Government.[12]

An obvious aspect, of course, was that the United States contributed about half of the theatrical rentals for the industry, so both
domestic and foreign markets had to be taken into account.

It was clear in the early 1940s that the end of the war would bring
about a reorganization of world markets, and that American exports,
motion pictures among them, would be affected. Many foreign countries, drained materially and financially by the war, would find more
than adequate justification for resurrecting trade barriers in order to
protect domestic manufacturing, as they had done in the prewar
decades. They would need to conserve scarce foreign exchange,
rather than face even larger trade deficits at a time when their economies could hardly tolerate them. American film distribution companies had fought against trade restraints in the 1920s and 1930s, but
the postwar period clearly presented greater dangers prompted by
greater economic difficulties abroad. Some markets, moreover, would
be in such terrible condition at war's end that it would make no

sense for each American company to establish its own distribution subsidiary to handle what little business was to be done.

Joint action by American companies seemed an appropriate manner in which to confront these problems. The Motion Picture Producers and Distributors of America, Inc. had an International Department that represented members in trade matters overseas in the pre-war period, but something more seemed to be needed once the war ended, especially if distribution of American films was to be merged in some markets.

The government also was concerned about the status of international trade when peace would come, and feared massive protectionism that could hurl the world toward another economic crisis. While the general principle of free trade needed to be upheld around the globe by the United States government, it turned to the private sector for support and policy guidance in specific fields. It was not surprising, therefore, when in early 1944 the Chief of the Motion Picture Section of the government's War Production Board urged the film industry to set up a permanent organization for presenting to the government that industry's global trade needs and for drafting specific recommendations for unhindered access to world markets after the war. 'Unless the industry lays the groundwork in advance for presenting its case,' Chief Harold Hopper warned, 'it will miss a golden opportunity. The proper committee or agency should be set up now to begin preparing a program.' Mr Hopper pointed to the dangers of inaction:

> Without a properly organized committee to keep the United
> States Government and all its agencies, as well as foreign
> nations, thoroughly conversant with the needs and requirements
> and problems of the industry, there is little hope that the motion-
> picture producers of the country will be given proper
> consideration at the peace table or in the domestic affairs of
> foreign nations.[13]

Discussions in 1944 and early 1945 looked toward devising an appropriate mechanism to achieve these goals. The International Department of the MPPDA already constituted one form of response to these demands, but it was not until the establishment of the Motion Picture Export Association Inc. (MPEA) on 5 June 1945 that the architecture was completed. The MPEA was incorporated under provisions of the Webb-Pomerene Export Trade Act of 1918, which provided certain exemptions from antitrust laws for cartels created solely to engage in foreign trade. The founding companies were Columbia, Loew's, Paramount, RKO, 20th Century-Fox, United Artists, Universal, and Warner Bros. They empowered the MPEA to divide markets among members, set rental prices on films, establish terms of trade, negotiate film import agreements abroad, represent members before foreign governments and trade associations, collect and disseminate intelligence about overseas markets, etc. A unique feature of the Association was that members soon granted it exclusive licenses to distribute their films in thirteen foreign areas, one of which was Germany.[14] By the end of 1951, though, the companies had set up their own separate distribution operations in Germany and in most of the other original joint markets.

The United States Treasury Department (under the Trading with the Enemy Act) did not authorize the MPEA to operate in Germany until 4 June 1946. But American films entered the market before then, distributed by the Psychological Warfare Division and the Office of War Information, to which American companies licensed their pictures.[15] The actual commercial distribution of films by the MPEA in the US Zone of Germany was permitted by American Military Government authorities as of 1 February 1948.[6]

The concern of the Allied Powers was not only to disarm Germany but also to launch an intensive program of ideological re-education to counteract the effect of Nazi control. The film companies' vaults contained thousands of pictures, many never released in Germany, that the Military Government might have used in its re-education campaign. Describing the American industry's activities in this post-war period, Eric Johnston later told a Senate committee:

In response to urgent requests of top United States occupation officials, American feature pictures were sent into Germany . . . as soon as the fighting stopped . . . American leaders recognized that these non-propaganda [entertainment] pictures would assist during the critical post-war period in conveying to the people of the occupied areas an understanding of American life and democratic institutions. The films were the first real contact between America and the former enemy . . . The film industry provided the pictures at no profit to itself but rather at an actual loss for out-of-pocket expenses.[17]

I don't know of any industry giving away cloth or clothes or steel or anything, but we gave away films, not only gave them away but paid for the means of showing them in dollars out of our own pockets, at an expense of about $500,000 a year.[18]

Of course, films are not consumable in the same sense as cloth or steel, and distributors have long known that films have a long life in which their ability to produce revenue is often not exhausted. Moreover, such exhibition of pictures, as Mr Johnston described, can be seen as a loss leader in which companies forgo revenue at one moment to make it up later. Nonetheless, Mr Johnston claimed that the industry was actively cooperating with the government, and that the companies were disregarding profit in favor of a more philanthropic posture. The record, though, suggests a somewhat different state of affairs.

Exhibition of motion pictures was permitted at the end of July 1945, when cinemas were allowed to operate in the American Zone, but the plan for reopening them could not proceed as rapidly as authorities desired. According to one account written by a participant in the Military Government, 'the real difficulty in getting more motion picture houses opened lay in the short supply of films.'[19] The Military Government did not have enough titles at its disposal, and it faced a shortage of prints as well.

From the end of hostilities until mid-1946, only forty-three American features were released with 1,049 prints. By mid-1947 the total was increased by eighteen features, which circulated in 334 prints. In the year ending in mid-1948, twenty-one features were released in 268 prints. In the first half of 1948, the MPEA was processing only seven prints per title for use by the Military Government, whereas Eagle-Lion (a British company) was preparing thirty prints of each title, including those in Technicolor. There were at this time, 2,245 cinemas in the combined American and British zones and their sectors of Berlin.[20]

The difficulties could have been avoided had it not been for the 'inability of the American motion picture industry to cooperate along policy lines laid down by the United States Government for the occupation of Germany.'[21] By controlling the supply of films, the American majors hoped to obtain from the Military Government concessions that would have bettered their position in the German market. To cope with the film shortage, Military Government decided late in 1945 to permit the exhibition of German pictures that had been found politically harmless. By May 1948, three German distributors in the US Zone were licensed to handle fourteen old German films, with 198 prints, that had been released for use by the military authorities in charge of property control. German distribution companies from the British Zone circulated another five films in the US Zone.[22] There were, in addition, old German pictures that had been distributed well into 1948 by the Military Government, but it was 'prepared to withdraw all these prints (some 700) from circulation,' an MPEA report disclosed, 'as soon as we, the free traders, are in a position to cover the requirements of the exhibitors with a sufficient number of prints.'[23]

The demands American companies were making on the Military

Government 'were so inconsistent with occupation policy' that the two parties 'failed to reach a mutually satisfactory agreement.'[24] Toward the end of 1945, General Robert McClure had numerous discussions in the United States with representatives of the companies in order to resolve the problems that were hampering the re-education program. But upon returning to Germany, he was forced to conclude that the industry wanted to 'utilize the military occupation to establish an exclusive position for American films and American distribution machinery.'[25] The aim of the Military Government, however, was to create a free and competitive market, and eventually to revive the German film industry.

One aspect of the dispute was how the MPEA would be paid for its films, and how it could dispose of its earnings. Under the occupation authorities' program, revenue from the showing of American films was accumulated in accounts blocked by the Military Government, to which the MPEA had to apply for permission to spend these Reichsmarks. This currency could not be converted into dollars, nor could it be used outside of Germany, and the Military Government severely restricted how the MPEA could use it in Germany, given the delicate economy. Items in short supply, such as automobiles and new office equipment, could not be purchased by the MPEA, while used equipment, available on the black market, exceeded the price levels set by Allied and German control authorities. Office furnishings, consequently, had to be rented. Some blocked earnings were allowed to be spent to cover expenses of visiting film production units, and small sums were permitted for the exportation of dubbed prints. In 1947 and 1948, paper for advertising posters could not be bought because there was no official allotment for that purpose, and supplies of photographic stock for stills were practically non-existent. The MPEA had planned to publish novelizations of films, but it could not proceed because there was not even enough paper for textbooks. Two plants in the Russian Zone were manufacturing film base, but they only accepted dollars for payment.[26]

American interests also tried to buy cinemas in Germany, and expressed a desire to obtain minority holdings in the film studios of Bavaria, Munich, and UFA Tempelhof, when those facilities were being liquidated. Basically, these requests ran counter to the policy of the US Department of State (and of the British Foreign Office), which wanted to protect the fragile German economy from the infiltration of foreign capital and control. Moreover, occupation authorities sought to rebuild a film industry that would be German-owned, -operated and -financed, and they believed this goal could not be achieved if parts of it became American subsidiaries. As a step toward that objective, the Military Government encouraged politically clean German film-makers to apply for permission to organize production companies. By mid-1948 two German pictures had been completed in the US Zone and a third was in production; five had been made in the British Zone.[27]

Another source of friction was the quality of films the MPEA was offering. The Association insisted only its members should be permitted to export to Germany. 'This ran straight into strong opposition from Military Government,' one observer has claimed, 'which wanted to include independent producers in order to obtain the best product.'[28] An MPEA internal report written in 1948 revealed that to 'overcome the constant negative attitude of Milgov representatives toward our product, we have introduced special showings of every picture released, for invited guests, and we feel that we are convincing the authorities that the product selected for German audiences is of high class.' Nevertheless, the MPEA admitted that the 'attitude of the German press is, generally speaking, negative to our product.... [T]heir freedom of press is employed as a destructive force.' On the other hand, the MPEA claimed, '[o]ur pictures are very successful with the German public.'[29]

In February 1948, the MPEA officially took over distribution of American pictures from the Information Services Division of the Military Government. The Association was operating six offices in the US Zone and two in the British Zone, with the head office in Berlin where it could be in immediate touch with Military Government authorities. Shifting distribution directly to the MPEA did not, however, change how the Association was paid for its pictures or what it could do with its money. Earnings continued to be unconvertible into dollars and difficult to spend. By mid-1948 the MPEA had accumulated RM 75 million in its blocked account held in trust with the Military Government, and RM 5 million from its own operations. Rental revenue was averaging RM 800,000 weekly, and a good 'A' picture with sufficient prints could earn RM 3 million in the combined American and British zones.[30]

Film companies were not the only ones vexed by this financial situation. Publishers also were affected because, for example, some American authors hesitated to sell German-language rights to their works as long as earnings were blocked and could not be exchanged into dollars. American government officials, prompted by media representatives, realized these matters could hinder the re-education program in Germany, and looked for a solution that would accommodate the specific needs of the private sector while achieving the broad goals of the state. The answer was the Informational

Media Guaranty Program (IMG), launched in 1948 under the aus-
pices of the Economic Cooperation Administration. The Program
established a mechanism by which the American government could
pay dollars, at attractive rates, for certain soft foreign currencies
earned by American media exporters, provided the communications
material earning the money reflected the best elements of American
life. This Program was advantageous to film companies because it
encouraged them to have their pictures distributed and exhibited in
soft currency countries with US government assurance that some of
the revenue would be available to them in dollars. Implicitly, the
Program supported the foreign operations of American companies
and made Hollywood's films an official export of the United States.
Thanks to public policy, selected American films went into the world
with the rank of ambassador.

German currency was reformed while the IMG Program was
getting underway, and the Deutschmark superseded the Reichsmark
as the official unit. But conversion of the new currency into dollars
on the open market was still not authorized. The blocked earnings
problem would have continued to plague American media operating
in Germany had not the US government inaugurated the IMG Program. It is quite possible, however, that despite industry threats to
halt trade altogether, exports to soft currency areas such as Germany
would have continued, even without government assistance, and that
the film companies saw this help as just one more way they could
benefit from state largesse. In 1950 Francis Harley of 20th Century-
Fox International Corporation told a meeting of the MPEA board of
directors that they should complain to the government because

the delay in Washington in reviewing these pictures [for IMG
aid] had been very harmful to the companies and that as a result
a number of them had been forced to send in pictures [to foreign
markets] without submitting them for [prior] approval ... A
number of those present [at the meeting] expressed the contrary
opinion, that it might be very dangerous to make a point of this,
inasmuch as there appeared to be a strong feeling in Washington
that ECA assistance to the movie industry was unnecessary since
the companies would feel compelled to send in their product
even if such assistance were not forthcoming.[31]

Films covered by guaranteed dollar conversion had to meet the
selected criteria established by the Economic Cooperation Administration:

The films eligible for IMG coverage include only those which
present a fair and essentially accurate picture of American life, or
which, regardless of subject matter, have sufficient distinction of

production, design, or acting, to reflect credit on the culture of the United States.[32]

Pictures not approved still could be distributed abroad, but their earnings in Germany would be blocked. Even taking that into account, the Program still benefited American distributors. Not surprisingly, they quickly increased their exports to the German market and were eager to fill their ECA dollar quotas.

Internal correspondence at Warner Bros., for instance, reveals that an ECA-approved package being distributed in Germany in 1951 included good pictures as well as some 'which are doing very poor box-office.' In order to increase the latter's revenue, and thus their dollar conversion value, a branch manager reported that 'everything is being done to expedite the execution of our existing contracts and these pictures are included in every [exhibition] contract wherever possible and you may be sure that nothing is neglected in this respect.'[33]

A Warner representative in Frankfurt reminded branch office managers of 'the importance of concentrating all your efforts on obtaining quick playdates and the maximum possible business on the group of pictures for which we receive ECA Dollar guarantees.' He pointed out that Warner at the moment was 'mainly concerned about the business you have been doing on *Possessed*, *Conflict*, *Dark Victory*, and *Hasty Heart*, and which is so far below the average of what we are doing on some of our other weaker pictures, that we are afraid that you have not given these pictures sufficient attention.' The Warner official told his managers to 'instruct your sales personnel to make every effort to include these pictures in every possible unsold situation,' and that the company 'will not accept any cancellation [by exhibitors] of any of the ECA approved pictures.'[34] Meanwhile, the Warner representative in charge of the German market was instructed to 'initiate a Drive for more bookings, playdates, etc. to build up the grosses so that we will, before June 30th, 1952, gross sufficient to obtain the full amount guaranteed' by the current ECA contract. The matter was urgent to Warner officials because 'it does not appear that the pictures [involved in this contract] will do enough to cover the $292,000' that the ECA intended to provide.[35]

The IMG Program's first media contract was executed with the MPEA in December 1948 and covered selected films released from 1 August to the end of the year. The value of this contract was $230,000. Subsequently, it was extended six months and increased to $457,000. During this period, the MPEA agreed to distribute thirty prints each of eight color and forty-four black and white features, plus a number of shorts. In the last half of 1949, IMG guaranteed

$636,000 for MPEA films. To cover the following year, contracts were drawn for more than $3 million, and for the 1951 program, the American companies suggested an increase to $4 million.[36]

Concerning only the German market, from the inception of the IMG Program until its termination there in 1955, the US government executed seventy contracts and made payments of somewhat more than $7 million. American film companies accounted for close to 70 per cent of these dollar conversions. On a global basis, from the beginning of IMG until mid-1966, American film distributors received almost $16 million. The Program in Germany, therefore, represented almost a third of all government payments to US motion picture companies.[37] That IMG had been lucrative to those interests is beyond question. Indeed, when Congress considered an appropriation to the United States Information Agency in 1959, one Representative attacked both film industry lobbying and the IMG Program, asserting that because of its payments the 'Motion Picture Export Association has been given a pretty good ride on the informational media gravy train.'[38]

Because of the IMG Program, as well as the strengthening of the German economy that foretold the approaching conversion of marks directly into dollars, the interests of the American distributors changed. Whereas in the immediate postwar years they severely restricted their exports to the German market, their new policy became one of sending as many films as they felt could be played off profitably. To accomplish that, the MPEA, as a central bargaining agent, devoted its energies to thwarting any restrictions that would impede American companies' access to that market. As in dealing with other problems, MPEA officials went directly to the highest levels of government. In a letter to Secretary of State Dean Acheson in 1949, MPEA president Eric Johnston pointed out that the Joint Export and Import Agency of the Military Government was considering implementing a film import quota for the western zone. Mr Johnston urged the State Department 'to take the strongest possible stand against the imposition of a film quota in Germany' because (according to the MPEA version of history) 'we know from actual experience that film quotas are detrimental to the home industry.' Moreover, a 'film quota would be a negation of America's national policies and traditions and would not help the revival of the German motion picture industry.' On the other hand, Mr Johnston alleged, the exhibition in Germany of American films *would* help that revival because '[g]ood pictures are made where there is competition and not where there is artificial protection.'[39] (In retrospect, one wonders how Mr Johnston could seriously make this pro-competition argument when the US Supreme Court a year earlier had upheld the antitrust convictions of eight MPEA members for conspiring to restrain competition and for monopolizing the film business in the United States.)

Military Government officials not only apparently understood that increased MPEA exports to Germany could threaten the recovery of the country's film production, but also seemingly anticipated that the IMG Program would encourage American distributors to saturate that market. Indeed, this is exactly what occurred. In the 1948–49 rental year only sixty-four American films were released there. But during the following year, the number jumped to 145, in 1950–51 to 202, and in 1951–52 to 226. (By contrast, in the three-year period from the end of hostilities until mid-1948, only eighty-two American features were released.) These pictures, moreover, were not necessarily new, for of those released up to April 1951, about 20 per cent had been produced prior to 1940.[40] The willingness of the government to exchange soft currency for dollars, a program enacted with great encouragement from the private sector, proved to be a substantial stimulant for the exportation and exhibition of American motion pictures in Germany. Additionally, the Program's inauguration suggests that film industry interests were more influential with federal government officials in Washington than with Military Government authorities in Germany.

The effort to derail the Military Government's consideration of a film quota was not an isolated incident. Throughout the early 1950s, the MPEA waged a continuing battle to prevent any restrictions on American films in Germany. Attempts to protect the market were inspired, in part, by the troubled financial condition of local production. Capital for film-making was difficult to obtain because banks could lend money at high interest rates to other sectors of the economy with less risk than is customary in motion picture production. Forty-three of the fifty-seven production companies in West Berlin had not completed a film by 1950,[41] and studios in Munich often went unused for months at a time because no companies had funds for production. Even if capital could have been found for making films, they would have had to squeeze into what theatrical screen time remained after American films were exhibited.

Interests in the German film industry pressed their government for measures to ameliorate these conditions and to advance their own business. German government authorities responded in March 1950 and proposed substantially reducing the importation of American motion pictures to about 100 annually. During this period, however, the German parliament could not act autonomously because the Allied High Commission had power to veto any legislation enacted that, in its view, violated the Commission's own laws or did not enhance the country's rehabilitation and reconstruction. Pertinent to motion pictures was Law 5, on 'Freedom of press, radio, information, and entertainment,' which was part of the occupation statutes enacted in September 1949. Article 1 of this law declared:

The German press, radio and other information media shall be free ..., [and the] Allied High Commission reserves the right to cancel or annul any measure, governmental, political, administrative, or financial, which threatens such freedom.[42]

It was upon this authority that the Commission in June 1950 rejected the Parliament's proposal for officially reducing the importation of Hollywood's films. Implicitly, the American ideal of free trade was imposed on Germany, and it was based on the belief that because the United States had no governmentally initiated film quotas, then neither should other countries have. But the Commission's power to reject the import quota was merely implied in Law 5, which was generally vague about film matters anyway. Also unclear was whether the Commission would maintain its stance in the future, especially when faced with German arguments that a quota was designed to *preserve* the domestic industry and that such encouragement was needed for a competitive market.

The pressure building up from German advocates of protection, as well as uncertainty over the Commission's future actions, obviously signalled to the MPEA that this situation was far from settled and required further attention. The need to plan their 1951 export programs, and to make sure they could distribute the volume of pictures adequate for their own commercial needs, prompted American companies again to enlist the aid of the American government. MPEA president Eric Johnston and vice president John McCarthy informed the Association's board of directors' meeting on 10 October 1950 that they would confer in a few days with Mr Webb, Under Secretary of State, and Mr Perkins, Assistant Secretary of State for European Affairs, and that 'they would advise these officials that the Association considered unrestricted motion picture importation into Germany as an absolute necessity.' If any restrictions had to be imposed, then the MPEA representatives were prepared to say that 'the Germans should be permitted to apply an internal screen quota only,' which would reserve a small percentage of theatrical playing time for locally made films. Mr McCarthy feared, though, 'that the State Department officials might not agree with this viewpoint and in particular that they might feel that some import restrictions must be imposed until such time as the Germans join the International Trade Organization [GATT].'[43] Mr McCarthy asked the board to instruct him whether they could propose to State Department authorities a minimum number of import licenses that would be acceptable to MPEA members.

Minutes of this MPEA meeting disclose considerable discussion about the position the Association would present to the State Department. Morton Spring of Loew's International Corporation argued that he could not see why any import restrictions should be agreed to by the MPEA. Others at the meeting felt 'Messrs Johnston and McCarthy should be empowered to mention a figure to the State Department officials since otherwise the Association might be considered unreasonable by the US Authorities and might not be supported by them if the Germans later imposed stringent import restrictions unilaterally.' Discussion then centered on 250 pictures per year, or twenty-five per MPEA member company. But Francis Harley of 20th Century-Fox International Corporation pointed out that 'it would be exceedingly dangerous if one or more companies would not be able to use all of the import licenses granted to them and that for this reason the Association should be careful not to ask for more pictures than the companies actually intended to import into Germany.'

Arthur Loew of Loew's stated he could not understand why some companies with fewer films available still insisted on equal distribution of import licenses, 'particularly if the number was as high as twenty-five pictures per company.' Some members then conceded that 'they could or would in all probability not import twenty-five pictures into Germany annually.' Mr McCarthy considered it 'virtually impossible' that the State Department would accept the 250-picture figure anyway.

The strategy finally adopted at this meeting was that Messrs Johnston and McCarthy 'should ask for unrestricted importation first, and if the State Department insisted on having a figure which the Association would be willing to accept, then to indicate that 200 pictures annually would be acceptable.' This level, however, would be applicable only until Germany joined GATT, 'whereafter there should be no restriction at all on importation but merely an internal screen quota.'[44]

According to a trade press report of the meeting at the State Department, the MPEA delegation argued that 'Germany is the focal point in the current battle of ideologies,' and that while millions of dollars were being spent on Voice of America broadcasts, it would be 'illogical to restrict the powerful message that American pictures could carry to the Western Zone' of Germany.[45] The Association's representatives claimed that if the State Department wanted widespread dissemination of the American message, then the government should inform the Allied High Commission to strike down any further attempts to limit importation of American films. The MPEA insisted that the Germans were wrong to believe that American companies would flood the market in the absence of a formal import quota.

Immediately after the October 1950 meeting in Washington, the State Department informed American authorities in Germany as well as German officials that it was opposed to an import quota. This reinforced the High Commission's action earlier in the year and placed the government on record once again as supporting the export business of American companies. Without an official quota on imports, MPEA members could determine what they themselves believed was a suitable number of pictures for the German market. In essence, the American government opposed a German quota on political grounds, but the American industry was at liberty to institute its own control for commercial reasons.

Following his meeting with State Department officials at which he argued against an official import quota, Mr McCarthy travelled to Frankfurt where he met with German film industry representatives to discuss a *voluntary* limit on the number of American pictures in the market. German film interests, which had been frustrated by the High Commission when they attempted to have their government legislate a quota, now tried to bargain directly with the MPEA for an unofficial ceiling to prevent their market from being suffocated.

The agreement worked out between the MPEA and the Spitzenorganisation der Filmwirtschaft called for American companies to limit themselves voluntarily to about 200 films annually in the German market. Although that was lower than the 250 figure discussed at MPEA board meetings, it was clear American majors did not necessarily always have that many pictures suitable for export. Consequently, the voluntary ceiling hardly constituted a hardship on them, and because there was no force of law behind this Gentlemen's Agreement, no action could be brought against American companies if they did exceed it. In view of the needs of the German industry, this agreement 'was not successful.' According to a report published by the US High Commissioner for Germany, 'foreign competition continued to plague the German motion picture industry ... since many of the companies did not adhere to their self-imposed quotas.'[46]

The agreement reflected, of course, the poor bargaining position of the German industry. On another level, however, it represented the power of the business and government sectors in the United States to impose their will on foreign countries, not only on specific matters such as this, but also more generally when broader issues of trade and competition were involved. Decisions on particular problems, film importation in this instance, were embedded in a much larger context whose dimensions, especially in the postwar period, were circumscribed by the needs of the American private sector working through government.

Voluntary import controls after 1951 continued to be the result of strained negotiations as the German industry, spearheaded by producers, sought to have imports held below 200 each year. American distributors, supported by the State Department, successfully beat back these efforts as they did others, including a German proposal in 1954 to reduce imports to 160 American pictures and to tax their earnings. A few years later, American interests similarly thwarted a German plan to set an age limit on US films to stop importation of old pictures that had not been released in the market. German producers also tried to obtain reciprocity by being guaranteed the distribution of their pictures in the American market, or at least some financial support to enable them to distribute and publicize their films in the United States. This proposal, according to an MPEA representative, was 'shot down immediately.'[47]

The persistence of the MPEA brought handsome rewards for American companies. From 1951 through 1958, an average of 225 American films were released annually in Germany. The number did not fall below 200 until 1959,[48] but that was due to declining film production in the United States, rather than to weakness at the bargaining table. In 1955 and 1956, Germany was the fourth largest foreign market for MPEA companies (behind the United Kingdom, Italy and Canada), and in 1957 it moved to third position. Their gross billings in Germany in those years were, respectively, $22.4 million, $23.8 million, and $26.9 million. During that period, revenue from the German market increased from 7.3 per cent to 8.4 per cent of total foreign earnings. By 1957, Germany constituted 4.4 per cent of the entire *world* market for MPEA companies.[49]

Throughout its campaign to maintain unrestricted access to the German market, the MPEA, as we have seen, operated on commercial and diplomatic levels. It did not neglect the public front, though. At a 7 June 1951 meeting of the MPEA board of directors, Mr McCarthy suggested that it would be desirable to send a public relations expert to Germany to get 'together with certain German community groups which were presently showing a pronounced anti-American bias.'[50] Three months later, Mr McCarthy reported that 'he had temporarily engaged Mr [Frederick] Gronich to perform certain public relations functions with German groups such as religious and educational bodies in order to clear away presently existing misunderstandings regarding American pictures and that Mr Gronich has already obtained considerable success.'[51]

When television was inaugurated, the MPEA had to insure its access to that market, just as it had done earlier for the cinema market. The MPEA's *Interim Report on Television* described the strategy it was using:

> In Germany, where the new commercial network is scheduled to
> begin operations in January 1961, Mr [Leo] Hochstetter [MPEA
> representative in Frankfurt] has been in constant touch with the
> executives of Deutschland Fernsehen [sic] and Freies Fernsehen
> GmbH, the operating company for the upcoming network and
> the basic program contractor, respectively. Just as, some 18
> months ago, MPEAA, Frankfurt was largely responsible for
> eliminating a proposed ruling that would have banned American
> features older than two and half years from German television,
> Mr Hochstetter had been working toward liberalized trading
> conditions for the new German network. A principal objective is
> an increase in the planned proportion of film to live
> programming during the early stages of operation. Precedents set
> at the beginning are likely to influence programming patterns for
> years to come.[52]

The MPEA had claimed consistently that exhibition of its films abroad had an Americanizing effect because 'each film ... carries important social and ideological by-products which have a tremendous impact on film goers around the world.'[53] 'Another by-product of Hollywood movies,' American distributors always alleged, 'is that they serve as global showcases for American techniques, products and merchandise.'[54] These were certainly self-serving arguments to advance to the American government when foreign markets, such as Germany, threatened to restrict importation of US films, or when American distributors objected to currency conversion restraints. In the absence of broadly based empirical testing, these kinds of claims went unchallenged, or at best were refuted or confirmed by anecdotal evidence. It is quite likely, though, that the effects of American pictures abroad (as is the case with media content in general) were, and are, mediated by a variety of circumstances. A public opinion survey commissioned by the United States Information Agency, and carried out by private contractors abroad in mid-1962, found that American commercial movies had very mixed impact on audiences' impressions of the United States. Positive effects offset negative ones for an 'even split' in France and Great Britain, but 'the gains from American commercial movies appear to be substantial in West Germany and Italy.'[55]

The economic aims of the American companies found a convenient linkage with the presumed ideological impact of their films, and these worked themselves out through policy positions taken by the American government and the industry as both operated in postwar Germany. Although films' role in the re-education plan can be subject to various interpretations, it is clear that on the commercial side the American program was eminently successful because the importation of US films has never been officially limited in Germany. Basically, the American industry had unhindered access to that market and was able to impose its own conditions on it.

The development of the film market in Germany demonstrates a complex set of relationships between the government and the private sector in the United States, and between them and comparable entities in the Federal Republic of Germany. Another aspect of these webs of influence and power involves the effort to destroy postwar concentration in the film industry.

The motion picture business had been organized by the Nazi regime under UFI, a large holding company, one of whose subsidiaries was Universum Film AG (Ufa). Like widespread interests of leading firms in other nations, the UFI trust included film production, domestic and international distribution, exhibition, laboratories, and music and script publishing among its many activities. American, British, and French occupation authorities agreed to reconstitute the industry on a thoroughly competitive basis, not only to mirror the general classical ideal of a market economy, but also undoubtedly to strike at this cartel in particular. After all, occupation authorities were not oblivious to the needs of their own domestic film industries, which would be threatened by the resurrection of a strong and highly centralized industry in Germany. In the prewar era, UFI had been a powerful challenger in Europe to British, French, and American film interests, but occupation authorities planned a film industry of small independent units. In contrast to vertically integrated companies, especially in the United States, the western powers wanted separation of production, distribution, and exhibition, and there was to be competition within each of these levels. This policy was heartily endorsed by the MPEA, which on numerous occasions transmitted its concerns to occupation authorities. The Association pressed the Military Government, which had custody of the UFI combine, to sell various parts of it, not just to fragment the firm but because American interests hoped to buy some of these properties.

The first concrete action to decartelize the industry was taken in September 1949 when the American and British Military Governments promulgated Law 24 - the 'UFI Law' - which was supplemented by Ordinance 236 from their French counterpart. Law 24, according to its preamble, sought to 'dispose of such [motion picture] industry property in a manner best calculated to foster a sound, democratic and privately owned motion picture industry in Germany, organized so as to preclude excessive concentration of economic power.'⁵⁶ The Law authorized a Liquidation Committee, which was established in February 1950, to which the Military Government passed title to UFI properties. The Committee was empowered to sell these at public auctions, but buyers could not be government bodies, political party officials, former high-ranking Nazis, or previous important employees of UFI. Non-Germans could acquire no more than a quarter interest in any of the production studios.

By the time this plan could be put into effect, Military Governments had transferred their own authority to the Allied High Commission and to a reconstituted central government in the Federal Republic of Germany. Civilian authorities requested clarification of the former Military Governments' UFI Law, whose legal status was now somewhat ambiguous. The High Commission then promulgated Law 32, which repealed Law 24 and French Ordinance 236, but perpetuated the basic policy line. Powers of the Liquidation Committee were transferred to a newly created Deconcentration Committee. Moreover, the High Commission pledged to revoke its own Law whenever the German government enacted legislation leading to film industry deconcentration. Meanwhile, the High Commission proceeded with its own program to dispose of UFI properties, but there were no measurable results. The American High Commissioner for Germany reported:

Extensive but unsuccessful negotiations have been held with various groups who expressed interest in buying these properties. The major obstacle to selling them has been the lack of liquid capital in Germany. Banks have been unwilling to lend money to finance the purchase since very high rates of interest can be obtained in making industrial loans with less inherent risk than in the motion picture industry.⁵⁷

These efforts to dissolve UFI were criticized by segments of the German press and government, who argued that the current 'financial difficulties of the motion picture business' were a greater danger to growth of the film industry 'than another motion picture monopoly in the hands of a few big companies.'⁵⁸ Some government officials, furthermore, urged the High Commission to suspend its efforts and to leave the job to Germans. Dr Rudolf Vogel, who headed the parliament's committee for press, film and broadcasting, declared that forced deconcentration was 'an act of mistrust' and that it was contradictory for the High Commission to dissolve UFI when similar large companies existed in the United States and Great Britain. According to the trade newspaper *Variety*, Dr Vogel insisted that the matter 'has nothing to do with security. Today the question is whether – five years after the capitulation – it is still possible to squander German property without the participation of the Germans.'[59] Other government officials charged that the basic aim of deconcentration was to impede the growth of competition from the German industry, and that it was entirely 'for the one-sided benefit of foreign interests.'[60]

Continued opposition from Germans, as well as the credit problem facing potential buyers, eventually obliged the High Commission late in 1951 to curtail its attempts to dissolve UFI. Title to these properties gradually passed to the federal government in Germany, and the transfer was completed by the end of 1953. As of that time, one observer has reported, the 'deconcentration of the UFA–UFI properties into economically viable and competitive units [had] not yet been accomplished.' Experience with the coal, iron, and steel industries had shown that 'deconcentration is a very long drawn out matter,' and this certainly was confirmed by the UFI case. For the film industry, 'it is perhaps too much to expect that future developments will be along the lines desired' by the Allied High Commission for Germany.[61] Indeed, control of much of the UFI properties was transferred in 1956 to a holding company in which several major German economic and banking interests were involved.

In consideration of the needs of a growing capitalist economy in Germany, it made little sense to turn the clock back to a much earlier era of small business entrepreneurs, energetically competing among themselves for market shares, when the history of capitalism clearly revealed the long-term propensities for capital concentration and centralization. Germans in government and in the private sector recognized this, and were aware that their interests would be handicapped in the global postwar economic reordering. Although a broad program of deconcentration could have appealed to the small business sector of the nation, restoration of the country's economic prowess and its position in Europe could not be based on a tiny enterprise model, especially in key industries. The inauguration of the European Economic Community confirmed this, because by reducing internal barriers to trade it created larger markets to be served by large firms. The position that undercut occupation authorities' plans represented the needs of major financial interests that resisted the dispersion of economic power and the retardation of the country's emergence from ruin.

This sector believed that capital multiplication and accumulation could be facilitated by concentration of resources and that unbridled competition was something to be avoided, regardless of what classical economic theory taught. Decentralization seemed a retrograde step, especially in those industries that could contribute to Germany's economic recovery. On the most general level, then, the needs of the economic system played important roles when the state confronted and responded to the deconcentration issue. Indeed, the state was the mechanism through which economic interests worked in their own behalf. Whereas a century earlier they might have relegated the state to a passive position, in the postwar period it was clear the state could be made an active participant.

When he was Minister of Economic Affairs, Ludwig Erhard assessed what was then called the German economic miracle and attributed the country's growth to a social market economy policy:

My use of the term 'social' is not intended to refurbish tacitly continued capitalistic methods, but to indicate a definite departure from the old liberalism which, as is generally known, cast the state in the role of night-watchman in the nation's economy.

What 'Social Market Economy' implies is that the state is given not merely the function, but in fact a real responsibility for imposing on the economy certain politically desirable maxims and employing the broad range of instruments of economic policy in such a manner that the free decisions of men of all categories in the course of their economic activities will nevertheless lead to the desired result.[62]

As applied to the motion picture industry, it would seem that this policy entailed maintaining the UFI properties intact, as a strong hub around which the rest of the business could revolve. This, as has been shown, was opposed by both the American industry and the American government for economic and political reasons. Yet the American position was not able to prevail completely. The UFI monopoly was broken by the rise of independent companies, but dissolution of the UFI structure never proceeded according to plan.[63] Deconcentration was, therefore, an issue over which German and American industrial interests fought not only directly but also and most fiercely through their respective governments. That the German film industry never managed to attain a really solid economic posture is not necessarily due to faulty assumptions behind efforts to prevent decartelization. A survey of other European film industries shows they, too, suffered many blows, not the least of which were the spread of television, the continued American presence in their markets, and their inability to penetrate the United States market.

The status and nature of motion picture production in the Federal Republic of Germany since the war is all too frequently described in individualistic terms. That is, the kinds of films made are attributable to the inclinations, training, or artistic conceptions of specific directors, for instance. While individuals may leave their mark, they clearly work within the confines of a private enterprise economy that establishes expectations of what films should be and do. Moreover, numerous historical forces have shaped the context of that economy, and the specific contours of the film business in it.

With particular reference to Germany, the American government and the American industry played significant roles in determining how the market would develop, and in whose favor. German economic interests also were important in this regard because they contested the authority of the American state and private sectors to impose their will.

At least as far as the United States is concerned, the complexity of relations between the government and the film business suggests that while the two can be in substantial agreement on the broadest level of principle, there have been instances in which they have had different interpretations of the way to achieve goals. In general, though, the industry found the state to be an active and effective advocate that used diplomatic power to further the interests of the private sector. Events in postwar Germany demonstrate that there is hardly an adversarial relationship between state and business, and that their partnership might best be described as a coalescence of interests.

Notes

1 Congressional Record – *State*, 22 March 1950, p. 3766.
2 'Can America afford to be silent?.' *Department of State Bulletin*, 14, 6–13 January 1946, p. 8.
3 'Freedom of the press – world-wide,' *Department of State Bulletin*, 14, 3 February 1946, p. 160. This is a transcript of a radio broadcast featuring William Benton and FCC Commissioner Paul Porter.
4 Copy of speech, 15 June 1949. Ellis Arnall was a former governor of the state of Georgia.
5 *Congressional Record – Senate*, 22 March 1950, p. 3764.
6 *Ibid.*, p. 3766.
7 *Variety*, 7 January 1953.
8 *Variety*, 28 January 1953.

9 *Overseas Information Programs of the United States,* Part 2, Hearings, Subcommittee of the Committee on Foreign Relations, US Senate, 83rd Congress, 1st Session (Washington: Government Printing Office, 1953), p. 236. It is, of course, quite imprecise to use the term 'free' without saying in relation to what. Only the most naive would contend seriously that there are no constraints on the production of media content, film in particular. The mere fact that theatrical films are commercial products – commodities – introduces them to a whole range of general and specific factors that shape what films are and should do.

10 *Ibid.,* p. 272.

11 *Ibid.,* p. 279.

12 *Motion Picture Trade Distribution Practices – 1956,* Hearings, Select Committee on Small Business, US Senate, 84th Congress, 2nd Session (Washington: Government Printing Office, 1956), p. 357. As of 1947, the International Division of the Motion Picture Association of America was developing 'a method to eliminate the showing outside of the United States of American motion pictures that do not accurately and truthfully portray American life and institutions.' The Division also had created an International Information Center 'which advises the studios on their scripts to avoid offense to foreign peoples – their customs, languages, and institutions.' Because the majors' films were distributed jointly by the MPEA in many foreign countries, including Germany, it was possible for the MPEA to review them carefully for suitability. The Department of State thoroughly supported this private sector effort and instructed embassies abroad to cooperate by informing American companies about audience reaction to their films. (Letter from Gerald Mayer, Managing Director, International Division, Motion Picture Association of America, to the US Secretary of State, 5 November 1947.)

13 *Congressional Record – Senate,* 22 March 1944, pp. 2878–9.

14 The MPEA initially was licensed by its members to distribute their films in the Netherlands, Germany, Austria, Yugoslavia, Hungary, Rumania, Bulgaria, Poland, Czechoslovakia, Soviet Union, Netherlands East Indies, Japan and Korea. By the beginning of 1952, individual companies had started releasing their own films in the Netherlands, Germany, Japan, Korea and the Netherlands East Indies; individual service to Austria began in August 1952. Countries in the Soviet sphere stopped importing American pictures toward the end of 1948, but the MPEA continued to export directly to Yugoslavia through 1956. Joint distribution to other areas apparently did not resume until the mid-1960s, when the MPEA was licensed to handle the films of its members in Burma, Indonesia and Pakistan. This arrangement lasted until the early 1970s.

15 Letter no. 28 from Herbert Erlanger, Motion Picture Export Association, to Directors of the MPEA, 4 May 1950.

16 *Report on Germany,* prepared by Marian Jordan, MPEA representative in Germany, 10 May 1948; circulated with Letter no. 50 from Irving Maas, Motion Picture Export Association, to Directors of the MPEA, 14 May 1948. Cited hereafter as *Report on Germany.*

17 *Overseas Information Programs of the United States,* p. 232.

18 *Ibid.,* p. 285.

19 Albert Norman, *Our German Policy: Propaganda and Culture* (New York: Vantage Press, 1951), p. 9.
20 *Report on Germany.*
21 Norman, *Our German Policy*, p. 61.
22 *Report on Germany.*
23 *Ibid.*
24 Norman, *Our German Policy*, p. 61.
25 *Ibid.*, p. 64.
26 *Report on Germany.*
27 *Ibid.*
28 Norman, *Our German Policy*, p. 64.
29 *Report on Germany.*
30 *Ibid.* Translating these values into equivalent dollars is fraught with many difficulties, not the least being the establishment of an appropriate exchange rate. The Jordan Report does mention, though, that the Joint Export and Import Agency of the Military Government was then using a rate of 1 Reichsmark to $0.30 US, or 3.3 RM to $1.
31 Minutes of a Special Meeting of the Board of Directors, Motion Picture Export Association, 26 October 1950.
32 Correspondence to the author from Contracts Officer, Informational Media Guaranty Division, United States Information Agency, Washington, DC, 23 October 1963.
33 Letter from Joseph Westreich, Warner Bros. Frankfurt office, to J. Hummel, Warner Bros. Paris office, 7 March 1951.
34 Circular letter from Joseph Westreich, Warner Bros. Frankfurt office, to branch managers in Berlin, Dusseldorf, Frankfurt, Hamburg and Munich, 9 March 1951.
35 Cited in unsigned letter to S. Carlisle, Warner Bros. Pictures International Corporation, 13 March 1951.
36 The IMG Program also covered print media. Among the many publishers and distributors to receive IMG payments were Reader's Digest $2.3 million, McGraw-Hill Book Co. $3.6 million, and Time Inc. $2.6 million. These amounts covered the period from the inception of the Program until 30 June 1966.
37 *US Informal Media Guaranty Program*, Hearings, Committee on Foreign Relations, US Senate, 90th Congress, 1st Session (Washington: Government Printing Office, 1967).
38 *Congressional Record – House of Representatives*, 26 May 1959, p. 9128.
39 Letter from Eric Johnston, president, Motion Picture Export Association, to Dean Acheson, Secretary of State, 13 July 1949.
40 Henry Pilgert, *Press, Radio and Film in West Germany, 1945–1953*, Historical Division of the Office of the United States High Commissioner for Germany, 1953, p. 97; and *Overseas Information Programs of the United States*, pp. 264–8.
41 Pilgert, *Press, Radio and Film in West Germany, 1945–1953*, p. 85.
42 US Department of State, *Germany 1947–1949: The Story in Documents* (Washington: Government Printing Office, 1950), p. 609.
43 Nineteen countries met in 1947 and 1948 in an attempt to establish the

International Trade Organization, out of which grew in 1948 the General Agreement on Tariffs and Trade. Thanks to extensive cooperation between the American government and MPAA–MPEA officials, the GATT treaty prohibited signatory nations from using film import quotas, but allowed them to establish cinema screen quotas, which American film companies considered the least offensive form of domestic protection.

44 Minutes of a Special Meeting of the Board of Directors, Motion Picture Export Association, 10 October 1950.

45 *Variety*, 25 October 1950.

46 Pilgert, *Press, Radio and Film in West Germany, 1945–1953*, p. 97.

47 Stephen Beers, MPEA Representative in Frankfurt, interview with the author, 11 December 1962. American interests were able to exert pressure in other matters, one of which was rental rates. Early in 1948, the German Price Control Authority limited rentals to a maximum 43 per cent of the box office. The MPEA protested this ceiling, stopped sales of films, and induced the German exhibitors' association to request the Authority to withdraw this rule. In its place, the MPEA agreed to voluntarily limit rentals to 45 per cent, or up to 50 per cent on sliding scales, until the end of 1948. The Authority subsequently rescinded its regulation of rental rates. (*Report on Germany*)

48 Spitzenorganisation der Filmwirtschaft, *Filmstatistiches Taschenbuch*.

49 Letter from Eric Johnston, president, Motion Picture Export Association, to Jack Warner, president, Warner Bros. Pictures Inc., 24 November 1958.

50 Minutes of a Special Meeting of the Board of Directors, Motion Picture Export Association, 7 June 1951.

51 Motion Picture Export Association of America, *Interim Report on Television*, 21 October 1960.

52 Motion Picture Export Association of America, *Interim Report on Television*, 21 October 1960.

53 Motion Picture Association of America, *1951 Annual Report*.

54 Motion Picture Association of America, *1952 Annual Report*.

55 United States Information Agency, Research and Reference Service, *The Impact of American Commercial Movies in Western Europe*, R-166-61(R), December 1962. According to the USIA, this was the only research it had undertaken on this subject as of 1976.

56 Pilgert, *Press, Radio and Film in West Germany, 1945–1953*, p. 87.

57 Office of the US High Commissioner for Germany, *Report on Germany*, 21 September 1949–31 July 1952, p. 116.

58 Pilgert, *Press, Radio and Film in West Germany, 1945–1953*, p. 89.

59 *Variety*, 20 December 1950.

60 *The New York Times*, 12 August 1949.

61 Pilgert, *Press, Radio and Film in West Germany, 1945–1953*, p. 105.

62 Ludwig Erhard, 'A new bond between economists,' *The German Economic Review*, 1:1, 1963, pp. 3–4.

63 Universum Film went through a period of reorganization, diversification, and economic instability, culminating in bankruptcy in 1962. Two years later, its remnants were purchased by a German publishing house.

Bibliography

This bibliography is a selective guide to writings about the American film industry. Like the anthology itself it does not give equal weight to all aspects of the industry but rather tries to represent the field of study of that industry as it is presently constituted – and it thus suffers from the same emphases and omissions as the book as a whole. The bibliography also includes a brief list of publications which provide a context for some of the developing debates in film studies against the background of which analyses of the industry have always taken place.

Books on the American film industry

Balio, Tino: *United Artists: The Company Built By the Stars* (Madison: University of Wisconsin Press, 1975).

Balio, Tino (ed.): *The American Film Industry* (Madison: University of Wisconsin Press, 1976).

Baumgarten, Paul A. and Farber, Donald C.: *Producing, Financing and Distributing Films* (New York: Drama Book Specialists, 1973).

Bernstein, Irving: *Hollywood at the Crossroads: An Economic Study of the Motion Picture Industry* (Hollywood: published by the author, 1957).

Bluem, A. William and Squire, Jason E. (eds): *The Movie Business: American Film Industry Practice* (New York: Hastings House, 1972).

Carmen, Ira H.: *Movies, Censorship and the Law* (Ann Arbor: University of Michigan Press, 1968).

Cogley, John: Report on Blacklisting 1: Movies (Santa Barbara, California: Fund for the Republic, 1956).

Conant, Michael: *Anti-trust in the Motion Picture Industry* (Berkeley and Los Angeles: University of California Press, 1960).

Crowther, Bosley: *The Lion's Share: The Story of an Entertainment Empire* (New York: E. P. Dutton, 1957).

Daly, David A.: *A Comparison of Exhibition and Distribution Patterns in Three Recent Feature Motion Pictures* (New York: Arno Press, 1980).

Dunne, John Gregory: *The Studio* (New York: Farrar, Straus & Giroux, 1969).

Dyer, Richard: *Stars* (London: British Film Institute, 1979).

Facey, Paul W.: *The Legion of Decency: A Sociological Analysis of the Emergence and Development of a Pressure Group* (New York: Arno Press, 1974).

Fadiman, William: *Hollywood Now* (New York: Liveright, 1972).

Fernett, Gene: *Poverty Row* (Satellite Beach, Florida: Coral Reef Publications, 1973).

Fielding, Raymond A.: *Technological History of Motion Pictures and Television* (Berkeley and Los Angeles: University of California Press, 1967).

Fordin, Hugh: *The World of Entertainment* (New York: Doubleday, 1975).

French, Philip: *The Movie Moguls: An Informal History of the Hollywood Tycoons* (London: Weidenfeld & Nicolson, 1969).

Gomery, Douglas: 'The coming of sound to the American cinema: a history of the transformation of an industry' (PhD dissertation, University of Wisconsin, 1975).

Goodman, Ezra: *The Fifty-Year Decline and Fall of Hollywood* (New York: Simon & Schuster, 1961).

Guback, Thomas: *The International Film Industry: Western Europe and America Since 1945* (Bloomington: University of Indiana Press, 1969).

Hall, Ben M.: *The Best Remaining Seats: The Story of the Golden Age of the Movie Palace* (New York: A. N. Porter, 1961).

Hampton, Benjamin B: *History of the American Film Industry: From its Beginnings to 1931* (New York: Dover Publications, 1970).

Handel, Leo A.: *Hollywood Looks at its Audience* (Urbana: University of Illinois Press, 1950).

Huettig, Mae D.: *Economic Control of the Motion Picture Industry* (Philadelphia: University of Pennsylvania Press, 1944).

Inglis, Ruth: *Freedom of the Movies* (Chicago: University of Chicago Press, 1947).

Jacobs, Lewis: *The Rise of the American Film* (New York: Harcourt, 1939).

Jobes, Gertrude: *Motion Picture Empire* (Hamden, Conn: Archon Books, 1966).

Kennedy, Joseph P. (ed.): *The Story of the Films as Told By Leaders of the Industry* (New York: A. W. Shaw, 1927).

Kindem, Gorham: *The American Movie Industry: The Business of Motion Pictures* (Carbondale: Southern Illinois University Press, 1982).

Klingender, F. D. and Legg, Stuart: *Money Behind the Screen* (London: Lawrence & Wishart, 1937).

Lewis, Howard T.: *The Motion Picture Industry* (New York: D. Van Nostrand Company, 1933).

Lovell, Hugh and Carter, Tasile: *Collective Bargaining in the Motion Picture Industry: A Struggle for Stability* (Berkeley: University of California Institute of Industrial Relations, 1955).

McCarthy, Todd, and Flynn, Charles (eds): *Kings of the Bs* (New York: E. P. Dutton, 1975).

MacGowran, Kenneth: *Behind the Screen* (New York: Dell Publishing, 1965).

Madsen, Axel: *The New Hollywood* (New York: Thomas Y. Crowell, 1975).

Mayer, Michael F: *The Film Industries* (New York: Hastings House, 1973).

Moley, Raymond: *The Hays Office* (New York: Bobbs-Merrill, 1945).

Murdock, Graham: *Patterns of Ownership, Questions of Control* (London: Open University, 1977).

Neale, Steve: *Cinema and Technology: Image, Sound, Colour* (London: Macmillan, 1985).

Nizer, Louis: *New Courts of Industry: Self-Regulation Under the Motion Picture Code* (New York: Longacre Press, 1935).

Powdermaker, Hortense: *Hollywood: The Dream Factory* (Boston: Little, Brown, 1950).

Price Waterhouse: *The Motion Picture Industry* (New York: Price Waterhouse, 1917).

Pye, Michael and Myles, Lynda: *The Movie Brats: How the Film Generation Took Over Hollywood* (New York: Holt, Rinehart & Winston, 1979).

Ramsaye, Terry: *A Million and One Nights: A History of the Motion Picture* (New York: Simon & Schuster, 1926).

Randall, Richard S.: *Censorship of the Movies: The Social and Political Control of a Mass Medium* (Madison: University of Wisconsin Press, 1968).

Ricketson, Frank, H.: *The Management of Motion Picture Theatres* (New York: McGraw-Hill, 1938).

Roddick, Nick: *A New Deal in Entertainment: Warners Brothers in the 1930s* (London: BFI, 1983).

Ross, Lillian: *Picture* (New York: Rinehart, 1952).

Ross, Murray: *Stars and Strikes: Unionization of Hollywood* (New York: Columbia University Press, 1945).

Rosten, Leo C.: *Hollywood: The Movie Colony, the Movie Makers* (New York: Harcourt, Brace, 1941).

Schary, Dore: *Case History of a Movie* (New York: Random, 1950).

Seabury, William Marston: *The Public and the Motion Picture Industry* (New York, Macmillan, 1926).

Stanley, Robert: *The Celluloid Empire: A History of the American Motion Picture Industry* (New York: Hastings, 1968).

Toeplitz, Jerzy: *Hollywood and After* (Chicago: Henry Regnery, 1974).

US Temporary National Economic Committee: *Motion Picture Industry: A Pattern of Control*, Monograph 43 (Washington DC: Government Printing Office, 1941).

Wasko, Janet: *Movies and Money: Financing the American Film Industry* (New Jersey: Ablex Publishing, 1982).

Watkins, G. S. (ed.): *The Motion Picture Industry* (Annals of the American Academy of Political and Social Science 256, November 1947).

Articles

Allen, Jeanne Thomas: 'Copyright and early theater: vaudeville and film competition', *Journal of the University Film Association*, no. 31 (Spring 1979), pp. 5–11.

Allen, Jeanne Thomas: 'The industrial context of film technology: standardisation and patents', in *The Cinematic Apparatus*, ed. Teresa de Lauretis and Stephen Heath (London: Macmillan, 1980), pp. 26–37.

Allen, Robert C.: 'Contra the chaser theory', *Wide Angle*, vol. 3, no. 1 (1979), pp. 4–11.

Allen, Robert C.: 'Film history – the narrow discourse', in *Film: Historical-Theoretical Speculations: The 1977 Film Studies Annual* (Part 2), ed. Ben Lawton and Janet Staiger (Pleasantville, New York: Redgrave Publishing, 1977), pp. 9–17.

Allen, Robert C.: 'Motion picture exhibition in Manhattan: 1906–1912; beyond the nickelodeon', *Cinema Journal*, vol. 18, no. 2 (Spring 1979), pp. 2–15.

Andrew, Dudley: 'The postwar struggle for color', *Cinema Journal*, vol. 18, no. 2 (Spring 1979), pp. 41–52.

Batman, Richard Dale: 'The founding of the Hollywood motion picture industry', *Journal of the West*, no. 10 (October 1971), pp. 609–23.

Beaupré, Lee: 'How to distribute a film', *Film Comment*, vol. 13, no. 4 (July–August 1977), pp. 44–50.

Bertrand, Daniel, Duane Evans, W. and Blanchard, E. L.: 'Investigation of concentration of economic power', study made for the Temporary National Economic Committee, Monograph 43, *The Motion Picture Industry – A Pattern of Control* (Washington DC: Government Printing Office, 1941).

Bordwell, David: 'Camera movement: the coming of sound and the classical Hollywood style', in *Film: Historical-Theoretical Speculations: The 1977 Film Studies Annual* (Part 2), ed. Ben Lawton and Janet Staiger (Pleasantville, New York: Redgrave Publishing, 1977), pp. 27–31.

Borneman, Ernest: 'Rebellion in Hollywood – a case study in motion picture finance', *Harpers* (October 1946), pp. 337–43.

Borneman, Ernest: 'United States vs. Hollywood: the case history of an antitrust suit', *Sight and Sound* (March 1951), pp. 448–50.

Branigan, Edward: 'Color and cinema: problems in the writing of history', *Film Reader*, no. 4 (1979), pp. 16–34.

Buscombe, Edward: 'Bread and circuses: economics and the cinema', in *Cinema Histories, Cinema Practices*, ed. Patricia Mellencamp and Philip Rosen (Los Angeles: American Film Institute, 1984), pp. 3–16.

Buscombe, Edward: 'Notes on Columbia Pictures Corporation 1926–1941', *Screen*, vol. 16, no. 3 (Autumn 1975), pp. 65–82.

Buscombe, Edward: 'Walsh and Warner Brothers', in *Raoul Walsh*, ed. Phil Hardy (Edinburgh: Edinburgh Film Festival, 1974), pp. 51–62.

Cahiers du cinéma editors: 'John Ford's Young Mr Lincoln', *Screen*, vol. 13, no. 3 (Autumn 1972), pp. 5–44.

Campbell, Russell: 'Warner Brothers in the thirties,' *The Velvet Light Trap*, no. 1 (June 1971), pp. 2–4.

Cassady, Ralph Jr: 'Impact of the Paramount decision on motion picture distribution and price making', *Southern California Law Review*, vol. 32, no. 4 (Summer 1959), pp. 325–90.

Cassady, Ralph, Jr: 'Some economic aspects of motion picture production and marketing', *Journal of Business of the University of Chicago*, no. 6 (April 1933), pp. 113–31.

Comolli, Jean-Louis: 'Technique et idéologie' in *Cahiers du cinéma* nos. 229, 230, 231, 233, 234–5 (May 1971–September/October 1972).

Crandall, Robert W.: 'The postwar performance of the motion picture industry', *Antitrust Bulletin*, no. 20 (Spring 1975), pp. 49–88.

Davis, John: RKO: 'A studio chronology', *The Velvet Light Trap*, no. 10 (Fall 1973), pp. 6–12.

Dawson, Anthony: 'Hollywood's labor troubles', *Industrial and Labor Relations Review*, vol. 1, no. 4 (July 1948), pp. 638–47.

Dawson, Anthony: 'Motion picture economics', *Hollywood Quarterly*, no. 3 (Spring 1948), pp. 217–40.

Dawson, Anthony: 'Patterns of production and employment in Hollywood', *Hollywood Quarterly*, no. 4 (Summer 1950), pp. 338–53.

Donovan, William and McAllister, Breck P.: 'Consent decrees in the enforcement of federal anti-trust laws: the moving picture industry', *Harvard Law Review*, vol. 46 (April 1933), pp. 929–31.

Ellis, John: 'The institution of cinema', *Edinburgh 77 Magazine* (1977), pp. 56–66.

Giannini, A. H.: 'Financing the production and distribution of motion pictures', *Annals of the American Academy of Political and Social Sciences*, no. 128 (November 1926), pp. 46–9.

Gomery, Douglas: 'Corporate ownership and control in the contemporary US film industry', *Screen*, vol. 25, nos. 4–5 (July–October 1984).

Gomery, Douglas: 'Failure and success: Vocafilm and RCA Photophone innovate sound', *Film Reader*, no. 2 (1977), pp. 213–21.

Gomery, Douglas: 'Problems in film history: how Fox innovated sound', *Quarterly Review of Film Studies*, vol. 1, no. 3 (August 1976), pp. 315–30.

Gomery, Douglas: 'Rethinking US film history: the Depression decade and monopoly control', *Film and History*, vol. 10, no. 2 (May 1980), pp. 32–8.

Gomery, Douglas: 'The economics of US film exhibition policy and practice', *Cinetracts*, no. 12 (Winter 1981), pp. 36–40.

Gomery, Douglas: 'The picture palace: economic sense or Hollywood nonsense?', *Quarterly Review of Film Studies*, vol. 3, no. 1 (Winter 1978), pp. 23–36.

Gomery, Douglas: 'Towards an economic history of the cinema: the coming of sound to Hollywood', in *The Cinematic Apparatus*, ed. Teresa de Lauretis and Stephen Heath (New York: St Martin's Press, 1980), pp. 38–46.

Gordon, David: 'The movie majors', *Sight and Sound*, Summer 1979, pp. 151-3.

Greenwald, William I.: 'The impact of sound upon the film industry: a case study in innovation', *Explorations in Entrepreneurial History*, vol. 4 (May 1952), pp. 178-92.

Guback, Thomas: 'Film as international business', *Journal of Communications*, no. 24 (Winter 1974), pp. 90-101.

Guback, Thomas: 'Theatrical film,', in *Who Owns the Media?*, ed. Benjamin H. Compaine (New York: Harmony Books, 1979), pp. 179-241.

Gunning, Tom: 'Weaving a narrative: style and economic background in Griffith's biograph films', *Quarterly Review of Film Studies*, vol. 6, no. 1 (Winter 1981), pp. 11-26.

Haralovich, Mary Beth: 'Sherlock Holmes: genre and industrial practice', *Journal of the University Film Association*, no. 31 (Spring 1979), pp. 53-7.

Harpole, Charles H.: 'Ideological and technological determinism in deep-space cinema images', *Film Quarterly*, vol. 33, no. 3 (Spring 1980), pp. 11-22.

Hellmuth, William: 'The motion picture industry', in *The Structure of American Industry*, ed. Walter Adams, revised edition (New York: Macmillan, 1954), pp. 360-402.

Hugo, Chris: 'The economic background', *Movie*, nos. 27-28 (Winter 1980-Spring 1981), pp. 43-9.

Jensen, Paul: 'The coming of sound', in *The Sound Film: An Introduction*, ed. Arthur Lennig (Troy, New York: Walter Snyder, 1969), pp. 77-110.

Jeter, Ida: 'The collapse of the Federated Motion Picture Crafts: a case study of class collaboration', *Journal of the University Film Association*, no. 31 (Spring 1979), pp. 37-45.

Joseph, Robert: 'Re: unions in Hollywood', *Films*, vol. 1, no. 3 (Summer 1940), pp. 34-50.

Journal of the Producers Guild of America, no. 14: 'A study of the economic condition of the motion picture industry in California', *JPGA* (December 1974), pp. 3-8.

Jowett, Garth S.: 'The first motion picture audiences', *Journal of Popular Film*, no. 3 (Winter 1974), pp. 39-54.

Kael, Pauline: 'Raising Kane', in *The Citizen Kane Book*, by Pauline Kael, Herman J. Mankiewicz and Orson Welles (New York: Bantam Books, 1974), pp. 1-124.

Kerr, Paul: 'Out of what past? Notes on the B *film noir*', *Screen Education*, nos. 32-33 (Autumn 1979-Winter 1980), pp. 45-65.

Kindem, Gorham: 'Hollywood's conversion to color: the technological, economic and aesthetic factors', *Journal of the University Film Association*, vol. 31, no. 2 (Spring 1979), pp. 29-36.

McGillian, Patrick: 'Bank shots', *Film Comment* (September-October 1976), pp. 20-5.

Merritt, Russell: 'RKO Radio: the little studio that couldn't', in *Marquee Theater*, ed. Hayward Allen (Madison, Wisconsin: WHA-TV, Channel

21, University of Wisconsin-Extension Television Center, n.d.), pp. 7–25.

Motion Picture Producers and Distributors of America: 'The motion picture industry', in *The Development of American Industries*, ed. John George Glover and William Bouck Cornell (New York: Prentice-Hall, 1932), pp. 745–61.

Murdock, Graham and Golding, Peter: 'For a political economy of mass communications', in *Socialist Register*, ed. Ralph Miliband and John Saville (London: Merlin Press, 1974), pp. 205–34.

Murdock, Graham and Golding, Peter: 'Ideology and the mass media: the question of determination', in *Ideology and Cultural Production*, ed. Michele Barrett *et al.* (London: Croom Helm, 1979).

Nowell-Smith, Geoffrey: 'Facts about films and facts of films', *Quarterly Review of Film Studies*, vol. 1, no. 3 (August 1976), pp. 272–5.

Odlum, Floyd B.: 'Financial organization of the motion picture industry', *Annals of the American Academy of Political and Social Sciences*, no. 254 (November 1947), pp. 18–25.

Ogle, Patrick: 'The development of sound systems: the commercial era', *Film Reader*, no. 2, 1977, pp. 199–212.

Ogle, Patrick: 'Technological and aesthetic factors upon the development of deep focus cinematography in the United States', *Screen Reader*, no. 1, ed. John Ellis (London: Society for Education in Film and Television, 1977), pp. 81–108.

Onosko, Tim: 'Monogram: its rise and fall in the forties', *The Velvet Light Trap*, no. 5 (Summer 1972), pp. 5–9.

Onosko, Tim: 'RKO Radio: an overview', *The Velvet Light Trap*, no. 10 (Fall 1973), pp. 2–4.

Powell, W. Dixon; 'MGM: the studio at its zenith', *The Velvet Light Trap*, no. 18 (Spring 1978), pp. 1–7.

Pryluck, Calvin: 'The aesthetic relevance of the organization of film production', *Cinema Journal*, vol. 15, no. 2 (Spring 1976), pp. 1–6.

Slide, Anthony: 'The evolution of the film star', *Films in Review*, no. 25 (December 1974), pp. 591–4.

Staiger, Janet: 'Dividing labor for production control: Thomas Ince and the rise of the studio system', *Cinema Journal*, vol. 18, no. 2 (Spring 1979), pp. 16–25.

Staiger, Janet: 'Individualism versus collectivism', *Screen*, vol. 24, nos. 4–5 (July–October 1983), pp. 68–79.

Staiger, Janet: 'Mass-produced photoplays: economic and signifying practices in the first years of Hollywood', *Wide Angle*, vol. 4, no. 3, pp. 12–27.

Strick, John: 'The economics of the motion picture industry: a survey', *Philosophy of the Social Sciences*, no. 8 (December 1978), pp. 406–17.

Wasko, Janet: 'D.W. Griffith and the banks: a case study in film financing', *Journal of the University Film Association*, vol. 30, no. 1 (Winter 1978), pp. 15–20.

Wasko, Janet: 'The political economy of the American film industry', *Media, Culture and Society*, no. 3 (1981), pp. 135–53.

Williams, Raymond: 'Base and superstructure in Marxist cultural theory', *New Left Review*, no. 82 (November–December 1973), pp. 3–16.

Wollen, Peter: 'Cinema and technology: a historical overview', in *The Cinematic Apparatus*, ed. Teresa de Lauretis and Stephen Heath (London: Macmillan, 1980), pp. 14–22.

General books

Adorno, T. W. and Horkheimer, Max: *Dialectic of Enlightenment* (London: Verso, 1979).

Althusser, Louis: *Lenin and Philosophy and Other Essays* (London: New Left Books, 1971).

Caughie, John (ed.): *Theories of Authorship* (London: Routledge & Kegan Paul, 1981).

McArthur, Colin: *Underworld USA* (London: Secker & Warburg, 1972).

Marx, Karl: *Capital: A Critical Analysis of Capitalist Production*, vol. 1, ed. Frederick Engels (New York: International Publishers, 1967).

Metz, Christian: *Film Language: A Semiotics of the Cinema* (New York and London: Oxford University Press, 1974).

Neale, Stephen; *Genre* (London: British Film Institute, 1980).

SEFT: *Screen Reader 1: Cinema/Ideology/Politics* (London: Society for Education in Film and Television, 1977).

SEFT; *Screen Reader 2: Cinema and Semiotics* (London: Society for Education in Film and Television, 1981).

Tudor, Andrew, *Theories of Film* (London: Secker & Warburg,. 1974).

Williams, Christopher (ed.): *Realism and the Cinema* (London: Routledge & Kegan Paul, 1981).

Index

288   *Index*